To Tipple A Prince

TO TIPPLE A PRINCE

Michael Hogan Godfrey
The Man Who Moved Hibbing

Daniel W. Lynch

NORTH STAR PRESS OF ST. CLOUD, INC.
St. Cloud, Minnesota

Copyright © 2010 Daniel W. Lynch

All rights reserved.

ISBN: 978-0-87839-369-5

Printed in the United States of America

Published by:
North Star Press of St. Cloud, Inc.
PO Box 451
St. Cloud, Minnesota 56302
www.northstarpress.com

Tipple—to drink liquor continuously in small amounts

Tipple— a place where or an apparatus by which (ore) cars are loaded or emptied.

This book is dedicated to the men and women of Minnesota's Mesabi Iron Ore Range who over the past ten decades have persevered under extremely difficult conditions and in the process raised families who have given back more to the state than they were given.

Acknowledgements

The author wishes to thank the Minnesota Historical Society's employees for more help than I can even remember; they and the society's facilities provide testimony to the professionalism and the resources so desperately needed by scholars. Also, the author wishes to thank in a very strong but general way the many fee offices on the Iron Range that allowed the author to examine and record material long thought lost. Also on my list is Hibbing Taconite for allowing me to explore the greatest open pit iron ore mine in North America, the Hibbing Historical Society for its assistance, the Iron Range Resources Center for allowing me to explore areas long hidden from public view, and lastly, a special thank you to Paul Aubin of Aubin studios in Hibbing for his assistance in locating some of the best photographs of the iron range ever taken.

Table of Contents

I	Time Passing: 1928 to 1890	1
II	The Penn Experience: 1890 to 1893	30
III	1893 Hibbing Stirs . . .	39
IV	. . . The Pot: 1912	74
V	Anticipation: 1913 to 1918	133
VI	The "Town" That Moved: 1918 to 1922	184
VII	And the Town That Didn't: 1922 to 1924	241
VIII	Where the Wind Hangs Heavy: 1925 to 1928	282
	Appendix A: Locating the Godfrey Underground Mine	317
	Appendix B: Defining the Mine	327
	Appendix C: Siblings	371
	Bibliography and Sources	375
	Index	379

Introduction

Iron ore has been here a long time. As the principal ingredient of steel, it has been the major contributor to the industrialization of the United States. In 1888, it started to ship from Michigan's Upper Peninsula. By 1900 major deposits had been discovered in northeastern Minnesota's Mesabi iron ore range.

In July of 1893 the Village of Hibbing had been platted and within ten years had become the dominant focus of the Mesabi iron ore range's activity as the Oliver Iron Mining Company started shipping massive amounts of ore from the largest concentration of ore deposits that has ever been found in the United States.

By 1918 it was more than evident that a major deposit of this precious ore was sitting right under the ever-expanding village of Hibbing. To the west, north and east of Hibbing the mines were already yielding their ore but mining could not expand to the south because the three major "additions" that comprised most of Hibbing were in the way. Mayor Vic Power, the perennial opponent of "the Oliver" was poised to stand in the way of any mining activity that would encroach on his citizens' rights and the sheer audacity of spending millions to move a town—and that seemed like the only option—seemed beyond comprehension.

Yet someone did plan the move and carry it out without a single whimper from "Victory" Power and with the full financial compliance of his employer. One entire addition of the village of Hibbing was moved two miles to the south, leapfrogging two other forty-acre plats, and replanted. Residences were moved, businesses re-established in a new town center, hospitals, apartments, hotels, banks were erected, parks created and land virtually given away for the village hall and one of the best known high schools in the state.

The man that did this while running the most successful complex of mines on the Mesabi Range, the sprawling Hull-Rust-Mahoning, was called a Prince of the Range and his name was Michael Hogan Godfrey. He had arrived on the range from the iron country of Michigan in August of 1893 and went to work for the Oliver as a clerk. In the next 35 years he never left its' employ and at his death in 1928, he was the District Manager of the Western Division of the Oliver on the Mesabi iron ore range.

I

Time Passing: 1928 to 1890

Introduction

The end of Michael Hogan Godfrey's life coincided with the beginning of the age of iron ore on Minnesota's Mesabi Iron Ore Range. Godfrey had been there at the beginning, a beginning that was slow, steady, and spectacular. The pioneers arrived after Frank Hibbing platted his village in 1893, and most of them came from the iron ore mines of Michigan's Upper Peninsula, the training ground for Mike Godfrey and the others even though the prospects there had been short lived. Once assembled in Minnesota, however, the cast was ready and equal to the long term task of creating the Mesabi Iron Ore Range. The end of the beginning thirty-five years later was more swift and silent.

The End Is the Beginning of History[1]

Fifty-three-year-old Thomas Jefferson Godfrey, local businessman and long-time post office official of Hibbing, Minnesota, exited the front (south) entrance of Hibbing's five-year-old Village Hall with an impending sense of dread on a cold, snowy Friday, January 13, 1928, and Tom was in a hurry to cross the recently paved and renamed Twenty-first Street E. (it had been Mesaba[2] Street E until two years prior) to his brother's house on the southwest corner (the intersecting roadway was Fourth Avenue E).

The house and the Village Hall faced each other across history much like old familiar friends. House and Hall were part of the heart of the Central Addition that formed the main business and residential dis-

Village Hall as seen from the front porch steps of Michael Hogan Godfrey's residence. The fence is no longer there and the car has been moved but the Village Hall has changed very little. This is the last view Mike Godfrey had of the town he lived in and did so much for. Photo circa 1925. Author's collection.

trict of the reconstituted village. Just ten years before the central part of what was once Alice, Minnesota, was nothing but a mud flat, barren of grass or tree. Now, it was the nerve center of the most prosperous city on Minnesota's Mesabi Iron Ore Range.

Tom was destined to see his fifty-six-year-old brother only once more (later that evening) and, although he remained living in Hibbing for another thirty-seven years, he never set foot in that house again. Thomas Jefferson and Michael Hogan Godfrey were not only brothers but true pioneers of Hibbing, having arrived in the village in 1893. They were well-known and popular members of the Hibbing and iron range community. In fact, Mike and Tom were as well known as the village's leading politician and his brother: Victor Leon the ten-term mayor and lawyer, and Walter J. Power, part time politician, lawyer, and land speculator.

Daniel W. Lynch

Tom Godfrey was no stranger to the Village Hall as he had served on and off as a Village Council trustee, recorder and secretary for nearly his entire time in Hibbing, in addition to running a men's clothing establishment and the post office. His brother Mike, sometimes referred to as the genial brother (being Irish that meant that he was not as good at blarney), had also taken some political jobs on the Mesabi Iron Ore Range early in his career but in spite of this his path and his future were far different than his brother's. Mike never worked for anyone but the Oliver; his brother tried that *only* once.

The three story Colonial Revival structure across from Village Hall was one of the last houses constructed by the Oliver Iron Mining Company in Hibbing. It was built in 1923, for Mike Godfrey who had by then served the Oliver for over thirty years and was now in his eleventh year as the Western District superintendent of mines. The Godfreys were a large family, with eight children, and the eight bedrooms and seven bath-

This view of the house on 404 Mesaba Street E is from the rear of the dwelling looking northeast from 4th Avenue E. The two-story sun porch is a latter addition and the fireplace chimney can be seen between the two windows on the third floor. Taken in 2003. Author's collection.

rooms came in quite handy. The first floor, where Mike lay bed-ridden, contained a fireplace, a kitchen, a study, a breakfast room, and the servant's quarters.³

The second floor was reached by way of a spiral staircase which even today some seventy years after the home was built is still the most striking interior feature of the house. The third floor was divided into two dormitory-like partitions where the Godfrey boys slept. The girls had bedrooms on the second floor. Mike's favorite Buick sat in one of the two stalls in the rear garage (not shown in the photograph above), which contained an upstairs apartment for the chauffer.

The staircase today. The carpet runner is a latter addition but the beautiful hand-carved banister stands out clearly. The living room and its fireplace are to the right. When Mike Godfrey died, he hadn't climbed those stairs in over two years. Taken in 2003. Author's collection.

Hibbing's current Village Hall (this was the second one) was built between 1922 and 1923 and dominates the block. The grounds take up half the rectangle framed by Howard Street on the north, twenty-first Street E. on the south with Fourth and Fifth Avenues E forming the western and eastern sides. The Village Hall and its immediate surroundings, which included the Hospital, the Oliver Club, and prominent residences, is the heart of the Central Addition.⁴ Its imposing Colonial front measures 126 feet and the building's depth runs to sixty-eight feet. The first floor's east wing contains the jail with eight cells for men and two for women. (This probably does not say anything significant about the crime rate at the time.)⁵ The clock in the central tower dominates the skyline today as it did seventy years ago.

Daniel W. Lynch

Immediately to the west (until recently) was the Hospital and immediately to the east was the Oliver Iron Mining Company Clubhouse. The village hospital was Hibbing's second; the first was the Rood Hospital in "Old North Hibbing" and the Oliver Clubhouse has given way to the present Library. The Androy Hotel is immediately to the north of the Library and shares the block. This is the core of the Central Addition in Hibbing. (The massive and beautiful High School is four blocks east of this area spanning Seventh, Eighth, and Ninth avenues E.)

The Central Addition of Hibbing was originally called the Larabee Forty, and Mike Godfrey's house sat facing the Village Hall not by coincidence or chance. The Oliver wanted it here. And the streets that sur-

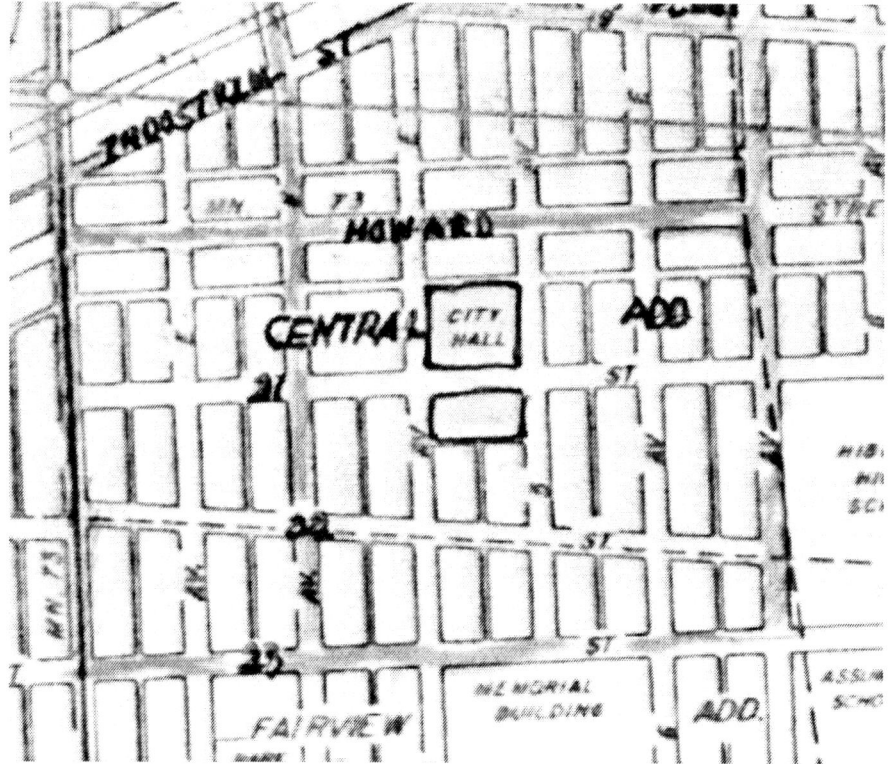

This is the Central Addition as it is laid out today. City Hall is in the center of the addition between 4th Avenue E. (on the west) and 5th Avenue E. (on the East). Howard Street is to the north and Twenty-first Street E. (originally, Mesaba) is to the south. This copy of the map was drawn in 1995. City of Hibbing, Urban Area, January 1, 1995. The scale is 1" = 1000'.

rounded this area, the buildings that dominated it, and the man who planned the Great Move were all laid out by Mike Godfrey and the Oliver. Their plan is still very much in evidence today. It was even more so yesterday.

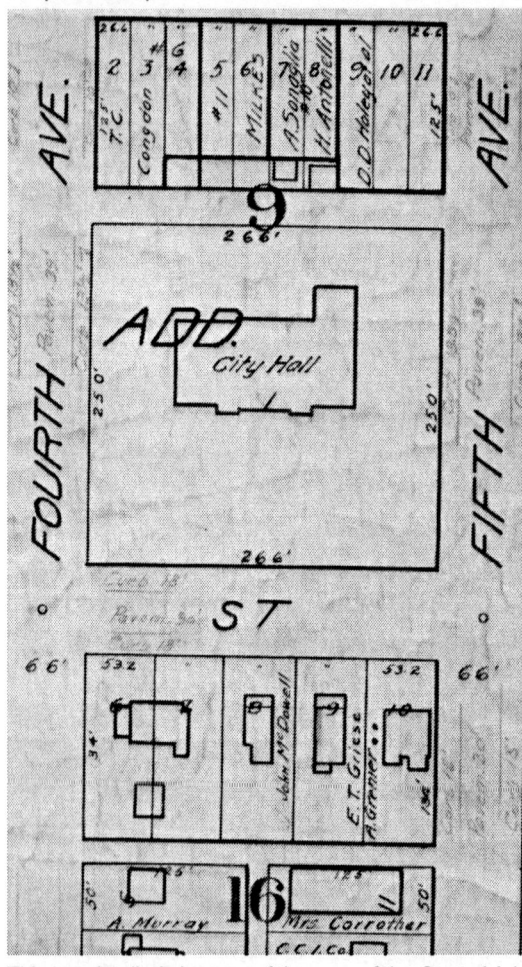

This is a detailed close up of the core of the Central Addition in 1921. It is the arrangement the Village of Hibbing (Village council) and the Oliver (read, Michael Hogan Godfrey) agreed upon before the Great Move. Mike Godfrey's house occupies two lots on the Southwest corner of Fourth Avenue E. and Twenty-first (Mesaba) Street E. Reproduced from a Map of Central and Park Adds, Hibbing, Minnesota, Scale 1" = 100'. Originally drawn on July 8, 1920. Author's Collection.

The Early Days

In 1855, the year the Sault St. Marie canal was opened enabling the mines of the Upper Midwest to reach the profitable eastern markets for the first time, the tiny settlement of Oneota (later incorporated into the city of Duluth), where the Merritt family lived, boasted a population of about twenty very hardy souls. In 1852, a trading post was established on what is now called Minnesota Point and Duluth continued to sprout little settlements on a regular basis until the Panic of 1873.

As Duluth grew slowly, reports were filtering back to this shipping center from a bug-infested, tree- and shrub-chocked swamp seventy-five miles to the northwest, of mineral deposits of unknown amounts. Richard and Henry Eames had reported on the deposits of extremely hard iron ore in the area, reports which were largely ignored but their reports of gold, which proved to be "fools gold" were not. George Stuntz surveyed the area and found deposits of ore he believed to be rich and extensive. So, he did the others one better, he brought back samples to Duluth to be assayed. Even though nothing much happened for a while it was evident that there was something "up there" and since it conveyed adventure and riches whatever it was, it was going to be unearthed and exploited eventually.

In 1878 Professor Albert H. Chester of Hamilton College and in the employ of Charlemagne Tower, advised Tower to dig in the region. In 1882 he did just that by forming the Minnesota Iron Company to mine ore and while they were at it with the foresight any successful investor needs—in this area—obtained a charter for a railway to run from the ore beds to Two Harbors, twenty-seven miles north of Duluth. Furthermore, the distance from the Iron Range to Two Harbors was one tough seventy-mile stretch of track that cost a considerable amount for the day ($2,000,000) and almost bankrupt Tower. The ore dock at Two Harbors was finished in 1884 and the Duluth & Iron Range railroad was standing by.

Then, on June 30, 1884, a steam locomotive called the *Three Spot* took on ten ore cars at the Soudan Mine near Lake Vermilion on the western end of the range and transported it to Two Harbors: Iron ore became a commercial commodity.

The Merritts

Chester and Tower in spite of their foresight had somewhat missed the mark. The really, really big deposit of iron ore was just to the southwest, and, what's more, it was nearly in plain sight. Since 1875, outcroppings had been reported on a regular basis. Professor Chester had made his obligatory visit but then things quieted down. It was left to the Merritt family of Oneota to draw the world's attention to what lay underneath all that oak, tamarack, jack pine, and endless swamp that formed the Mesabi Iron Ore Range.

In the meantime, ore trains poured into Two Harbors every day, dumping their mineral wealth into the waiting ore boats for the trip to the east and it seemed to the Merritts that the range of land to the southwest of the Tower area might also be developed. They left Tower on March 17, 1889, and headed southwest entering the area near Township 59 North, Range 18 West, Section 34.[6] They dug test pits here but found nothing. They moved south and tried again. This time they found ore and though it was sandy in color and soft to the touch they eventually learned that it was nearly sixty per cent iron. They sunk their test pit in 1890, and hit hematite ore almost immediately (in the NW ¼, Section 3, Township 58 North, Range 18 W). The Merritts knew a "find" when they had one and named the area Mountain Iron (wishful thinking but not inappropriate). They were just to the west of the great Z-fold in the rock at what is called the Virginia Horn. The ore in this area was almost sixty-five per cent pure. This was real news and like it should, it spread fast and wide and the iron ore rush was on. From December of 1890 to October 1892, 127 companies were incorporated to explore for this ore. The Merritts incorporated twenty of them.

It was no easier shipping ore from this part of the range than from the Vermillion area, and the Merritts were well aware of it. After considerable effort they did raise the funds for a railroad (the Duluth, Missabe & Northern) which ran for forty-two miles and connected to another railroad, the Duluth & Winnipeg. Ore started moving along this line in October of 1892. Even though the rush was on the Merritts were about to be derailed.

The Merritts overreached at this point by building their own railroad down

Daniel W. Lynch

This picture first appeared in 1903 (as far as I can determine). It was part of a Department of the Interior Monograph of the United States Geological Survey, volume XLIII, published by the Government Printing Office, Washington, D.C., 1903. It is the first train load of iron ore from the Mesabi Range in 1892. The first ore shipment was divided among four companies: the Thomas Furnance Co., Carnegie, Steel Co., the Isabella Furnance Co., and the Oliver Iron and Steel Co.[7] The steam engine and ore cars are parked on a Duluth, Missabe and Northern Railroad ore dock. None of the individuals are identified and from the manner of dress the weather was mild.

to the ore docks in Duluth instead of relying on the Duluth & Winnipeg. To do so, they had to borrow the money and borrow a lot of it. Right in the middle of building their railroad the Panic of 1893 hit and credit dried up and banks called in their loans. The Merritts went to John D. Rockefeller and borrowed the money. By the time the panic settled, Rockefeller controlled the road, the Merritts went off in search of copper and gold and the Iron Range stood at the precipice of greatness.

The ore was found thirteen feet below the surface in Virginia (then called Missabe Mountain), which came to the attention of Mr. Henry W. Oliver of Pittsburgh who was in Minneapolis attending a Republican[8] political convention when word traveled south. With a gambler's sure instincts Oliver wasted no time in investing and within four months had a lease taken out on Missabe Mountain for a guaranteed royalty. He was here to stay and ore now became the central focus in the historical process that was the drama of the Mesabi Iron Range.

To Tipple A Prince

Townships 57/58 North and Ranges 20/21 West

That drama was unfolding twenty-five miles away to the southwest, right on the edges of ranges 20 and 21 West, townships 57 and 58 North, and right there, there was a lumber camp. Not a big one by any means nor in any way unusual. This camp, later to be called Hibbing, was sitting atop the largest concentration of high grade iron ore ever found.

Franz Dietrich von Ahlen

Franz Dietrich von Ahlen was born in Germany in the Hanover province in 1856. At age eighteen, he immigrated to Wisconsin using his mother's name. Little is known about Frank Hibbing's background in Germany or of his stay in the Midwest but what is known suggests a man in a hurry with a real taste for adventure: he worked for a while as a farmer and in a shingle factory, studied law, cruised timber, prospected for iron ore, helped plat the town of Bessemer on Michigan's Gogebic Range and in 1887 arrived in Duluth. That didn't last any longer than any of his other endeavors. In 1888 he headed northeast. That proved to be his undoing for he stayed awhile.[9]

The Mesabi Iron Ore Range

The Mesabi iron ore range is approximately 110 miles long, from Birch Lake on the northeast to Grand Rapids in the southwest. Divided roughly into three sections, an Eastern section runs from the Birch Lake-Babbitt area to Mountain Iron and from Mountain Iron to Buhl as the Central section and from there to Grand Rapids as the Western section but this is a loose scheme. The center of the Mesabi Range is approximately at the Z-Fold (look at it as running north and south) which is an interruption of the NE-SW line of the Mesabi. The fold is a relatively short distance running from Virginia on the north point to Eveleth on the south point, corresponding to the Missabe Mountain and Fayal mines, respectively. In this view, Hibbing is about twenty-five miles to the southwest of Virginia and is actually in the center of the Western District of the Olivier Iron Mining Company's operations.

Daniel W. Lynch

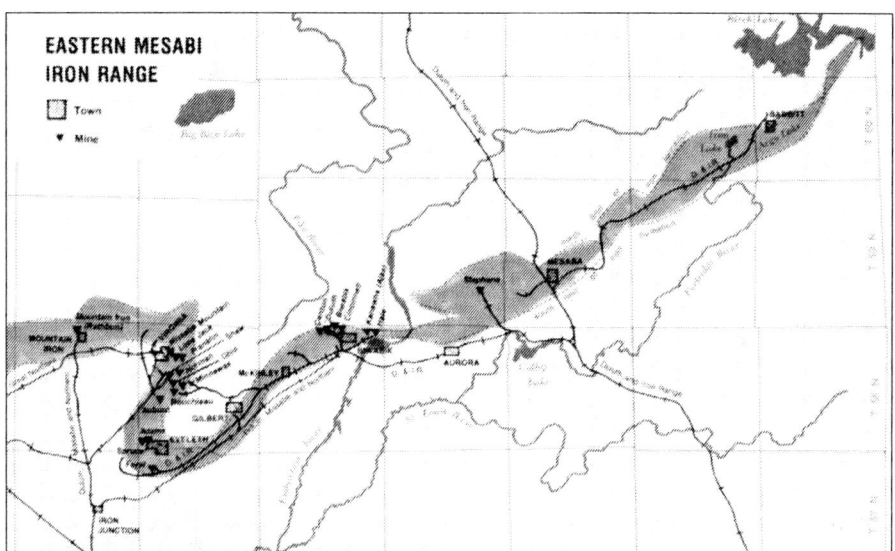

The Easter Mesabi Iron Ore Range. The Z-Fold can be seen clearly in Township 58 North, Range 17 West. Follow the route of US Highway 169 and the fold becomes much more pronounced: at Virginia Hwy 169 heads due south in the form of Hwy 53 until it reaches Eveleth where it then splits off as Hwy 135, heading first east and then northeast. From David A Walker's book: Iron Frontier: The Discovery and Early Development of Minnesota's Three Ranges.

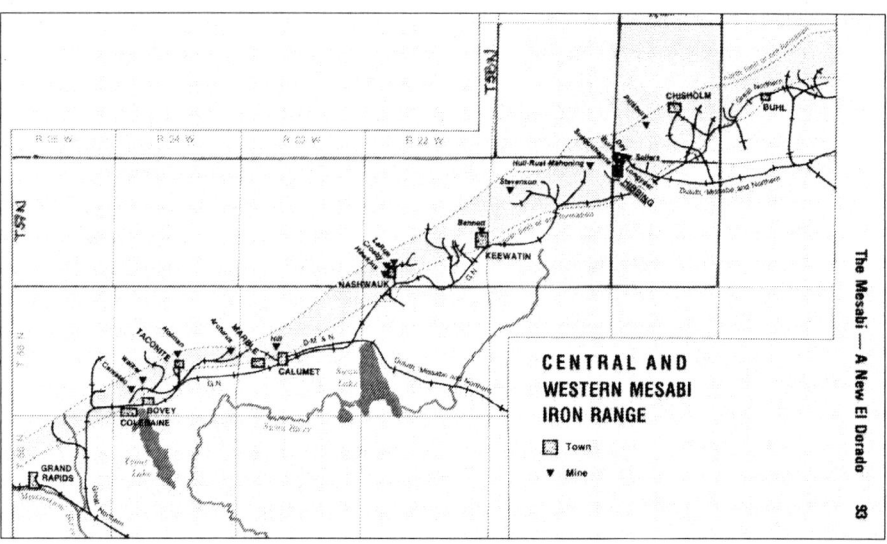

This is the Western Mesabi Iron Ore Range. Hibbing is 'nestled' in the crossroads at Township 57/58 North and Ranges 20/21 West. It is about 45 miles Northeast of Grand Rapids where the westernmost mines, the Tiogas, are located. Mike Godfrey was to serve the Oliver along the Mesabi in one capacity or another, from 1893 to 1928, from Coleraine to Virginia. From David A Walker's book: Iron Frontier: The Discovery and Early Development of Minnesota's Three Ranges.

To Tipple A Prince

Frank Hibbing and Township 58N

Three years after he set out for the northwest, Frank Hibbing found himself on Minnesota's Mesabi Iron Ore Range. He had spent the previous three years exploring, timber cruising, scouting the land. These years were apparently productive for he returned to Duluth in 1891 and took out a lease, granted him from Wellington R. Burt, to mine iron ore in an area bounded by Township 58 North, Range 20 West. But he was not granted mining rights in the entire Township, being restricted to nine sections in Township 58 North-Range 20 West: 13, 20, 21, 23, 24, 28, 31, 32, and 34.

Thus, he was not free to explore or mine ore just anywhere. His rights were restricted to certain sections, each being one square mile. One square mile of surface terrain that is more swamp than anything else, with no roads, no train tracks, nothing but some old trails which were mud most of the year (frozen the rest of the time) and dated back to French fur trading days. Frank had the mineral rights to nine square miles of nearly impassable earth but in addition to that these squares did not adjoin one another.[10] But he—and we—had a guide, the rectangular survey and for the next two years he used it to good effect. He found what he was looking for and he platted a town.

Townships, Sections and Forties

This business of Townships, Ranges, Sections, "north forties,"[11] is going to come up again and again and the site of many events, such as the moving of Old North Hibbing, or the locations of mines, such as the Hull, the Rust, or the Mahoning for example, require a detailed knowledge of how the Mesabi Iron Ore Range (and the rest of the United States) was laid out by surveyors long before the advent of GPS.

Maps represent areas of land and water. They are divided for easy reference by line grids. The north-south lines are called Meridians and the east-west lines are called Parallels.[12] Between the Meridian lines are six mile-wide columns called Ranges. Six mile-wide rows intersect these six-mile wide columns forming Townships. The township is thereby thirty-six square miles. Ranges are numbered from east to west, consecutively, starting with Range 1 west of a Meridian. In Minnesota this is either the fourth or fifth Meridian. Townships are numbered from south to north, consecutively, starting with Township 1 at a certain baseline. For Minnesota this baseline, drawn in 1855, in part forms the border between Kansas and Nebraska.

Township 58 N, Range 20 W is a thirty-six square mile area (23,000 acres) of land and water and swamp and underbrush and dense overgrowth that is 58 rows north of the baseline and 20 columns west of a meridian. For Minnesota's Mesabi Iron Ore 'Range', this is the 4th Meridian. (Townships in Minnesota west of the 4th Meridian are numbered below 100; those west of the 5th Meridian are of course numbered 100 or above.)

The thirty-six units in a township are called sections. Each section is 640 acres, a half section (½) consists of 320 acres and a quarter section (¼) consists of 160 acres. Each 640-acre square in the Township grid has a number assigned to it starting with the number 1 in the northeastern-most corner and snaking back and forth so that the northwestern-most corner is number 6, the southwestern-most corner is 31 and the southeastern-most corner is 36. (North on a township layout is always at the top with east to the right (south is always at the bottom and west is always on the left).

Township 58 N, Range 20 W

Frank Hibbing's sections in Township 58 N, Range 20 W, where he had mineral rights are in gray. Someone else had the rights—or they were as yet unassigned—to the other sections. What should be obvious is that the numbers above and below each other are not consecutive.

Finally, each numbered section is sub-divided into sixteen smaller units called "forties" (forty acres each). This scheme becomes increasingly important as we go on.

References to objects, locations, and features inside a section follow a somewhat different nomenclature. For this purpose, sections are divided into four equal parts and each 160 acre part is assigned a compass designation: NW, NE, SE, SW. Shown below is a section divided into its four standard parts.

Each 160-acre quadrant here is then further sub-divided into forty-acre units and each is assigned a familiar designation: NW, NE, SE, and SW. The result is what is depicted below. Shown here is a section with each forty identified as a surveyor would label it (or a mining company or a village council).

Hibbing Sets Up Shop

Michael H. Godfrey Arrives
In March of 1892, a certain captain Cohoe found ore thirteen feet below the surface in the vicinity of present day Virginia. Henry Oliver heard of it and was duly impressed so he invested immediately. Frank Hibbing, meanwhile, was busy exploring to the southwest. While he was doing so, in June of 1893 to be exact, a young man of twenty-one arrived in the area and went to work in Virginia for the Biwabik-Mt. Iron Company[13]— a subsidiary of the Oliver Iron Mining Company at the Minnewas mine. He was single, carried his mother's family name of Hogan, spoke French, and had a bookkeeping background in the iron ore industry. He was most recently from the Menominee iron ore range in the Upper Peninsula of Michigan and he was Irish. This was a bit unusual as the Irish formed only a small segment of the Mesabi ethnic mix. This was Michael Hogan Godfrey and he was one determined young man. He immediately went to work as a Timekeeper in the Accounting department of the mine and settled in Mountain Iron for the next two and a half years.

Daniel W. Lynch

Frank Hibbing may have heard of the recent arrival but if he did there is no record of it. In any event, Hibbing had something else on his mind: he had a town to plat. On June 6, 1893, he filed the papers in Duluth, the seat of St. Louis Country. A.J. Trimble and H.L. Chapin, a civil engineer, did the paperwork and the layout. Among the original landowners were two, soon to be important names in Mesabi lore, Martin B. Hull (yes, *him*) and Marshall Alworth. Hull had a mine named for him and Alworth had an office building.

Frank settled for the town. The plat called out the required locations, names, and boundaries of streets, individual lots or parcels, lot lines, land dedicated to public use such as parks and cemeteries, and other boundary dimensions. The original specifications called for the purchase of eighty acres of land in Township 57N, Range 20W the SW½ of the NW¼ of Section 6. This area originally ran from North Street on the north down to South Street on the south and from First Avenue on the west to Fifth Avenue on the east. The remaining forty acres to the east of this were laid out but never developed. The exact center of the plat that is now called Old North Hibbing (originally it was the village of Superior) was one mile due north of the intersection of North Street and First Avenue. First Avenue is also a town line, which divides Range 20 West from Range 21 West. And this was all too soon to become another famous landmark: the northeast corner of the Mahoning mine.

The *plat* for the town may have covered eighty acres, but the entire *incorporated* Village of Hibbing with a population at that time of 326 hardy souls, was two miles square as the village encompassed no fewer than four adjacent sections: Township 58N, Range 20W, Section 31; Township 58N, Range 21W, Section 36; Township 57N, Range 21, Section 1 and Township 57N, Range 20W, Section 6 (where Hibbing chose to place his town), each section being 640 acres for a total of 2,560 acres. If it weren't for the mines nearby that would have given each resident eight acres of space.

To Tipple A Prince

That space, however, dwindled fast as underground mining rapidly gave way to open pit mining. Instead of sinking twenty-five-foot square vertical shafts 300 feet down into the mineral deposit, open pit mines simply "peeled" the earth ("overburden") away, exposing the ore to steam shovels and ore trains. In 1893 this was in the future and the future was fast approaching.

Pentecost Mitchell Arrives

One part of that future arrived very early in the year with the arrival of mining Capt. Pentecost Mitchell who reported to W.J. Olcott (working out of the Duluth, Minnesota, office) the general manager of the Mines for the Lake Superior Consolidated Iron Mines Company. Mitchell was born in Hancock in Michigan's Upper Peninsula in 1861. The Panic of 1873 had made working a necessity, and Mitchell went to work initially on the Marquette range in Negaunee (some twenty miles to the east of Champion) and then later in Bessemer in the Gogebic range. In 1886 he was working in the Ironton mine in Bessemer and later, in 1889, he was superintendent of the Comet mine at Wakefield, again on the Gogebic. He arrived on Minnesota's Mesabi Iron Ore Range in 1894 and was put in charge of the Hull, Rust, Burt, Pillsbury and Lake Superior mines for the Lake Superior Consolidated Iron Mines Company (eventually a subsidiary of U.S. Steel). He was made general superintendent of the Oliver mines in 1903. At that time, he had charge of the Oliver properties not only in Hibbing but in Chisholm as well, a nearly identical path followed later by Mike Godfrey. In 1906 after twelve years in Hibbing, he became the general manager of the Oliver and moved to Duluth. He became vice-president in 1909 and held that post until 1928 when he succeeded Olcott as president. He retired in 1931.

Within ten years, the area around the north part of Hibbing was quickly becoming home to parts of the Mahoning mine, the Rust, Penobscot, Sellers, Burt, Pool, Day, Laura, Morris, Webb, Susquehanna, Boeing,

Daniel W. Lynch

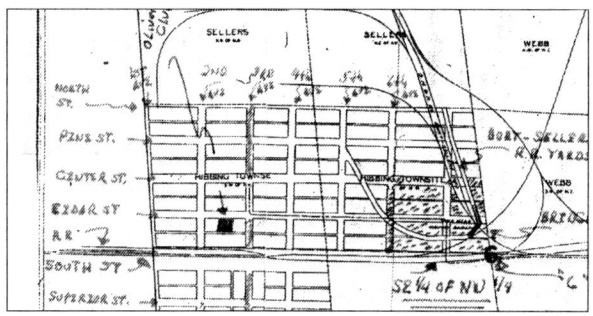

"Section 6, SW½ of the NW¼" is what Frank Hibbing applied to plat. In the graphic above this is the area running from First Avenue, east to what would have been 7th Avenue and from North Street south to the Railroad tracks/Railroad Street. This depiction of Old North Hibbing appeared in the April, 1907 edition of the Mesabe Ore and *Hibbing News*. North Street runs along a boundary line as does First Avenue. South Street runs parallel to and south of the Great Northern Railroad tracks. The area east of 5th Avenue E. never was built up, no streets were paved, nor were lots occupied. The closely spaced lines between streets represent alleys. Superior Street begins the Pillsbury Addition which was platted later. Pine Street was to become the center of the business activity.

and Philbin mines, as well as part of the Longyear mine, and part of the Northern Pacific holdings. By the time the consortium of fifty-three mines became the conglomerated Hull-Rust-Mahoning it was evident that those holes in the ground were going to displace more than just people.

The Village of Hibbing was becoming the center of the mining business in this part of the range. Growth was to be rapid but not without order, except for the fact that the original plat—apparently unknown to all - was sitting right on top of one massive deposit of iron ore and the ore wasn't going to move.

Hibbing and the Mesabi Iron Ore Range 1893

In August of 1893 Mike Godfrey was transferred to the Mountain Iron Mine to supervise the accounting department. In part this was because he could read French which he had learned in his younger days. In addition and perhaps more importantly, he had a good background in bookkeeping which he learned while working for three years for the Penn Iron Company back in Michigan.

Hibbing itself was starting to change. Lots were assigned and the first two businesses were opened. The Murphy brothers had the first business, a general store which initially was housed in a tent. Second place in the sweepstakes went to James Gandsey who, having just arrived from the Gogebic range in Michigan with his sixteen-year-old daughter in tow, opened a grocery store. He and his daughter were to figure prominently in Hibbing's and in Iron Range history in the not too distant future. For now they operated the grocery store.

In the meantime the typical sights and sounds that mean civilization were being seen and heard in the small village. Mr. and Mrs. Edward Champion became the parents of the first child born in the new village. The child, a boy, was named Philip. And a Mrs. York, from where is not known, became the first woman to officially settle into town (later she married and became Mrs. William Wills) while the dubious honor of being the first to officially die also went to a woman, Mrs. Charles Gourdette. This created a difficulty of some magnitude as there was as yet no cemetery. So, the coffin was hauled to the east end of town where it was buried, thus forming the beginnings of the village's first cemetery. This was at the east end of Superior Street.[14].

Another indication that civilization was beginning to take hold was that of the first election for president of the Village Council and the honor was accorded to J.F. Twitchell on August 8, 1893. He won in a landslide having had no opposition at all. This time. Twitchell was to have a long and colorful history with the village but at the time of his election his political career was just starting. Until now he had enjoyed life as a time-keeper, store-keeper and as a cashier for Granville & Sullivan, the contractors who were doing the construction work on the extension of the Duluth, Missabe & Northern railway which was running from Wolf to the newly minted village of Hibbing. Good connections are the good neighbors of good beginnings.

Michigan's Upper Peninsula and Its Three Iron Ore Ranges

There are six principal iron ore ranges in the United States. Three of them are in Michigan's Upper Peninsula and the other three are in Minnesota. We will return to Minnesota's principal range, the Mesabi, a little later but

Daniel W. Lynch

for now lets note that its development began initially in the 1890s and really took off ten years later. This places its development later than Michigan's but many of Minnesota's iron ore pioneers were previously pioneers in Michigan. (Mineral rights holders[15] it should be mentioned followed suit.)

Marquette, Menominee, and Gogebic
Michigan's Upper Peninsula contains the Marquette Range, the Menominee and the Gogebic ranges. The Marquette Range was the first to be discovered around 1845 near Negaunee but the ore shipments didn't start in earnest until 1855 with the completion of the canal at Sault Ste. Marie. Mining operations on the Menominee Range began around 1870 but shipping was delayed until the Chicago and Northwestern Railway Company ran a line from Escanaba to Quinnesec in the heart of the range. In 1878, when Mike Godfrey was six years old, five mines were in active operation: the Breen, Cyclops, Norway,[16] Quinnesec, and the Vulcan. The Gogebic Range was producing iron ore by 1884, near the town of Wakefield where Pentecost Mitchell worked for a time. Loosely put, the three ranges run in a general east/west orientation and are southeast of Minnesota's Mesabi Range.

All three ranges were to benefit from the industrial boom that followed the conclusion of the Civil War. By 1920, Michigan's three ranges were shipping around ten million tons of ore annually.

It was in this area and in this industry that many of Minnesota's men of iron got their first exposure to the red dust that was to dominate their lives and that of their families'. It was here in the Upper Peninsula of Michigan in the heart of the iron ore boom that Mike Godfrey got *his* start. His parents had *their* start thousands of miles to the east, on the other side of the ocean, in Ireland.

Robert Godfrey and Bridgit Hogan
Robert Godfrey, Michael Godfrey's father, was born on August 15, 1843, at the very beginning of the Irish Potato Famine (1845 to 1848) that

decimated the island. During this time, nearly twenty-five percent of the population either died or emigrated. The devastation was so bad that the decline in the use of the Gaelic language is traced directly to this period. Robert was raised in County Tipperary[17] near the west coast of Ireland, an area with some of the island's most fertile and picturesque countryside. County Tipperary is bound by tree-covered mountains to the south and west and is cut in various places by powerful rushing rivers. It is south of Galway and northwest of Dingle.

What is really significant about Robert's early life is that his family[18] did not leave the area or the island. Either the potato famine passed them by or they found ways to deal with it but the fact remains that Robert stayed until he was almost twenty-three years old.[19]

Michael's mother was Bridget Hogan also of County Tipperary (or, again, Tipperary Town) where she was born on May 30, 1846. Her father was a James Hogan and her mother's name was Margaret.[20] Her family stayed the course during the famine as well.

In 1866, when Robert Godfrey was twenty-three and Bridget Hogan was twenty, each emigrated to Holland, Michigan on the west coast of Lake Michigan (due west of Detroit by several hundred miles). Although there is no record of their having known each other when they were growing up, it is probably not by chance that they emigrated the same year and settled in the same town. By chance or by design, Robert Godfrey and Bridget Hogan married in 1866 in Holland and settled down to farm and raise a family. The first of ten children, Mary was born a year later in 1867 while the family was still living in Holland. Anna, the second child and second daughter was born in 1868. William Emmett the third child in three years, was born in 1869, in Ishpeming about fifteen miles from Champion.[21]

The record is silent for the next three years but in the interim, the family of five moves to Champion, thirty miles west of Marquette, where

Daniel W. Lynch

the fourth child, a second son, was born on April 13, 1872. In spite of the fact that he was the second son, he carried his mother's family name of Hogan and his grandfather's name of Michael, each case being a clear break with tradition. The first son by tradition and practice almost always took both honors. Why this was not the case here is unknown but not necessarily significant.[22] Robert and Bridget stayed in Champion where they continued to farm and have more children. Robert, Jr., was born in 1873 and Thomas Jefferson—and that name cannot be a coincidence—was born in 1875. His birthplace is given as Norway, Michigan, which is about fifty miles from Champion. Six children in nine years—this calls for some relief and so it was three years before the seventh child, the third daughter, Theresa, was born in Champion.

On March 10, 1880, the fourth daughter and eight child, Catherine was born and her birth was recorded as being in Norway. Either the family moves around constantly between Champion and Norway or they could not settle on the best hospital. What is most likely is that Robert sharecropped on farms but did not own one causing the family to move with the availability of jobs. Agnes Lorette, better know all her life as "Meme" arrived on July 18, 1881. But seven years passed before Winifred, the tenth child and sixth daughter was born on May 10, 1888. That ended child bearing for Robert, forty-five, and Bridget, forty-two. But Bridget was to live for another thirty-four years and Robert another forty-two. In 1888, Michael was sixteen and had nine living siblings and they were living in Champion east of the Gogebic Iron Ore Range and north of the Menominee Iron Ore Range, about equidistance between the two.

It had been a remarkable journey in mid-century for Robert and Bridget, from Ireland to America, from a European culture to an emerging one, from a settled environment to an expanding one. America's Civil War, which didn't really touch the new family, was over but still in the recent past and the Godfreys up until now farmers, were about to enter an entirely new way of life for the family of twelve. Mike was the fourth oldest child and hadn't done anything of note up until now nor had he the opportunity but he was about to change his life and we have no idea why. And then there was that large family.

James Gandsey and His Daughter, Cecelia

The upper peninsula of Michigan in the late 1880s and 1890s was as swampy and thick with underbrush and devoid of roads as was northern Minnesota. It had three iron ore ranges as did northern Minnesota. And, even though they didn't know of each other, the Upper Peninsula and northern Minnesota were about to have something else in common: the Gandseys and the Godfreys.

A long, very long 120 miles east of Champion, rests one of those little villages that sit snugly in the heart of a small farming area and have little if anything to distinguish it from any other small village. Newberry was typical of the area and of the time which may have had something to do with the Gandsey family's eventually leaving although there is no way of knowing for certain.

What we can say is that James Gandsey was born in 1855 in Ireland and immigrated to the United States around 1874. In 1875 we know that he was married to Bridget Annie McCarthy and they had a daughter, Mary. At this time they were living in Wisconsin but move shortly to Newberry, Michigan, where their second daughter, Cecelia, was born in 1877. Bridget disappeared from the historical record at this juncture as did Mary, who reappeared only briefly in 1889, when she was recorded as dying at the age of fourteen in Newberry. Her sister Cecelia was twelve years old at this time and something of an aspiring actress. Cecelia was on record in a handbill dated April 18, 1893, when she appeared on a Tuesday evening in the Temple of Fame, as a Famous Woman of Modern and Ancient Times. The price of admission to see Cecelia's interpretation of Helen of Troy was twenty-five cents.

Daniel W. Lynch

In less than a year, Cecelia and her father would be in North Hibbing where James Gandsey will open a grocery store and Cecelia will end her aspirations to be an actress and start to socialize. But that is getting a little ahead of things.

1889 and A Mystery Involving Michael Godfrey
Mike Godfrey graduated from High School at the age of seventeen in Champion. Even though there are no indications in the family stories, slim as they are, that he was a scholar or adventurer Mike Godfrey now sets out on the adventure of a lifetime: he heads over a thousand miles away to a school in Joliette, Canada! By boat. And train. To a school that even Van Brunt[23] couldn't name. To study bookkeeping, in French.

This is the Patriarch and his brood. Robert, Sr., is in the center of the first row with his wife, Bridget, on his left. Michael is the one with the mustache third from the left in the back row. In the back row on the extreme left is Mary, first child (1867-1939), to Mary's left is Thomas Jefferson, sixth child (1874-1965), to Thomas' left is Michael, fourth child (1872-1928), to Michael's left is Winifred, tenth child (1888-1955), to Winifred's left is William, third child (1869-1961), to William's left is Robert, Jr, fifth child (1873-1963), to Robert's left is Anna the second child (1868-1960). The front row on the extreme left is Catherine, eighth child (1880-1965), to Catherine's left is Theresa, seventh child (1878-1959), then we have Robert, Sr. (1843-1930), his wife, Bridget (1846-1922), and on the extreme right is Agnes, ninth child (1881-1969). This picture was taken in Hibbing, Minnesota, sometime before 1897 when Michael married Cecelia. Michael and his siblings are all grown and the whole family did not assemble as a group in Hibbing until approximately Mike's wedding. Author's collection.

To Tipple A Prince

When I read this I thought what initiative, what determination, what maturity. After a moments' reflection, I thought, what is going on here? This sounds ludicrous even without reflection. But why is this mention even in the standard text? This is one of those things in a person's life that maybe even if you had some source material on it you still couldn't explain why. In our case, there is simply no good explanation for this journey if indeed there is *any* explanation.

It has been suggested that Mike had a burning quest for higher learning but, if so, it lasted barely a year before he returned, if not to his senses, at least to Champion. There are and were good schools closer to Champion (in Marquette, for example) where he could have gone to study accounting or bookkeeping and he would have had to travel no more than fifty miles to do so, not over a thousand miles. A romantic interest has been suggested as a possible cause but if love was the theme of this quest, it is still hard to support this idea as the lady in question (her existence is never referred to) would herself had to travel the same distance either to go to school in Joliette, Canada or to return there after visiting Champion. Love may be strong but it is rarely that impulsive over such vast distances (with apologies to Helen and Paris).

What is claimed at least by Van Brunt and repeated ad nauseum is that Mike Godfrey traveled over a thousand miles to attend a school in a remote location forty-five miles northeast of Montreal, Canada, in an area which then as now, is predominately French-speaking. To get there in 1888, you had one option and that was to take a boat across Lake Superior (a distance of 800 miles), then use the railroad to travel to Montreal and then travel by one means or another up the Assumption River to Joliette. That is an impressive trip for a young man of seventeen or eighteen to take, especially in light of the fact that he did not at that time speak French. But, according to Van Brunt this is where Godfrey went to school and this is where he picked up his knowledge of the French language which helped him get his first important job.

Daniel W. Lynch

On the other side of the story, there is a school there today and there *was* a school there in the 1880s. Today, it is associated with the University of Montreal and is still, as it was when originally founded, school and seminary. Its origins go back to 1846 when one Bartholomew Joliette called upon the congregation of the Clerics of Saint Viateur, France to teach at the newly established Joliette College. The school was founded to teach mathematics, botany, agriculture, the English language (!), and bookkeeping. And it is bookkeeping that Mike Godfrey, aged seventeen or so, a thousand miles away from home, and speaking little or no French, studied for a year. That is perseverance of an extremely high order and supporting this improbable story is the fact that for all his adult life Mike Godfrey knew how to persevere in the face of considerable odds. And according to his family he did indeed know some French.

Also supporting this story is Mike's Catholicism which he practiced devoutly all his life as did his children. One last item is worth mentioning: there is a brief reference in the *Mesaba Ore and Hibbing Daily News* of July 22, 1916, that Mr. and Mrs. J.J. Cox (Anna Godfrey, Mike's sister) were visiting friends in Montreal and Quebec, Canada. Maybe Mike had relatives in that remote corner of Canada who told him of this place where he could both study for a career and practice his religion. And learn French. Maybe.

1889 and 1890

In 1889, Mary Gandsey, Cecelia's sister, died in Newberry. In 1889 Mike Godfrey came home from Joliette, Canada to Champion. He was not going to stay long. Whether or not he intended to return to school is not known but the fact that he went immediately to work indicates that money was becoming a serious concern in his plans. Mike headed south to Norway about fifty miles away, the

Les Clerics de St. Viateur today. From the Web site of Simonneeddy's Joliette Travelogues, 2004. Two photographs are spliced together but the picture is nonetheless clear.

heart of iron country in the Upper Peninsula. Norway is next door to Iron Mountain. (Mike Godfrey's first job on the Mesabi Range in Minnesota was in Mountain Iron.[24])

It was here that Mike Godfrey began his career in the service of the United States government as a postal clerk for the Norway Post Office where he joined his brother, Thomas Jefferson who had started earlier in the year. However, Mike's time with the Norway Post Office is difficult to follow. The records are scanty and the little we do know seems a bit larger than life, but some aspects of Mike Godfrey's life and career *were* "writ rather large." What we do know of Mike at this juncture is that he went to work in the Post Office at the age of seventeen or eighteen as a clerk near the end of 1889 or the beginning of 1890, where he remained for a short time, rising to the position of Assistant Postmaster.[25]

Sometime in 1890, Godfrey left the employ of the government (J.H. Gee replaced him and promptly disappeared from history.) and went into private industry taking a job with the Penn Iron Company as a timekeeper/bookkeeper/accountant in one of the company's two stores. He reports directly to the Supervisor of Accounting. It is here that he is credited by Van Brunt of obtaining the job due to his working knowledge of French.

The Hull/Rust/Mahoning, looking east. April 2002. The North rim is to your left, the South rim to your right. The center section of the photograph is the original area of the Sellers mine. The present Observation building is just outside the picture to the right. Authors Collection.

Daniel W. Lynch

The Penn Iron Company had two company stores where the miners could charge for items such as food, clothing, and equipment. Before the men were paid the company deducted the amount of the bill from their paycheck. The Penn company mines that Mike would have been familiar with at this time included the Breen, the Cyclops, the Norway, the Quinnesec, and the Vulcan. All of which constituted one very large operation but Mike saw himself at the wrong end of the business. He was ever restless with the ambition of youth and moved on quickly from the store to the Accounting Department at the mining part of the business. Here is where his real learning took place. It was here that Mike Godfrey was to get his first real taste of the iron ore business and the opportunities it offered.

* * *

Notes

The oblique reference is to a passage in T. S. Eliot (In my beginning is my end.) My intention is to convey the idea that history unfolds chronologically (i.e., currently) but is viewed most effectively in retrospect. The writing of history requires a perspective, an understanding of events that have concluded.

[1] This word, which is a transliterated rendering of an Ojibwa word meaning "Giant Hills", can be spelled in numerous ways, such as "Mesaba", "Missabe" , "Mesabi", "Messabe", "Misabe" and so on. For consistency, I will use the convention of using "Mesaba" when referring to the local paper, *The Mesaba Ore and Daily News*, or the Village street now known as East Twenty-first Street; and when referring to the D.M.&I.R., I will use the railroads' spelling of "Missabe". For all other cases I will use the 'official' spelling of "Mesabi". If Nicollet had a better ear he could have done better than "Missabay".

[2] He died at 10:50 pm.

[3] *Hibbing Daily News and Mesaba Ore*, 5 March 1920. This reference fixes the cost at $1,657,000. The original brick Village Hall in Old North Hibbing stood three stories high and had an impressive 75' deep by 144' wide footprint. It could not be moved as too many lamp posts along the only route (down 3rd Street E.) would have to be removed, the street widened and additionally, the building was tied up in the 'North Forty' litigation which was to last for years. Eventually the Oliver Iron Mining Company (represented by Mike Godfrey) would buy the building for $240,000 and tear it down.

[4] Arnold R. Alanen, *A Field Guide to the Architecture and Landscapes of Northeastern Minnesota*, Vernacular Architecture Forum 2000, Pines, Mines and Lakes, June 7-10, Duluth, Minnesota (Madison, University of Wisconsin, 2000), 2-78. Professor Alanen mentions what is a (currently) popular belief that the dwelling resembles Boston's famous Faneuil Hall. The *Hibbing Daily News and Mesaba Ore* of May 1, 1923, reflecting popular opinion of the time, claimed that it more closely resembled Philadelphia's Independence Hall. Local pride makes good news even if it is not based on critical analysis.

To Tipple A Prince

[5] Townships, ranges, sections, "forties", are terms used almost exclusively by surveyors, farmers, and civil engineers but need some explaining before the casual reader can use the concepts those terms convey as easily as the professionals do. We will go into considerable detail when we come to the platting of North Hibbing. For now it is sufficient to know that a Township is 36 *square* miles and all subdivisions of that area are also squares.

[6] *Skillings Mining Review*, October 27, 1928. Vol XVII, No. 25, page 4.

[7] Maybe it was coincidence maybe not, but later events would demonstrate that being Republican was an advantage when you worked for the Oliver.

[8] David A. Walker, *Iron Frontier: The Discovery and Early Development of Minnesota's Three Ranges*, Minnesota Historical Society Press (1979), p. 94. Walker's book is an excellent work and he is very careful to cite his sources, which are considerable. The Frank Hibbing material is drawn from Hibbing's obituary in the *Duluth News Tribune*, July 31, 1897.

[9] The map on the previous page (from Walker) has Township 58N, Range 20W shaded in yellow but the Sections are not delineated. What I am trying to show is where all this activity took place and using a Minnesota highway map just won't do. We need United States Geological Survey (USGS) maps or their equivalent to locate the areas and places we are describing.

[10] Appendix A goes into greater detail in order to locate an underground mine shaft: a 200 sq ft needle in a 23,000 acre haystack.

[11] Around 1790, local officials in what is now Ohio, encountered the problem of measuring, marking, and describing property lines. The system they devised to satisfy those needs was called the rectangular survey. The name comes from the checkerboard appearance that survey lines give to a map.

[12] Testimony in the *State of Minnesota, District Court, County of St. Louis, 11 Judicial District, Henry P. Reed, et.al. Plaintiffs vs. Village of Hibbing, a Corporation, et.al, Defendants*, page 248.

[13] This was not going to last as the ground was later needed for the Buffalo & Susquehanna mine.

[14] In some quarters, the mineral rights owners are called "miners hemorrhoids" - with a touch of irony - by miners, the men who dig the ore.

[15] This mine was still producing in 1890 when Mike Godfrey was a robust teenager living in town with his family. Godfrey was born in Champion near the Marquette range, grew up in the Menominee range and spent his career on the Mesabi range, an Irishman who spent a lifetime in red ore. Mike was a very introspective man but I wonder if the contrast ever occurred to him.

[16] He may have been born in Tipperary Town but the sources are not clear. His death certificate states Tipperary and does not distinguish between county and town. The town of Tipperary is five miles southeast of Limerick.

[17] His father's name was Michael but his mother's name is not known. This is of some interest as Robert's sister signed his death certificate and wrote that she did not know their mother's name. Something is amiss here but it's only suggested.

[18] He was to die at the age of 87, of a cerebral hemorrhage, on October 17, 1930, in Hibbing, a widower for the last eight years of his life. He saw his son Michael die two years previously.

[19] Bridget dies on June 8, 1922, in Hibbing, of chronic myocarditis, at the age of 76.

[20] For unknown reasons, his mother's name on his death certificate is Mary. 'Mary' is not even close to 'Bridget'.

Daniel W. Lynch

[21] Parents did not name their children by whim in this era, particularly Irish ones and so it may be significant that the first son did not receive his mother's maiden name or his father's name or his grandfather's name. It could have been that he was not expected to live, the infant mortality rate being quite high. William did live, however, and eventually settled in Mahoning Location west of Hibbing on Minnesota's Mesabi Iron Ore range. Michael who took the dual honors of Hogan and Michael, was born on the 13th of one month and died on the 13th of another. William did not die young; Michael did.

[22] *Duluth and St. Louis County, Minnesota. Their Story and People.* Van Brunt, Walter. Ed. Vol II, Pg 891. The American Historical Society, N.Y., 1921. One last mention is instructive: Van Brunt wrote this text when Mike Godfrey was very much alive and living on the Mesabi range. He is neither cited as the source, nor in confirmation of the facts.

[23] Minnesota's Mountain Iron rates quite high on the iron range lore gauge: the first iron ore mine brought into operation (by the Merritts); the first Mesabi mine reached by railway was the Mountain Iron mine and of course, the very first shipment of iron ore from the range was from Mountain Iron (that's it pictured on page 25).

[24] *Norway Current*, Norway, Michigan. April 28, 1917. Norway was then and is now in the Pine Creek area along with some ethnic sounding places such as Swede Town and Belgium Town. At this time in Pine Creek certain nationalities would settle in a certain area when they first arrived, language often times being the lure. Pine Creek is farming country, criss-crossed by rivers and creeks. Pine creek itself was used by the early loggers to float their logs down to the Menominee and Sturgeon rivers.

II

The Penn Experience 1890 to 1893

Introduction

The iron ore industry became a big deal in Michigan and a big business in Minnesota. The major player in the mining business on the Upper Peninsula was the Penn Mining Company which was every bit the major influence but not the market dominator that the Oliver Iron Mining Company was to become in northeastern Minnesota. The early similarities between the Menominee and the Mesabi were more than coincidental: the men that started the first range went on to build the second one as well.

Getting Started

Mike Godfrey went to work in the Accounting Department of the Penn Mining Company in Norway, Michigan, in the summer of 1890. He started in the company store but soon felt the need to move on. It didn't take long to figure out that the experience he needed was in the iron ore *mining* business, not in the *general store*. And iron ore in the Upper Peninsula in the last decade of the nineteenth century was fast becoming very big business. And the area in and around Norway on Michigan's Menominee iron ore range was an ideal place to start.

Daniel W. Lynch

The Menominee Iron Range

Fifty years before Penn starting mining operations on the Menominee range the local Indians were telling stories of great fields of iron and one of those stories reached the clerical ear of Father Bourion and from him and the Indians, these tales eventually reached the right people and mining operations east of Champion began soon after. By 1864, the Jackson, Cleveland and Lake Superior mines were producing varying degrees of iron ore.

In 1866, brothers Thomas and Bartley Breen, residing in Menominee, some fifty miles south of Norway, heard the tales of iron ore deposits scattered around Norway and went looking. In September, 1877, a shipment of twenty-five carloads or iron ore was made from the Breen mine (this was not the first shipment) but in 1878 less then a year later, the Breen mine was closed down and vacated. At the same time, in August of 1878 the Norway mine was opened up by the Menominee Mining Company. Then the Cyclops mine was opened up in 1878 as was the Perkins (originally the Saginaw). The industry was beginning to grow but as is the case throughout the ore business at this time, success was dependant on capital, lots of it.

By 1890, there were forty-seven mines operating on the Menominee iron range and thousands of Cornish, English, Swedish, Polish, and a mixture of Finns, French, German and Italian miners were working these mines. The ore business was volatile, the miners no less so.

Norway

Norway is 326 miles north of Chicago, Illinois, about 300 miles east of Minneapolis, Minnesota, and 160 miles west, by rail, of the Sault St. Marie locks. It sits two miles east of the Menominee river which divides Michigan from Wisconsin. Norway was platted in 1879 and incorporated in 1891, with an incorporated area much larger than the original plat which managed to cover a mere 306 acres of the nine square miles that comprised the city area.[1] Norway had sixteen miles of streets, four of which were graded and it was connected by telephone to Iron Mountain. Although there were only twenty-seven subscribers, the lines were usually busy. The phone exchange was located in the town's only drug store, owned by a Mr. Patenaude, who managed the dual task of also being the County Coroner. Norway had originally been mostly swamp but with platting came drains and sewers and run offs. But the high ground went to the Penn Mining Company with its mines running from the Black Hills on the West to the Brier Hill mine on the east (further east but not on high ground were the Curry and the three Vulcan mines).

The origin of the Norway name is in dispute but there are two claimants: the founder seems to have been Norwegian but the mighty pine that dominates the area and dominated the early industry, may have been a more influential factor. In 1888, Norway was rebuilt after a fire leveled the town with the predictable results of driving land values through the roof: during the rebuilding an acre of land which went for $700 before the fire now went for $7,000.

The population of Norway in 1890 was 4,000.

The Penn

In the Spring of 1890 the Penn Mining Company applied its engineering skills to the task of sinking a vertical mining shaft six feet by thirteen feet through sixty feet of quicksand into the heart of an ore deposit in the vicinity of Norway. An Irishman by the name of Kelly supervised the job.[2] The mines (among them, the East and West Vulcan, the Norway, the Cyclops, the Curry) that formed the core of the Penn's operations were purchased from the Menominee Mining Company.

Its labor force numbered some 750 men. This is the place and environment that Mike Godfrey encountered in 1890.

Ore Pockets and Underground Mining

The Penn Mining Company and most other mining concerns of this era were limited due to the constraints of technology for underground ore mining. The technology, the equipment necessary for open pit (stripping) mining were not yet available.

Iron ore is found generally in separated pockets, not in veins like coal. The hard ores are generally found near the top of the iron formation. Each pocket of ore becomes a mine—an underground mine—and each underground mine has a cluster of shacks and outbuildings to support it and the men since they were almost always in a remote, inhospitable location. The "location" after a while became semi-permanent as the mine wasn't about to move and the men had no intention of moving either as long as their basic needs were taken care of.

At first the ore was near the surface and was simply dug up and hauled away but as time went on this became increasingly difficult as the ore was further down. Too much overburden to strip away and inadequate equipment to do the stripping. Shafts then had to be sunk and the ore mined underground and brought to the surface through a shaft sunk to the level of the ore body. But before the ore could be mined someone had to determine if it *should* be brought to the surface: what was the quality and the quantity of the ore. Would the cost of the operation be justified when the ore was sold. This determination had to be made first.

This is where the diamond drill came into play. It was first used on the Menominee range in 1877 to cut out a core which could be brought to the surface and its strata examined to determine the location and depth of the ore body and the nature and quality of the overburden through which the ore shaft would have to be sunk. By taking a number of cores at strategic spots the potential tonnage and quality of the ore body could be forecast.

If the forecast was promising enough, work began on sinking the main shaft. Simultaneously, the surface buildings were erected: the hoist house (also called the engine house as this is where the generators were installed that did the hoisting), the dry house (shower hall), blacksmith's shop, carpenter's shop, storage rooms for equipment such as drills and blasting materials, and a repair shop (essentially to repair the drills). Additional areas on the surface had to be graded or prepared for trucks, railroad beds (to haul the ore off the property), storage for reserve ore (during most of the Winter the ore could be mined but not shipped-the lakes were frozen), and for waste ore. A head frame or housing for the skip cars that hoisted the ore to the surface had to be constructed.

The main shaft was usually sunk along the edge of the ore body rather than into it. The main shaft had to support an immense weight as ore was hauled to the surface and it needed as strong a surrounding material as it could have, material that was not going to be 'mined out'. Radiating out from the main shaft (rarely were there two main shafts) were the drifts that ran through the ore to the edge of the ore body or to the edge of the property (where the mineral rights stopped), whichever came first.

Once all that was done, the ore could be extracted from the ore body, taken by one means or another to the main shaft and hoisted to the surface. Three methods were tried. The first was called the "open stope" method. Using this method, drifts were driven from the main shaft into the ore body and large 'rooms' were left behind as the ore was removed, containing pillars (of ore) to hold up the roof. Much ore was left behind for this purpose, particularly if the ore body was soft. Another method involved creating an empty room about seven feet square and then holding up the roof of the room with large, sturdy wooden pillars at the corners. This also was very costly as wood for the purpose was at a premium and the cost and complexity of the method multiplied if the body of ore required more than one layer of rooms. The third method was the caving method where, again, rooms are created (the size varied), starting at the top horizontal layer. Once the ore is removed from the room the supporting wood frames are taken out, the ceiling or roof (also called the "back") is cleared of loose material and the ceiling/roof/back, and the overburden, are allowed to cave-in under their own weight naturally. All the ore on that level is mined before the process is repeated at the next horizontal level down.

Daniel W. Lynch

There is a good deal more involved in all this such as how the air in the mine was kept fresh, how was water pumped out, how were the drills supplied with power. But the basics are few in number: mine the ore, haul the ore to the surface, transport the ore to market, dig more ore. This was the environment that Mike Godfrey stepped into in 1890. It was underground mining of iron ore at its most basic and Mike learned quickly even as the methods of mining and the industry it supported changed.[3]

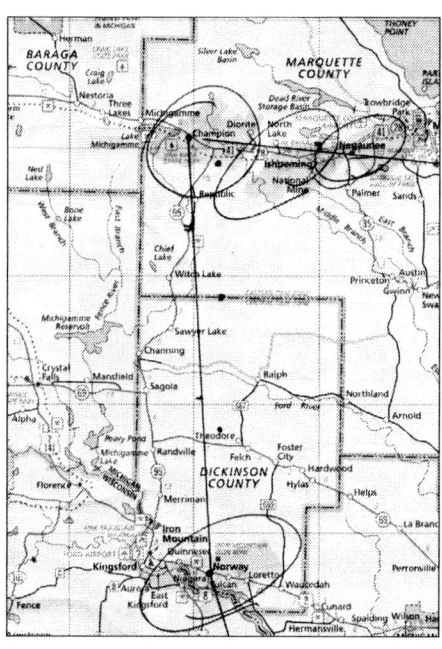

Michigan's Upper Peninsula from Champion where Mike Godfrey was born and raised and went to school to Norway about fifty miles away where he started his career in the mining business working for the Penn Mining Company. This country is a mixture of farm land, swamp, bog, and forest. It's both rugged and beautiful and the countryside in and around Norway then and now is dotted with the shafts of underground mines (mostly capped). Norway is just east of Wisconsin's border.

Mike started work as a clerk in the company store in 1890, due in part to the fact that he spoke and understood French. As has been noted before, "his work had much to do with handling trade and other work involving the use of the French language." He must have been industrious to a fault as he was transferred and promoted into the Penn Mining Company's Accounting Department by 1892.

While he was busy with his career at Penn, his brother Thomas Jefferson was attempting to forge a career in the mercantile store business. We know this as the *Norway Current* made mention in the September 1893 edition that "Thomas Godfrey, son of Robert Godfrey of Pine Creek is clerking at W.M. Ramsdell's store. He was let go on September 2nd as W.M. Ramsdell found it necessary to cut down his expenses and Thomas Godfrey, his clerk, was let go on Thursday." Tom was now out of work and looking for something new to keep him busy and secure, as was his younger brother, Mike. Mike's job (and it is not clear if he was let go, left, or received a promotion into another area) was taken over by Arthur Voligny of Iron Mountain on April 1, 1893. Within a space of six months the two brothers were most likely both out of work and, having no immediate obligations and being possessed by the energy of youth, were understandably looking for new world's to, if not conquer, at least explore.

While Mike and Tom were toiling away in the heart of the iron ore district of the Upper Peninsula, other events of no less importance were taking place. In 1891, Frank Hibbing started to explore the Mesabi Iron Range country of Minnesota. In late 1892 or early 1893, James Gandsey with his sixteen-year-old daughter Cecelia in tow, moved from Newberry, Michigan to Hibbing, Minnesota. James's brother Miles went with him. James opened a grocery store. Miles career on the other hand is more obscure and there is no record of what he did, at least at first. Later, Miles is found to be occupying the position of Assistant Postmaster. His boss is none other than Thomas Jefferson Godfrey.

Frank Hibbing

By the time in 1893 that Frank Hibbing platted the eighty acres that bear his name, he had lived in the Midwest for nineteen years and in Minnesota for barely seven years. He had married Barbara Lutz who had emigrated from Germany the same year Frank had (1874) but there is no record they had known each other while living in Germany, nonetheless each had eventually settled in the same small town (Stevens Point) in Wisconsin. (It is worth recalling that Robert Godfrey, Sr., and Bridget Hogan had something of the same experience leaving Ireland and then eventually settling in the same small town in Michigan.)

When Frank and Barbara were married in 1885 Frank took up real estate in Duluth but with a singular lack of success, causing his return

The Hull/Rust/Mahoning. Looking west. This photograph was taken in April 2004 on the floor of the mine. The South rim is to your left, the North rim is to your right. This area as most of the rest of the mine in the photo has been under water for nearly forty years and there is almost no vegetation in those areas. The water has a very low oxygen content. Photograph is in Author's collection.

to timber cruising and ore exploration. So, it was somewhat natural that having found several rich deposits of ore in the midst of a wilderness of underbrush and swamps, that Frank would combine several past and present talents (or maybe, *traits*). He platted a townsite in the heart of Minnesota's Mesabi Iron Ore Range, bought some real estate and invested in some mineral rights. (Most of which he later sold.)

Mike Godfrey

In September of 1893, Mike Godfrey transferred to the Accounting Department of the Mountain Iron mine where he was assigned to supervise the mine's payroll, accounts payable and receivable, and the paying of local taxes and mineral royalties. The exposure he needed later to supervise mining *districts* was being acquired right here on a smaller, more manageable scale early on in his career. He was to prove himself a fast learner.

To Tipple A Prince

Hibbing with its 326 residents and 2,560 acres of developed and undeveloped real estate was just down the road. It had the ore and a burgeoning business district and the intrepid beginnings of a social scene. The lures were obvious and Hibbing was not that far away for a young man on his way up in the business world.

* * *

Notes

[1] The Village of Hibbing employed the same approach on Minnesota's Mesabi range three years later. A clear case of history repeating itself. A large portion of Norway's original town site rested in a swamp, an early characteristic of Hibbing's townsite as well.

[2] Either the Irish are naturally gifted at supervising shaft sinking or Kelly got lucky. There just are not a lot of Irish in this story even when you count the Godfreys. But, to be fair, the first mayor of Norway was Irish: Mr. R.C. Flannigan. He, like the great mayor of Hibbing, was first a lawyer.

[3] This brief description of an underground mining operation applied equally well to Minnesota's Mesabi Iron Ore Range.

III

1893 Hibbing Stirs . . .

Introduction

The signs of civilization are both social and political and Hibbing was characterized by each in the nearly decade and a half from 1893 to 1906. Two railroads, the Duluth, Missabe & Northern and the Great Northern reached Hibbing; hotels were being constructed, churches established, houses numbered, businesses inaugurated. Hibbing was stirring as the Oliver was establishing itself as the premier mining presence on the range and Mike Godfrey was part of this endeavor. Godfrey married, tried politics not for the last time, and started his climb up the Oliver's management ladder. John C. Greenway also started his climb up the Oliver's ladder by organizing the Canisteo mining district (southwest of Hibbing) and Vic Power stepped confidently onto the political stage in Hibbing. And a little Location by the name of Alice made itself quietly known.

North Hibbing and the Pioneering Early Days

While Mike Godfrey was sharpening his craft and gaining experience first in Virginia and then in Mountain Iron, Pentecost Mitchell was gaining his in Hibbing running the Lake Superior mine, later renamed the Burt-Poole. Like most of the mines in the area the Burt-Poole started as an underground mine until the technology came along which could cost-effectively strip millions of tons of surface material away before the real business of extracting iron ore could begin. Mitchell at this time and for a long time thereafter was to report to W.J. Olcott (in Duluth) the General Manager of all the Lake Superior Consolidated iron mines for the Rockefeller interests.[1]

In 1893, the first two businesses in Hibbing were opened. The Murphy brothers had the first, a general store, and it was housed in a tent. Second place honors went to James Gandsey as he steps into the limelight (in the history in Hibbing) for the first time with his grocery store. Gandsey, who was also unfortunate enough to be Hibbing's second mayor, did have a first place blue-ribbon distinction of sorts. He was the first store owner to be robbed. Of a ham. By one Paddy the Pig.

Although Hibbing was hardly out of its social swaddling clothes at this point, being barely six months old, with several of its businesses operating out of tents, the Panic of 1893 still fresh in most minds, 1894, 1895, and 1896, still managed to find change and progress on several fronts.[2]

The First Pioneer Ball
The social new year took some little time getting underway with the holding of the first Pioneer Ball on January 24th. This was more than just a dance it was the official beginning of the Hibbing Pioneer Association, which recognized the first settlers. Unofficially, this was to include those who worked or lived in "Old North Hibbing" at any time in the years between 1893 and (approximately) 1903. The qualifications were somewhat loose but included (or where limited to) general recognition by one's fellow citizens.

The Pioneer Ball dance and inaugural social event took place in the 'new bank building', a wooden structure that was later to become Ryder's furniture store. Tickets hopped off the shelf at $1.50 a piece. The floor managers were—in no particular order but of some importance —J.F. Twitchell (the first mayor and he was soon going to resign), G.G. Robinson, Dan McFadden, Mrs. J.J. Stuart and taking her place on the social and historical platform of Hibbing for the first time, Miss Cecelia Gandsey all of seventeen, daughter of James Gandsey, the grocer and political figure.[3]

Daniel W. Lynch

This secular event was followed by a non-secular event at about the same time. The Blessed Sacrament Catholic church was established to cater to the souls of a large segment of the population. The organizers were John M. Gannon (although there is no further reference, this has to be the senior John Gannon; his son will become an important legal and political figure in about twenty-five years time), Mrs. Susan Gandsey, Gladys Gandsey, James Gandsey, Miles Gandsey, A.M. ("Archie") Chisholm, W.E. Godfrey, Thomas Jefferson Godfrey, and Michael Hogan Godfrey. Mike was to serve as the First Trustee, another indicator of the esteem his contemporaries held him in. It is obvious that the organizers were leaning into the Irish wind. Eventually, they were to set sail in a joint endeavor on the high seas of matrimony.

The summer of 1895 witnessed the arrival of the Duluth, Missabe & Northern railroad to Hibbing where it built a depot at the south end of third street. Hibbing's first Village Hall was also put up during the year. But something else more serious was at work as the Oliver began building its first headquarters on the Mesabi Range, north of the Third Avenue and North Street intersection.

Starting at "The Oliver"
In the spring and summer of 1895 the brothers Godfrey were starting to move around a bit as they settled in to life on the frontier, as were many other families. In April of that year Thomas Jefferson Godfrey moved in with his brother Michael and stayed for nine months while working as a timekeeper for the Oliver Iron Mining Company. Mike was himself moving further into the Oliver[4] fold by going to work in September in the Burt mine (north of North Hibbing) as a Clerk and Timekeeper. He was now a direct report to Pentecost Mitchell. (The Burt holdings—this is the "fabulous" Wellington R. Burt—rested their western shoulder on the Range line that became First Avenue in Alice, later Hibbing. The Day holdings were on Burt's eastern shoulder.)

Within ten years the Duluth, Missabe & Northern deport had a neighbor and competitor, the Great Northern railway. The Great Northern is on the left. A DM&N steam locomotive No. 23 waits between the two depots on its own rails. Hibbing Historical Society.

Dedicating the Hotel Hibbing

No sooner had the Godfreys started working in one of the local mines than it was back to the social whirl with the dedication of the Hibbing Hotel in February (the 22nd) of 1896. The Summer of 1895 had just witnessed the Duluth, Missabe & Northern railway establish its first depot in Hibbing at the south end of Third Avenue (about three years to the day since W.J. Olcott had to travel from Virginia to Hibbing on horseback). Before the figurative dust had settled on these two constructions it was time to dedicate the first hotel in the new, raw frontier town where the streets were still a mud slogging nightmare. This hotel and this event were important for two good reasons: as noted, it was the first hotel in Hibbing and everybody and his cousin showed up for the event. *And* Mike and Cecelia were there too . . .

The Hibbing Hotel was opened with a Grand Ball (dances being community events in those days, not just a sport for the young) and attendees came from as far away as Grand Rapids on the southwest (forty-five miles away), Duluth on the southeast (some eighty torturous miles away) and Virginia off to the northeast (again, some forty or so miles through the woods and swamps). This was not an easy journey and in February the weather could be really, really bad. This onslaught of dignitaries and good neighbors required the services of a Reception Committee to welcome all the travelers and make them feel at home. The committee consisted of— at least in part—a F. Brady, F.H. Dear, P.F. Eagan, Garry Graham, A.M. Chisholm (who started one of the first banks in town), Dr. D.C. Rood (the first licensed physician in Hibbing), Pentecost Mitchell (whom we have met before), James Gandsey (he of the lovely daughter), Michael H. Godfrey, and the catch of the social season, Frank Hibbing (his wife attended the dance as well). And that was just the *reception* committee! This did not end the social formalities, however, as such a heavyweight assemblage had to have the support of a Seven Man Floor Committee as well. This committee included the future Postmaster, village council trustee, local busi-

Hibbing Hotel. The hotel that started it all. This picture was taken in 1905 and the hotel was a popular spot for dinning or dancing or just getting together. It was the site of many charity balls and fund raisers in Hibbing's early days and was well known for its excellent meals and fine accommodations. It was built by Frank Hibbing and opened in 1896. Later, it survived the journey to South Hibbing as part of the Great Move. Aubin Studios.

nessman, and prominent future member of the Hibbing School board when *the* high school was being designed (his name still graces the plaque inside

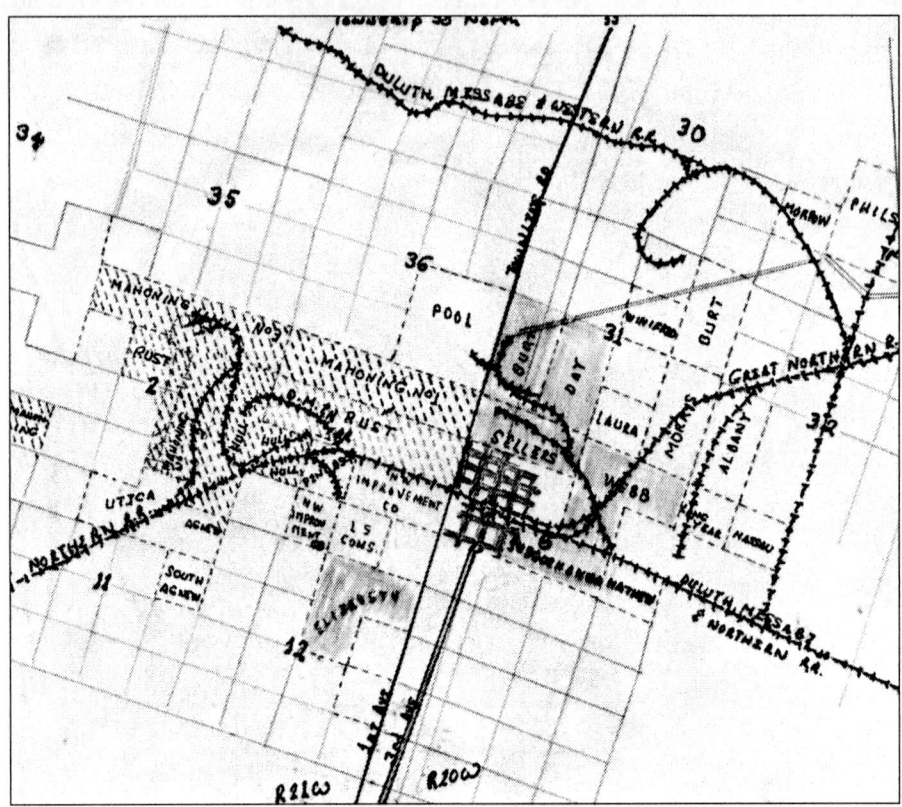

This drawing is copied from the Geological Map of the Mesabi District, Minnesota, drawn by C. K. Leith, U.S. Geological Society, 1903. Ten years after the founding and platting of north Hibbing, it is obvious that the original townsite is surrounded on three sides by mining activity. The west, the north, and the east 'forties' are already spoken for by one or another mine, mining company, and mineral fee owner and there is only one 'exit' and that is to the south. This is where the Pillsbury Addition would be platted and then just south of it, the Southern Addition. Third Avenue would run through the heart of each. This map also shows the prominent part that railroads played in mining activities and town development. One other note, the 'forty' adjacent to and east of the Lake Superior Cons ('L.S.Cons') became the location of the second headquarters of the Oliver in Hibbing and many of the foundations are still there. (The Elizabeth is now the Scranton.)

A further word is in order: it is entirely the author's observation that anyone looking at this layout now—or then, especially then—would logically conclude that if the west, north, and east areas adjacent to Old North Hibbing were as rich in ore as drill cores had already proven them to be, then the area in their cross-hairs, at this time occupied by the townsite, would also be rich in iron ore. This is an important factor to keep in mind as we trace the development, movement, and politics of the Old North Hibbing townsite, particularly when we come to the "Vacation Case."

the front door), Thomas Jefferson Godfrey, Mike's older brother. Cecelia has enough company by this time to require her own reception committee.[5]

Hibbing's incorporated area covered four square miles but only a small portion was platted and eventually occupied for one overriding reason: there was no other place to build. Expansion was limited to the south and in only a short time the Pillsbury Addition was platted immediately to the south of "North" Hibbing and then the Southern Addition was platted immediately to the south of the Pillsbury. Third Avenue was the principal north-south corridor through all three "additions." Pine Street in "North" Hibbing was the early center of business activity for all three additions. Surrounding everything was iron ore mining activity. Hibbing or North Hibbing sat at the juncture of four thirty-six-square mile townships.

Hibbing's incorporation encompassed four sections spread across two ranges (R 21 & R 20) and two townships (57N & 58N) but only one section was platted and occupied. Iron ore mining prevented expansion in all but a southerly direction. The Pillsbury and Southern additions were platted and occupied but then "North" Hibbing had to move in the only direction it could go—south. (And at that it was only some political maneuvering that prevented Hibbing from becoming part of the Alice mining location.)

This confinement should be kept in mind as we progress through the narrative of Hibbing's early days and the roles of certain important officials and of the Oliver's part in Hibbing's historical development. The confinement wasn't a major factor in the early days (although it was *a* factor) and wasn't prominently mentioned in the historical texts but it was there, quietly gathering energy until there was no escaping the inevitable. Then, moving the town became the only alternative but the arrangements were something else and the consequences worthy of all the ink spilled on them.

Organizing the Political Front
While Mike and Thomas J. were scouring the range for jobs and Cecelia and her Father were getting established in the newly minted frontier vil-

To Tipple A Prince

lage, politics continued in the form of setting up the Village Council and electing village officials, most especially the Village president, or mayor.

Fred Twitchell[6] was to assume office as the first president of the Village in 1894 but he resigned later that year and the second mayor, James Gandsey, took office. Gandsey held the job for the remainder of 1894, all of 1895 and 1896. Gandsey was re-elected in 1900 after spending four years running his grocery store, raising his daughter, and re-marrying (Susan Murphy)[7], by whom he had three more children, Gladys (1897), James (1901), and Roger (1903). Cecelia was to get some early lessons in child care as a teenager, a valuable experience as time would demonstrate.

The Oliver's Headquarters

The Oliver Iron Mining Company was one of the earliest mining companies on the iron range and it was well organized and well run from the

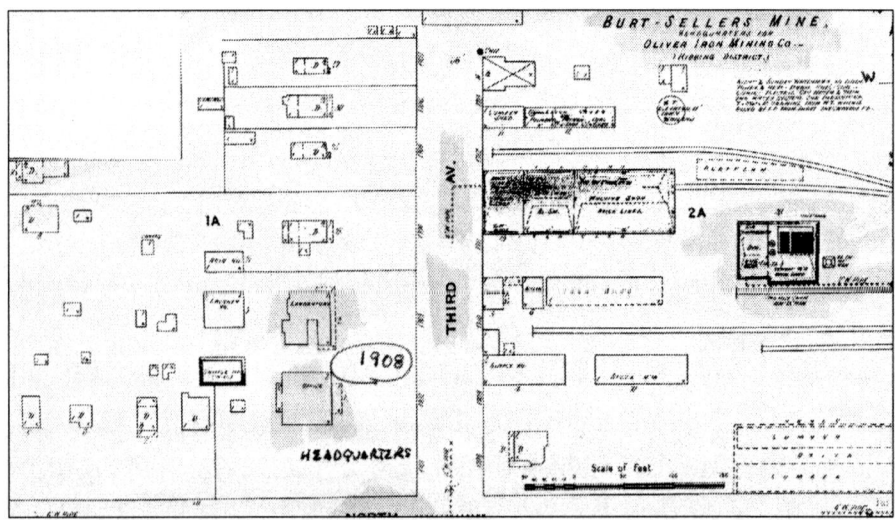

This is the Oliver's first North Hibbing headquarters complex. It was located on the northeast corner of the intersection of North Street and Third Avenue. Since this is a Sanborn Insurance Map great emphasis is laid on the availability of water and the means to deliver it. Underground street pipes are identified, the water tower's location is carefully noted as is its elevation and capacity. In 1908 this was Pentacost Mitchell's domain. The site was dismantled (in part) when Old North Hibbing had to move and was re-assembled west of First Avenue between Washington and Garfield. The Headquarters building remained pretty much intact but the Laboratory structures changed. The one building that did not make the trip from the original site was the crusher.

very start. As the immense deposits of ore were located and analyzed, the Oliver knew it was in for a long haul and built headquarters facilities in several of the range towns to reflect their long range plans. They built impressive building sites in Coleraine, Hibbing, and Virginia.

Mike Godfrey would have been quite familiar with this complex as he started his career with the Oliver as a clerk and bookkeeper for the Burt mine (an Oliver operation) and he would have worked here at the headquarters building at the corner of North Street and Third Avenue. The Burt and Day mining operations were due north of this spot.

Mike, Marriage and Politics

Mike was now, in 1895, and 1896, settling in working and living in North Hibbing. He and his younger brother, Thomas Jefferson, were now living on Third Avenue in the Pillsbury Addition. "T.J." as he was more generally known to the family, was listed as a timekeeper for the Oliver. He was to stay with his brother in this bachelor paradise for nine months. Mike continued to work for the only employer he was to know for the next thrity-three years but by 1897, T.J was, among other things, a member of the Hibbing Fire Department.

Mike had returned to live in Hibbing after a sojourn of two years and four months of living in Mt. Iron. By this time, he and Cecelia Gandsey were hardly strangers. They were both living in the village of Hibbing where the population hovered around 300 or so, living within the confines of some eight square city blocks and had already attended two of the Village's biggest social affairs, the last in February of 1896. If that wasn't close or often enough, Mike (and T.J.) was a regular attendee at the only Catholic church in the Village, Blessed Sacrament, where Cecelia and her father were also regulars.

The exposure and proximity enjoyed by the couple led exactly where you would expect it to, and on October 12, 1897, he and Cecelia were married in her father's home in North Hibbing. Attending for the groom was the entire Godfrey clan from Michigan.[8] It is not known how long the trip took but October in the Upper Peninsula of Michigan can be unpredictable, only somewhat less so for the upper confines of Minnesota's Mesabi Iron Ore country. And 300 miles is still 300 miles. I found no record of or even if Mike and Cecelia may have had a honeymoon but Mike was but four years into his job as clerk/timekeeper and that did not place him too high on the company ladder but his father-in-law James Gandsey was well connected and had some means from his business efforts. (There is a family tradition among the Godfreys of a succession of summers spent on Lake Esquagama, east of Gilbert, Minnesota, some fifty miles away and a honeymoon may have been the opportunity that launched a tradition.)

Mike and Cecelia settled in to life in the Pillsbury Addition of Hibbing (on Third Avenue) and almost immediately things began to change as Mike decided to do his civic duty (perhaps influenced by Cecelia and her politician father) and run for Village Recorder which he won in 1898 in a "landslide" over J.B. Connors, 208 votes to 192. Miles Gandsey, Cecelia's step-brother, followed up this civic emphasis with his election as Village Recorder. In 1899 Miles again made Village Recorder but Mike, running against a more worthy opponent, got trounced by Max Rogalsky 248 to 151.

This was not to be the end of Mike's political endeavors but for now it looked like a good thing as the couple's first child, James Robert, was born right before Christmas on the 23rd of December.[9] James is to remain in Hibbing his whole life except for a brief attempt at college, and an abortive enlistment in the army (more about this later on as the record is very confusing). He marries Margaret McHardy, one of two sisters, and has three children, William who dies when he is but three days old, a second son, Michael Peter and a daughter, Claire. Both become teachers. He died suddenly in testate at Hibbing's General Hospital at the age of fifty-four while living at 512 East Sixteenth Street across from Bennett Park.[10] He was the vice-president of the First American National Bank on Howard Street at the time of his death.

Mike's brother's were also busy in the mining industry at this time: Robert J(ohn) and Thomas J. are both working for the Oliver and living together on Railroad Avenue in North Hibbing and William Emmett is at work in the Sellers mine as a teamster.

1900: A Pivotal Year

Mike with his colors in high evidence, attended the Republican Party convention in Duluth in May of 1900 with Archie Chisholm and S.R. Kerly but they were not the only Hibbing activists to attend the convention. Pentecost Mitchell, Mike's supervisor at the Oliver and C.M. Atkinson, the editor and proprietor of the *Mesaba Ore and Hibbing News*, were in attendance as delegates from the Sixth District Congressional Contingent that was to nominate Page Norris. Hibbing's Republicans were not noticeably shy about their political allegiances and all in one way or another were to play important roles in local politics and were to eventually make their mark on the historical stage.

No sooner had Mike returned from the Duluth Republican Convention than he joined a newly minted socially conscious lodge, the Modern Samaritans. This organization was founded with the sole purpose of "administering to the needs of wayfarers who had fallen victim to the rapacity of robbers." I have to assume from the meager clues in that statement of intent that getting robbed while in or on your way to Hibbing must have been a considerable problem. This council started with twenty-three members and Walter J. Power, brother of the later mayor, Vic Power, was one of the founders. It was, naturally, given the times, a fraternal organization.

Mike was also mindful of some other pressing needs and in that light he and Cecelia purchased a home on Mountain Iron Road in Virginia from a Mr. Halvorsen. This must have quite a purchase as Halvorsen had to journey from Two Harbors to close the deal and Mike was moving his emerging family a considerable distance from Hibbing. Mr. Halvorsen returned to live in Two Harbors with his two daughters and Mike and his pregnant wife settled in for the long haul.

The deal on the house was finalized on June 23rd and five days later Mike attended his brother's (Robert in this case) marriage to Maud Garrity at the Blessed Sacrament Catholic church. On June 30th he saw his brother T.J. off on a summer vacation in Chippewa Falls, Wisconsin to (it was then said) visit friends. It was to prove a fruitful visit as five months later on November 12th in fact, Thomas Jefferson Godfrey married Miss Lucy Bronsky of (yes) Chippewa Falls, Wisconsin, and this marriage, like his brother Michael's, occurred in the home of the bride. Lucy Bronsky was not only fair she was also a niece of Archie Chisholm, friend of Michael's. She was later to teach school in Hibbing for a year. For the time being, the couple took a week off for a honeymoon before settling in the Pillsbury Addition.[11]

Before his brother married in November, Mike was involved in organizing the St. Louis County and Minnesota State Republican political campaigns. These campaigns were to see Mike once again re-united with Walter J. Power (brother of the future mayor and political independent). The campaign's particulars landed on the front page of the August 25th edition of the *Hibbing News*. C.W. Atkinson was a very vocal Republican and this may have had something to do with the fact that other leading Republicans, especially those who were active in the party, were mentioned so often. In any case, it did not hurt their reputations or for that matter, circulation.

In October Mike found time for a business trip to Duluth, some eighty very difficult miles away and upon returning he was off on a duck hunting trip with his father-in-law and J.J. Cox (the town druggist) on Lake Winnebegoshish.

Blessed Sacrament Catholic church, North Hibbing around 1900. Mike and Cecelia's children were baptized here. Aubin Studios.

Mike must have been very busy at home and the office at this time as he virtually dropped from sight if the paucity of news articles is any indication. He had a newborn son to care for and a job to manage so political activism may have taken a back seat.

But not for long and by the time the elections for Village offices rolled around again in the early part of 1901, Mike was campaigning for Village Trustee which he won handily over Leo Mitchell. "Landslide Mike" had a plurality of forty-three votes. His brother Thomas Jefferson also served as one of the Village trustees. And it was about this time of the year that Cecelia was pregnant for the second time. On November 1st Cecelia delivered a baby girl, Miriam Cecelia.[12]

Mike had now been on the Mesabi for eight years, an employee of the Oliver for seven, married for four, elected to public office twice, and had two young children. He was ready for more, more public service, more advancement, and more accomplishments (not to mention more children).

Hibbing at this time was undergoing its own version of a metamorphosis. Its population had jumped from 300 to over 5,000. Mining was bringing prosperity to the Iron Range and to Hibbing for the first time.

1902: The Oliver Shakes Things Up

By 1902, the Oliver had maintained large and ever-growing mining operations on the Iron Range and it was time considering the explosive growth to adjust its administrative arrangements, so the Oliver shook up its management profile with the result that Mike Godfrey went from clerk/bookkeeper to General Surface Foreman for the Oliver's Hibbing District and

W.J. Olcott now became the general manager of all U.S. Steel's mines in Minnesota, Wisconsin and Michigan. Olcott was jumping from one industry to another but the leap was really from one aspect of iron mining to another: from the railroad which hauled the ore over steel rails to the company chiefly responsible for mining that mineral those rails owed their existence to. W.A. McGonagle of the Duluth & Iron Range railroad became the assistant to the president of the Duluth, Messabe & Northern railroad.

It was on this occasion that Pentecost Mitchell became resident superintendent of ten of the Oliver's iron ore mines. And as Charles Skillings special correspondent for the *Duluth News Tribune* put it, Mitchell was to become one of the most successful mining men in Lake Superior Country. The *Hibbing News* noted in its edition of August 9th, that Mitchell was ably assisted by W.E. Wessenger and Michael Godfrey, "who is another valuable man in the service of the company and assists Mr. Mitchell with the work at the Clark and Chisholm mines and [who] will probably look after the new mine now being opened."

This new mine, Oliver's tenth in the district, like the other mines worked by the Oliver was an underground mine and it was predicted to be a productive one. The estimate was that the resources of the mine could reach twelve million tons of iron ore. This was to be named the Glen mine and its importance can be gauged by the size of the Location that was being built by the Oliver to support the miners who were to work this corner of the Iron Range. It was estimated that some twenty-four to forty cottages would be necessary. In fact, the Glen Location eventually housed a first rate school, community center and post office.[13] Hibbing now had 8,000 people living within its village limits.

It was also sometime later in the year that in recognition of his unofficial position as Mitchell's assistant, Mike Godfrey was officially promoted to assistant superintendent of the Clark, Chisholm, Pillsbury and Glen underground mines. His brother, Thomas Jefferson wasn't doing all that badly either. He was in Duluth on February 21st for a meeting of the Chief Clerks of the US Steel company.[14] He was also a Hibbing Village trustee.

The assistant superintendent position put Mike ever more into the public eye by increasing his exposure to more public mining activities and organizations such as the Lake Superior Mining Institute where he was the visible public spokesman for the Oliver. He represented the Oliver in August of 1902 before the Institute and again on July 11th of 1903 at the Institute's eighth annual meeting. He will be a member of the organization for the rest of his life and acquire some of his most notable public exposure as a result of this commitment.

It was only two weeks later on July 30th that the Godfrey's third child and second son, Thomas Clark Godfrey was born. He later marries Dehlia McHardy, sister of his brother's wife (James and Margaret) and has three children, Tim, Barbara, and Betty.[15] He is a widower at the time of his death (age seventy-three), of chronic myocardial failure (like his father), has worked all his life for the Oliver (like his father) and is living in the Androy Hotel which his father helped bring into being during the Great

This photograph of the Godfrey Location (right center) and Glen Location (background far right) was taken sometime between 1928 and 1935 by Aubin Studios. The view is to the East. The Godfrey underground mine started production in 1928 and about this time the Godfrey Location and the Glen Location merged. This is the only photograph the author has ever been able to find showing both locations. The Godfrey underground mine is a quarter mile due south of the Location. Photograph in Author's collection.

Move. He even tried college for a while[16] but preferred the mines and never rose higher in the Oliver hierarchy than foreman. His middle name may derive from one of the mines, the Clark, which his father was supervising at the time of Tom's birth.

Superintendent, 1904

The Chisholm, Clark, Glen, and Pillsbury mines all began as underground mines as did almost all other mines of this early era, for the technology to economically strip 200 to 250 feet of material (called "overburden") off the top of the ore was not there yet and would not be until the advent of steam. Nevertheless, these were not small operations by any means.[17] In 1904, the Chisholm underground mine shipped 170,000 tons of high grade hematite, the Clark mine 300,000 tons, the Glen 170,000 and the Pillsbury 230,000.

In the last week of January 1903, the Minnesota Iron Company had its name changed to the Oliver Iron Mining Company by its parent the U.S. Steel Company. Two years before this, U.S. Steel had changed the names of its divisions to reflect the state where its mining activities occurred but Henry W. Oliver objected to this arrangement and after two years of negotiations, U.S. Steel accepted his preference.

There were fifteen such mines in U.S. Steel's Mesabi inventory and they were divided into three divisions, each division headed by a full superintendent, and the three divisions reported to the District Superintendent Pentecost Mitchell, whose headquarters were on North Street in Hibbing. Mike Godfrey was superintendent of the Chisholm Division, Eastern Division Properties. (As assistant superintendent, Mike initially had nominal charge of two mines, the Chisholm and the Clark. Shortly thereafter he acquired nominal charge of the other two: the Glen and the Pillsbury. This promotion put him in day-to-day operational charge.)

Godfrey took his business responsibilities and familial obligations as seriously as his civic duties and in this light he stood for office almost as soon as he was transferred to the Chisholm area. He was elected to the Chisholm Village Board as a Trustee for 1904.[18]

Although not much is known of Godfrey's record on the village council it is known that on one occasion, Mike Godfrey supported, indeed pushed for, a review of the effect on private homeowners of some purposed sidewalk improvements along Maple Street and First Avenue. The improvements were a known necessity but the cost seemed disproportionate.

This was in December of 1904 and it looks like someone wanted Mike Godfrey's name to figure more prominently than it normally was, elections for the following year's elective offices were not all that far away. Mike and his wife took care of that in their own way: Marjorie Helen Godfrey's birth closed off the year in grand fashion on December 8th. Mike and Cecelia now had two sons and two daughters and as would become obvious as time moved on, it was but a nice start. Marjorie herself is something of a mystery. Her father established a larger trust fund for Marjorie than for any other family member. She was cared for by her oldest sister (Miriam) for over forty years supposedly because Marjorie was emotionally and mentally challenged. But she was enrolled in the University of Minnesota for some two quarters which does suggest something else altogether.[19] At a minimum, a high school diploma is required.

She died in the care of the Leisure Hills Health Care Center in 2000, the last offspring of Mike and Cecelia's to die.

Hibbing: Some Toes Test the Historical Landscape
The saga of the Mesabi Iron Range's interurban electric trolley car line saw its inaugural appearance in April of 1903 when the proposed village ordinance granting a franchise to the Mesaba Electric Railway Company was discussed at a council meeting. The franchise fronted by a Duluthian, O. D. Kinney for some investors 'out East' was granted but the company had to agree to extend the tracks from Sellers Street to Pine Street, along Third Avenue (in North Hibbing). That amounts to an

extra six blocks of trackage and one very large expense. This saga of the Interurban Electric Trolley car line was to drag on for quite some time with some unusual twists and turns.

Walter J. Power was about to be joined on Hibbing's historical stage by his brother Victor L. Power. In spite of the fact that Walter was the older of the two brothers and had settled in Hibbing first, had served as the Village attorney and was a successful local businessman he was eclipsed by his wife, Dottie, who operated a mercantile business and by Vic who enjoyed a successful political career.

Of the two Godfrey brothers, Michael was older and better known because of his role in Hibbing's history, but T.J. stayed the longer course due more than anything to his longevity. But T.J. did more than just live a long time. The better known of each pair, Mike and Victor, died relatively young; the lesser known pair, Thomas and Walter, lived long and well.

In May of 1903 Victor L. Power made his entrance as word was received that he had passed his examination at the Chicago Law School and had been admitted to the practice of the bar in the state of Illinois. Walter and Victor along with their father (a lawyer and then U.S. District attorney in Michigan) and their two additional siblings formed a coterie of five attorneys in one family.[20]

Victor wasted little time shaking the raw dust of Chicago off his suit coat and formed a partnership with his brother in January, 1904, after studying for the law in Minneapolis for six months. In February he passed the Minnesota bar exam. Walter, who really did not like second place, was Mayor of Hibbing at the time.[21]

Ordinance # 50

Hibbing closed out the year with an effort titled Ordinance # 50. It required the numbering of houses and lots. First Avenue was to be taken as the starting point (it was and of course still is a township line) and the first number at the intersection of any Street and First Avenue would be 101. For avenues, North Avenue would be the starting point, (To start further north of North Avenue put the surveyor in a real hole.) the houses and lots on both sides of every street and avenue were to be numbered alternately, odd numbers on the west side of avenues and the north side of streets, even numbers on the east side of avenues and the south side of streets

Hibbing's status as something other than a raw frontier village would continue to be emphasized in 1906 with the passage of more ordinances. Number 57 provided for the punishment of prostitutes and forbid the operation of houses of prostitution; number 58 suppressed gambling within the village limits and ordinance number 59 suppressed disorderly houses, taverns or saloons. Hibbing was cleaning itself up and learning that a moral house is a necessity when a town or village reaches a certain size.[22] It was a lesson that Victor Power would draw upon when he became president of the village.

Mike's Sojourn in Chisholm

Mike Godfrey's name was really being emphasized after all: in February of 1905 when the *Chisholm Herald* under a banner headline "The Election" spelled it out. "Mike Godfrey, currently a village trustee and superintendent of the Clark and Chisholm mines will head one of the two tickets for mayor of the village. William Grant is , oh, well, everybody knows Bill Grant the landlord of the Grant Hotel."

Mike Godfrey was expected to carry all four districts in Chisholm and win going away thereby unseating Mayor Grant.

Grant who had been born in Canada in 1863 was nothing if not colorful. He had moved to Duluth in 1882, and then to Ely in 1890. He made his way to Chisholm a year later. His three story Chisholm hotel was his second endeavor of this kind; previously he had owned a hotel in Eveleth. He was indeed well known but not just for being the mayor. Grant had been elected mayor two years before but he and the village council of trustees did not see political eye to political eye. One of those

To Tipple A Prince

trustees was Godfrey. In July of 1903, Grant was also elected treasurer of the school board and in no time at all charges were brought against him for miss-appropriation of funds. Rather than fight that battle in court, Grant resigned. Grant's hotel had a rather unsavory reputation which may or may not have helped his political career.

Somehow or another Grant became a favorite of the working man in Chisholm and he pulled off one very stunning upset according to the *Chisholm Herald*. In its March 15th issue the Herald's writer was somewhat poetic as the said that "the surprise factory of the whole range worked overtime here yesterday, and then the next day it snowed." Grant had defeated Mike Godfrey and absolutely no one had seen it coming, least of all the *Herald*. But predictions that fall need an explanatory crutch and the *Herald* had one: the fight was after all between the town's people and the mining companies. Labor punched Steel squarely in the nose and the Godfrey ticket, with the sole exception of one village trustee, Peter Johnson, went down for the count. Grant earned 289 votes to Godfrey's 250.

According to the *Herald*, "it was the fiercest political battle ever fought here and the scars remaining will be many." The *Herald* was prescient. From reading several accounts of the election it is evident that the fight was between labor and steel much more than Grant versus Godfrey and it was one of the first visible signs of a problem that had been growing for years and was now old enough to stand on its own. The economic imbalance between employee and employer was teetering. When business creates settlements it also creates, whether or not it foresees the consequences, expectations among the settlers. In a land as raw as the Mesabi Iron Range, this was going to get ugly.

Although the social consequences were to create some considerable turmoil, Godfrey did not lose much of his popularity and Grant did not enjoy his. He died of pneumonia on February 10, 1906, leaving behind a wife and fifteen-year-old daughter. The day before, Chisholm voted to add another forty acres to the village in the southwest.

Daniel W. Lynch

Before that was to happen, however, things were stirring off to the west of Hibbing.

John C. Greenway Leaves Michigan
John C. Greenway was leaving Ishpeming, Michigan, for the iron ore deposits of the Western Mesabi. Iron range newspapers were well aware of his accomplishments and reputation on the Marquette Range and were pleased that the Oliver saw fit to have him on the Mesabi. Greenway and the President of U.S. Steel, F.F. Cole and W.J. Olcott, general manager of the Oliver were seen touring the Western Mesabi in February of 1895.[23] Greenway was thirty-two years of age and had started as a machinist's helper for the Duquesne Furnace Co (Mike Godfrey who was to play an important role in Mr. Greenway's career, was thirty-two years of age and had started as a clerk with the Oliver.)

Things Get Deadly Serious
While Greenway was settling into his new role for the Oliver on the Western Mesabi, and Godfrey was taking care of the Oliver's business to the northeast of Hibbing, the Mesabi Iron Ore Range was about to see some news come from an unexpected quarter. On April 15, 1905, the men who dug the ore on the Mesabi Range made news of their own: they struck the Oliver! And they weren't very gentle about it either.

Two hundred men working in the ever-expanding Hull-Rust operation led the strike and in no time they and 1,500 co-miners stopped work at the Burt mine. A mob attacked the strippers whose job it was to remove the overburden from on top of the ore and two miners were killed in the riot.[24] The Duluth police department in the person of the Sheriff (Bates) and seventy-five of his "deputies" were called in to restore order. The local papers which were decidedly pro-business referred to the strikers as sullen, ignorant foreigners who had no grievances. Even at this distance that seems like a one-sided viewpoint.

To Tipple A Prince

The strike which began at the Hull-Rust quickly spread to other mines. The men, essentially contract miners, went from mine to mine promoting their cause and the strike. They wanted ten cents more per car for loading the ore and that according to the paper would bring them an average of seventy two cents per car. Over three hundred men marched on the Pillsbury, Glen, Clark and Chisholm underground mines, all of which fell under Mike Godfrey's supervision. Godfrey had closed the Clark but rallies at the Glen, Chisholm, and Pillsbury led to walk-outs. Tensions ran high at first but quickly flattened out and a week later an uneasy peace was holding. Sheriff Bates went home to his sick wife and his deputy, Michael Hogan (no relation to Mike Godfrey), went home for his father's funeral. The strikers slowly went back to work.

Not once in the week long melee did Godfrey's name come up even though four mines under his supervision were struck. He received no public criticism and it may be that the miners, who were well aware of his reputation, may have calculated that by striking certain mines retaliation would either be mild or non-existent and that a silent, sympathetic ear might be listening. Godfrey, however, made no public announcements or comments. A wise council was playing it close to the vest.

Godfrey did not however stay low for long and on July 15th at the annual election of School district #27 which was held in the Glen Location school house, Godfrey served as an election judge. He liked politics, sometimes as a candidate, sometimes as a delegate, sometimes as an election official but he never lost his interest in the process of how things work politically or how politically things work. In any case, Godfrey was doing something right as far as his management was concerned.

Reorganize and Prepare
Late in July, on the 22nd to be exact, the Oliver Iron Mining Company announced another of its re-organizations this time of the group of mines in and around Hibbing, now some fifteen in number. This district was

Daniel W. Lynch

now given a new Office of Assistant General Manager of the Hibbing Group of Mines and W.J. West was appointed to fill the role. This was a new position created to reflect the growing size and complexity of the Oliver's operations in this area. Open pit mining was just around the corner and the Oliver wanted to be placed at the intersection of Open Pit and Steam. West, who did not always enjoy the best of press, had formerly been the superintendent of the Hull and Rust mines for the Oliver a position now given to Mike Godfrey. W.M. Tappan took over Mike's former duties with the four underground mines. Mike was now in a position of authority in the heart of the Mesabi Iron Ore Range and at the technological intersection that was to profoundly reshape the iron ore industry.[25] Time did not hang heavily on the change.

Up until now (1905) the major mines of the Oliver were underground operations and the Hull, the Rust, the Mahoning and others were no exception. But things were changing as the scale of operations expanded - or maybe the scale of operations changed because of the technology involved. Likely, they were intertwined. The Hull mine had shipped around 250,000 tons of ore this shipping season. The Rust was keeping pace and was to ship about the same amount. All three mining properties were to the west of North Hibbing and they dominated the landscape being almost a mile in width at this time. Their properties adjoined even if their operations did not. But Mike Godfrey and the Oliver changed the nature of this activity as they changed the landscape. Stripping work was begun in the fall and continued with fervor throughout the winter. Open pit iron ore production was to begin in these mines in the summer of 1906.[26]

As stripping continued that winter Godfrey received more good news: in February he received his fourth promotion in twelve years with the Oliver. For a man who started his iron ore career as a clerk this was a fast track indeed. This promotion found Mike as assistant general superintendent to William J. West who was assigned Pentecost Mitchell's old job. The duties were in this case expanded rather than changed. Mike still held sway over the Hull and Rust operations while taking on the new responsibilities.[27] Cecelia contributed her part to the advancement of the cause by having her fifth child, a boy named Paul Francis.[28] This was the third son for Mike and Cecelia in ten years of marriage. There was a certain symmetry to the couple's lives even if they did not sense it: three sons, four promotions, five children, ten years. The bookkeeper from the Pine Creek area of Upper Michigan had arrived but he was not yet at his destination.

Head frame of the Rust underground mine. The Hull, the Rust, and the Mahoning mines, as well as the other fifty or so mines that comprised the Hull group mostly started life as underground operations where no overburden was removed and men and ore descended and rose through a shaft that was capped by a head frame. Shown here is the headframe to the Rust mine in 1900. The ore was pulled to the surface and emptied into the center of the headframe, called a pocket, whence it was dumped into the ore cars underneath. Courtesy of the Minnesota Historical Society.

General enthusiasm for this mining official reached a new peak during the year when his name was floated as a possible mayoral candidate in the upcoming elections in Hibbing. But as the paper pointed out Hibbing politics were peculiar and there were instances where a ticket that had been in the public eye for a month or so, was withdrawn the day before the election. This time Mike withdrew himself but only after waiting a month to see how things played out. He may have allowed this grace period just to stay on the good side of his fellow Republican and newspaper magnate, Claude M. Atkinson.[29]

Godfrey, W.J. West, G.H. Thompson, and Robert Murray did not waste the year, however: they put in considerable effort that season raising funds,

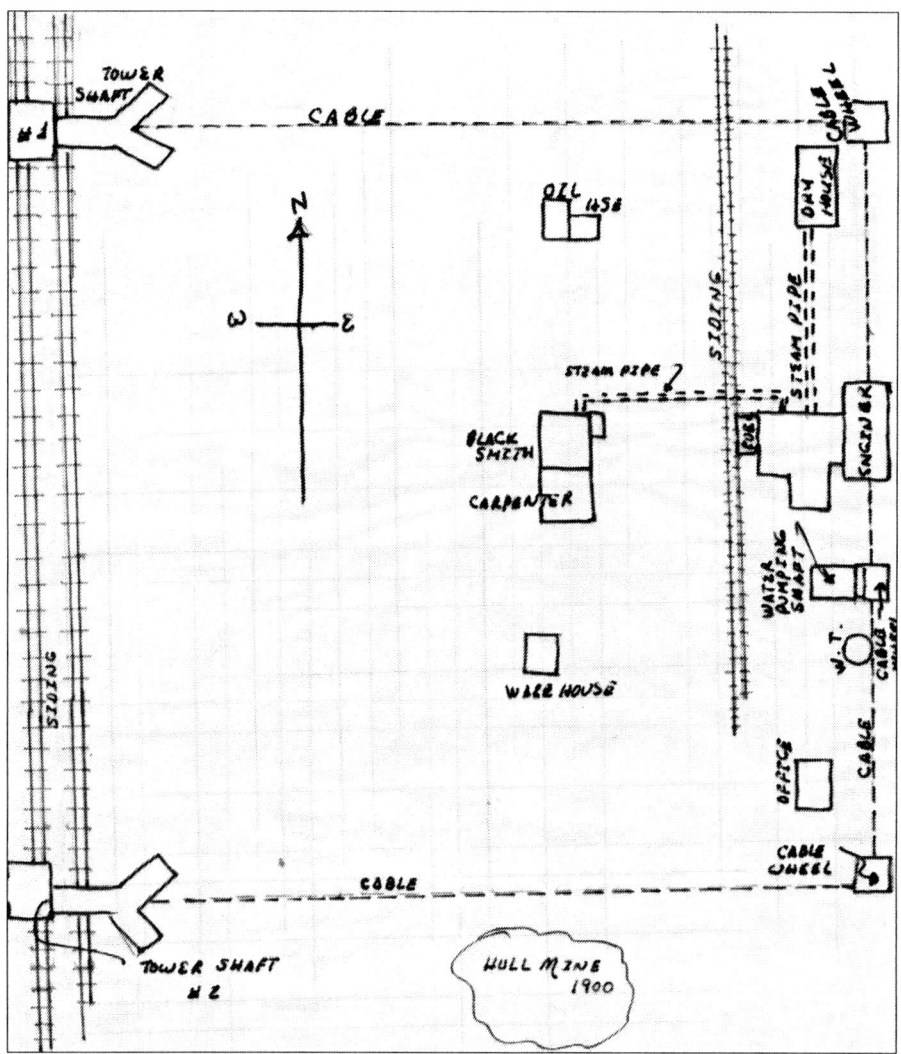

Hull underground mine site layout. An underground mine consisted of more than just a shaft to bring ore to the surface. This layout shows all the necessary elements, the Dry House where the men changed, the Blacksmith and Carpenter's shops, the Water Pumping Shaft which was necessary in a "wet" mine to remove the water constantly seeping and flowing into the mine, and the Engineering or Hoist House which was the most important element of all: it contained the power source and hoist which lowered the men into the mine and brought the ore and the men to the surface.

some $4,500.00, and started the first curling club in Hibbing, an edifice some ninety by 200 feet. It was located near the baseball park.

To Tipple A Prince

It Was Known

The year ended with an item in the *Mesaba Ore and Hibbing News* that went virtually unnoticed in the rush of ordinary events which to an extent it resembled. On December the 29th the paper described the Hull-Rust ore body as adjoining the Mahoning ore body, the two opening into one another as a tremendous excavation that would extend over an area of several square miles, *including portions of the townsite of Hibbing* [author's emphasis]. The depths of overburden amounts to one hundred feet and heretofore this was considered as entirely beyond the scope of steam shovel stripping, but no longer stands in the way of open pit works. What the editor is stating here is that there are no limits to the size of an open pit iron ore mine. The mining will go where the ore is rather than limiting itself to what it can remove. And the townsite is right in the middle.

This suggestion now seems obvious and may have been just as obvious at the time but if so the mining officials were mum about it and the public seemed oblivious to the possibilities. If a 10,000 pound elephant sits right on top of your ore it is probably better to keep quiet about it until such time as you can gracefully finesse the elephant to move. *This, in any case, was the first public, printed hint that Hibbing had a problem and no one, at least publicly, was doing anything about it.*

Of Yards, Round Houses and Hotels

As the mining industry began its shift from numerous underground operations to much larger open pit activities, massive piles of earth and rock were beginning to take up more and more land as the result of stripping operations but iron ore, too, was about to contest for the shrinking available land unless it could be transported somewhere else. And the sooner it was transported to a shipping point, the sooner it could reach the mills where it could be turned into steel. Creating gigantic piles of iron ore that dot the landscape produces neither efficiency nor profits.

Iron ore shipments by rail had to increase from the traditional loads to much larger shipments to meet the increases brought about by open pit mining methods. The Oliver Iron Ore Company and the Duluth, Missabe & Northern railway company worked together to handle the new traffic loads that were in large part going to the port of Duluth from where they would be shipped over the largest inland waterway in the world to the steel mills further east.

Increased rail traffic necessitates larger "yards" where ore car trains from each mine carrying varying grades of ore are sorted by grade and by customer and re-assembled into new trains that meet shippers' and customer needs. The iron ore trains from the mines of the Mesabi range from Virginia to Hibbing operated by the Oliver Iron Mining Company converged at a spot one and a half miles northeast of Hibbing, east of the Hull-Rust-Mahoning complex, at the Mitchell yards. These yards were to handle the increasing iron ore train loads from the Oliver properties on the Mesabi range for the next fifty years and although they were closed in the sixties and the rails removed and the ties buried under tons of rusting salvage junk, their remnants can still be discerned even today.

On the 24th of May, 1906, as spring began, the Duluth, Missabe & Northern railway began the construction of a "round" house (trainmen have a habit of calling any structure designed for locomotive maintenance, round, but Mitchell's locomotive repair shop was about as rectangular—220 feet long, sixty feet wide—as it gets). This repair shop was constructed of concrete and brick and could accommodate up to twelve locomotives at a time. The yards were to eventually have seven tracks for the marshalling operations, three additional tracks would pass through the engine repair structure, another track would bring coal to the furnace/boiler, a by-pass track and a RIP track. The yards also contained a very large wye (pronounced and shaped like the letter "y") to reverse locomotive direction, a water tower, coal station, and depot. The northern side of the yards contained the Great Northern by-pass tracks which paralleled the DM&N tracks and left the area under a double-overpass that supported the Interurban Electric trolley car line. In 1906, this operation was initially responsible for handling over 8,000,000 tons of ore from the H-R-M and the mines north and northeast.[30]

Around this huge area devoted to railway activity was another area of equal importance, the Mitchell Location. The Mitchell Location not only housed the workers who built the yards and the officials who ran the yards, but also a post office (called the Redore), and initially, a 100-border hotel (a second one was added later) for the D.M.&N. employees. The location consisted of thirty-five lots, twenty dwellings, fourteen garages, two rooming houses, and a railway depot for passengers.[31] The location's personal dwellings occupied the areas adjacent to and on either

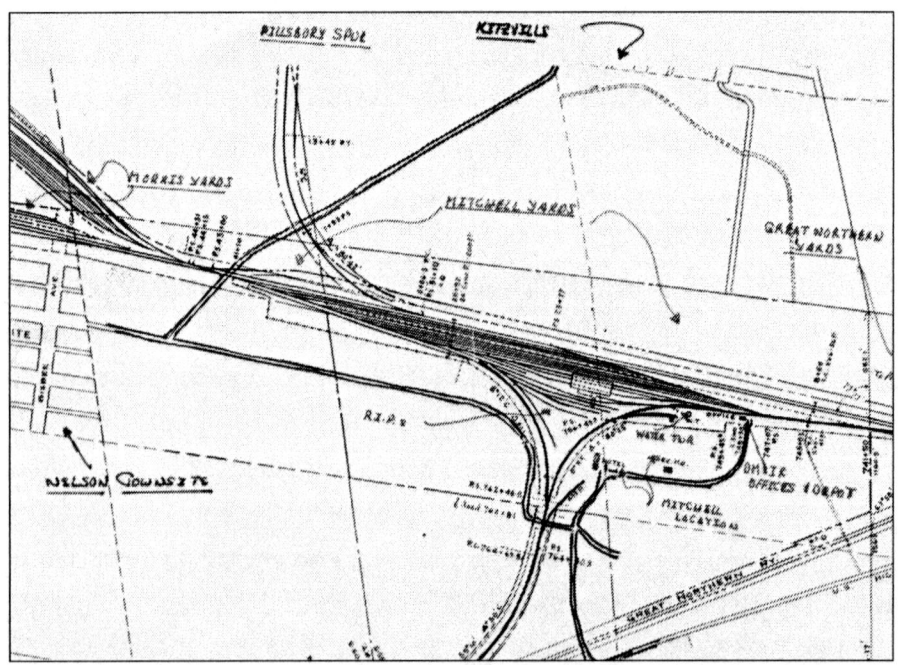

This is an overview layout of the Mitchell Yards as it looked in 1926. The Mitchell Location was to occupy positions on both sides of the railway wye. The 'round' house is right of center in the complex of tracks. The yards were just to the east of the Nelson townsite which was platted but never occupied and the Morris Yards led to the Webb underground mines (2) and the Laura. The Pillsbury spur ran north and then turned east near what is now Hwy 5. The site today is a salvage business,. The property runs northwest to southeast for over a mile. Author's Collection.

side of the wye. The Mitchell Hotel was still serving meals in 1960 and the manager, a Mrs. Isabelle "Blondie" Nosan made the best homemade pot roast on the Iron Range.[32]

The Mitchell Location, which was intended to house the D.M.& N. (later, D.M.&I.R.) workers in the marshalling yards and the necessary officials administering the yards, was to have its own long and colorful history and was still carried on the local maps in the mid-fifties (the Redore Post Office was still there). It was one of the few Locations to last, principally because like the Kelley Lake Location on the other side of Hibbing, it did not support a mine but rather a railroad (Kelley Lake serviced the Great Northern). However, like all settlements built almost entirely of wooden structures it had its problems with fire.

In March of 1907, the expected happened: the landmark Mitchell Hotel burned to the ground putting quite a few residents out in the cold. If being March wasn't bad enough the fire compounded its miseries by starting at three o'clock in the morning when the heated bricks that surrounded the front surface of the fireplace caught fire. The Hibbing Fire Department was called out (locations did not have their own facilities) but found it impossible in the smoke and general confusion to connect its hose to what few hydrants there were around. The hotel's water supply was equally useless as a fire fighting source as its basement water supply had been shut off to prevent its freezing during the night and no one could be found in the general melee that could turn it back on. Although no one died in the blaze, the manager, Mrs. John McPhail lost her furniture, bedding and other material necessary to carry on the business. She had no insurance, her husband was out in Arizona recovering his health, and she had three little children. The hotel's value was $5,000.[33]

Hibbing and Alice in 1906

While the Oliver Iron Mining Company was planning for the future, Hibbing was adding a "forty" to the village of Alice. The population of Hibbing

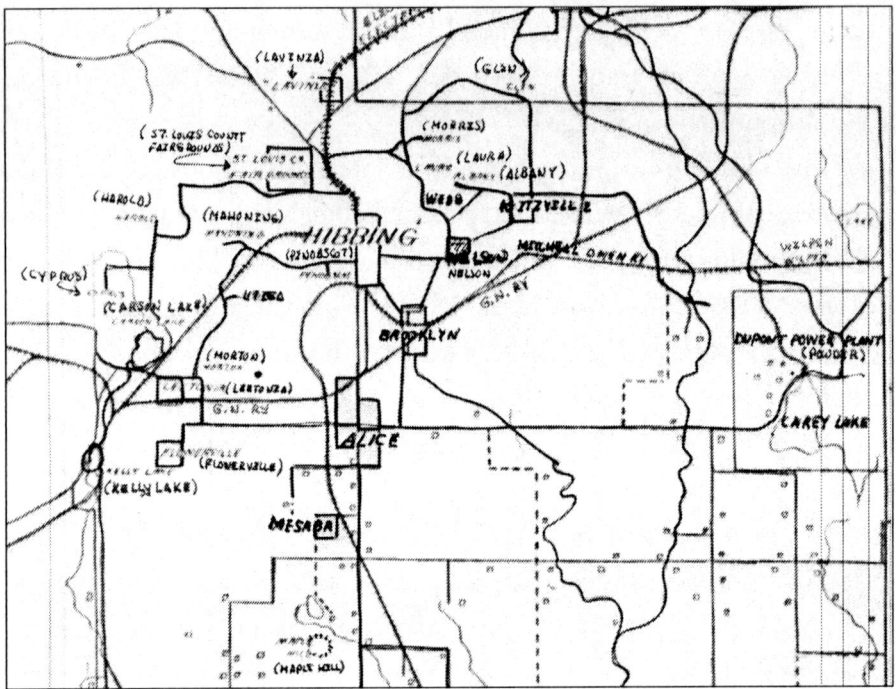

The Village of Hibbing in 1906 occupied the area half a mile north of the Village of Alice. Alice was started by Brian O'Rourke as a location about ten years before and was growing as fast as Hibbing. Hibbing was not in the best position to expand except to the south and Alice, which had city services and room, was more than willing to accept Additions. Mike Godfrey and the Oliver were well aware of this and took advantage of the sole remaining "forty" in the heart of Alice and bought it. At the time of the purchase, the Central Addition to Alice/Hibbing consisted of a few trees and a lot of mud. As a result of this purchase and the re-location of the business district in "Old North" Hibbing, the "Hibbing" of today is the "Alice" of yesterday. The map was a reprint that appeared on April 18, 1914, in the *Missabe Ore and Daily News*.

was nearing 10,000 hardy souls and the village was filling out in the form of a new Addition, the Western. The Western Addition occupied forty acres west of and adjacent to First Avenue, anchored on the south by Howard Street and on the north by Cody Street, a piece of land described by the promoters as being on the gentle decline to Penobscot Creek. The Great Northern Railroad tracks nearly cut the addition into two triangles. B.H. Hayes and Thomas Breen were the principal investors behind the platting.

Daniel W. Lynch

The Hull/Rust/Mahoning. Looking east. April 2004. Vegetative life on the bottom is sparse. The Observation Building is in the distant background on top of the photograph. Taconite operations will eventually encompass this area as well. Author's Collection.

* * *

Notes

[1] Olcott had the distinction of visiting the Hibbing area in the Summer of 1892 with Frank Hibbing. The two arrived on horseback as the railroad at the time went no further than Virginia. Olcott was not associated with the Oliver Iron Mining Company at the time, however. Olcott testimony in the *Henry P. Reed, et al., Plaintiffs vs Village of Hibbing, A Corporation, et. al., Defendants*, 1921. We will deal with what Olcott testified to later. For now, the reference is used solely to establish presence.

[2] Well, almost. Mrs. David Graham of Hibbing with a practiced eye for the dry detail that makes history so interesting, noted in 1894 that three "sporting" ladies were registered (yes, *registered*) in the Village of Hibbing. *Mrs. David Graham, papers on file with the Minnesota Historical Society, 345 Kellogg Boulevard West, St. Paul, Minnesota*. The 'papers' are in the form of typed items by Mrs. Graham, based on her recollections, diaries and local and state newspaper and magazine articles.

[3] I can't prove it but I suspect that both James Gandsey and Mike Godfrey also attended the event. James because he was a true Hibbing pioneer, local businessman and the father of Cecelia, who at the tender age of seventeen—floor manager notwithstanding—would not be allowed to attend a nocturnal dance unescorted. Mike was also a true pioneer and on the rise in the social and political atmosphere of the Iron

To Tipple A Prince

Range. James Gandsey would never have let his only child and unmarried daughter attend any social event alone, particularly one with such heavy political overtones. His political career would never have left the confines of his grocery store if he had. Mike had to be equally careful. He was single, a pioneer with some political aspirations, a Catholic, and he well knew the value of connections. Besides, he had his eye on Cecelia as would soon become obvious.

[4] For thirty years while the author was growing up every reference to the Oliver Iron Mining Company was limited to "the Oliver", never the Oliver Iron Mining Company or a variant, just The Oliver. I did not realize it at first but The Oliver was as familiar and as paternal to the Godfrey family as IBM was to a whole generation of its employees. Cradle to grave security, familiarity, and comfort. "The Oliver" was the pater familias and the Godfrey children used the same tone in referring to the company as they did when referring to their father. I think there was another reason and I'll touch upon that later. But it did not escape my notice that this (sometimes mixed) reverence was also adopted by other descendents of Pioneer Hibbing residents when referring to the Oliver.

[5] This material is drawn from various accounts in the *Hibbing News* of February, 1896. A clue as to the reason for the paper's emphasis on this dance, other than the fact that it was the only newspaper in town and it may have been a slow news day, is contained in the masthead for the paper where the editor refers to the "Home Newspaper of Republican principles and the representative mining Journal of the Mesaba Iron Range." The dance included a number of soon-to-be prominent Republicans, among them Mike Godfrey.

[6] Fred Twitchell was to die in Phoenix, Arizona in 1932, after a long and peripatetic career, or series of careers, in and out of Hibbing.

[7] The second mayor's second wife was the first school teacher in North Hibbing.

[8] This included Mikes parents, Robert 54 and Brigit 51, and his siblings, nine in all: Mary, at this time around 30 years old; Anna, aged 29; William, 28; Robert, Jr., 24; Theresa, 19; Catherine, 17; Agnes, 16; Winifred, 9. Thomas Jefferson, who was already in Hibbing, 23. The occasion must have proved propitious as Mike's family moved *en masse* to Hibbing a year later. Cecelia was given by her father and her step mother. The *Norway Current* (Michigan) of 23 October 97 was of the opinion that the wedding was a quiet one witnessed only by family and friends. Somewhere around 20/25 Irish and the wedding was a quiet one? Hmmm. The Rev. Gamache, a relative, performed the ceremony.

[9] Cecelia was no sooner out of the hospital than she was back into the social life of Hibbing attending a St. Valentine's Day party in February of 1900. Typical stays in the hospital for newly minted mothers in those days was nearly a week. Cecelia either had a remarkable constitution or an exceptionally easy pregnancy and delivery. The former seems more likely.

[10] I will go into greater detail later on but for now it is sufficient to mention that James would be barely 15 years old when World War I broke out and not yet 19 when it ended. He was by all family accounts diagnosed with a liver problem while in the army and medically discharged (his name is featured on a Hibbing High School plaque outside the front entrance) but there is a 'but' here which will be discussed later. His death certificate lists a hardening of the arteries condition (first diagnosed in 1918) and nephrites, also dated to 1918.

[11] Thomas was now employed in the Pillsbury mine for the Oliver working as a timekeeper.

[12] Miriam like her sisters went on to earn a college degree but she was the only one to go east: she graduated from one of the Seven Sisters and then returned home to care for an invalid sister (Marjorie) and teach. She never married, remained in Hibbing for the rest of her life and died of congestive heart failure in Hibbing's General Hospital in 1975. To her students she was nick-named 'fish hook' for a pin she constantly

Daniel W. Lynch

wore on school days. She had Bob Zimmerman in one of her English classes and considered him a quiet and serious student, more interested in poetry than either the classics or grammar.

Mike laid out special provisions in his will for any of his children should they wish to pursue a higher education at any institution of higher learning. Six and a half years of education along with any of the additional expenses that go along with such an education were to be paid for by a trustee. His daughters all took advantage of this benefice and completed a higher education.

[13] Although this is getting ahead of the story, the Glen Location was for a short time to have a very special mining official as its guest. Mike Godfrey was to live in the Glen Location for a while according to the *Duluth News Tribune* on March 7th, 1903. Moreover, the Godfrey Underground mine located south of the Glen mine was to have its own Location. The Godfrey mine's water supply in fact served as the Glen Location's water supply for awhile and later the Godfrey Location 'merged' with the Glen.

[14] *Duluth News Tribune*, Charles Skillings' byline. T.J. worked for the Minnesota Iron Company, one of two iron ore mining companies owned by US Steel; the other was the Oliver.

[15] Only Betty stays on the Iron Range and eventually marries the step brother of the prosecutor of the Charles Manson family.

[16] More about this later. Tom had many opportunities to go to college but had no taste for it. The Godfrey women had the taste. Perhaps the reason the boys did not pursue a higher education can be found in their father's example: Mike arrived on the Iron Range with little higher education and rose to the top of his profession. The sons may have felt the same future was in store for them.

[17] Steam, at least in its embryonic form was not long in coming. The Hull and the Rust mines which were being worked as underground operations put out bids for stripping off the overburden at the end of the 1903 shipping season.

[18] This position was not mentioned in the *Hibbing News* but when, on February 27, 1904, Godfrey did visit friends in Hibbing the News saw fit to call attention (on the 27th) to the visit mentioning that "there is always a fellow feeling here about this season of the year for the genial Michael." While it may seem like nothing more than a good way to sell newspapers (and it probably is) it should be kept in mind that a visit from a village no more than 5 or 10 miles away took the better part of half a day to travel over the rutted, water logged, mud strangled trails that we call roads. Visits were accomplishments as much as they were occasions.

[19] Marjorie's share of the estate was to be 19% as apposed to the 12½ that other members of the family received, save one: Thomas Clark the second son (he received 6%). She not only attended the U. of Minnesota for two quarters but she lived with her brother during that time. James never discussed this. Secrets have silence for offspring.

[20] And this sibling was a sister, May, who practiced law in Chicago and provided the housing for her brother, Victor, while he studied the law.

[21] Walter did not stand for re-election as he was the active managing partner for a copper mining investment in Arizona and Sonora, Mexico.

[22] In the February 1906 census, Hibbing claimed to have a population of 10,000.

[23] Just in case someone missed it, four pages later the *Mesaba Ore and Hibbing News* connected the dots and carried the announcement that the Oliver Iron Mining Company had acquired the lands of the Canisteo Iron Mining Company of the Westerly end of the Mesaba range. The Canisteo Company's leading investors were C. A. Congdon and G. G. Hartley of Duluth. The Canisteo had developed two mines of great value by this time in the Bovey area and the Oliver already was working three others. There is a rich history here

that needs more exposition in some other context. Here it is important to note that Cole and the Power brothers, Walter and Victor, were partners in the Cananea Mining Company, which was incorporated in Bisbee, Arizona. This is the area that Greenway was to settle and work in (for Cole) after Olcott fired him from the Oliver. It could be—but is difficult to prove—that Olcott felt squeezed between his superior Cole on the one hand and his subordinate Greenway on the other and removed the lesser obstacle. This is speculative but what is fact is that from a very early period F.F. Cole the head of U.S. Steel and John C. Greenway, a superintendent for the Oliver, were good friends and Greenway's visit to Cole—without Olcott's knowledge—was to have fateful consequences for Greenway.

[24] The two men, Leander Koski and John Logga, were both in their thirties, un-married and Finnish, which at the time did not help their cause. The fact that they were employed by a Minneapolis contract firm didn't help much either.

[25] Underground mines at this time were just beginning to go electric. The area had 65 such mines and a power plant was 65 miles away. The recent improvement in the efficiency of electrical machinery and application over long distance transmissions was making it possible to use this power. Open pits were such huge operations that electricity would not have been cost-effective. Mike was in the center of the open pit story but when he died an underground mine was named after him and it boasted the very latest in electrical improvements and innovations. Mike would have smiled at the irony.

[26] The Burt-Poole mining operations just to the north of the Mahoning had been converting to open pit for the last three years but this was the first year that ore production was possible: the overburden was over 60 feet in depth in this area and it wasn't going to move by itself. It is also pure overhead. Nothing is salvageable from it and once it is removed from the ore body, it still has to be *moved* somewhere *out of the way*. And if that doesn't prove to be daunting enough, you can't just dump several million tons of the stuff on your neighbor's lawn.

[27] Although not part of his new duties Mike was called upon to give the keynote address at Mitchell's going-away luncheon.

[28] Paul is a mystery for the most part. He never had a Social Security card and seems to have drifted from one job to another. He once gave his occupation as Machinist Helper and at the age of 17 was carried on the rolls of the Oliver as a Technician. Mike kept him nearby in the laboratory in North Hibbing. He never married and died in the Anoka State Hospital in 1957.

[29] Atkinson was soon to enjoy a nice sinecure himself as Hibbing postmaster, a job he held until Mike's brother Thomas Jefferson replaced him.

[30] Ironically, this huge operation, which was designed to handle the increased ore traffic from the Oliver's open pit operations and the development of which occurred on Godfrey's watch, was later, beginning in 1927, to handle all the ore coming from an underground mine named after and in honor of Mike Godfrey. This mine which we will discuss in detail later, was touted as the most modern of all the underground mines on the Mesabi Range and lasted as a going operation into the 1960s, by then having shipped some fifteen million tons of ore.

[31] The terms, "lots" and "dwellings" were apparently used instead of "real estate" as the latter term suggests permanence and individual ownership. A location was never designed to be permanent and the sole owner of property was the mining company that bought the land, built the structures, and possessed the surface and mineral rights.

[32] The Mitchell operation was so promising that several investors jumped at the chance to plat yet another Addition in the vicinity, this time just to the east of the main village of Hibbing. It would adjoin the west

end of the Mitchell Yards and be called Nelson. Walter Power had something different and definite in mind when he applied for the plat as the initial, and *only*, lots for sale were to be restricted to the business interests on the main street, Carmen. This plat was surrounded by the Buffalo and Susquehanna, Webb, and Longyear mines thus restricting its expansion possibilities even more than Hibbing itself. Since it was surrounded by railroad tracks and the mines they served, it is probably only natural that the first 96 lots were purchased by the Duluth, Missabe & Northern.

[33] There is no further mention of what may have happened to Mrs. McPhail and her children but perhaps she took fate's shove and worked on improving her health and fortune with her husband.

IV

. . . The Pot: 1912

Introduction

Hibbing was still growing during this period and, although there was some disagreement with the census takers, its population stayed close to ten thousand.[1] Mining activity continued to grow faster than anticipated as circumstances and technology made it possible to convert from underground mining methods to open pit ones. These two factors hinted darkly at consequences for both the village of Hibbing and the Oliver Iron Mining company that—even when presented with the evidence—Hibbing ignored, but Godfrey did not: he paid close and careful attention (and quite soon so was Hibbing's Victor Power).

But this slowly developing drama took backstage while another drama developed over on the Canisteo district to the southwest of Hibbing where the legendary John C. Greenway was making quite a name for himself before running right into an iceberg by the name of Olcott. At this juncture, Godfrey in his quiet way stage-managed a smooth transition, saving both Greenway's reputation and job. All this was ignored while a certain Mrs. Liend, an owner of a boarding house in North Hibbing and one of the lesser known personages in this complex series of events, obtained some satisfaction for her loss and in the process assisted in sharing Hibbing's future.

A Quiet Beginning to the New Year

Mike Godfrey was occasionally known to enjoy a good cigar and at the beginning of the year he most likely sat in front of his fireplace at 302

Daniel W. Lynch

Sellers Street in the Pillsbury Addition—the Forty immediately to the south of Hibbing—and enjoyed the quiet satisfaction of a good smoke. He had been on the range for a little less than fifteen years and had not only made quite a career for himself but had brought a fair measure of security to his growing family.

In fact, he was literally surrounded by family. His parents were three and a half blocks away on 415 Garfield Street, one brother lived a block and a half away on 429 Mahoning Street, another brother, Thomas Jefferson lived a block away at 222 Sellers Street (he also ran a very successful men's clothing store at 426 Sellers, in direct competition to the Itascan mercantile store run by Walter Power's wife). His sister, Agnes, a nurse, lived with "T.J." on Sellers. A third brother lived in the Mahoning Location west of Hibbing with his wife. He and Cecelia were successfully raising five children—James Robert, eight; Miriam Cecelia, six; Thomas Clark, four; Marjorie Helen, four, and Paul Francis, one—and Godfrey had just been promoted.[2] Life was looking good to Godfrey as he looked back over his leaving the wilderness of Michigan's upper peninsula. He was just thirty-four years of age, married to the mayor's daughter, and secure in his position with the Oliver Iron Mining company which had more economic muscle on the Mesabi Range than any other mining company, indeed, more than *all* the others. Godfrey and Hibbing were keeping apace.

Of course when things are looking that good it's time to celebrate before reality sets in and so Mike and Cecelia attended Hibbing Lodge No. 1022's first annual Charity Ball on the 17th of January. The Benevolent and Protective order of Elks was staging a dance and dinner to raise money for a special account to help the working poor. Every person fortunate enough to receive an invitation was expected to contribute a donation, even if they couldn't attend the dinner. The announcement in the *Mesaba Ore and Hibbing News*[3] predicted that anyone who missed the event would regret it for the rest of their lives as this event was the most brilliant function in the social annals of the city. Mike was on the reception committee as was his brother T.J., and a newcomer to the social whirl (and a bachelor to boot), Victor L. Power, recently of Chicago. Either the presence of such men of stature or the grandness of the occasion enticed over 160 couples to attend.

While Mike was enjoying his cigar, and an occasional dance, he was still superintendent of the Hull and the Rust development which was turning two formerly productive underground mines into open pit behemoths. That tends to keep a man busy but in spite of the obligations he already had on his plate someone (probably his friend Atkinson) slipped a notice into the paper in March speculating on Godfrey's possible candidacy for mayor. This would have embarrassed Dr. Howard Weirich, the incumbent, no end. Mike never came right out and denied the story but it did *not* reappear in subsequent issues of the paper. Godfrey did not publicly declare for candidacy either.[4]

In and Around Hibbing

While Mike Godfrey and the Oliver Iron Mining Company prepared for the future, Hibbing was not standing still (so to speak). It was expanding. No sooner had Hayes and Breen platted[5] the Western Addition than they were applying to plat the forty acres adjoining the southern boundary of the Western, which was to be called the Roosevelt Addition. The two additions formed the western boundary of the (yet to be named or platted) Central Addition.

To the north of Old North Hibbing, the Burt mine had begun surface stripping preparatory to the beginning of open pit mining in this area. The Oliver, in anticipation of this event, had already purchased several lots on the west side of Old North Hibbing south of Washington Street, and was moving a large number of dwellings from the area of the Finntown location to this newly acquired area, which was *not yet platted* (author's emphasis). (The Oliver may have been anticipating.)

Daniel W. Lynch

In 1909, the Board of Supervisors of Stuntz township voted to build a road from Hibbing to the Mitchell Location. As an item of excitement this did not rank high on any scale but it was an indicator of the importance of the location, as well as of roads and bridges. The Mitchell Location was growing fast and a number of D.M.&N. and Great Northern railroad officials had moved in and had to travel to Duluth (eighty miles away) to do their shopping. The only alternative was to take an unscheduled train to Hibbing. And that wasn't a passenger train, either. A road to Mitchell— one mile to the northeast of Hibbing— would also enable the merchants of Hibbing to send delivery teams to Mitchell. Goods, services, traffic, could move between the two centers which had not been possible

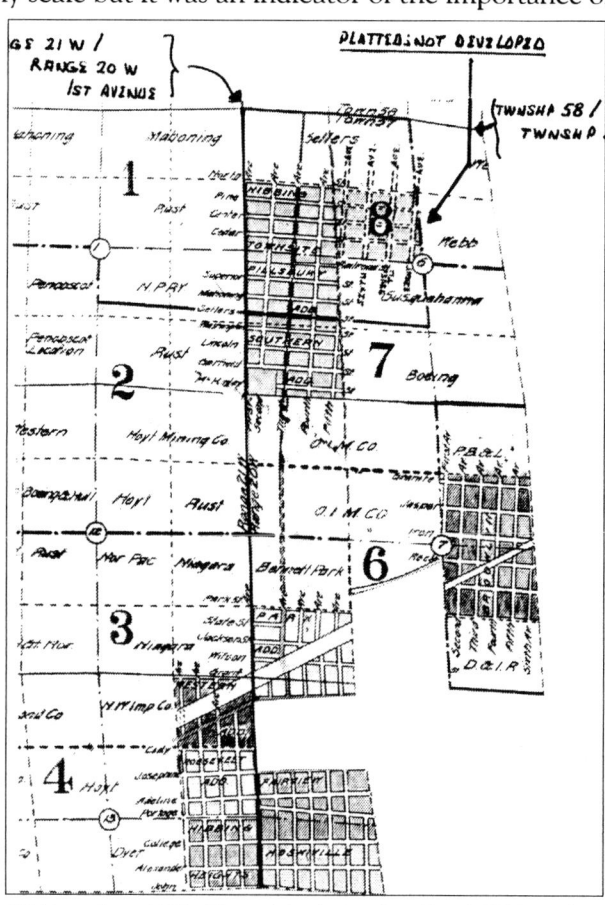

Hibbing circa 1906. The original plat that Frank Hibbing filed specified that Hibbing was located in Township 57, Range 20W, in the SW half of the NW quarter of Section 6. The line at the top of the map divides Township 58 (above the line) from Township 57 (below the line). Range 21W is to the left of the line in the center of the layout and Range 20W is to the right of the line. The red line just to the left of the big 8 is the border to the east part of the original plat which was not developed. The large numerals are voting precinct designations. Hibbing's expansion proceeded in a leapfrog fashion, first to the southeast and then (largely) to the south. Everything else was privately owned, including the mineral rights. Kitzville to the northeast and Nelson to the east are not shown. *Mesaba Ore and Hibbing News.*

previously. This problem of getting customers to merchants and of delivering orders from merchants to customers grew exponentially as the population grew.[6]

To make the point even more emphatic, for example, a trip taken by Mr. H.P. Reed—who will play a much more important role later on—on June 19, 1909, by car to Coleraine, about twenty miles away, took over two hours and ten minutes, which for the time was considered a near record.[7]

Alice Expands and Incorporates

Hibbing continued to expand all during this period by (primarily) platting new Additions to the Alice Location. In October of 1909, the fifty-one-acre Fairview Addition was platted and Bryan O'Rourke began building almost immediately on what the brochure described as a level plateau. John A. Healy owned a "forty" to the south of the Fairview and he started platting immediately. By now, there were no fewer than five additions to Alice: the Western, the Roosevelt, Hibbing Heights, Koskiville (Healy's) and Fairview, in that order.

Remember that the original plat of Hibbing was eighty acres and to the south of this was added the Pillsbury Addition and the Southern Addition, and over to the east we had Brooklyn, South Brooklyn, Nelson, and Kitzville (distant northeast).

Expansion was to the south and to the southeast and northeast of the original plat, just about anywhere except to the immediate north or west (the eastern plat of 1893 had not been and was not to be, developed). Hibbing was growing alright but didn't seem to recognize that there were unmentioned and unrecognized limitations. As long as land was available (and it was), the direction seemed unimportant.

However, this is only part of the story. Hibbing's expansion was not a simple one of adding Additions to the current ones. It chiefly involved leapfrogging a mile or so south of the Southern Addition, placing plats in several discontinuous and in some continuous locations. This general—but unincorporated—area, (at least some of it) was claimed by Alice, at one time a typical mining camp Location. Alice's precise boundaries are not easy to delineate but two references are useful: the map in Chapter III on page XX shows that the Range 21W/Range 20W boundary line (First Avenue in old "North" and present day Hibbing) runs straight through—in a north/south direction - the center of Alice, Brooklyn being to the northeast of Alice.

The other reference seemingly contradicts or maybe *refines* the first.

In January of 1910, the *Mesaba Ore and Hibbing News*[8] reported that the residents of the rapidly growing settlement a mile south of Hibbing felt that they must have a government (i.e., incorporate). This rapidly growing settlement south of Hibbing, according to the paper, contained three parcels of platted land with several hundred residents: Hibbing Heights, Roosevelt and Western Additions, all on the west side of the Range 21W/Range 20W township boundary line (the plats east of the line are not mentioned).[9]

An application for incorporation had been made in 1909, but incorporation was not possible then because the platted tracks were separated from Hibbing by sections of "unorganized" land. Such was still the case. Brooklyn was denied incorporation with Hibbing for the same reason. The residents of this platted area weren't about to wait for creeping Additions to join the two areas (and it is a good thing they didn't as the "unorganized" areas are still pretty much unorganized) and applied for incorporation as a village (as Hibbing was) to be named Alice. These are the platted tracks west of the range line. This matter was to be decided by the voters on April the 2nd when the Board of County Commissioners specified that the residents of Sections 12 and 13, Township 57, range 21W were authorized to cast their ballots. (They voted for self-incorporation.)

As the *Missabe Ore and Hibbing News* put it,[10] "The territory proposed for the new village of Alice is located one mile south of Hibbing and with the encroachment of mining operations upon the village [i.e., Hibbing] it will be but a *short time before a large number of residents will look toward this southern territory for their homes.*" [Emphasis mine.] This was in 1909, nearly a decade before anyone did anything about it and then it was certainly not the Village: Hibbing stood by and watched. The paper could see it but the village was seemingly turning a blind eye to the matter. The mining companies were indeed encroaching on a part of the Village of Hibbing ("Old" North Hibbing). In fact they were about to excavate the place, whether on not carting it off was made part of the deal.

Mining encroachments or not, the village went right ahead with what it considered the necessities of city life, this time it was the building of a new City Hall to replace the current wooden one. This was to be a three-story light-colored pressed brick seventy-five-by-125-foot structure that was to rise impressively along Second Avenue. It contained the village's, fire department and National Guard Armory's offices. The jail was also housed within its impressive White Bedford rock lined walls.[11] The interior of this nearly dead-on-arrival edifice was faced with White Marble and White enameled brick. The burial cost $130,000.

. . . and Expands Again

After its recent incorporation Alice held a special election in August of 1911 and voted to bond the village in the sum of $150,000 in order to construct a water works and install a sewer system. This was not a bad idea in a village growing as fast as Alice was especially in light of next-door neighbor Hibbing's growing interest in expanding.[12] A year later or on December 21st, Alice continued to press its expansionist point by voting to annex six sections—240 acres—of *valuable iron ore-bearing land* lying a mile and half west and south of its boundaries. The justification for this affront to mining company interests—the Utica, Morton, and part of the Scranton mine stood right in the path of this expansion—was that 146 residents lived in the annexable territory. This expansion effort offered a dress-rehearsal of the conflict to come: the mining companies needed ore and the villages that dotted the areas in question either sat on top of that ore or tried to annex ore-bearing areas for expansion. The need for more ore and the need for more urban space were growing faster than plans could accommodate.

The total amount of available land remained, as always, fixed.

Eight Hundred Men Are Put Out of Work
Mrs. Elizabeth Hukari Liend Files Suit

Hibbing woke up on Saturday the 10th of February 1912 to an unexpected headline: TWO MINES CLOSE. EIGHT HUNDRED MEN ARE OUT OF EMPLOYMENT. OLIVER COMPANY CLOSES DOWN HULL-RUST AND BURT-SELLERS AFTER INJUNCTION IS SERVED. If this headline in the *Mesaba Ore and Hibbing News* wasn't enough, the reason for the mine closings at first blush seemed even more bizarre. It seems that a local woman, Elizabeth (Lizzie) Hukari Liend had filed an injunction against the Oliver Iron Mining Company ordering them to cease mining operations and blasting so near her property! Now, that takes starch. The Oliver was the largest iron ore mining company in the state, employed more miners than any other company in the entire Midwest and paid more taxes than anyone around and a local business woman said, Stop Mining Near My House! Someone had forgotten to explain Robert's Local Rules of Mining Etiquette to the lady and she was mad.

The headline also suggests something else: the editor's attitude towards the Oliver. It is not absolutely definitive as an explanation but Claude M. Atkinson, the owner and editor of the *Mesaba Ore and Hibbing News* was a life-long Republican and a friend of Mike Godfrey's. He was also pro-big business (as his many editorials make clear).[13] The sense one gets from reading the articles and editorials of this period leave one with the impression that the Oliver was nearly helpless in the face of this unfair (and unexpected) lawsuit and not only did they have to cease operations in their two biggest mines but they had to reluctantly lay off 800 men in the process.

To Tipple A Prince

Mrs. Liend retained Victor L. Power as her legal council. She was not only mad she was serious.

Mrs. Liend (she was married but her husband seems not to have been part of the suit) owned property at 331 Pine Street, a hotel/boarding house and a– as the paper put it—monster barn where she stabled horses. This was no overnight affair either. Mrs. Liend had owned the property and had run the businesses for over fifteen years. The hotel/boarding house brought in over a $100 a week and the barn stables brought in another $72.00 per month. Roomers couldn't get any sleep and the horse owners were afraid that a rock would come hurling through the roof of the barn killing their horse.

Mrs. Liend had tried to sell her property for a fair price to the Oliver but they had not responded.

This case brought several factors to the public's attention. These factors had been there for some time but had not been acknowledged. What initially looked like a straight foreword case of cease-desist and response turned out to be a fairly tangled affair.

The injunction was issued by Judge Martin Hughes of the Eleventh judicial district and in it he called for the Oliver to cease blasting in the Sellers pit and cease its encroachment (mining activities) on Fifth Avenue. The Oliver rather liberally interpreted the order to stop blasting not only on the east side of the Village (the Sellers side) but on the west side as well (the Hull-Rust operations). Fifth Avenue was on the east side of town where the blasting and the encroachment were, not the west side. The injunction most emphatically did not apply to the west side of the Village. In as much as the Oliver had lawyers too, they knew that perfectly well.

The Oliver did not like the injunction. Judge Hughes was an official of the court that they would have to meet again (and who would again rule against the Oliver[14]). This time around the officials of the Oliver felt that the feeling against the company was sufficiently bitter that it was better to shut down both mines rather than risk contempt of court.

Daniel W. Lynch

For the Record

The historical background to this event was of a simple nature. The Village of Hibbing platted two "forty's" back in 1893. They joined each other to form an east-west axis running from First Avenue on the far west to Eight Avenue on the far east and from North Street on the Township 58/57 boundary line to South Street paralleling the Great Northern railroad tracks. The forty on the west side was platted (First to Fourth Avenue, north to South Streets) and occupied by the Village and in fact it became over the next twenty years *thee* Village. The east plat (Fifth Avenue to Eight Avenue) was never developed or occupied but was still legally part of the Village of Hibbing.

During the years following Frank Hibbing's platting of his village the Oliver had dug up and demolished several streets, alleys, and roads that were part of the east plat without filling a legal notice or taking any legal action. The avenues that were elimi-

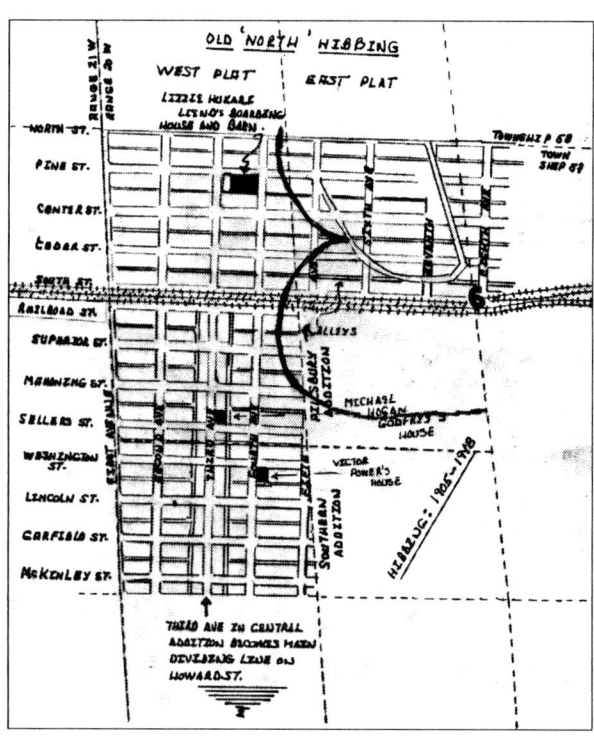

Shown here is Hibbing in approximately 1912. Elizabeth Hukari Liend's house and barn face the giant Sellers pit just to her east and are considerably removed from the west side of the village where the Hull-Rust complex was being developed. The heavy double semicircular lines represent the westernmost expansion of the Sellers mine (top arc) and the Susquehanna mine (bottom arc) and the Oliver operations at the time. The business district centered on Pine Street was cut off between Fourth and Fifth Avenues but was not yet directly affected. It would be when the Sellers and Susquehanna mines caused the viaduct over the Sellers on the far east to be removed. This was the principal access route to Chisholm, a village northeast of Hibbing. Drawn by the Author.

nated were the Fifth, Sixth and Seventh and the streets were North, Pine, Center and Cedar east of Fourth Avenue. The east plat, in fact, whatever its condition had been part of the original plat and had never been formally or legally abandoned by the Village of Hibbing. The Oliver owned most in not all of the lots in the area that they dug up but they were still obligated to give legal notice and the Village was obligated to give notice if the Oliver did not. Everybody went mute.

The result of all this silence amidst all this digging was that the Oliver's mining operations were creeping closer and closer to Mrs. Liend's property. The noise and the yawning pit were ruining her businesses. Her property's value was dropping as fast as the pit was expanding and the Oliver was not about to reimburse her for the loss.

The Oliver Files Its Response
The Oliver fired back in March contending with a blanket denial of most of the allegations and a specific charge that whatever interest Mrs. Liend had in certain lots is subject to the mineral lease of the property held by the Lake Superior Consolidated Iron Mines which gave the company the authority to enter the property and remove all ores. What isn't clear but what is implied is that Mrs. Liend had no surface rights if the mining company needed to remove ore by virtue of its mineral rights. The Oliver further contended that where it has dug into property on Fifth Avenue and Pine Street, it has only done so where it owned the abutting property and that the Village never improved the roads anyway.

The Judge Files His
This is where the matter stood for the better part of eight months waiting the court's judgment which was rendered (finally) in the first week in December. Judge Martin Hughes of the Eleventh Judicial District filed his decision making the temporary restraining order, granted back in February, permanent and so ordering the Oliver to pay costs. The Oliver Iron Mining

Company was enjoined from cutting into or across Fourth Avenue or Pine Street or making any further encroachments into the vicinity of Mrs. Liend's property. Not only was the Oliver told to keep its digging away from Mrs. Liend's property but it was further enjoined to "conduct its mining or stripping operations in the future so as not to prevent the reasonable and convenient occupancy of Mrs. Liend's premises and it must carry on its operations so as not to shake or jar the plaintiff's premises in such a way as to cause the breaking of windows or other damage."

No matter how you word that, Lizzie Liend had a very successful day in court.

But it was not to be the final chapter in this on-going tug of war between the needs of the mining companies and the rights of the local property owners. This decision applied to the property of Mrs. Liend but as the paper pointed out, it was of equal interest to all holders of property within the vicinity of the two big mines.

A Perspective of Sorts
Claude Atkinson tried to put the whole matter in some kind of perspective in an editorial in his newspaper.[15] His view was an attempt to show that each side had a good argument which would be helpful to everyone but in the end his approach was more wishful than convincing.

He felt that the businessmen and citizens of Hibbing were entitled to know what the intentions of the company were in regard to further encroachments into the area of the west plat and that the mining companies were entitled to know whether they were going to be hindered in carrying on their operations in the future. Once a full understanding was reached on each side, he felt, "everything will run smoothly." It wasn't immediately apparent what a full understanding amounted to or how it was to come about.

But Atkinson had more than this on his mind. As he said, "the Ore has it for publication that the present intentions of the company are not to cut further into the village than it has already, and those plans are expected to stand for several years." "Several years" is one very amorphous phrase. But Atkinson's source went on to say that when the time arrived that more property was needed by the company (i.e., the Oliver) for its mining operations it would pay a fair price. Maybe. The source is not identified. Atkinson closed with a warning: "A fight between the people and the Steel trust can only result in hardship and suffering to many. If the corporation officials in New York get their backs up it will be a prolonged fight in which the people of Hibbing will eventually be the losers."

The Steel trust was more reassuring, at least officially so. Oliver officials, this time from the Duluth Headquarters office, said categorically that they would not have to encroach on the improved district of Hibbing, with the possible exception of one or two lots, for the next fifteen years or possibly longer. And the company had no plans to move the Village of Hibbing as some reports would have it. Such a report was *without foundation*.[16] [Emphasis mine.] A report without foundation was denied with a response without veracity. In today's vernacular, that isn't even "good spin."

Southeast Quarter (SE¼) of the Northwest Quarter (NW¼) of Section 6, Township 57N, Range 20W
While the Oliver was waiting to take its lumps in court it was not standing still. In May, the general superintendent of the Oliver, William West, presented a petition for the Lake Superior Consolidated Iron Mines asking the Village of Hibbing to give up the use of the east ends of North, Pine, Center, Cedar and South streets to the sectional line (running about half way between Fourth and Fifth Avenue) and Fifth Avenue from North Street to South Street (effectively, the whole of the East Plat) in order that the mining work may be carried on in the ever expanding Sellers Pit. This was accepted by the Village Council.

This is the same pit giving Mrs. Liend cause for court action. And the Village Council accepted the idea! Victor Power, counsel for those opposing the granting of the petition, stated that in his estimation the council should not have anything to do with the petition as the mining companies had already taken up the matter of streets and avenues in the Judicial Court in Duluth. Accepting the petition would be legalizing an illegal action.

The Judicial Court in Duluth was indeed taking up the matter.

Enter Judge Cant of the Judicial Court in Duluth

In August of 1912, Judge Cant of the Judicial Court in Duluth handed down his ruling and this time the Oliver got something for its courtroom efforts. Judge Cant ruled that the Oliver could mine—the vacation petition was granted—that part of the plat of the Village of Hibbing which lay east of the West forty (the East, undeveloped, Plat) that adjoined the Sellers pit (the whole forty in other words since the pit adjoined the entire plat).

But as few things in life are free, neither are victories in court. The judge granted the petition on condition that the mine owners and operators compensate certain property owners named in the judgment, excluding owners of property between Third and Fourth avenues. (They were on the wrong side, the west side of the line.)

The Memorandum

But Judge Cant was not going to let the matter rest with a mere judgment for the petitioners. He quite clearly saw the situation in its entirety and laid out observation in a case memorandum. His observations were prescient.

- The vacation serves private interests (the mining companies and fee holders) and not the public welfare. The forty acres being vacated is platted land [This is the East Plat]. Immediately to the west is another forty acres of platted and entirely occupied land [This is the West Plat.] The dwellings in this area are a mixture of business, residential, and public [City Hall, library, court house, and so forth] This section had long been considered the active business center of the Village and now one or more of its main avenues and/streets which carry residential and business traffic, local and outside the community, have been cut off.

To Tipple A Prince

- All direct communications to this business section from the east will be effectively cut off. Nearly the entire surface of the vacated land has already been excavated to an average depth of seventy-five feet and the mining companies have proposed an excavation of an additional 200 feet.
- The business section is a peninsula surrounded by excavated areas instead of water. The excavation on the east connects with a deep excavation immediately to the north and this connects to another deep excavation to the west.
- Except from the south [Pillsbury and Southern Additions], it is unapproachable from any direction except at the *extreme northwest corner where a viaduct has been constructed* [Author's note: this viaduct or bridge loomed ever larger as time went on.] over the excavated area and it is over this viaduct that there is travel to and from the village.
- To travel east from anywhere in "Old" North Hibbing you first have to get to Washington Street (and if you came from the north that meant Third Avenue as that is the only route across the railroad tracks) and then go east.
- Property devoted to business will sustain a greater proportion of damage than that devoted to residence purposes.
- As to the amount of damages, my opinion is that the property owners have overestimated the same.

This memorandum laid it all out for anyone who wanted to see the future and not too many looked. North Hibbing (when years later the West Plat was moved to the Central Addition just to the east of the Western Addition of Alice, North Hibbing became "Old" North Hibbing) was being isolated as, Judge Cant called it, a peninsula. The businessmen would take the brunt of the isolation and this was noticed by the Oliver. They would have something in mind when the time came and that extended to the residential property owners as well. For now the mining companies had what they wanted but they too could read the tea leaves: if rich, high grade ore lay to the east, north and west of North Hibbing, what was under the remainder of that Peninsula?

The viaduct or bridge across the Sellers Pit, looking Southeast into North Hibbing. This is the viaduct that Judge Cant had in mind when he referred to the "viaduct on the extreme northwest corner". The extreme northwest corner of the East Plat of "Old" North Hibbing. This should be a continuation of First Avenue. Also called the North Street bridge as North Street intersects First Avenue at this juncture. Removal of this bridge cut off every town and location north of this mine from the business districts of Hibbing. Aubin Studios.

It is inconceivable that the mining companies, especially the Oliver, didn't ask themselves that question and didn't come up with a definite answer.

Looking to the Civil Future

Vic Power, who had been building his law practice slowly and for the most part off stage, was now stepping into the public eye. Back in April of 1907 he had authorized a bill to provide the larger towns of the Mesabi

To Tipple A Prince

Iron Range in St. Louis County with a District Court (for civil matters), for at least one or more terms a year. In this Mr. Power proved to have foresight equal to his legal abilities. The future would hear many such cases on St. Louis County's Mesabi Range.

Up until this time, district court was held in Duluth which was seventy-two miles and many hours away, causing many to think twice about initiating civil matters. Individual litigants were often required to spend time over several days or weeks in the Port City and that could drive the cost of a suit beyond one's means.

The bill as passed called for District Court sessions in Hibbing for a specified period each year. Mr. Power, Mr. Hughes, and the Oliver were to enjoy the benefits of the bill oft times in the future.

For now, things in the legal world on the Mesabi Iron Range, at least for Victor Power, remained relatively quiet.[17]

As if he didn't have enough to do in court or while convalescing in the hospital, Power was all over the Hibbing landscape. In addition to his legal practice and the introduction of legislation in 1910, he fronted a company that entered the interurban electric trolley car fray. The Northern Traction attempt was still in process but was not yet a going concern and there was a real need for trolley car service between the towns on the Iron Range.[18] As noted before, a car ride from Hibbing to Coleraine took over two hours (over really bad rutted dirt roads), and train facilities on the Range were for the transportation of iron ore, not passengers. And at that, if you weren't going to or from Duluth, trains were almost nonexistent.

This new company of Power's would take a western route out of Hibbing instead of Northern Traction's eastern route. The line would leave the west end of town and travel northward over the steel bridge at the end of First Avenue and then follow the rock formation in a northeasterly direction to Chisholm. The route was carefully chosen so as to avoid iron ore deposits on the way. The steel bridge was another matter.

Daniel W. Lynch

Both proposals were for electric car lines to service the area but a third proposal also launched in 1910 was to utilize gasoline-driven cars. This effort was headed by H.P. Reed, F.H. Dear and H.J. Breen. The route it chose out of town was to the south along First Avenue, to Alice.

A Civil Union
A civil matter of a different sort commanded Vic Power's attention and time in the Spring of 1910. In April he married Miss Percy Garner in Manistique, Michigan. Miss Garner was well known in the Hibbing area having been in charge of the millenary department at the Itasca Mercantile Company (Vic's brother's wife ran the establishment[19]). Father Power lived in Manistique but Mother Power lived in Chicago and it was to Chicago that the couple traveled to enjoy the honeymoon. Upon returning to Old "North" Hibbing, the Powers moved to 408 Mahoning Street, just around the corner and a block away from Mike and Cecelia Godfrey and their brood.

Civil Suits
When, in June of 1912, the Oliver circulated a petition among the local businessmen (particularly those along but not limited to Pine Street) asking the Village Council to vacate certain streets and avenues and the petition reached the council which found itself in favor, Power stepped up to the legal/political plate at a council meeting and speaking for those opposed to the granting of the petition pointed out that the mining companies had already taken up the matter in Judicial court in Duluth and that, if they accepted the petition, the council would be taking the matter out of the hands of the Judicial court.

But A.R. Crassweller, Duluth counsel for the mining companies, while mentioning that granting the petition would enable hundreds of miners to return to work, also managed to mention the obvious: the East Plat was undeveloped and the petition would do no more than return the section to what it would have been had the city never plated it in the first place. Or, if you're not going to do anything with the place why not leave it alone and we'll take care of it.

In Power's view, granting the petition—according to the revised laws of 1905—would be the same as legalizing the illegal action of the mining company. The council understood the finer points of that argument and turned down the petition. This, however, was not the last time the Village Council would come face-to-face with the dilemma of what to do with the issue and it was not the last time Vic Power would take a legal/political position that opposed the mining interests. This stance would later serve Victor Power quite well on his political journey. The more he looked at the Council's actions the less impressed he became.

Petitions were one thing, court actions another and Power had two of them on his hands this year. Near the end of the year, Power represented Louis Malleta, who like Mrs. Liend, had a grievance against the Oliver.[20] Malleta owned a small jewelry store at the east end of Center Street, a block south of the Liend property. Louis was losing customers to the fast encroaching Sellers mine. He too was seeking a restraining order against the Oliver to stop their blasting and from further cutting into the banks along the side of his property. It didn't help his business to have "large rocks and boulders" plummeting through his roof. Malleta's action was complicated by the fact that the Oliver had offered him $4,000 for his property (worth half that by the assessor) and he was holding out for $15,000. (The Oliver was not limiting its acquisitions to the Malleta property and had purchased a number of properties surrounding Malleta's. They had the mineral rights; now they needed the surface rights as well.)

It was a good year all around for Victor Power as Mrs. Liend's suit, which she had filled in February, reached court settlement status in her favor in December in no small measure due to Victor Power's efforts in her behalf. Three major actions against the Oliver placed Vic Power directly in the path of the Oliver's mining intentions and with success comes confidence. Victor Power was coming into his own as a public advocate for the "little guy" in and around the Range and was becoming equally well known as a critic (all right, opponent) of mining company policies. Quite often, this sort of combination makes men think of the bigger picture.

Frank and Mike

No matter who you are, the opportunities for doing public good are seldom lacking. And so it was that in April, with the Charity Ball not yet behind him than Godfrey was called upon to solicit funds for the creation of a statue commemorating the achievements of Frank Hibbing.[21]

A monument committee had been created and fund raising was to begin immediately. Mrs. Frank Hibbing, widow of Frank and resident of Duluth and owner of the Hibbing Hotel, had been in communication with the Hibbing Agricultural Association and given them permission to erect such a memorial to her late husband. The State of Minnesota not to be outdone, I suppose, and in a rare burst of public largesse toward residents of the Mesabi Iron Ore Range, donated forty acres of ground one mile west of Hibbing for the location of the venerable statue and park.

Victor L. Power. This photograph from a 1915 edition of the *Mesaba Ore and Hibbing News* seems to catch Vic Power in a pose where he is off thinking of the larger picture. It strikes the author as being reminiscent of Jacques Louis David's painting of another well known politician from the French revolutionary period.

Frank Hibbing Statue. This statue resides in Frank Hibbing Park, a quiet alcove situated on 19th Street, between 8th and 9th Avenue, a block north of Howard Street. But it is not the original. This is a 1941 version sculpted by Robert C. Mitchell. The original has been lost forever. Author's Collection.

To Tipple A Prince

Michael Hogan Godfrey, circa 1917. This picture shows Godfrey in front of his house on Mountain Iron Road in Virginia on Easter Sunday. It was probably a very cold day but it really would have made no difference to Godfrey: he wore a hat in public practically all the time as did most businessmen (it was a different era). Author's Collection.

Stripping Continues

Few of the operations Godfrey oversaw at this time were as important as turning the Oliver's underground operations into open pit excavations. The Winter season, roughly December thru March, saw the Oliver push hard at stripping one and a half million yards of surface overburden from the Sellers mine, the Hull-Rust mine, the Burt mine, the Morris mine, and the Pillsbury mine. These mines comprised an area half a mile square and the overburden had now been stripped off to an average depth of sixty feet. That left some twenty more feet to remove before the ore was completely exposed to full open pit mining methods. The overburden was being removed by forty-two-ton steam locomotives. The Hull and the Rust stripping operations alone saw the removal of nearly ten million cubic yards of earth.

The Hull mine and the Rust mine were among the original holdings of the old Lake Superior Consolidated Iron Mines Company and formed the original nucleus of the Oliver Iron Mining Company operations. They were among the first mines to make shipments from the Hibbing district, having been worked separately by the underground system until two years ago. The first shipment of iron ore was made from the Hull in 1895 and its output by this method up until now has been about 1,900,000 tons while the Rust, which also made its first shipment in 1895, had up until then shipped about 1,600,000 tons. These two mines formed the nucleus not only of the Oliver's earliest ore-shipping mines

The Hull-Rust today. This view is looking to the Southeast from about 1500 feet and it shows what the HR looks like as it is being mined of its Taconite. The gray areas are Taconite and it is mined much as coal is: drill holes, blast, scoop up the remains, haul it away to be processed. The water depth in the center is between fifty and a 150 feet. Author's collection.

but they also formed the nucleus of the one of the largest man-made holes in the ground anywhere.

The stripping operations—which saw four shovels working the Hull-Rust and three working the Mahoning—had formed a continuous, three quarter long open pit mine, with the two mines being next-door neighbors.[22]

Tragedy Strikes the Godfreys

The year started out well for Mike Godfrey with his superintendency of the Hull and Rust mines gaining him wide recognition for fairness among both his superiors and the miners. Iron ore shipments were running at record levels. Underground mining was being phased out and open pit mining was being phased in without noticeable difficulty. The Oliver was not enjoying noticeable success in court but judgments had been relatively small and had not so far impeded mining activity. Then, just as the year entered its fourth quarter, tragedy struck Michael and Cecelia.

The announcement was terse and final: on October the 14th Mr. and Mrs. Michael Hogan Godfrey lost their two day old son. No other details were given and none were needed. The funeral was two days later on Monday. The boy would have been the Godfreys' sixth child. He had not been named.

This apparently lead to a period of quiet mourning for the couple and little is mentioned in the papers. Two months later, Mike and Cecelia left the colds of northern Minnesota for the climes of Wyoming, Utah, Colorado, Arizona, and Mexico for a much needed vacation. They were gone almost a month before returning to life in Hibbing with its welcome rhythms.[23]

The March of Mines

In April of 1908, the Oliver announced more ambitious stripping plans for the Hartley, Sellers and Hull-Rust mines. Stripping operations had

Washington Street. Looking east from the Oliver Iron Mining Company Headquarters complex. Notice the unique five-globed street lamps which were characteristic of Old "North" Hibbing. Circa 1918. Aubin Studios.

progressed to such an extent at the Sellers that underground mining was abandoned and open pit mining was so extensive that it carried completely around the north end of the Village. In the summer, the stripping at the Hull-Rust complex of mines was creating a yawning open pit some one and a half miles long. This stripping of overburden from the Hull-Rust and the stripping that began in May for the Mahoning marked the beginning of the single, open pit iron ore complex we know as the Hull-Rust-Mahoning. The Sellers mine which was surrounding the Village was also expanding as overburden was peeled away and in August over thirty houses were being removed in the eastern part of the Village to make way for more stripping. The Village of Hibbing was beginning to look like a peninsula jutting defiantly into an empty ocean. And the mining companies were nowhere near done. The August 22, 1908, edition of the *Mesaba Ore and Hibbing News* had it correct: "it is in fact only a question of time when the town itself will be fairly engulfed. Already, the Sellers pit is within three blocks of the Post Office and the main business portion of Hibbing. The ore deposits extend southerly into the town for blocks yet. Eventually its stripping will be undertaken and when this is done there must be of necessity a wholesale removal of buildings."[24]

The Village still didn't seem to be listening. The Village Council announced in May financing plans for purchasing lots at the corner of Second Avenue and Center Street for the new three story Village Hall which was to begin construction in a year. The Village already owned two lots at the corner and was now purchasing a third.[25]

The Oliver was contributing to the general feeling of complacency, whether intentional or not, by going ahead with its plans for an employee clubhouse. Godfrey had already paid one visit to Proctor to appraise the DM&IR railroad club house and to pick up ideas for the Hibbing version. Along with his secretary, Mr. William F. Kohagen, and his planning department, most of which was headquartered in Duluth, Godfrey and the Oliver came up with a final design that almost dazzled. The design called

Village Hall. Old North Hibbing at the corner of Second Avenue and Center Street. This building which was built in 1909 replaced the earlier one and housed all the Village's municipal departments. There was also an armory on the third floor. It cost $130,000 to build and measured seventy-five by 125 feet. Aubin Studios.

for a $25,000 two-story, fifty-by-nintey-foot, wooden structure containing Reading and Reception rooms, a Kitchen and a Dinning room and naturally a Billiard Hall. The basement housed two complete bowling alleys. Just in case anyone should look askance at the plans a fine dancing hall graced the second floor. The club house would occupy the better half of a block (actually eight lots) on the south side of Cedar Street between Second Avenue and Third Avenue. This perched the structure north of the railroad tracks and if any part of Old "North" Hibbing was to find its way to the bottom of the HRM mine, this section would.[26]

Dividing It Up

The new year is a time for both private resolutions and public announcements and no sooner had various individual resolutions been laid to rest

Oliver Iron Mining Company Clubhouse. Circa 1915. This is the employee clubhouse that the Oliver constructed in 1908/1909 (it was dedicated on New Years Day). The location is on the south side of Cedar Street between Second and Third Avenue in Old "North" Hibbing. It was later moved to the corner of Fifth Avenue and Mesaba Street (present day Twenty-first Street), the site of the present day library. Postcard from a Bloom Brothers Imprint. Minneapolis, Minnesota.

than the Oliver Iron Mining Company announced its resolution: the Hibbing Mining District was being divided. The iron ore operations were simply too big and too difficult for one general superintendent to manage and so the spoils had to be divided. U.S. Steel wasted no time in making the announcement on the 2nd of January, 1909.

The announcement was heralded on the front page of the paper: DISTRICT DIVIDED. OLIVER IRON MINING COMPANY CUTS HIBBING DISTRICT IN TWO.[27] What had been known as the Hibbing District of the Oliver Iron Mining Company, a subsidiary of the U.S. Steel Corporation, were now two districts, each under the management of a general superintendent. William J. West the superintendent of the Hibbing District was now the general superintendent of the Hibbing District but the district and Mr. West's responsibilities had changed. The Hibbing District now encompassed the Oliver's mining operations west of the Pillsbury mine such as the Winifred, Morris, Sellers, Burt-Pool,

Hull, Rust and two new properties to be developed in 1909 (presently, unnamed). Godfrey's responsibilities encompassed the Pillsbury mine and all Oliver operations east of there such as the Glen, Clark, Chisholm, Leonard, Monroe-Tener, Myers and the Hartley. This entirely new district carved out of the old one was to be called the Chisholm District. The Chisholm District was so new in fact that it did not even have an office. That was to be built 'later in the year'.[28] Godfrey, however, did not have the luxury of waiting for the construction of a new headquarters building or for even one of his own: he took a temporary—it was to last over a year—dwelling at #85 Monroe Location, just south of Chisholm, five miles northeast of Hibbing. Cecelia stayed home in Hibbing with the children and Mike started a daily commute. Mike Godfrey had come a long way from Norway, Michigan, in the heart of the Gogebic Range in 1893 and now, fifteen years later, he sat on top of the management hierarchy of the Oliver Iron Mining Company's Mesabi Range operations in the heart of northern Minnesota.[29]

The Monroe Location. Mike Godfrey's home (left foreground) as he assumed the duties of general superintendent of the Chisholm District. The Monroe Location is long gone but in 1909 it looked like it might last. No attempt at a landscape aesthetic is evident as Locations were generally functional. However, flower gardens added color and such efforts were sometimes awarded prizes. Iron Range Research Center; now, *Minnesota Discovery World*.

Daniel W. Lynch

Things were so busy and the lack of planning so noticeable that Godfrey was called to Duluth to consult with his superiors, Pentecost Mitchell and W.J. Olcott. He was there for three weeks and stayed at the GitchiGami Club while in the city.[30] Not only were mining districts being divided but administrative duties had to be re-arranged and re-assigned, and managerial duties and responsibilities had to be re-defined. It is one thing to divide a mining district in two by drawing a line through it but it is another thing entirely to re-arrange duties and authorities. There are some very large egos involved and various considerations have to be placated. It won't do to lose your top talent over a minor contretemps. Besides, Godfrey and West already had plenty to occupy their time.

An Ongoing Problem Finds a Solution

Miners like to drink. And when the ordinary comforts of civilization are absent—comforts such as churches, medical facilities, sports arenas, and family organizations—and brutally hard work abounds, drinking can become a personal, social, and business problem. The mining concerns were particularly sensitive to this when it came to their employees: work time lost due to drinking resulted in ore not being mined and profits being low-

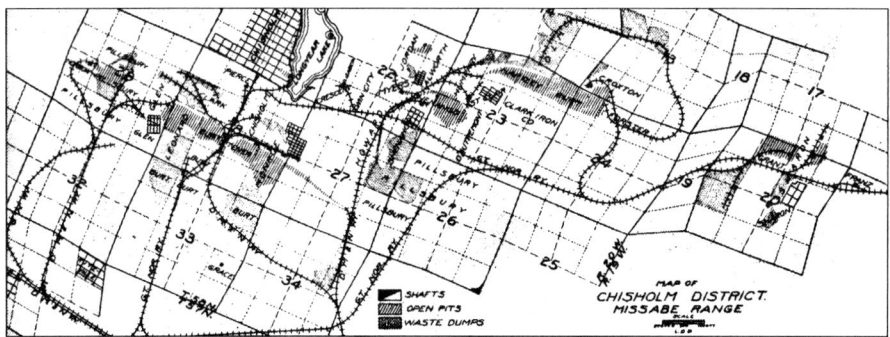

Chisholm District. Township 57N, Range 20W. This is the picture that greeted Mike Godfrey when he took charge in 1909. The ore deposit in this area ran southwest to northeast as it did over most of the Mesaba Range. Notice the prevalence of railroads. There was simply no other way to transport iron ore from the Mesabi Iron Ore range to Duluth or anywhere else except by steam-driven locomotives. Charles E. van Barneveld, Iron Mining in Minnesota, Bulletin, No. 1, The University of Minnesota, Minnesota School of Mines Experiment Station (1912), Minneapolis, MN. p. 151.

ered and sometimes it also meant increased medical expenses. This was not a unique problem limited to just the iron range but it had a heavy impact in what was at the time nearly a frontier of forest, swamp, and rock.

There wasn't much the mining companies could do about the proliferation of bars, saloons and taverns that plagued iron range towns along this frontier but they could address the problem in their own back yard Locations. A letter survives indicating how the Oliver felt about the problem and what they were willing to do about it. The letter is from Godfrey to his superior in Duluth, Pentecost Mitchell, and it is dated August 14, 1909. It is in response to an inquiry Mitchell had made as to a recent policy decision on the part of the Duluth Headquarters.[31]

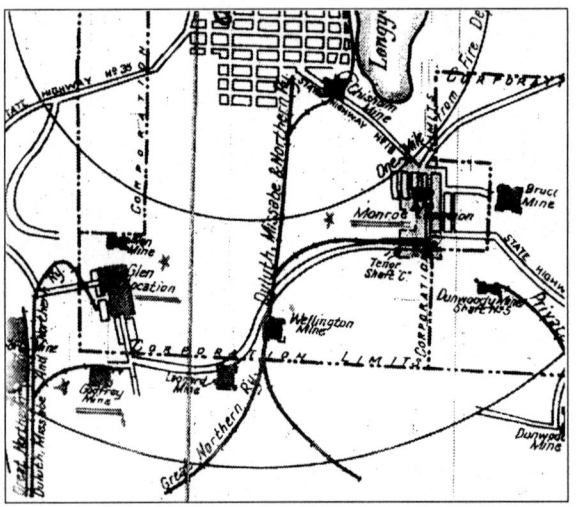

From a Sanborn Fire Insurance Map dated 1930. Chisholm is at the top. The Monroe Location is approximately a mile to the southeast of Chisholm and Longyear Lake. The Glen Location and the Godfrey mine—much more about that later—are approximately a mile and a half southwest of Chisholm.

There seem to be two points in Mitchell's inquiry that Godfrey is responding to: the stopping of liquor sales by the Oliver at some locations (but not at all of them) and the problems and benefits resulting from that policy. The Oliver wanted to ban the sale and distribution of liquor from their mining Locations because in their opinion it resulted in crime, lost work time, accidents, the spread of disease, strikes, unhappiness, and premature death. They were also concerned that men would gravitate to those locations were liquor was permitted, abandoning the locations where it was not.

Godfrey is basically telling his bosses what they wanted to hear but the letter appears to reflect his own beliefs as well. He begins by emphasizing that he believes that prohibiting the distribution of intoxicating liquor to Oliver employees at Oliver Locations during the strike of 1907, was one of the wisest policy decisions the Oliver ever made. Since then this general policy had been used to target the specific locations of Myers, St. Clair, Glen and Clark. To quote directly from the letter:

> During the strike it was argued, and I think wisely, that if any trouble occurred it would have its origin at those "blind pigs"[32] where men and women congregated and drank to excess, that argument still holds good.

But the heart of the letter is the second paragraph where practically all the issues are commented upon:

> Prohibiting the delivery of beer on our mining locations has improved conditions as far as disturbances, fighting, shooting, etc. are concerned. Of late there has been very little complaint from the men because beer was stopped, though complaints were common at first. It has, I believe, tended to make the men more contented, steadier, and has materially increased their efficiency, besides lessening the possibilities of accidents as men are now reporting for work sober rather than in a semi-dazed condition as frequently happened in the past and men do not remain away from work as long on pay days and holidays as under former conditions. It has not resulted in driving the men into the saloons of the village, as is evidenced by the fact that a considerable number of saloon-keepers at Chisholm are opposed to the closing of the "blind-pigs", claiming that is has hurt their business.

In short, conditions have improved since we instituted the policy of preventing the sale of beer on our property. The men are more efficient, (read more productive), and accidents—always a prime concern of Godfrey's—are also down. All of which were true. Also true was the fact that "sick time" right after payday was also down. Godfrey may, possibly, be quoting himself, however, when he claims that the closing of the blind-pigs on Oliver property has hurt the liquor trade in town. If anything it would have helped business in town. A dry miner does not head home immediately if beer is unavailable in a location although he may wait a little longer between drinks.

So far as Mike Godfrey was concerned not a single man had quit because of the policy and he goes on to claim that "the large exodus of men from this Range has gone from points where liquor was permitted." Whether or not that was true is arguable but Godfrey is clear in his message that beer is the cause of many problems that the Oliver has encountered over the years and that nothing but good has come from the company policy. Mitchell and Olcott must have felt good about that. In case Mike missed a point or two somewhere along the line, he closes with a resounding declaration:

> Existing conditions at our locations are I sincerely believe a direct benefit to the men, their families, the company and the nearby villages, and we know from incontrovertible evidence that "Blind-pigism" is of all causes the most frequent source of poverty, unhappiness, immorality, crime, disease, accident and death.

Wow. Godfrey could have made a living writing for the Temperance Union. Men who do not drink—and Godfrey rarely drank—tend to take a less than charitable view of those who do and this letter does reflect such an underlying conviction. It is also true that the Oliver was concerned with lost time, accidents (often resulting in the death of a miner), lack of productivity and so forth but it is hard if not difficult to prove that the sale of beer lead to strikes or that the closing of blind-pigs hurt the liquor trade in town or that men were leaving town because beer was being served nearby.

Overall though, excessive drinking constituted a problem at many mining locations and removing the source of the problem to a remote village probably did not hurt. Accidents were certainly down when beer was unavailable but those were *mining* accidents, whatever other kinds of accidents may have been prevented is hard to tell. I think, and Godfrey does touch on the issue, that the men were getting a pretty good deal with cheap rent at a company location and the company did have a right to regulate the sale of liquor on its own premises.

The Oliver Makes Its Move

Now that the Oliver had the Mesabi Iron Ore Range divided up between the Hibbing and Chisholm districts and iron ore mining was progressing at a rapid rate from underground operations to open pit ones and, that Old "North" Hibbing was eventually going to be swallowed up by constantly expanding mining activities, it was time to move headquarters. With Old "North" Hibbing surrounded, on the west, the north, and the east, by mining activities the headquarters complex of laboratories, blacksmith shops, carpenter shops, administrative centers, and railway access, had to move or it too would wind up at the bottom of what was fast becoming one great big giant, open pit.

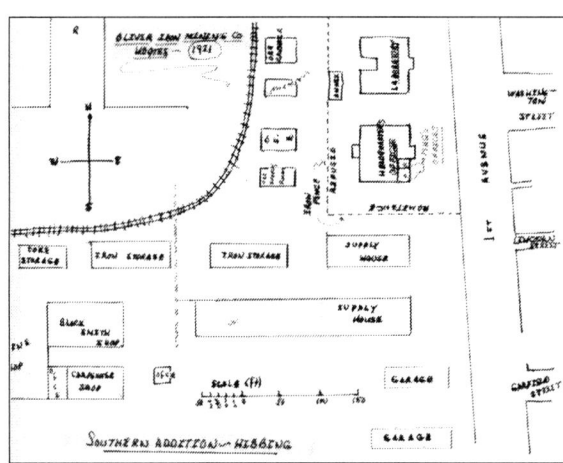

Oliver Iron Mining Company Headquarters Complex. This is a layout of the Oliver headquarters complex as it looked later in 1921. The previous site was abandoned because as the Oliver announcement said, "it is necessary to give up the ground for mining purposes." The Sellers open pit mine was about to swallow it. The new site is still there but the buildings have long been bull dozed into oblivion. Hibbing has replaced some of the street lamps that are so unique to the area and some of the street signs. Only the Oliver Avenue sign is missing. The east side of First Avenue is now a camp ground. Redrawn from *Mesaba Ore and Hibbing News*.

In October 1909 the Oliver announced that it was going to move its headquarters from the intersection of Third Avenue and North Street (also the administrative headquarters of the Sellers mine complex) to a twenty acre site west of First Avenue between Garfield Street on the south and Washington

Street on the north. This put the Oliver's headquarters on the west side of the Southern Addition of Old "North" Hibbing. It also put it out of harms way.[33]

Whenever the Oliver wanted to promote what it was doing it called in a reporter from the *Mesaba Ore and Hibbing News* for a thoroughgoing explanation of the facts. The paper obliged with an excellent run down.[34] Under a banner headline on the front page that proclaimed, **WILL REMOVE HEADQUARTERS. OLIVER IRON MINING COMPANY TO BUILD NEW SHOPS AND OFFICES,** the article went on to detail the new headquarters site.

> All the buildings will be erected on a much larger scale than those now in use. The office will be a handsome three-story structure with a basement and will be modern in every detail. The machine shop will be a model of its kind. The dimensions of the building will be 115 by 215 feet and like the old shop it will contain machine, blacksmith, and carpenter shops. The machine shop now in use if sixty by 190 feet and is far too small for the demands made upon it.
>
> The foundation for the engine house is already will along and that will be the first building to be completed. The office will occupy the most commanding site on the plot, and the ground will be leveled and terraced.

But the many new and much larger buildings[35] were not the main feature of the place and if you visit this site today and walk around in the weeds and scrub brush for awhile you will find out what was: tracks! And a lot of them because, "it is the plan to have the marshalling yards of the Sellers, Burt, Pool, Hull, and Rust mines at the south end of the twenty acre site which will insure a permanent yard for these mines, for the reason that the overburden at this point is so heavy as to preclude the idea of stripping." In other words, it was not cost effective enough to remove what ore there was.

Five open pit mines all with their railroad facilities in one place is an operation befitting the size of the mines being served. Rearranging all that trackage in fact took over a year and the ore outlet for leaving the mines had to be changed from east to west. The reason for the re-orientation of the outlet, however, had more to do with the Buffalo & Susquehanna's decision to strip its property (for open pit mining) southeast of the Sellers and Burt-Pool mining activities and this cut off the eastern outlet of those properties.

That wasn't the end of the story and the consequences of the next act were to be felt many years later when the act had to be undone. In creating the new Western outlet for the ore it was found necessary to dig out the highway which was the extension of First Avenue and this cut off access to and from the west and north end of Old "North" Hibbing. Any village, location, settlement, road—in short goods, services, and people—currently using that road was now cut off but the mining company knew a controversy when it created one and so it announced that it was to construct a steel bridge, three hundred feet long and at a cost of over $80,000.00 over the open pit at that point, which would restore communication to the west and north.

The article concludes by noting that when the new buildings are ready for occupancy the old ones would be dismantled and any other

Oliver Iron Mining Company Headquarters, Old "North" Hibbing between Garfield and Washington Streets. From a penny postcard, postmarked Hibbing, Minnesota, May 27, 1912. The Laboratory is the building on the corner and the Headquarters building is next door (south of) to it. The front of each building opens onto First Avenue which runs north and south and forms the boundary line between Range 21West and Range 20 West. Postcard from a Bloom Brothers Imprint, (1910), Minneapolis, Minnesota.

buildings on the site would also be removed which would then allow the open pit operations to extend "down to North Street and the resultant open pit would extend from the Mahoning on the west side of the Village to the Sellers on the east, a distance of nearly two miles." Two new mines, the Dell and the Arno, west and southwest of the Mahoning were to open early the next year when stripping concluded. Emptiness was enclosing Hibbing.

A Mesabi Iron Ore Range Mystery

Almost lost in the general excitement of the announcement and initial clearing and construction was an event that sent shock waves through much of the mining community and in towns and villages alike: John C. Greenway, general superintendent of the Canisteo District of the Western Mesabi had been fired!

Greenway had been headquartered in Coleraine for about four and a half years and was immensely popular, probably at that time the most popular mining official on the Mesabi Iron Ore Range, just ahead of Godfrey. Something was very wrong in the Canisteo for this to happen. There had been no forewarning and in fact the local papers were a bit vague as to not only what happened but whether or not Greenway had been fired or had resigned.

But this was real solid news and it was a jolt. Nothing like this had happened before to so popular or highly placed a mining official, at least not one working for the giant Oliver Iron Mining Company. What was this all about?

John C. Greenway was a very well-connected graduate of Yale University who knew his way around mining camps having started in the business in 1894 in Homestead, Pennsylvania, where he worked for the Pittsburg Steel Company, beginning at $1.75 per day. From there he went to the Upper Peninsula of Michigan and worked for the Oliver in Ishpeming. During the Spanish-American war he rode with Teddy Roosevelt's Rough Riders, distinguishing himself at San Juan hill, and was promoted to Captain of Volunteers. He and Roosevelt remained close. Greenway was also a good friend of William Howard Taft. In October he and T.F. Cole, the president of the Oliver Iron Mining Company, had spent a month together visiting Cole's copper holdings in Mexico and Nevada. Greenway was obviously well-connected.

The events leading up to Greenway's departure are summarized nicely in Boese's book[36] but they bear repeating. Sometime in November 1909, Greenway received a confidential letter from John Carse who worked in U.S. Steel's New York office. Carse was informing Greenway that the president of U.S. Steel, Judge E.H. Gary, had made some inquiries about the Canisteo District and wanted to talk to John. Greenway had been planning to go to New York in January anyway and he said he would be glad to meet with the judge then. Carse wrote back and suggested he meet with the judge forthwith. Greenway requested a leave from Olcott without telling him what he was about to do and proceeded directly to New York. Greenway and Gary had their conversations,[37] Greenway returned home, Olcott requested his presence in Duluth, Greenway traveled to Duluth and was fired.

Here is how Boese puts it:[38]

> Arriving in Duluth in mid-December, Greenway went to the Oliver Iron Mining Company's headquarters in the Wolvin Building (Author: on Superior Street, the main thoroughfare in Duluth) where he was ushered into Olcott's office. There he was abruptly confronted with questions concerning his recent trip to New York. Greenway had no choice but to acknowledge that he had been involved in discussions concerning his district with the top officers of the United States Steel Corporation. Olcott flatly stated that he considered Greenway's participation in those discussions, carried out without his knowledge, to have been an act of disloyalty to himself and to the Oliver Iron Mining Company.
>
> A quite astonished John Greenway was requested to tender his immediate resignation.

Greenway pointed out that he was asked by the president of U.S. Steel (to whom the Oliver also reported) to keep the discussions confidential. This cut no ice with Olcott who repeated his charge that Greenway had been disloyal.

This is little to go on in this mess without a few additional points of interest: Olcott had been president of the Oliver for only a short time before this incident and may have felt a bit insecure about his own position when a subordinate and a superior were having private talks, private talks he had not been privy to; a U.S. Steel second vice president by the name of Kerr, the official who initially told Olcott of Greenway's conversations with Gary, was also the official whom Olcott checked with and who consented to, the firing.

Kerr's real reason for telling Olcott of the talks has never been examined in any detail and it would be interesting to hear his side of all this. It was after all Kerr's initiative that lead to Greenway's firing and Kerr's consent that made it possible. However, office politics being what they usually are, the parties to the intrigue—if that is what is was—are the only parties that aren't going to issue any clarifications.[39]

And they didn't.

A Simple Twist of Fate

The news that John C. Greenway had "resigned" or had been fired, news accounts were not clear, would have rung the phone sitting on Godfrey's desk even before the news reached the men's room. Olcott or his secretary would surely have told his general superintendents what had happened even if he was not clear on why. Godfrey had just begun to take charge in Chisholm when he heard the news. What Olcott did tell Godfrey and the other general superintendents is not known but no sooner were they informed of the act than it became general knowledge that Mike Godfrey was being asked to go to the Canisteo District and take over Greenway's responsibilities.

Godfrey must have been somewhat taken aback as such firings were not common in the Oliver world and he, himself, had just got into the rhythm of operations in the Chisholm area. Now, he had to travel to the other end of the Mesabi Range and take over an operation he was not familiar with, from a man of immense ability and popularity, in the dead of winter, with no advance notice, before his family had even had time to unpack in the Monroe Location? Fate does not require preparation.

The Christmas Day edition of the Hibbing paper on page 4 reported that: GODFREY MOVES UP. RUMORED THAT M.H. GODFREY WILL SUCCEED GREENWAY AT COLERAINE. Michael H. Godfrey was being introduced as the new general superintendent of the Canisteo District. He and his general manager McLean had arrived just the night before on a special train from Chisholm and President W.J. Olcott and vice-president Pentecost Mitchell arrived the following day from Duluth.

Boese[40] has a nice first hand account and tells it best:

> Later in the day McLean left for Duluth, and Godfrey took over Greenway's offices and a small room upstairs to serve as a sleeping accommodation. He did not seem to be enjoying his situation at all and told Greenway's secretary that he "did not care about coming here, but came as it was the wish of the officials." In the midst of the uncertainty and confusion, the secretary went to the train depot to welcome Greenway's parents and sister, but they had learned that something had happened and did not arrive.

Oliver Iron Mining Company Headquarters building for the Canisteo District, Coleraine. It is used by the local school district today but the company's name can still be clearly seen above the doorway. Mike Godfrey stayed here for two weeks until Greenway's (equally) surprising return. But he had to come back on a more permanent basis when Greenway left for good. Author's Collection.

Godfrey must have been very uncomfortable. He was using another man's secretary and was aware that Greenway's family was to arrive by train that day. And he gets the upstairs cot for the night. He was to remain here for the next two weeks as the drama held all in suspended inaction. The drama had a turn or two left.

Greenway "Rehired"
As if he had never left, John C. Greenway returned to his job as general superintendent of the Canisteo District during the first week in January 1910. U.S. Steel rescinded Olcott's decision and re-instated Greenway. Greenway's only comment on the incident was that the firing was a mistake. Olcott's comment was equally helpful, "If Greenway says he is coming back, it must be true." That from the man ordered to reinstate Greenway. Not only were the men unwilling to talk about the affair but they never again had a warm working relationship, just a cool, distant businesslike one.

On January 8th the *Mesaba Ore and Hibbing News* had a delightful, tongue-in-cheek reference to the whole incident. The column was headed: PLEASANT VACATION and went on to say that John C. Greenway, superintendent of the iron mines of U.S.S. in the Coleraine District of the Mesaba Range returned Saturday after a pleasant visit with Eastern Friends and seems to be well pleased with the visit. Godfrey returned to the Chisholm District and his family.

But not for long.

Winter stripping in the Chisholm District gave way to spring mining all across the Mesabi Range in 1910 while Greenway got busy with building the Trout Lake Concentrator. Summer would bring the inevitable mosquito invasion while open pit mines shoveled ore into waiting trains and the steel mills of the East turned out steel for the ever-hungry American industry.

July's Good News-Bad News
First, the Good News
By July the mining season and the shipping season were well under way with open pits set to ship record amounts of iron ore. But in July Mike

and Cecelia celebrated the birth of their sixth child, third daughter, Elizabeth Ann. The lucky couple spent the entire week at the hospital in Chisholm[41] as they were worried that fate might take away their second child in a row. Fate waited for this child. Mike and Cecelia now had an even pairing of three girls and three boys.

Then, the Bad
In July as Mike and Cecelia were celebrating and adjusting to another household member, John C. Greenway was resigning. He left Minnesota in July to assume a new position as general manager of the Superior & Pittsburg and Calumet and Arizona Copper companies centered in Bisbee, Arizona. He was given a royal send off by the grateful citizens of Coleraine at an outdoor picnic. He felt good about what he had accomplished in Minnesota but looked foreword to the new challenges out West.

He never mentioned Olcott again.

Mike Godfrey's name was suggested as a possible successor. Men[42] in close touch with the Oliver Iron Mining Company said that it is likely that general superintendent Godfrey of the Chisholm District would be Mr. Greenway's successor.

But . . .
On July 16th the Oliver confirmed the rumors: Michael Hogan Godfrey, age thirty-eight, currently general superintendent of the Chisholm District for the Oliver, was being named as the general superintendent of the Canisteo District. The reporter for the *Mesaba Ore and Hibbing News* placed Godfrey in the forefront of those Oliver mining administrators that had a place reserved in the local hall of ore fame. As the paper said, "Mr. Godfrey is accounted one of the most successful mining superintendents in the Lake Superior region, and is well qualified to overcome the difficulties that constantly confront the mining man in the successful operation of the mines along the western end of the range. The new

To Tipple A Prince

Canisteo superintendent is particularly well known in Hibbing, where he spent many years in connection with mining operations carried foreword by the old Lake Superior Consolidated Iron Mines Company and the Oliver Iron Mining Company."

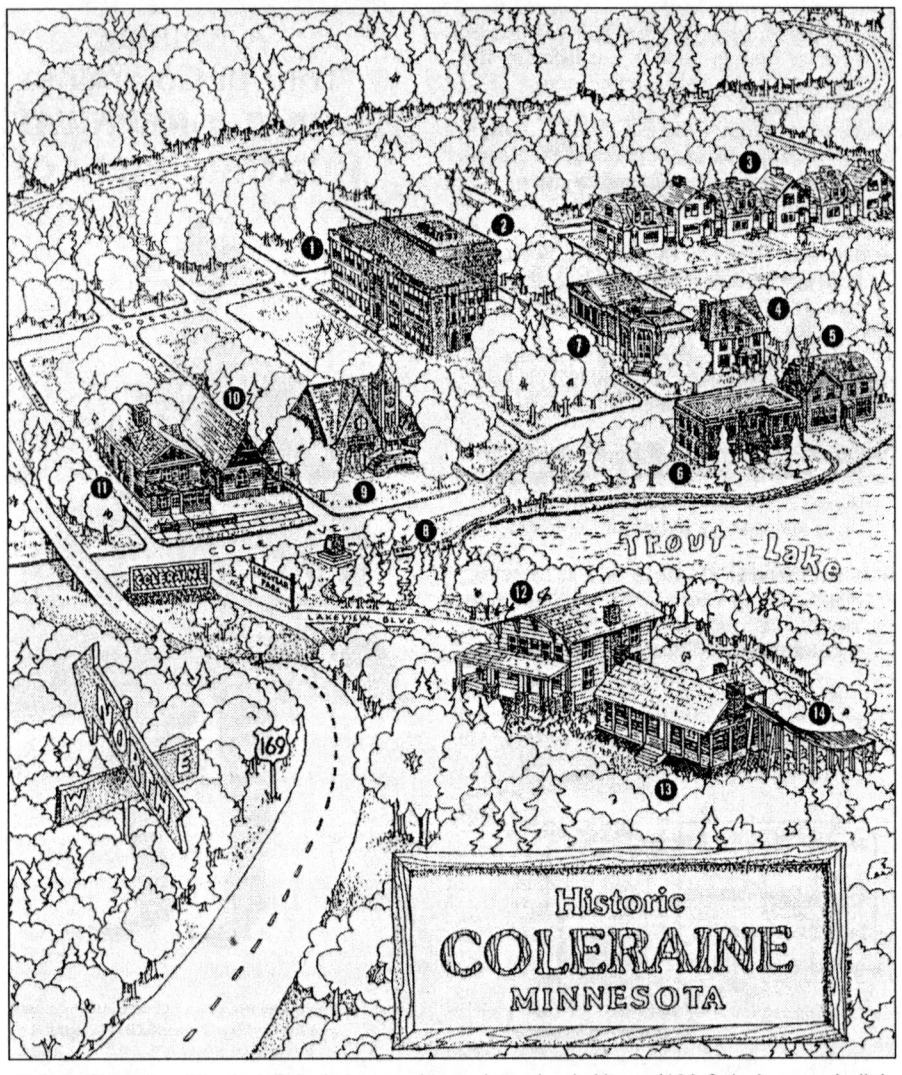

Historic Coleraine. Number ❺ is the general superintendent's Home (100 Cole Avenue, built in 1910) and ❻ is the Oliver Iron Mining Company office (200 Cole Avenue built in 1909). The Trout Lake Concentrator was on the southeast side of Trout Lake. All the Godfrey children remember the view of the lake which was the first time they had such a view in the many places they lived. Sketch by Rhoda Nyberg.

Godfrey's career credits were then listed in chronological order but the author of the information had been on the iron range at least for a while and was well aware that Greenway's shoes were not small. "The Canisteo District," he went on, "is a difficult one for a stranger to fill, for the reason that Superintendent Greenway was an exceedingly popular man, but Mr. Godfrey will fill the bill, because he is just as popular here as Mr. Greenway was at Coleraine, and the trait will soon manifest itself to the end that the loss of Mr. Greenway will be assuaged by the presence of the new superintendent, and he will soon be right at home." A little local pride crept into that send off but Godfrey was to justify the praise more than once. He had now been with the Oliver for sixteen years.

He was succeeded as general manager in Chisholm by A.J. Sullivan, of the Fayal District.

Cecelia had to pack again.

As Cecelia packed and Mike prepared, the Mesabi Iron Range, Hibbing in particular, was treated to the spectacle of a few bricks flying about.

Godfrey Becomes Postmaster
The Duluth Evening Herald started the fray on the 14th of July with the publication of a letter it had received from A.E. Pfremmer of Hibbing, one of the owners of the *Hibbing Tribune*. It seems that Clarence B. Miller who was running for reelection to Congress had given the appointment of Postmaster in Hibbing to one Thomas Jefferson Godfrey, instead of giving it to Grier H. Thompson, L.C Newcombe, R.L. Griffin, F.A. Lass, D.D. McEachin, or to Mr. Pfremmer. According to Pfremmer, he was promised the job by Miller back in November. And during the winter Miller (according to Pfremmer) had told several people that Pfremmer was the man for the job now that C.M. Atkinson, was stepping down after four years at the helm.

Mr. Pfremmer was really upset and went on to say that T.J. Godfrey was the brother of Godfrey, the Oliver Iron Mining Company superinten-

To Tipple A Prince

dent recently appointed to succeed J.C. Greenway at Coleraine. It was, Pfremmer contended, through his [Mike Godfrey's] influence that he [T.J. Godfrey] was recommended for the job. The *Bovey News* on July 23rd chimed in by repeating the story but it added an "ataboy" by pointing out that Hibbing was indeed indebted to Mr. Atkinson who modernized the service until Hibbing ranked among the best post offices in the country. The lily got a good gilding there. Naturally, they had to suggest something was amiss by making sure that everyone understood that T.J. was related to Mike Godfrey, the superintendent of the [i.e., Bovey/Coleraine] district.

The general superintendent's House. 100 Cole Avenue. Coleraine. The frame structure has multiple gables and roof dormers. This is the house that Cecelia and Mike and the children moved into in the fall of 1910 when John C. Greenway moved to Arizona. One child, the seventh, a daughter, was born here.44 Author's collection.

In August, President William Howard Taft, appointed Thomas Jefferson Godfrey, lesser known brother of Michael Hogan Godfrey, and local merchant, Postmaster of Hibbing. Thomas Jefferson you remember had had post office experience back in Norway, Michigan, so this job was not entirely new to him. T.J.'s salary was to be $2,600.00 a year.[43]

Mr. A.E. Pfremmer sold his interest in the Hibbing paper and de-camped for Florida.[45]

T.J. moved to 426 Sellers Street. As the paper noted, Mr. Godfrey was to continue in the clothing business while letting Leo J. Kilduff run the store. In the event that second class postmasters were to go under civil service rules—and it looked like President Taft was going to authorize this[46]—Godfrey would hold the position as long as he liked.

Mike Godfrey said nothing about this, at least in public, and went duck hunting in Bow String country for a week. He had a lot to think over.

Safety at Work

The Oliver for all its emphasis on shipments and its sometimes seeming indifference to its workers and their plight was aware—with an occasional timely prod from U.S. Steel—of the connection between reducing the number of accidents as a means of increasing productivity and came to hold safety in high regard. In late November 1910, the Oliver held just such a meeting for its general superintendents, Master Mechanics and other officials of the company, in Hibbing.

The purpose of the meeting was to examine the use of safety devices for the miners and to work out safer methods of operating in the mines. Mike Godfrey, who had long advocated stressing safety as a day-to-day concern was chairman of the committee that examined safer methods of work and the installation of safety appliances in underground mines. In 1910, the Oliver had ten underground mines in operation on Minnesota's iron range and a number of them in Michigan. There were four in the Hibbing District: the Winnifred, Harold, Mace and Mississippi and six in Chisholm: the Glen, Clark, Chisholm, Monroe, Leonard and Myers.

Godfrey's committee met on Tuesday and Wednesday of the third week in November in Hibbing and then traveled to Chisholm to examine conditions there, finally ending up spending the better part of the week in Ironwood, Michigan.

This concern with safety was to return constantly in Godfrey's career, the Oliver's and U.S. Steel's. In fact, in September of the following year, the Mining Captains Institute met in Coleraine at Godfrey's urging to lend what emphasis as they could to the issue of safety. City Hall and Godfrey had the honor of hosting the meeting.

To Tipple A Prince

A certain Captain Vickers, from Biwabik, gave the first presentation on the methods he used to teach his wards the importance of First Aid. This was an important point as safety methods had to be ported from mine to mine and the best way to do that was to hold classes that the *miners would* attend. The results were noticeable in the areas of transferring injured men from the scene of an accident to the emergency room of a nearby hospital, in the treating of hemorrhages from wounds, and in the use of first aid for even seemingly minor wounds. Men taken off the line for even minor injuries returned to work sooner than if they had let the injury linger before reporting it. Improved methods of sinking, drifting, stopping, slicing and pumping were also looked into because more efficient methods of mining also reduced accidents. A special committee looked into the handling of explosives.

The Mining Captains institute gathered its information by means of its meetings where it read and discussed issues presented in professional papers. It then circulated any information of value by publishing it where it did the most good: where the miners could see it and in a form that was easily understood.

The Trout Lake Concentrator. 1912. Designed by Oliver Iron Mining Company engineers and built by the American Bridge Company. The equipment inside was supplied by Allis-Chalmers of Milwaukee, Wisconsin. The structure was 255 feet long, 162 feet high and 124 feet wide and was approached by an enormous berm 4,000 feet long, 125 feet high which was connected to the mill by a steel trestle 650 feet long (above on the left). Today all that is left of this enormous structure is a field of wild flowers and weeds. Charles E. van Barneveld, Iron Mining in Minnesota, Bulletin, No. 1, The University of Minnesota, Minnesota School of Mines Experiment Station (1912), Minneapolis, Minnesota. p. 183.

After four days of that anyone could use a break and Mike Godfrey was there to supply it. On Saturday after lunch Godfrey gathered the assemblage and took them through the principal buildings in Coleraine, after which he took them on board the Godfrey Special Touring Train for a trip through the various open pit mines of the Canisteo and Walker Districts. The highlight of the tour was an in-depth look at the Holman mine near Taconite and the nearby Trout Lake washing plant.

That evening in the hopes that a good meal would reinforce the day's lessons, Godfrey hosted a banquet at the Park Hotel in town. The meal and the usual speeches lasted until 8:00 p.m. at which time the participants returned to City Hall where the Coleraine city band played until very late.

The Mining Captains Institute came away with high praise for Mike Godfrey, the Coleraine members of the institute and the people of Coleraine, "all of whom had done all in their power to make the stay of the mining captains an interesting one." [47]

Of Hospitals and Houses
Hospitals
When Godfrey took over in the Canisteo one of his first priorities was the health and safety of the men who worked for him. Safety slogans and improved mining operations do reduce down time but along with vigilance on the part of the men, they could not reduce down time to zero because they could not eliminate accidents with their attendant injuries. Godfrey had several requests in this regard.

Early in 1911[48], he wrote to the president of the Oliver, W.J. Olcott, requesting appropriations for a field hospital for the Hill mine and some "cottages" (worker housing) to be built in Marble (near the Hill mine). He was specifically asking for the monies to build one twenty-eight-by-thirty-two-foot Emergency Hospital costing some $5,000, one four room cottage, three six room cottages, costing about $5,000, and two frame Boarding Houses, running about $6,000.

The amounts being asked for were non-trivial ones and Godfrey needed to support his requests. He was ready for this as by now he understood what expenses Olcott would want details on and which ones he would pass on without comment.

The hospital for the Hill mine was necessary because there was no facility at the mine where injured men could be treated before moving them to a more permanent treatment center. And the nearest hospital was in Coleraine, some nine miles distant. Secondly, there were already 600 men employed at the Hill mine and a 'material increase' in men was forecast for the coming year: accidents in an employment force of this size are inevitable (even if the number is deceasing). Worst of all, when an injured man needed treatment for a serious injury, he had to wait on a cot in a warehouse or shanty while the Oliver lined up track rights on a DM&N line to Coleraine for one of its engines to run on.

If this sort of arrangement persisted Godfrey and the Oliver could see a serious public relations reaction.[49]

The hospital that Godfrey envisioned would have a lower floor for patients and an upper floor for a resident physician.

Houses
As to why Godfrey was making a request that the Oliver build some houses,[50] he explained to Olcott the request for a four-room and three six-room cottages was justified because the mine was going to increase its hiring of skilled labor by seventy-five men and although Godfrey does not say so directly, these were going to be married men and they would have families. These cottages would be built in Marble where the Oliver had already constructed fifty-six cottages and had sold some twenty-fire of them back to the employees. The cottages were a good investment: the married men had a place for their families that was close by and would consequently be less tempted to indulge in the partaking of alcoholic spirits.

The two frame boarding houses were also for skilled laborers, young skilled ones (i.e., single). Godfrey once again betrayed a typical concern of Oliver management (and maybe the zeal of an Irishman who rarely drank) when he went on to justify the expenditure because, "a number or our young men are obliged to *board in saloons* and other *unwholesome* places in Calumet, and which is something over a mile distant from their work, and they are not always in the best of condition when they come to work, and it was *to correct this condition that the request was made.*" Godfrey probably did not have bed and breakfast establishments in mind when he referred to "unwholesome" places.

For Good Measure
There was also an element of politics here as Godfrey did not want U.S. Steel headquarters involved in the transaction but he is circumspect about it to a fault. He says, "We purposely held down the number of houses asked for so that the appropriation might be made a local one and we could get quick action on the same." Involve headquarters and you could wait forever. The requests were granted.

Camps, Concentrators, Churches, and Contributions
If Olcott thought he was going to get off lightly he was going to have to wait a bit. Godfrey's administrative skills and local needs combined to push him into writing another letter dated the 27th of January. (The 26th must have warmed him to the task.) The shopping list this time was for two, twenty-by-sixty-three-foot timber-frame camps for use in connection with the Washing Plant (on Trout Lake). The camps were needed to accommodate two groups of foreign workers for the coming season especially when bad weather set in. Not to mention that housing between seventy-five to ninety Bulgarians and Austrians in one dwelling was asking for trouble. The men were then living in Bovey and Coleraine and it has to be assumed that the men had to walk to the Concentrator which was no easy task even though the distance was relatively short. Godfrey makes a point of mentioning that they had a high rate of absenteeism when the weather got really bad. Miners at this time rarely owned cars. The request was granted.

To Tipple A Prince

The rest of the year saw no less activity in the realm of public relations good will building. The Methodists of Marble were given two lots in the original plat for a church and later in the year when it was ascertained that it would cost more than originally thought, were granted a donation by the Oliver to finish building; the Catholic Church in Marble also received a substantial sum to build its church; St. Joseph's Catholic Church in Grand Rapids (about ten miles from Coleraine) was granted a large donation to their building fund to help them rebuild their church which had been destroyed by fire; the Fourth of July celebrations in Coleraine and Marble were partially underwritten by the Oliver.

Godfrey and the Oliver did not limit themselves, however, to just donating necessary monies to help build a community's infrastructure or for its entertainment, helpful as these donations were, they also understood that men, given the chance of rehabilitating themselves, would be productive (not to mention, grateful) employees. A letter exists from Mike Godfrey to F.H. Whitney, warden of the St. Cloud State Reformatory,[51] offering employment in the Canisteo mine to two men about to be released on parole from the reformatory.

Sanitation
One response[52] of Godfrey's to an inquiry by Olcott is interesting for two reasons. First, Olcott's inquiry has not been preserved and it hints at something larger (perhaps an inquiry by state officials) and secondly, Godfrey takes two pages to delineate the various procedures and safeguards taken to insure good sanitation.

Under the general rubric of "What are we doing to keep the sanitation of our workers homes at a high level," Godfrey describes nine initiatives that were undertaken after consultations with experts. The first six initiatives deal with employee residences. The employees homes are furnished with good water and where possible, are connected to sanitary sewage lines; a health office, generally a physician along with the police, enforce health regulations; if the water quality is questionable, wells are dug; residences are well built (generally the best in the vicinity) and the lots are graded; ice—for refrigeration in the Summer - is examined by the health authorities, and garbage is collected regularly. The last three initiatives deal with work situations. Machine Shops for the Oliver mines have sanitary change houses of modern design and have stools, urinals and shower baths, employing men with obvious physical defects are not hired, and lastly, Godfrey's favorite concern: a great deal of time and money (this is the only place that the cost of something has come up) is being put into accident prevention. Some 20% of the employees were being protected by mechanical guards, 18% partially so and in the Canisteo, Godfrey and his safety officer were trying to perfect a human guard to take care of the balance of the men. On balance then it would seem that Godfrey provided a very detailed response to Olcott's request, way out of proportion to the mention unless we assume that Olcott wanted not only an affirmative response but a detailed one as well.

A Trip

After the flap over his brother's appointment to Hibbing Postmaster, Mike (and Thomas) assumed a low profile and said nothing about either's role in the affair. There was really little reason for either of them to say anything but it didn't help their No-Influence case by traveling to Washington, D.C., in March 1912 to visit none other than Congressman C.B. Miller. The brother's Godfrey also made stops in New York City and Philadelphia. No reason was announced for the trip. But they were the better judges of the situation and nothing arose as a result.[53]

The Most Successful Meeting in the Organization's History

Late in June 1912, the summer outing of the Northern Minnesota Editorial Association was held in Grand Rapids. This was one very good time to get some good publicity for the Oliver and its operations that wouldn't hurt after the public relations mess that firing John Greenway created.

These were newspapermen and they reached the general public in a way that the Oliver couldn't no matter how many press releases they issued.

The newspapermen assembled early on Friday morning at the Hotel Pokegama where they had their headquarters and met to discuss the issues of the day and to plan for the day's activities. By afternoon they were ready for a woman's suffrage meeting that was held in Grand Rapids' City Hall. That was followed up on Saturday morning with a softball game.

The Association assembled in force in front of the hotel in the afternoon and traveled the distance to Coleraine some nine or so miles away by car where they were met by Godfrey. He greeted them all as they drove up and had them board his Oliver train that the visitors enjoyed so much they dubbed it the "Mike Godfrey See Coleraine First" observation train. After a visit to various mines with Godfrey providing the commentary, they swung by the massive Trout Lake Concentrator where they were given a guided tour of the facility. With the sound of rock being crushed by metal and sand being blasted with water still in their ears the visitors assembled outside for the return trip to the Oliver building where, as the paper[54] put it, "Godfrey answered their questions faster than the reporters could ask them."

An Unusual Problem

Sometimes a labor problem is not the looming prospect of a strike nor unemployment, sometimes the labor problem is a lack of labor and Godfrey and the Oliver Iron Mining Company faced just such a problem on the Canisteo District in the summer of 1912. Olcott and Godfrey were in correspondence over this difficulty in June. Godfrey's observation was that men were leaving one or two at a time every day and had been for some time but the cause in his opinion was not dissatisfaction with wages or conditions. The cause was a combination of factors one short term and one potentially long term.

The previous summer, the Canisteo District laid off over a thousand men and most of them headed off to Northwestern Canada or back home to Europe and they were not returning. In fact, according to Godfrey, *none* had returned. That was one aspect of the problem. The other aspect was that the men that the Oliver generally relied upon to strip or mine in a region, common laborers, wanted not only work but they wanted to work *regularly*. The men did not appreciate working six or seven months and then getting laid off. This was a real hardship for both single men and married men but especially married men as they could afford neither unemployment nor moving.

This problem in the summer of 1912 did not resolve itself quickly and Godfrey and Olcott were still wrestling with the problem. In October Godfrey was still confronted with the problem of men wanting continuous employment. Some seventy-eight men had permanently left the Oliver's Canisteo, Holman, and Hill mines (locomotive fireman topped the list) and the Trout Lake Concentrator (car spotters and drillers) in the last month. Practically everyone had given the same reason for leaving: they needed a job where they could reasonably be assured of continuous employment. The Canisteo was also losing men from the Oliver's Engineering department and the Laboratory, approximately a dozen good men (three of them wanted to go back to school) left for better prospects. Each category was headed by married men, the stable backbone of the Oliver's labor force. This problem was to grow over the next several years.

The News Improves

Things were looking good in the fall of the year and Mike and Cecelia were able to step out and attend an evening's entertainment at the Oliver Clubhouse in Hibbing. I can just imagine Cecelia's relief when the evening's entertainment, consisting of a series of lectures on mine safety and a movie on mining in the region, concluded.

Mike and Cecelia were back in Hibbing on November the 16th to visit friends for the evening. Although the paper does not say so, it can be "imagined" that they visited their friend and owner of the *Mesaba Ore and Hibbing News*, C.M. Atkinson who was having his fiftieth birthday.[55]

The shipping season was slowly drawing to a close on the Great Lakes as fall descended into winter and the mines were converting from mining iron ore to stripping overburden to expose next season's deposits. Equipment was idled, examined, and sent to maintenance sheds for repair. Many men were furloughed as stripping replaced mining. Some men were transferred to the few underground endeavors that needed replacements for injured, or missing, men.

Godfrey tackled his paper work in preparation for next season's activities as a major conflict overseas grew more likely and the planning had to expand to meet the anticipated increase in production. Godfrey would have been very busy at this time and by now he realized that the Oliver Iron Mining Company had a high regard for his abilities and accomplishments. He had served in a subordinate superintendent's capacity in Hibbing, assumed a commanding role in supervising the Oliver's operations in the Chisholm District, and now had secured the Oliver's interests in the Canisteo District. He had no reason to believe that this was the end of his ascension through the ranks of the Oliver's administrative hierarchy but neither did he know where he would be sent next or when. If things could settle down for a while at the large general superintendent's house on Cole next to the Oliver's headquarters that would be all right. Cecelia who moved bag, baggage, and kids every time Godfrey was promoted, undoubtedly felt that a nice long, slow winter holiday season followed by a long warm spring would be a nice idea for a change. With seven kids of various inclinations and personalities in tow, packing to go somewhere was probably not high on her agenda. Anyway, the Range seemed reasonably quiet.

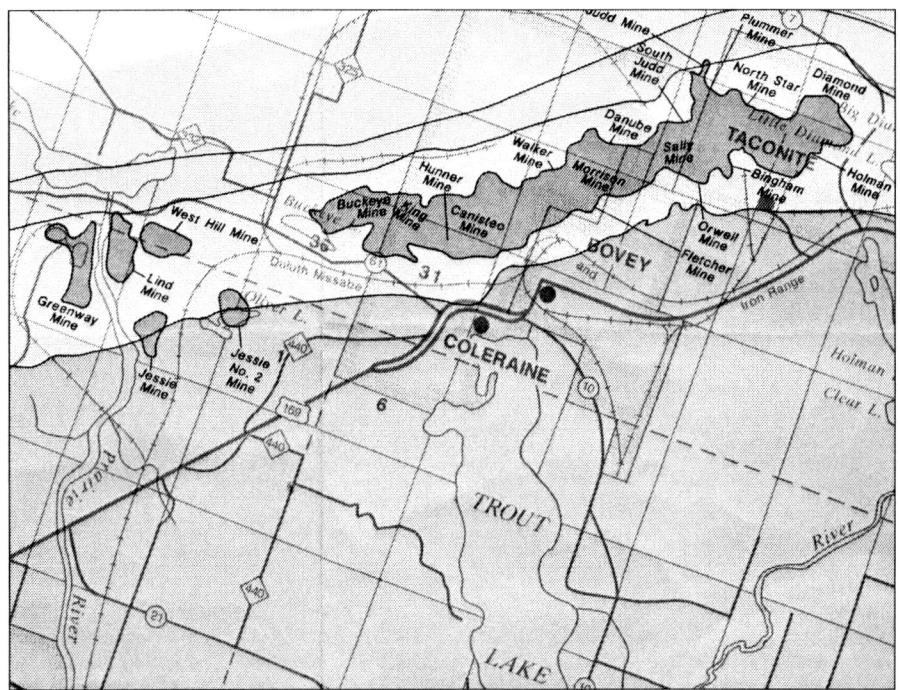

The Central section of the Canisteo Mining District. This is John C. Greenway country and Mike Godfrey tread very delicately while serving as general superintendent here for three years. The map is a later edition, circa 1955. Minnesota Department of Natural Resources.

But when you are in a business as volatile as iron ore mining, time always seems to be running out and market demand never seems to stand still.

* * *

Notes

[1] On June 8th, 1907, the *Mesaba Ore and Hibbing News* put the total at 12,000.

[2] As assistant general superintendent of the Hibbing Group of mines, reporting to William J. West. Mike had, in this and in his former capacity, direct responsibility for the operations and development of the Hull and Rust mining complexes.

[3] January 5, 1907. The article also makes note of the fact that the ten month old (incorporation was on April 26, 1906) lodge's colors were purple and white. Current membership was at 85 (the original membership had been a healthy 26) and climbing.

[4] The notice appeared in the March 9th issue.

1. M.S. Hawkins, Supt., Virginia, Minnesota
2. Pentecost Mitchell, Vice President, Duluth, Minnesota
3. W.J. Olcott, President, Duluth, Minnesota
4. J.H. McLean, General Manager, Duluth, Minnesota
5. M.H. Godfrey, Gen. Supt., Virginia, Minnesota
6. R.R. Trezona, Gen. Supt., Fayal Mine, Eveleth, Minnesota
7. O.C. Davidson, Gen. Supt., Gogebic & Menominee Ranges, Iron Mtn., Mich.
8. J.H. Hearding, Ass't. General Manager, Duluth, Minnesota
9. W.H. Johnston, Gen. Supt., Marquette Range, Ishpeming, Michigan
10. Charles Trezona, Gen. Supt., Vermilion Range, Ely, Minnesota
11. W.J. West, Gen. Supt., Hibbing, Minnesota
12. Frank Keese, Supt., Ishpeming, Michigan
13. D.E. Sutherland, Ass't. Gen. Supt., Gogebic & Menominee Ranges, Ironw
14. A.T. Sullivan, Supt., Chisholm, Minnesota
15. R.T. Mitchell, Gen. Supt., Adams & Spruce Mines, Eveleth, Minnesota

Oliver Iron Mining Company, officers and superintendents. October 18, 1912. W.J. Olcott is the stern-faced gentleman front row, center. Mike Godfrey is on the far right, first row. He is at this time forty-six years old and still looks ten years younger. Pentecost Mitchell is to Olcott's immediate right; J.H. Hearding is in the middle row behind and to Olcott's right. Digitally altered. J.R. Zweifel, photographer. S3012b26, Northeast Minnesota Historical Center, Duluth, Minnesota.

The Hull/Rust/Mahoning open pit mine. 2000. The view is from the east end of the mine, looking west toward the current Taconite operations. The Webb Locations are to the right (North) and present day Hibbing is to the left (South). The location of the photographer (the author) is next to a chair on a cliff overlooking the mine. Every year the chair is there and it is cleaned each year. There are no cigarette butts, no paints, no debris anywhere around. Someone on the Mesabi's Iron Ore Range has the soul of a poet or the heart of a photographer. This is an extremely beautiful spot and very hard to get to. Author's collection.

Daniel W. Lynch

[5] This seems like a good time to introduce a subject of less than broad interest: platting. When a quarter section is platted the plat is a piece of land identifying the location and boundaries of street rights-of-way, individual lots, and other site information (for example, the names of the streets). The plat shows features such as lot lines, utility easements, setback lines, and land dedicated for public use (such as parks). There are five categories in the series, enough to cover any stage of development. A plat at its most basic is nothing more than a developer's desire to develop property. It is also a necessity when obtaining a building permit.

[6] According to the government's latest figures, the population of Hibbing was 8,500. Hibbing seemed to calculate the population at nearly double that. The difference was probably in who was considered a resident and whether or not the resident resided in a) 'Old' North Hibbing, b) the Pillsbury Addition, c) the Southern Addition, an d) addition to Alice, or e) one of the nearby Locations. If you lived in the 'Old' North Hibbing-sponsored Roosevelt Addition to Alice and shopped in 'Old' North Hibbing, you probably were considered a resident of Hibbing. The Feds probably didn't have that broad a method of counting.

[7] *Mesaba Ore and Hibbing News*. H.P. Reed is to return to these pages later on as he liked to not only travel but he was also a local businessman, an 'Old' North Hibbing real estate businessman.

[8] On January 22nd.

[9] There are no mentions of shopping districts either, which may have figured into the calculations of merchants in Old North Hibbing when it became evident they had to move. Somewhere south.

[10] On March 12th.

[11] The entrance was also framed with the same White Bedford rock and the doorway was enhanced with paneled glass. The structure had a full basement containing gentlemen's and ladies Comfort Stations. This design feature was carried over into the present building.

[12] Putting aside its intrinsic value to the development of the village, someone managed to take a contrary point of view. On August 19th, Deputy US Marshal George J. Mallory of Duluth served the village and its board of trustees with an injunction calling for such city works to cease. It is not clear what George L. Burrows a citizen of Michigan had in mind when he did this but that certainly didn't stop him (he may have been a fee holder with mineral rights). He was ultimately not successful much to the village's relief.

[13] To be fair, Atkinson, whatever his bias, ran editorials and articles where he preached the necessity of the two parties for getting along. Mutual need was one of his more powerful arguments. In this case, Mike Godfrey and the Oliver got off the hook: they had other reasons for succumbing to this injunction and high on the list was the pressure that 800 out of work men and their families could bring to the town's attitude towards the single solitary woman who dared to defy the Oliver. The Oliver was not a beanstalk and Mrs. Liend was no "Jack." But . . .

[14] That case involved the Buhl school district and their allocation of funds collected from the Oliver. Judge Hughes again ruled against the Oliver and in the only time his family *could ever remember* their father speaking out about or *against a judicial official*, Mike expressed his belief that the ruling against the Oliver was a ruling against him, personally. Buhl in the euphoria following its victory named its high school after the good judge. History is replete with the irony and enjoyed such a taste of it when, years later, a valedictorian graduate of Buhl's Hughes High School became the college roommate of the author, a grandson of Godfrey.

[15] Back in February when this issue first became a pressing one.

[16] Exactly who said this is not specified but without doubt it was first cleared by Olcott.

[17] Vic Power may have been a powerhouse attorney - and we will hear more about that shortly—but it appears that he paid for it physically, spending time either in Hibbing's Rood Hospital or down in St. Mary's Hospital in Duluth. In November 1908, he spent over a week in St. Mary's with what was described as 'stomach trouble'.

To Tipple A Prince

[18] By mid-May of 1910, Robert F. Berdie and his company had managed the paltry feat of laying two blocks of ties and rail *in* Hibbing but that was all. His franchise was revoked. This at first did not deter Mr. Berdie who continued to lay tie and rail from outside Hibbing in the general direction of Chisholm. While he was at it Berdie traveled to Chicago to get backing for his charter airplane service on the Mesabi Range. As a promoter, Berdie was full of ideas, some of them way ahead of his time (and way beyond his finances), but as an administrator, he had the energy but not the skill.

[19] Dotie may have even introduced them.

[20] Baldwin and Baldwin of Duluth represented the Oliver Iron Mining company in each action and didn't cover themselves in glory by losing both suits.

[21] The amount to be raised was $5,000.

[22] Stripping was generally restricted to the winter months and iron ore mining to the warmer months not because the ore was too difficult to remove from its confines in cold weather but rather because the ore once removed from the pit could not be shipped while the Great Lakes were in deep freeze. It made sense to expose/strip the overburden from the ore body in the winter months which you intended to mine in the summer months.

[23] While Mike and Cecelia were traveling, the Hibbing Ski Club voted Mike a directorship along with his colleagues, William J. West and W.M. Tappan.

[24] And three years later the Village finished constructing a brand new court house.

[25] The Village Hall was one very impressive building but that didn't help when it came time to move the edifice during the time of the Great Move. The Village Hall and the St. Louis County court house shared the same fate: neither was moved but due to its location (in the Southern Addition), the courthouse survived until the mid-1950s.

[26] It should be noted that even though it looks like the Oliver was oblivious to the encroachment of its own mines upon Old 'North' Hibbing and was just asking for a major loss on its own investments, that wooden structures are much easier to move than brick ones. Neither was the building of such a beautiful club house for employees an attempt at misdirection: the Oliver was rarely that subtle and it was in the mining business not in the real estate business and you do not take your general superintendent and put him in such an embarrassing position.

[27] *Mesaba Ore and Hibbing News*, January 2, 1909.

[28] With mining operations virtually exploding in the transition from underground operations to open pit ones and the possibilities and changes in operations that that entailed, the office complex was not at the top of the Oliver's ToDo list. Assigning responsibilities was.

[29] I don't want to make too much of this but Michael Hogan Godfrey was Irish and if you take a look at the ethnic breakdown of the nationalities that settled and developed the Mesabi Iron Ore range, you aren't going to find the Irish on the list. Their numbers are usually listed with "Others".

[30] This prevented him from catching the Lyceum theatre's production of "Ben-Hur: A Story of the Christ", presented for the first time in Hibbing. Victor Power, James Gandsey, Martin Hughes and wives were all in attendance.

[31] One of the more intriguing aspects of the correspondence that Mike Godfrey had with his superiors in Duluth is that he first hand wrote his letter and then had it typed. It would appear from the word-for-word rendition of the typed copy that Mike did not re-read the letter before signing it. Every grammatical and spelling mistake in the hand-written original was faithfully rendered in the final text. Which leads one to

wonder why the original was handwritten in the first place? The person typing the correspondence surely did not pay any attention to the content and Mike couldn't type.

[32] "Blind Pigs" were unlicensed establishments in Locations or in unincorporated areas were liquor was sold and consumed.

[33] The announcement didn't say that but it would have made no sense to spend the amount of money that it took the Oliver to move the entire headquarters complex some twelve or so blocks, not to mention the staggering amount of trackage it had to pull up and re-deploy, unless numerous test drillings confirmed this as an area free of marketable ore. Moving headquarters once cost quite enough, thank you, and even the Oliver wasn't about to repeat this expensive an operation again. Careful was the watchword here and it resulted in a new headquarters in the heart of the Oliver's massive mining operations that never moved again.

[34] This article appeared in the October 9th addition of the paper.

[35] The headquarters building design was changed shortly before it was built and this resulted in a two-story design instead. Godfrey's office in 1917 until his death—as noted by the author in the layout—was on the front of the building in the southeast corner, right inside the front door to the left. What that IRON FENCE where Admittance [was] Refused was all about I have not been able to ascertain. If there was such a fence no evidence of it remains.

[36] Donald L. Boese, *John C. Greenway and the Opening of the Western Mesabi*, (Grand Rapids, Minnesota, Greenway Book, 1975), Chapter 8.

[37] Boese reports that they discussed the Great Northern Properties' holdings on the iron range.

[38] On page 169.

[39] For example, why John Greenway consented to talks on such a confidential basis has never been explained and Greenway who was certainly no neophyte in the business world ever gave much of an explanation. Such a request to keep the matter confidential from his boss could not help but raise suspicions in Greenway's mind but he never gave voice to them. This whole affair had the scent of a setup.

[40] On page 174.

[41] The Monroe Location had no hospital facilities. Elizabeth Ann turned out to be the darling of her Father. Of all the daughters she ranked as the most favored. When Mike was terminally sick with heart problems, his most favored daughter died at the age of seventeen in November, 1927, but the family felt that the news would crush him and so they did not tell him of her death. He never found out as he did not long outlive his daughter.

[42] *Mesaba Ore and Hibbing News*, July 2, 1910. The men were not named.

[43] Thomas Jefferson Godfrey worked for the Oliver Iron Mining Company until 1904, when he went into the clothing business.

[44] This was Jane Winifred. Jane was one of the more unusual of the children. She took secretarial school in Duluth and later went on to graduate from the University of Wisconsin in Madison, WI. Later, she moved to New York, had dinner with the Sulzbergers, took steno from Arnold J. Toynbee, worked on the Manhattan Project, joined the Red Cross with her four roommates, went to North Africa, married an Irishman in Egypt, and lived most of her next thirty years in Saudi Arabia.

[45] He returned a year later and bought the newspaper in Eveleth, Minnesota. Maybe the warm climate was difficult to adjust to.

[46] He did.

[47] Itasca Iron News, Bovey, MN, September 21, 1911.

To Tipple A Prince

[48] January 26th. Godfrey had already submitted a budget, Olcott wrote back for details and a breakdown of individual expenses. This letter is in response to Olcott's request.

[49] Mike put it this way: "This building would enable us to better care for our injured employees, increase the medical efficiency and eliminate any criticism, public or private, that might result from our present method of taking care of our injured employees."

[50] The Oliver's building houses was not new but since it was a large expense and also involved selling real estate, the Oliver was careful about what it did.

[51] Dated August 29, 1911.

[52] Dated December 8, 1911.

[53] This is the first time in eighteen years that the brothers were mentioned in the newspapers as having done something together. The next mention of togetherness would be in January 1928.

[54] On June 29, 1912 under the caption, "Were Royally Entertained. Scribes Enjoy three Days Real Outing. Grand Rapids Newspaper People Leave No Stone Unturned That Would Add to Pleasure. ... It was the most successful meeting in the history of the organization." Hard to imagine.

[55] Atkinson's first paper was the Mining News of Florence, Wisconsin, his second the Diamond Drill of Crystal Falls, Michigan, followed by the Independent in Rock Springs, Wyoming, the Eveleth Republican in Eveleth, Minnesota and the Northome Record in Northome, Minnesota. He bought the *Hibbing News* from C. A. Smith in May of 1899, later changing the masthead to the Mesaba Ore.

V

Anticipation: 1913 to 1918

Introduction

While Mike Godfrey was busy planning for next season's mining activities in the sandy ores of the Canisteo District, the central part of the Mesaba Range was slowly gathering the colliding forces of change. This is where the ore was, this is where the population concentrated and this is where local politics seemed most active. Stresses had been developing along lines that could for the most part be seen, even if not believed, and sooner or later something had to give more ground than was acquired even if the cost was daunting.

But it was one thing to build a city on a dream; it was a whole other thing to build it on a mountain of ore. For the Oliver, it was one thing to mine the ore, but it was a whole other thing to move a town.

What Alice Did

As Hibbing's population grew and the village expanded by gathering Additions to itself off to the south and southeast, Alice had growing ambitions of its own. It could not help but notice that Hibbing was expanding by acquiring and platting "forties" and thereby increasing its tax base and revenues. It was even challenging the Oliver and winning while Alice stagnated. Civic pride can remain quiescent just so long.

The location's first initiative fell flat. In the first week of January 1913, at a special election held at the Robert Pritchard farm just south of Alice proper, it was proposed to the voters (which *did not* include any residents of the village of Hibbing) that Alice annex six valuable sections of ore-bearing land which, not incidentally, included the Utica and Morton mines. The vote by those who lived in the annexable lands defeated the idea by a comfortable margin, forty-one to fourteen. Victory for Alice would have placed those in the annexed sections between a rock and a hard place, between the wishes of those residents of Alice (which the voters were not) and the economic muscle of the mining companies. Better what you have than what you can't have.

This vote did have the positive effect, however, of restarting the dialogue whereby Alice could annex itself to Hibbing but as before the residents of Alice needed to see some initiatives on Hibbing's part (paving roads seems to have been uppermost on their minds). It was a subject of conversation in Alice and had been for some time, that it was only a matter of time before the Village of Hibbing—at least that part of Old Hibbing that would be most immediately affected—started getting serious about moving en masse to the south thereby surrounding Alice. An extra six sections would have given Alice some leverage in the subsequent negotiations. Very little of the conversation seemed to include the possibility of the mining companies initiating (or, *forcing*) the move.

Alice initially settled for petitioning the new interurban electric trolley car line to extend its orange and dark green car service to the location.

Alice made another formal application for annexation before the Hibbing Village council in May. The new mayor, V.L. Power, turned the matter over to a committee which was charged with calling on the Commercial Club of Hibbing. The Commercial Club was in turn to present the package to the citizens of Hibbing for their response thereby insuring that the mayor would know the will of the people. If a more circuitous approach could be found it would be hard to imagine. The result of all this was that the village council decided on a more basic approach: it instructed the village attorney S.C. Scott to draw up a resolution favoring the consolidation. He did. The council voted approval in June. The measure went to Alice's council. In July it approved the measure. Hibbing and Alice were now one and the tax rolls increased by twelve hundred.

Everybody got busy on extending trolley car line service to Alice which would run south along Third Avenue and then cross over to First Avenue as it passed the Cemetery. It escaped no one's notice that this would make commuting between Hibbing and Alice so much easier that the *Mesaba Ore and Hibbing News* felt that it would even solve Hibbing's housing problem.[1] Extending electric trolley car service was one thing, paving Third Avenue for the full two miles was another. This was not accomplished until 1915.

The ETC

Traveling between Mesabi Iron Range towns, villages and locations was no easy matter during this era as the roads were rutted mud trails originally used by Indians, explorers, fur traders, and loggers. Real roads did not exist (neither did settlements for that matter) and travel from one place to another was arduous and time consuming. Ten miles could take the better part of a day. The need to have some kind of public transportation that could take residents from one end of the Range to the other in a matter of hours was obvious. Electric rail traffic designed for passengers had been tried before but failed for lack of funds. R.F. Berdie had originally tried but managed to lay only a couple blocks of track (in Hibbing) before giving up and promoting documentary films of the Iron Range.

Now, in 1913[2] the Mesaba Electric Railway Company established electric trolley car service that included stops at various places along its thirty-five miles of track between Hibbing and Gilbert.[3] The trolleys began service at six in the morning and the last run of the day was at 8:50 in the evening but that car stopped at Olcott Park on the outskirts of Virginia (not too far from the general superintendent's house) instead of proceeding on to Gilbert.

To Tipple A Prince

Electric Trolley Car Tracks. This view is looking south along First Avenue in Hibbing. First Avenue is the dividing line between the east and west (to the right) avenues in the Village. It is also a township boundary line. The tracks arching off to the left are running down the center of Howard Street (which is Twentieth Street, the next street south is Twenty-first Street). The first building on the left is the Delvic Hotel. The picture was taken sometime around 1922. Aubin Studios.

The Mitchell Bridge. This bridge which spanned both the Great Northern tracks on the left and the Duluth, Missabe & Iron Range railroad tracks running off to your right carried the Mesaba Electric Railway trolley cars over the tracks which at this juncture, were north and east of Hibbing. Note the two trolley cars on the tracks above (one at center span, the other at the north end). This bridge remains today but it is no longer split-spanned and crossing underneath it is only one set of tracks. The massive Mitchell Yards are 1,000 yards to the left of the switching tower. The view here is to the Northeast. The photograph is circa 1923. Aubin Studios.

Daniel W. Lynch

It would not be until several years had passed, in fact not until 1914, that a proposal was made to extend the line to the southwest, to Grand Rapids. And it wasn't until that same year that anyone suggested that the line be extended south from Hibbing. The capital expense involved in the extending the railway was all up front, the revenue stream was month by month. The population of the range increased regularly but not spectacularly. Unemployment was a frequent hazard of life on the Iron Range and this, additionally, tended to produce a certain degree of uncertainty in the business community. And there *were* competitors.

Finally, Vic Power

Victor L. Power assumed the presidency of the village council of Hibbing for the first, and far from the last, time in April of 1913. The relationship between Power and the Village of Hibbing was to last for some time and produce some really spectacular results. When he announced his candidacy in the *Mesaba Ore and Hibbing News* in March on the Progressive Ticket he was not an unknown entity in Hibbing or the Iron Range. He possessed a high profile having won several cases against the mighty Oliver and it didn't hurt that his brother was also a well-known lawyer and real estate investor. His sister-in-law was just as well known, if not better known, than either of her two male mentors. She ran a very successful business in Old North Hibbing and entertained frequently.

Once he decided to run, Power turned politician immediately and became coy about his plans. It took two weeks of "pressure" to induce him to announce his candidacy. His Progressive Party won easily even though the full ticket wasn't finalized until three days before the election. They defeated seven-time mayor, Doctor Howard R. Weirick (after whom Howard Street is named). Power had a mandate of sorts as he received 722 votes and Dr. Weirick took his lumps with only 369. The socialist candidate, Don Rogers, received took eighty-two votes and never ran again. The former blacksmith for the Oliver and University of Chicago-trained lawyer had arrived. He

To Tipple A Prince

**PROGRESSIVES START FIRE-
WORKS IN VILLAGE POLITICS**

VICTOR L. POWER HEADS NEW TICKET

Seventy-Five Progressives Gather at City Hall Last Night and Decide To Put Ticket in the Field to Oppose Administration and Socialist Forces. Battle Royal From Now Until Polls Close.

Progressive Ticket

For President—
  VICTOR L. POWER
For Trustees—
  JOHN CURRAN
  R. L. GEISELMAN
  B. J. BURROWS
For Recorder—
  D. D. HALEY
For Treasurer—
  No Endorsement

Victor L. Power announces his run for President of the Hibbing Village Council in 1913. The announcement was in March of 1913, he started office in April and began paving the roads of Old North Hibbing the same month. Definitely aggressive.

came from a family that included four lawyers and a judge. He was not destined to be a care-taker. The local paper called him a Progressive Aggressive.[4]

Whatever was going on in Hibbing politics, be it short-sightedness or untutored public pressure, it did not make sense to pave the streets of a village that was surrounded on three sides by gaping holes in the earth, holes poised to become continuous. But Power and the Village council went ahead anyway and started paving. One third of the streets affected were in the Southern Addition, one third was in the Pillsbury Addition and one third was in the original (western) plat.

Then Alice was annexed.

Then Vic Power stated reading village ordinances. In particular, Ordinance Number 99, passed in July of 1910. His excitement became a headline. Power concluded that the Village of Hibbing was losing $40,000 a year from uncollected taxes. And guess who wasn't paying? This was:

> A Story of Vital Importance to the Residents of the Village Because it Tells Plainly of the Conditions and it Speaks for the Future Actions of Mayor Power and the Probable Result.

Further reading of the headline summaries, elicited some qualifications from the writer:

> Mayor and Council to Take Immediate Steps to Place Property Where it will Add to the Income of the Village. Steel Corporation's Share of this Untaxed Property is but Ten Per Cent, the remainder is Chargeable to Other Concerns Operating Here.

The Oliver and U.S. Steel were only 10% guilty! Imagine the disappointment. But forty thousand a year is forty thousand a year. What had happened? It seems that Village Ordinance 99 had been passed at the request of the owners of some real property (read, land or real estate) in the Village that had an assessed value of over a million dollars. The owners wanted to be included within the Village limits and their wish was granted. *However,* the council did not forward a copy of this agreement to the Secretary of State (of Minnesota), consequently it was not binding and no taxes were collected. This oversight was rectified. Political capital accrued.[5]

Power was on a winning streak and things looked good for the coming year but things didn't quite work out that way.

A Ballet with Bills
In early December 1913, John Curran, a member of the Water & Light board for the Village received an early and empty Christmas present consisting of some 4,000 pounds of weightless coal, shipped to the Village via the D.M.& N railroad. Curran had been going over the Water & Light's bills for the month and noticed that there was an invoice from the Hibbing Lumber company (which sold the coal to the Village) for 8,200 pounds of coal. He thought that was odd, being an old railroad man, and did a quick calculation which resulted in a figure of 4,000 pounds for a car of coal. This led him to look through the stack of paperwork where he discovered that the D.M.& N. had *correctly* specified the car as containing 4,000 pounds of coal. Hibbing Lumber was billing the Village for over twice that weight!

Curran told Power and Power, ever the attorney, asked for a thorough accounting from Hibbing Lumber's F.W. Strang. Strang's analysis was then read in front of the Village Council at the end of January with C.C. Remington, president of the Water & Light Commission looking uncomfortably on. Strang checked the Freight Bills (from the D.M.& N.) against the Coal

To Tipple A Prince

Delivery bills (from Hibbing Lumber) and found that the Village had paid for two hundred and eleven thousand pounds of non-existent coal. Talk about burning money.

What had been going on under the wayward eye, quiet demeanor, and *signature* of Remington was that the Freight bills were being sent to the village by the railway company and the Coal bills were being sent by the Lumber company and the whole pile was being pinned together with the coal bill placed strategically on top. Efficient. Nice. Elegant. Remington was asked to resign and prudently, he did. Strang took a vacation.

More Bad News

That took care of that but life's twists and turns do not let up. Late in February 1914 Vic Power traveled to Chicago for his Mother's funeral. She had been living in Sioux City, Iowa but only for a short time.[6] He returned later in the week to see about getting re-elected and he won handily with a plurality of 1,178 votes by virtue of the fact that no one opposed him. (He had 700 some votes the previous year.)

That should have been good news but maybe it was just too much good news for Power spent the better part of the last week in March in bed with a stomach disorder. A second attack was so bad that Power had to be checked into the hospital for treatment. Power claimed it was indigestion. If it was, it was a very strange case of indigestion for it caused Power to check into the Mayo Clinic in Rochester, Minnesota, for tests. The indigestion must really have been strange indeed: the Mayo pronounced Power fit. Power then tried the University of Minnesota Medical Complex with the same lack of a diagnosis. So in April he traveled to Chicago for yet more tests. *Rochester, Minneapolis, Chicago?* For indigestion?

Third Time's the Charm

In April of 1915 Victor L. Power won election to the Village of Hibbing's highest office for the third time. But for the second time in his political ca-

The Mahoning 2004. Or, what's left of the Mahoning as Hibb-Tac's taconite operations move ever closer. The view is to the Northwest and the large rock formation in the center is called a miner's "horse." This photograph was taken half way down the south face of the old HRM complex. Author's Collection.

reer he had to run against opposition but he didn't even have to work up a sweat in defeating A.E. Templeton 1,469 to 241. This was getting to be a habit.[7] It may even have played a part towards emboldening Power for he now went to the mound against the mining consortium with an opening pitch guaranteed to get their attention: he raised the tax levy.

This time the tax bite was going to be noticed by everyone but most especially the Oliver and its brethren as the levy was being raised to the maximum extent allowed by state law, two percent of the Village's assessed valuation which brought the bite to nearly a million seven hundred thousand ($1,693,933.62) dollars. This was the largest levy ever made in Hibbing and was twice the previous years' total. The council and Power were not incrementally increasing the tax they were inflating it: the Village's valuation was raised to a staggering level of $84,000,000 and the levy on this amount was pushed to the legal limit. If this was a game of baseball, Power and the Village Council were rifling a high, hard one, on the inside of the plate, letter high (sometimes called a "brush back," to extend the metaphor a little further). And the mining companies responded by swinging for the fences. With money like this at stake, it would be an extra inning contest.

The lawyers for the mining companies took a month to ready their careful reply and in June they announced it: they refused the honor of paying their taxes! A headline read:

> Mining Company Declines to Pay Taxes in the Village of Hibbing, Accepts Big Penalty. Legal flight is opened up which may go to the United States supreme court. May be enjoined from shipping ore, Sensational developments in the controversy between taxpaying interests and Hibbing.[8]

The contest was on. It is important to see (and maybe to pick a nit as well) that the Oliver and the other mining concerns declined (refused) to pay their *first* quarter share of the tax levy, not the entire year's dazzling amount. The levy after all did not have to be paid in one lump sum. The amount initially at stake was a (paltry) $175,000, with a penalty of $37,500. And all this talk of tax levies was limited to municipalities, the mining companies didn't voice any concerns over school taxes which were also quite high. Behind the mining companies approach was a growing feeling that since they paid so much in taxes they should have some say in how the money was spent.

What might be more significant than the amounts at stake (and they *were* quite significant) is the fact that Hibbing was the only Mesabi Iron Range town so affected. The mining concerns certainly seemed to be getting along, fiscally, with everybody else on the Range but when it came to Hibbing. Hit a wall, called Power.

The immediate effect was to cut off Hibbing's supply of cash with which it met its payroll. Power reacted by declaring that in this chess game there were many ways to checkmate the move.[9] Power did have a few moves in his repertoire which he would soon use.

Virginia, which felt it was above politics of this sort, still enjoyed reading about those who found it irresistible to indulge. I guess if you can put a bad face on a problem, it is must be somebody else's. The *Daily Enterprise* dug up the fact that the Hibbing treasurer's report issued in January, showed that for the previous year the expenditures of the Village were over $1,200,000 which was more than the levy in Duluth a city much larger in area and far more populous. The expenditures in Hibbing amounted to $100 per person where it was closer to $5.00 a head throughout the rest of the state (for towns of comparable size).

 The Hibbing village council and its President made the next move near the end of July when they petitioned Governor W.S. Hammond to establish martial law in the Village so that the Village's affairs could be run by the state militia. This would not only ensure police and fire protection for the beleaguered city but would cast the cost onto the State. For good measure, Village Council and Power also asked the Governor to call a special session of the state legislature to enact legislation by which the mining companies could be prosecuted for conspiracy and be held criminally liable for damages to the life and property of the village. Some sailing ships are missing the main sail, this one was short a mast as well.

 The pressure, however, was on to settle as no one held all the cards in this game. Hibbing was feeling the financial pinch and the mining companies could not go on indefinitely running up fines while brawling with the local politicians for they realized that good community relations make for good business. Accordingly, in the first week in August, the mining companies' representatives sat down with Victor Power and the Hibbing Village Council in the President's office to talk the matter over. The mining companies were well represented by Carson Agnew of the Mahoning Ore & Steel company and the Oliver, the major player, sent none other than Michael Godfrey, the general superintendent of the Oliver in the Virginia District. Mike was familiar with Hibbing and its officials and was becoming well known as a mediator.

 The talks were described as friendly, frank, and cordial. The mining companies came to the table with some specifics: that Hibbing limit its expenditures to $22,500 a month; the mining companies would support construction of Hibbing's new water supply system (which was languishing without a budget) and the construction of a sewer system for Alice. Hibbing had to agree to maintain its levy at the previous year's amount, agree to fixed monthly expenditures, and not incur new construction expenditures.[10] The council did not sign a contract in the matter but they didn't refuse the terms either.

It was left to Victor Power to do that.

In September Power made a formal demand of J.A.O. Preus the state auditor to cancel the leases of the mining companies for failure to pay $750,000 in back taxes. Mining companies as far as Power was concerned are obligated to pay their taxes the same way individuals are. The state auditor has the right, indeed the obligation. To seize the lands and cancel all leases for failure to pay the taxes. Preus ever the politician wasn't buying this: he informed the local officials that it was up to the county officials to collect the taxes.

The stalemate continued.

In November the Village caved but not without some tense moments.

The businessmen of Hibbing decided to move the (nonexistent) negotiations off square one even if the mayor and the village council would or could not. The businessmen called for village expenditures per month of no more than $25,000, about the same amount that Godfrey and Carson Agnew worked out back in August. The usual impediment said "no." He would not consider a compromise. This is either a good negotiating ploy or stubbornness but in the end it didn't seem to be either one.

This time the mining companies brought in W.J. West the general superintendent for the Hibbing District who represented the eleven mining companies that were withholding their taxes. Monthly expenditures were to hover at $ 24,000 and the total levy was put back where it belonged (as far as the mining companies were concerned) at $750,000.

And just how had this problem arisen in the first place? Listen to Vic Power:

> In my opinion the local Range representatives of the mining companies have too little power in deciding questions effecting Range towns.[11]

Power expressed the opinion that if the differences between municipalities and mining companies were adjusted by local representatives of the mining companies instead of attorneys the spirit of antagonism which prevails here could be eliminated. If you don't tell U.S. Steel's headquarters what you are doing, it will work out better? That would be extremely unlikely in an organization as hierarchical as the steel industry but be that as it may, the seven months of antagonism between the two parties was at parade rest. For now.

The next time around, and there would definitely be a next time, the local representative of the mining companies did take considerable initiative but only after first clearing his approach with the President of the Oliver and the local businessmen took a short cut past the mayor and the mayor stood by and took most of the credit while getting a building named in his honor.

Fourth Time Isn't

Victor Power won his fourth election in as many years in March of 1916 and seemed to have finally struck a nice quiet spell for a change. There were no mining fights of any consequence to be won and the political scene tossed no challenges at his incumbency. It was winter on the Iron Range and things were slow and almost soundless for men and mines. Spring almost always brought renewed activity to each.

In June the International Workers of the World, the IWW, struck. Winter was over. The IWW launched its strike in Aurora at the Saint James mine and it spread westward rapidly. What was at issue were four things: an end to the "contract" system, an eight hour day, twice a month pay days, and a minimum of $2.75 a day wages.

The IWW also wanted to march through the streets of Hibbing and Power upheld their right to do so as long as they did so in a law-abiding manner. They did. But the other issues were not so easy to solve and time seemed to have more success than the strike. Wage problems were always the most difficult to solve because they were the most complex.

Wages for a miner varied depending on whether the work was done in a surface area (open pit), or in an underground mine, whether the mining was in a wet or dry area, and the job held, engineer, drill operator, shovel operator, blaster and so on.

On the face of it an eight hour day was already in place in open pits (and underground) but it depended at what point you started the clock running. If you were the Oliver, it stared running when the miner picked up a pick, so to speak. He may have spent an hour getting down to the bottom of the mine and then later in the day an hour getting out of the mine but that wasn't 'on the clock' as far as the bosses were concerned. The miners thought it was. The twice a month pay check problem was another of those questions that no one ever asks about unless they are paid only once a month. If you get laid off, or you quit, or get sick early in the month you have to wait the rest of the month to see a pay check. This results mostly in running a credit system on trust, there being no 'credit cards' at the time. A miner also had to pay for his tools and other equipment but the bill for those items didn't appear until the end of the month. And then it only appeared as a deduction. All this was classic in a mining industry but the contract system was the heart of the problem.

Miners on the Mesabi Iron Range fell into one of two categories: paid by the day (open pit) or on contract (underground). Contract work is a form of piece work where the miner contracted to mine ore for a certain price a carload. The price was set by the mine captain and varied day to day. The system was rife with possibilities for corruption. It was alleged that single men bribed the mine captains (real money changed hands) to get the soft ore to dig and that some unscrupulous married men bartered their wives while still others offered their carpenter skills for home repair. Drinks and cigars were common items of exchange. Mine captains could and did take advantage of this system and it is no wonder that this was attacked by the workers.

Underlying all these problems, wage inequities, length of the work day, price of a car load of ore and so forth was the uncertainty of the take home pay which, when combined with the seasonal employment uncertainty, led to one stressed-out work force. The miners were looking for stability, consistency, regularity and that is very hard to achieve in the iron ore mining business.

Carlo Tresca and other IWW organizers were arrested and held for murder in the first degree as accessories before the act. The theory being in this case that their incendiary speeches caused others to kill Deputy Myron from Duluth. The strike started to fizzle out at this point.

Power rode this one out too and ran unopposed for his fifth term. He garnered all 1,441 votes. There just wasn't anyone with the political clout to take on the four-time winner. Without opposition landslides are common.

Some History
In 1917, the iron ore range and the businesses and industries it supported was maturing. Twenty four years had gone by and everything was getting bigger. Wooden ore cars that carried twenty-one tons of ore each gave way to steel cars that carried forty-seven tons each. And in this year if you used the old cars it would have taken seven years to carry the output to Duluth's ore docks. Approximately 400,000,000 tons of iron ore had been shipped by this date. Enough material (ore and earth) had been mined and moved by this time to fill the Panama Canal excavations twice over. Steam powered locomotives called Mallets hauled the ore from the assembly yards outside of Hibbing (Mitchell and Monroe Yards) to the ore docks in Duluth or Two Harbors and these leviathans with

their coal and water tenders weigh in at 620,000 pounds. The wheel base for this hunk of black steel runs to over eighty-seven feet. The waiting ore docks in Duluth vary in length from nine hundred to two thousand three hundred feet and have been built sixty feet to eighty feet high in order that a boat can be loaded by using gravity to drop the ore through chutes out the different pockets built into the docks directly into the waiting boats. The newest dock constructed of steel and concrete made for the D.M.&N. railway cost a cool $3,000,000. There were some 400 boats in the ore carrying trade those days with a fleet capacity of 55,000,000 tons a season (around nine months).

This giant machine is necessary not only for the usual economies of scale but also because the mines themselves are not exactly just large holes in the ground, they can assume the proportions of canyons. To give an example that will seem obvious by now: the Hull-Rust mines to date had shipped 34,000,000 tons of ore; the Mahoning had given up 24,000,000 tons of those. And those mines were *underground* operations for the better part of a decade!

Local politics sometimes could seem unimportant to the men who ran those mines.

Power won his sixth term in 1917. Unopposed again. He had no reason to think that this term would be unlike any other but times change. William West was leaving and a new man with a familiar face and an impeccable reputation was arriving. The Oliver was shuffling the management deck again. Power's remark about local autonomy for Oliver officials was about to come true in a way that he didn't quite anticipate.

Back a Bit

As 1913 began, Mike Godfrey was busy attending to the details of administering the Canisteo District, principally stripping overburden off ore deposits to insure easy access to ore bodies when the spring mining season began. As was always the case with Godfrey, he was pressing his mine supervisors to make sure they understood the role of safety in the mines because it was not just a set of procedures for men to follow, it was a part of the culture. Mining activities had to be coordinated with U.S. Steel's plans/demands for the coming season, rail and lake transportation had be coordinated with mining activities, ore grades had to be determined, equipment had to be examined and where necessary, repaired or replaced.

And with seven children running around the house on Cole Avenue, Cecelia needed all the help she could get and the kids had to be looked after and managed. The winter season on the Mesabi Iron Ore Range never made any of these endeavors easy or simple. They were difficult, time consumptive and often, claustrophobic. When spring arrives on the Range everyone looks foreword to getting outside, breathing the scented air, and getting on with activities.

Godfrey was just enjoying the warmer weather in late May when Olcott and Mitchell asked him to come down to Duluth for a business planning meeting. Even Godfrey wasn't prepared for what the President and Vice-President of the Oliver had in mind. Cecelia was not overjoyed either.

June 6, 1913

The Virginia Enterprise of St. Louis County broke the news on June 6, 1913. The headline read: M.H. GODFREY IS NEW SUPERINTENDENT OF OLIVER. SUCCEEDS M.S. HAWKINS AS GENERAL SUPERINTENDENT OF VIRGINIA DISTRICT. ONE OF THE BEST KNOWN MINING MEN ON THE RANGE.

Mike, Cecelia, and the kids would have to move again, this time clear across the Range to Virginia, northeast of Coleraine, northeast of Hibbing, northeast of Chisholm. This was going to be a major move for everyone. The Virginia District was a big one and probably the second most important mining district on the Mesabi Range for the Oliver. It was a stepping stone and a proving ground and would the genial Mike be up to the task?

The Virginia Mining District. This is where Godfrey honed his skills for four years while Vic Power and the Oliver tried to figure out the future in Hibbing. Minnesota Department of Natural Resources.

Daniel W. Lynch

At this point in his career Mike was becoming fairly well known. He had served in Hibbing as a superintendent and as an assistant general superintendent and had served as the general superintendent of the Chisholm District. He took over from John C. Greenway and served with distinction as the general superintendent in the Canisteo District. This is a long time to serve in the public eye where mining officials on the Mesabi Iron Ore Range became almost as well known as Village politicians and in some cases better known.

The *Virginia Enterprise* understood the role of the mining official in the local community. The local editor characterized Godfrey as one of the best known and most popular mining men on the range.[12] The Enterprise knew as they put it, "that he was one of the most able executives in the employ of the company." It was in his favor that he was well known by both the public and the business community. It didn't hurt one bit that he knew how to boss mine captains, some of them as temperamental as opera stars, better than any superintendent up to that time. Godfrey could handle them all, businessmen, miners, captains, politicians, officials of the Oliver. One author referred to Godfrey this way: "he was rated a genius on the range."[13]

Hawkins stayed on in Virginia for the time being and LeRoy Salsich succeeded Godfrey in Coleraine.

Godfrey did not even have time to settle in before he had to prepare for the eighteenth annual Lake Superior Mining Institute's convention with its 300 or so delegates led by Pentacost Mitchell, one of Godfrey's bosses, at the helm. Godfrey was co-chair along with W.P. Chinn of Pickands-Mather, and W.J. West also of the Oliver. Mike was directly in charge of the reception committee of some eighty assistants that decided on what kind of entertainment was suitable for so many guests over a four day period.

The delegates arrived in Biwabik on Tuesday on the D.&I.R. railroad and were whisked away by automobile to the Genoa mine near Gilbert. They then proceeded to visit a number of mines on the route to

To Tipple A Prince

Eveleth. By that time the delegates were famished and stopped for a pre-arranged dinner at the Globe Hotel. After dinner, for those whose stomachs could take it a tour of the Leonidas was undertaken down to the 600-foot level. On the following day with the party somewhat on a roll, five mines were visited, the Norman, Alpena, Commodore, Union and Lincoln. Then the Virginia & Rainy Lake Company was toured for over two hours and the delegates were serenaded by the Mohami Band. The next day there was a baseball game in the rain at Oliver Park with a 6:30 p.m. dinner at the Elk's club as a chaser.

Then came business. The Roosevelt high school auditorium was the setting for a series of technical papers more or less with the theme "Mining Methods on the Mesabi Range". One long presentation compared the mining methods on the Iron Range of Minnesota (favorably) with methods in other parts of the country. Mike had "something out of the ordinary"[14] in store for everyone the next day in Hibbing. This was the St. Louis County fair (one of the first organizers of this fair was Thomas Jefferson Godfrey, Mike's brother) where horse races, vaudeville acts, and athletic performances were the order of the day. On the way back to Virginia, Buhl, and Chisholm rolled out the red carpet (iron ore red) where some more mines were visited.

Godfrey and his staff of eighty were praised for the clockwork efficiency with which the entire four days were run. With his boss looking over his shoulder this must have helped ease Godfrey into the Virginia District's mining activities.

A House Full of Kids

While Mike was living out of his suitcase and managing the Virginia Mining District the Oliver was thinking of his family and assigned one of their firms to design a house for Mike and his large family. It was loosely patterned after the one in Coleraine he and Cecelia had lived in while assigned to the Canisteo District. This one was considerably larger

The general superintendent's house in Virginia today (2003). It was originally located at 818 Ninth Street North on the other side of town. The street underwent a name change as well. It was first known (and sometimes is still known) as Mountain Iron Road. Mike and Cecelia lived here with their seven children beginning in 1913. An eighth child, Agnes Eleanor, was born here (and the only child born to the couple in Virginia) a year later in May. Author's Collection.

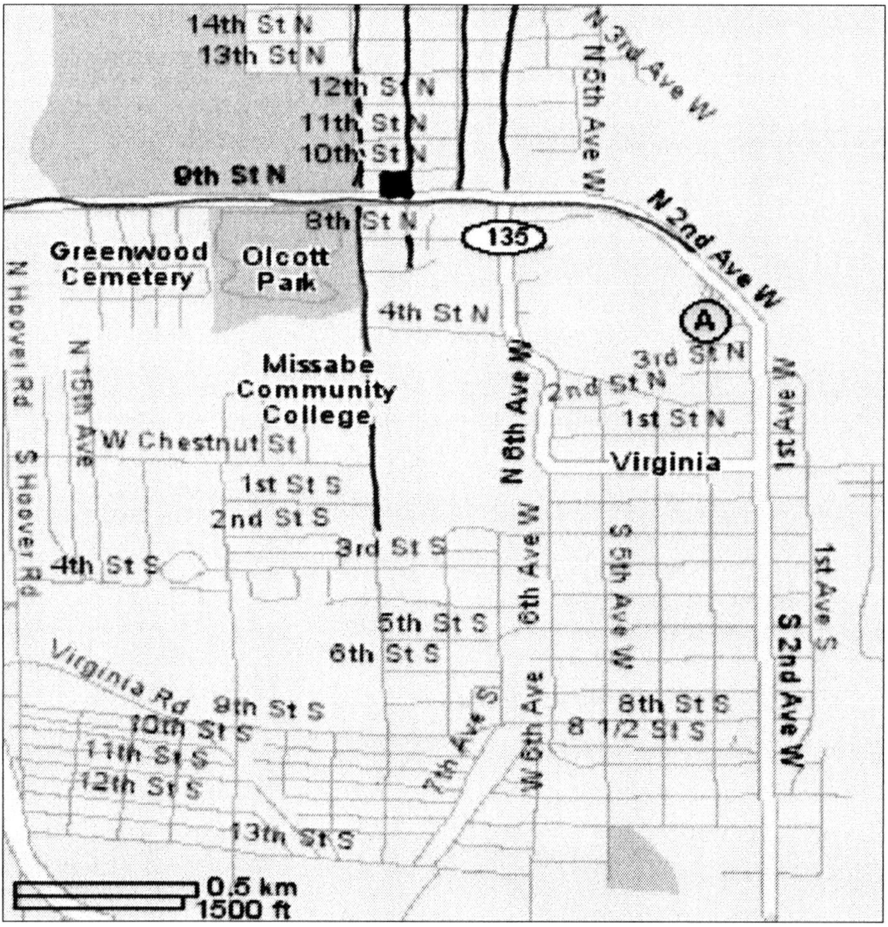

Modern map of Virginia with the general superintendent's house marked in shaded. The house was very near Cavalry Cemetery where the Godfrey's have a plot. North is at the top. Yahoo Maps.

and during construction, it attracted much attention. In November of 1913 it was nearly finished. The house was located just east of Olcott Park on a very large tract of land, some forty acres. The *Enterprise* predicted that it would become one of the finest residences in Virginia.

Safety First
It did not take long for Godfrey, once he had the feel of the district, to emphasize the importance of safety in mining activities. Just as he had done in the Canisteo District, Mike called on the experts and put their recommendations into everyday practice. In December, he called upon the United States Bureau of Mines in the person of Edwin Higgins to come to the district with his mine rescue car and demonstrate its use both in Virginia and throughout the Iron Range.

While the Bureau of Mines conducted its road show, Godfrey organized his office administrators in such a way as to put safety uppermost in their minds while they went about their mining activities. His managers, mine captains, and superintendents were put on notice to promote and maintain safety because it increased production. A committee was also appointed to present a comprehensive plan for carrying out safety procedures and safe practices down in the mines. He organized a Safety First club that had for its chief object the promotion of the Safety First movement in the mines of Virginia, Gilbert and Biwabik. He implemented practices that pioneered the promotion and use of first aid practices in the mines.

The Bureau of Mines joined him in the district in setting a uniform signal code for use in the mines. Safety by itself has little rationale other than reducing injuries but if you couple it with the economic twin of increased production, it takes on a whole new meaning and Godfrey knew it. This was sometimes a very hard sell to upper management (way down in Duluth) but eventually it caught hold and W.J. Olcott came out later in December with an Oliver-first, company-wide comprehensive safety policy that had the desired effect of putting teeth in all local endeavors.

Steam Shovel mining. The ore cars pass under the steam shovel on the way up and out of the mine. The Oliver preferred using rail to haul ore out of its mines. The shovel's bucket is over the next to last car. Photograph: Charles E. van Barneveld, Iron Mining in Minnesota, University of Minnesota, (Minneapolis, 1912).

Between journeys to Duluth to consult with Oliver officials and tending to business in the Virginia District, Godfrey had time to travel to Hibbing with Richard J. Mitchell, superintendent of the Eveleth District, to participate in Hibbing's twentieth birthday celebrations in August of 1914. Town officials and local businessmen gave them a royal welcome. Not every mining official on the range was accorded such a welcome and it is significant that this official was, even though he was forty miles down the road. In this area and in this business, your reputation precedes and follows you.

As another reminder of the esteem that Mike Godfrey enjoyed and from whom, when Mike and Edward J. Maney, superintendent of the Shenango Furnace Company spent several days in Hibbing in June of 1915, Mike drew the distinction of being referred to as General Manager and Prominent mining man from the Virginia District. Godfrey was a

To Tipple A Prince

Hibbing pioneer, it was noted, and formerly Assistant Manager of the Oliver Iron Mining Company's mines in the Hibbing District and he is deservedly popular with all classes. Mr. Maney managed the distinction of being "built along the same lines as the genial Mike."[15]

Things remained quiet in the Virginia District for the remainder of the year as winter stripping operations took up most of Godfrey's time but a visit in February of 1915 by President W.J. Olcott, Vice-President Pentecost Mitchell, and Chief Engineer G.E. Diehl from Oliver headquarters in Duluth to inspect the newly opened Sullivan underground mine, managed to keep things lively.

Nor Any Drop to Drink?

Sometime during Vic Power's argument with the Oliver, the question of Hibbing's water supply came up and with it the suggestion that it could be contaminated. This brought Mike Godfrey back to Hibbing in October 1915, to take a real close look along with the Oliver's Chief Mechanical Engineer, Spencer Rumsey and R.J. Moorehouse the engineer in charge of the work. They inspected the wells that the Oliver had originally dug and which were now being used by the Village for drinking water and found themselves very favorably impressed with the new water system. They went on the public record with their prediction that Hibbing had one of the finest water supplies in the state. That closed the matter as far as everyone was concerned.

Oliver Iron Mining Company Headquarters. Duluth headquarters where Mike Godfrey and W.J. Olcott met to discuss "the move." From here, orders went out to the Oliver's seven mining districts16 in northeastern Minnesota. A majority of the mines were in St. Louis County. Colorized postcard.

From Near and Far

But Godfrey and the Oliver continued to serve the local community and, from time to time, distant communities as well. In November 1915, Assistant Principal H.A. Hutchings of the East Technical High School of Cleveland, Ohio showed up in Virginia looking for a tour of the district's mines. He got one. Mike took him and the Virginia school board on a tour of the Alpena and Norman mines. It was Hutchings' first visit to the Mesabi Iron Range and to an iron ore mine. He left "agreeably surprised by the magnitude of the iron industry on the range."[17]

Godfrey and the other general superintendents of the Mesabi Iron Ore Range then met in Duluth in the first week of January 1916 to plan the coming year's mining and stripping activities. He felt that the coming season would be a prosperous one in all branches of the industry. Mike was of the opinion that the possible cessation of the war in Europe wouldn't make any material difference to the iron and steel industry. The Virginia District and the other six districts on the Iron Range were planning on working the mines and mills to capacity.

However, when he returned to the house on Mountain Iron road, bad news had arrived before he had.

First, Cecelia's Father

His father-in-law was very sick. After several weeks of doctoring himself with the help of his children, and several more weeks in the Rood Hospital, James finally consented to an operation (on—among other things—his gall bladder) at the Mayo Clinic. The operation was successful but he was left so weak he died shortly thereafter during the last week in January while recuperating in St. Mary's Hospital in Duluth. He was sixty-one years old.

James had been born in 1855 in Ireland and had immigrated to the Upper Peninsula of Michigan, married, and had a daughter, Mary, all before he was twenty. In 1893, he was living in Newberry, Michigan (and had a second daughter, Cecelia by this time) in 1893 when he moved to Hibbing (at about the very same time as Michael Hogan Godfrey) along with his daughter, Cecelia, and his brother Miles.[18] He opened Hibbing's first grocery store almost as soon as he arrived. He operated his grocery store until 1907, when he sold the lot to the Merchants & Miners State Bank. He also served as Hibbing's second mayor in 1894/1895 and served again in 1900/1901. He had been a member of the police force for the last three years before his death, courtesy of Vic Power.

Mike and Cecelia had remained close to her father since Cecelia's marriage to Mike and this certainly had its effect on them both. Her father had survived his operation but died in spite of it. Cecelia had to contend with this sudden death while taking care of her eight children, the youngest of whom was not yet two years old. Add moving every couple of years from one Range town to another (somewhat akin to moving to a foreign country in those days) and then add Mike's high pressure job to the mix and you wear down fast. Too fast.

Michael Hogan Godfrey and Family. This photograph was taken in 1913 with the then seven children: in the back row reading from left to right, James, Miriam, and Tom; in the middle row between Mike on the left and Cecelia on the right are, Paul and Marge; and down in front are Jane and Elizabeth. Authors Collection.

This had been a bad year for the Gandseys and the Godfrey's and it didn't take long for it to get worse.

Then, Cecelia and Child

The end came suddenly. Cecelia Helen Gandsey Godfrey died at 5:25 p.m., July 29, 1916, while battling eclampsia's[19] severest symptoms for half an hour. She was not yet forty years old and she was pregnant for the tenth time. The child was not delivered.[20] Mike and Cecelia had been married for not quite twenty years and her death was not expected. Coming just six months after her father had died, Mike must have felt like fate was taking a roundhouse swing at him. Her funeral procession included sixty-five cars and seven carriages. She was buried in the family plot in Virginia, a short distance from their house.[21]

Cecelia's grave marker. She is buried next to her husband, on his left. This is Calvary Cemetery and like all such places is quiet, beautiful and serene. On a gray day, however, the place has the feel of emptiness. The photograph was taken in the Summer of 2000. Author's collection.

Events at Hand

Mike had little time to grieve over his wife's unexpected death. He had eight children to take care of (although his oldest daughter, Miriam, at the time barely fifteen years old proved to be a big help as eldest daughters often are), and the Iron Range was going through one of its periodic convulsions: the IWW was out on strike. This kept Mike and the other district managers, general superintendents, mine captains and law enforcement authorities busy for several intense months.[22]

At one point over 1,500 miners were on strike in the Virginia District. Big Bill Haywood the general secretary of the IWW, issued a "Declaration of War" on United States Steel. His declaration was translated and printed in eleven languages and distributed in every mining town in Michigan, Wisconsin and Minnesota. At its height, over twenty thousand miners went out on strike for wages, safer working conditions, and better hours. The effects of the Mesabi strike, were noticed throughout the range as wages were increased, working conditions improved and more attention was paid to the miner's safety.

At one point during this tense turmoil of a time, Mike Godfrey traveled to Hibbing to visit friends and family (his brothers, sisters and parents still lived in Old North Hibbing, the Pillsbury Addition, and in the Mahoning Location). He was particularly pleased to sit down and chat with some of the men he knew when he first came to the Iron Range.

At one party with some old friends the current topic of interest—The Strike—came up which gave Mike the opportunity to say something in behalf of the mining interests and he was ready with a story drawn from his days at the Minnewas mine (in Virginia) in 1893 where he was working as a time-keeper.

Two hundred and forty men were on the job, and in August of that year the operating company was three months behind with the miners' pay, but that didn't bother the men so much as the lousy food served at the mine boarding house. Miners want good food and lots of it.

One noon Mike listened to the grievances of the men, particularly aimed at the boarding camp, where he also took his meals, and he was forced to agree with them that the food could be better, a lot better. But that was the only boarding house for miles around, and he could not suggest any remedy. He went into the office and talked with the mine captain, a bluff, red-faced, good-natured Cornishman, hearty and always hungry, when the captain, on looking out of the window, discovered the whole mine force idling about the shaft-house[23] though it was long after the one o'clock whistle had sounded.

"Wot the bloody 'el blong doin' out theer' lookee, Mike."

Mike replied that he didn't know what the blongs were doing out there, and suggested that they go on down and find out. Accordingly they joined the men, and the captain asked why they were not at their work.

"We're on strike," replied the spokesman.

"Wot fur," asked the captain.

Then the spokesman outlined the grievances, the poor grade of grub served being the principal one; in fact, it was the cause of the "strike."

"Well, damme, I'll go 'long with 'e, but where the bloody 'ell is us'ns to go to get better'n 'ere?" was the captain's rejoinder.

And the strike ended right there. There was no better food to be had in the whole range country in that day of early development, and the men finally decided that in such times of deep business depression they were lucky to get any kind of food, and with only the prospect of a pay day in the uncertain future.[24]

Mike had an obvious theme to his story but then so did the paper. What the writer had in mind was to emphasize that times certainly had changed on the Range since the early 1890s but Mike Godfrey had not and this was to his credit. As the Ore put it: "He's the same likeable chap and the advancement to the high position he holds hasn't put any foolish notions into his head." But that wasn't nearly enough for the writer or the editor. It was the fact that Mike was different from the other mining officials (*unnamed* officials) in that he had what the paper called an advance view of conditions and did not jump unless he can see clearly where he would land.[25] Translated, that reads that he could see the big picture and was conservative but not repressive.

Reading the tea leaves that the timing of some articles leads to, indicates that the Ore had some advance notice of what was about to happen on the Mesabi Iron Ore Range of northeastern Minnesota. This little anecdote didn't appear in the paper at this time by mere chance. This was excellent promotional material and a nice way to introduce readers to what was about to happen.

To Tipple A Prince

The Twain Meets

While Vic Power was rolling to his unopposed landslide in March for his fifth term, Mike Godfrey in the Virginia District and W.J. West in the Hibbing District were settling in for another year of making the Oliver Iron Mining Company the largest on the Mesabi Iron Range. But then the Oliver sent Godfrey west and West, well, he was sent east. Mike Godfrey was headed home to Hibbing and there he would stay. He did not move from here again. He and Vic Power and John Gannon and others now proceeded to write an enduring chapter of Hibbing's history.

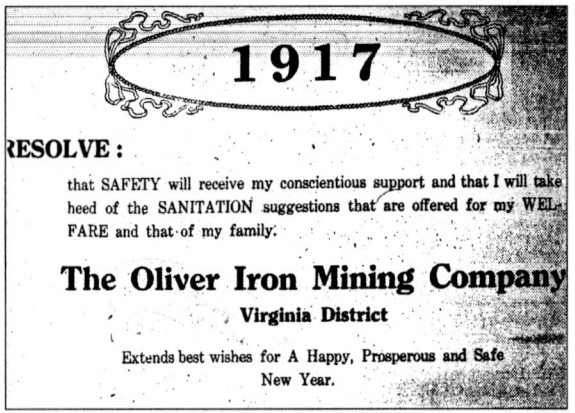

A typical example of the marketing techniques used by Mike Godfrey to sell safety to the general public. If he hadn't been supporting safety and better working conditions in the mining industry for over a decade, this would look very self-serving appearing just after the Wobblies Strike the previous autumn. The Oliver supported this emphasis after a few years of dragging its feet while it learned statistically just how effective safety could be: production inevitably went up as safety improved. As the miners could only agitate for safety, the mining companies had to implement and enforce it. *Virginia Daily Enterprise*, January 1, 1917.

April 1917, District Manager

At the end of March, the *Virginia Daily Enterprise* carried the announcement:

M. H. GODFREY AND W. J. WEST RECEIVE PROMOTIONS. CHANGE IN OLIVER COMPANY ORGANIZATION. By a change in the organization of the Oliver Iron Mining Company two of the best known mining men on the Mesaba range win will-merited promotions.[26]

What lay behind this double promotion and swap we can only guess as we are not privy to the Oliver's thinking but the promotions and announcements read like a recognition that time and circumstance were on the company's mind. The oracles in Duluth were removed only in distance from the economic, social and political pressures existing up on the Iron Range. Vic Power and his legal battles with the Oliver, his successive terms in office, mining strikes, and the emergence of open pit mining were all in evidence to Olcott, Mitchell, and others. The biggest iron ore producing district on the Iron Range had to reposition itself now that the war was winding down, to handle new mining methods, new markets and new men if it was to remain a player in this industry.

The Mesabi Range iron ore properties and the Vermillion range properties were now divided into two enormous districts. West received the mines east (really northeast) of Buhl and Godfrey received the mines from Buhl to the southwest through Hibbing. Each was given a new title to go along with his new duties and district, that of district manager. The change was to take effect on April the first. The West and East districts included some of the largest mining operations in the United States, not just northern Minnesota. The Hull-Rust-Mahoning-Burt-Day-Sellers-Pool-Susquehanna complex of mines produced an enormous amount of ore and were about to produce amounts that almost obscured the other districts. This range of mines also produced the first ore ben-

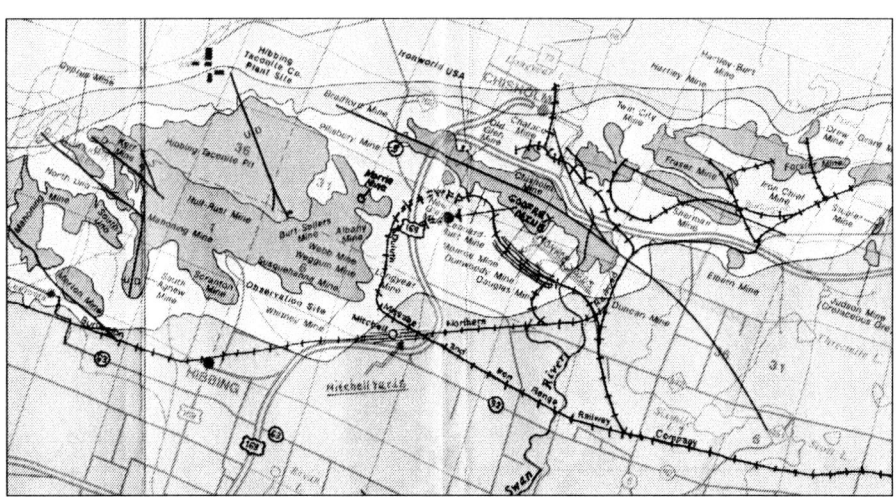

A partial overview of the Hibbing District. Mike Godfrey assumed the duties of general manager to handle this huge complex of mines, ore dumps, and railroads. Minnesota Department of Natural Resources.

eficiation plant (the Trout Lake Concentrator that J. C. Greenway had started on his own and then finished under Godfrey's direction) on the Iron Range to process the sandy ores of that district.

Godfrey was now one of the oldest continuous serving mining men on the Mesabi Range, having started in the Minnewas mine in Virginia in 1893 as a time-clerk, then working for the Merritts in Mountain Iron as a bookkeeper, then moving southwest to Hibbing where he was employed as an accountant then a mine supervisor. He had arrived with his brother, Thomas Jefferson, in the summer of 1893 and his rise had been steady. The *Virginia Daily Enterprise* on March 27th accorded him the honor of being generally well-liked by employees and townspeople and for being known all over the range for his squareness and sympathy in dealing with employees.

To put all this in human terms for his family this simply meant moving again. This time to 411 Sellers Street in the Pillsbury Addition. Wisely, maybe even with some prescience, he did not move into Old North Hibbing. His parents lived at 415 Garfield Street in the Southern Addition four blocks south. Again, not Old North Hibbing.

Honored Guest

Two days later (and this makes me think that company politics were of a general currency in towns and villages and not a matter of private corporate politics; someone had spilled the beans so to speak) the *Enterprise* under the head "Godfrey Will Be Honored Guest at Banquet Here This Evening" announced that 136 of Mike's closest Virginia friends would be getting together to honor him at a banquet dinner. Forest fires don't ordinarily spread that fast. The newly minted Fay Hotel was to be the site and 9:00 p.m. the time.

The plans had been put together in two days by a committee meeting in the library and they had restricted the guest list to only Virginians because if out-of-towners were to be invited the resultant crowd would be too large.

Daniel W. Lynch

The dinner started promptly at 9:00 p.m. as scheduled and for the next three hours "Mike" as he was referred to most of the evening, listened as miners, Virginia residents, common laborers, and fellow mining leaders, extolled his career and his achievements. Pioneers of Virginia who had known Mike Godfrey for more than a quarter of a century, were among the guests.

Toastmaster M.A. Murphy led off by emphasizing that Mike's promotion was the result of merit. Murphy, who knew how and when to tipple a prince went on to quote the citizens of Virginia extending their best wishes to Mike while he mentioned that Mike had a broad vision on every subject. He scored big when he said that this was the only time he had ever envied Hibbing as Mike Godfrey was headed there. Michael Boylan, the Mayor of Virginia, had the talent to put Mike's role in practical terms. Boylan saw that Mike had set a great example for the employers of labor because he believed in a square deal[27] for everyone and had been nothing but honest in all his dealings with the city administration. The Rev. Charles W. Ramshaw intoned that Mike had developed the spirit of unity in the Virginia community (and that was surprising as the IWW strike was not that long ago) as he was a man of character and knew how to deal sympathetically with all men. The head of the school board, Edward C.A. Johnson characterized Mike as a real community builder.

And this was only the start.

The Rev. Father W.J. Powers felt that Mr. Godfrey had no self-conceit. The assistant superintendent Charles Grabowsky lauded Mike's spirit of good-fellowship, his open-mindedness, his ability to treat everyone as a friend. He noted a trait of Mike's that had much to do with his success in the Oliver organization, "there never was a strain in the relations between Mike and his men."

When Godfrey had first taken over in Virginia some three years before, he extended the Oliver's resources to the independent Interstate Mining Company when their Lincoln underground mine had flooded. It had saved Edward P. Scallon's company from financial ruin and Scallon paid a personal tribute to Mike Godfrey.

Virginia's city attorney lifted his glass to "a Mesaba range that is producing great men," and S.S. Dahl felt that Mr. Godfrey was the "greatest of all mining men developed on this range." That may have been overstating things a bit.

A nice tribute came from Paul F. Chamberlain, an underground miner for the Oliver who had worked for Mike before. He laid heavy stress on the esteem that other miners felt for Mike and he and they understood Mike's success was due to his patience, loyalty and perseverance.

The Rev L.W. Gade had worked among Oliver families for awhile and had noticed that, as he put it, "corporations have souls. The Oliver with its homes, pensions, safety work and so forth shows its attitude toward humanity. Mr. Godfrey has to his credit the developing of excellent spirit here between capital and labor." The Rev. Gade concluded with the wish that "Mike would make Hibbing a city and take it out of the Village class." The clergy certainly covered the highs and lows that night. Three hours of this may have produced some audience fatigue but the evening was not quite over. President O.A. Poirier of the police and fire commission wrapped up the honors with his mention that "Mr. Godfrey had been instrumental in molding the policy of his company here."[28]

That last comment was the very thing on Vic Power's mind when he said that the local mining officials needed more say in the overall and day-to-day conduct of the Oliver's business on the Mesabi Iron Range. The Oliver was willing to listen and act upon Mike Godfrey's recommendations as they proved to be worthwhile, cost effective and had the consequence of placing the Oliver in a very favorable light across the towns and villages where Mike had been stationed. Olcott and others respected Mike and backed him up in matters of safety, labor relations, donations, medical care and a host of other initiatives. Now, they were about to go the distance with their local man. They weren't about to regret it. Vic Power's feelings on the subject are arguable.

Mike's comments were, mercifully, brief. "All my success has been due to the loyalty of my employees," he said and then concluded by saying, " My relations with my men and residents of Virginia have always been pleasant. Mr. West, my successor here, is the salt of the earth and a prince of a fellow."²⁹

The Hibbing papers let this opportunity pass for the simple reason that Mike was now headed their way and when he arrived they had their own version of a welcoming banquet ready.

Attorney W.J. Archer presented the guest of honor with a sterling silver centerpiece as a gift from those present. The guests arose and applauded as the gift was presented to Mike. The holder is shown. Author's Collection.

Honored Guest Déjà Vu

The news broke on March 31st under a front page headline announcing that a "**HIBBING BOY COMES BACK HOME**".³⁰ The rest of the article reads like a hagiography and that is probably what the author had intended. This was not just another phase in an endless game of management musical chairs. It looked like the real thing, a strategic move on the Oliver's part to place a well-known and former resident, and pioneer, in the most important job on the Mesabi Iron Ore Range at the time. Things had not been getting a whole lot better in the heart of the range over the last three years or so and the status quo was not, as they say, an option. Mining was big business and was on the verge of getting a whole lot bigger and social and political peace was a critical for growth. Bill West was a miner with a very broad range of knowledge about mining

To Tipple A Prince

and the mining industry. His skills seemed to be focus more on ore and not so much on the needs of those who mine it.

The article did not serve so much to introduce Mike Godfrey to the people of Hibbing as remind them of what he was like, what he had done, and what he was likely to do for the area. The article is worth quoting in full for it paints a clear picture of what Hibbing would come to expect.

> The Ore welcomes the return of Mike Godfrey to the Hibbing District, and believes *it will go a long way toward smoothing out some of the wrinkles of hate* [here and below author's emphasis] that have grown up amongst us by reason of conditions that none of us could control.
>
> Mr. Godfrey is to succeed William J. West as General Manager of the mines of the Oliver Iron Mining Company (United States Steel corporation) in the Hibbing District. Mr. West will be transferred to the Virginia district, where the corporation has work more fitting to his high talent.
>
> The arrival of Mike Godfrey brings a Hibbing boy back home, and his welcome will be a general one. That he is a faithful employee of the Steel corporation *has not effected his high standing with all classes* of people—he works in the interest of his employer, as every honest man does, and yet during all of the strife that has gone on between the Steel corporation, the miners and the "in betweens," *Mike has lost none of his popularity*. In fact, in the grievous stress of turmoil *he went freely between the lines* [the trench between Labor and Management] without the necessity of carrying the flag of truce. He is trusted and respected by everyone, and his coming to Hibbing is taken as the best move the Steel corporation has made since it first began to take the advice of its awful array of bone-head lawyers.
>
> If there is a *man that can heal the sore without leaving a vestige of a scar*, that man is Mike Godfrey, and he will succeed if his counsel is taken in the big office.
>
> The news of the approaching departure of Billie West, who has long lived with us and been of us, is received with deep regret by all Hibbing. But insomuch as it is to be, we all join in the wish that the new position will offer greater opportunity for the full exercise of his great mining knowledge.
>
> The transfer can in no way be taken as a reflection upon Mr. West as a gentleman, a good neighbor, a staunch friend, an ideal citizen, and one of the best iron ore miners that ever set foot on the Mesaba.
>
> Mike, we give you cordial welcome.
>
> Billie, good bye and God bless you.

Daniel W. Lynch

The Love Feast

But this was before the banquet which was to be held the following week. That event was announced with another front page headline on April 7th that read: **"HIBBING TO HAVE A LOVE FEAST"**. The article[31] reflected high expectations—if not reality—with Mike Godfrey's return and the editor was not shy in making his case. Hibbing was 'coming together' with the arrival of Mike Godfrey. At one point the editor became positively giddy at the thought of the Godfrey-West "coming and going" love feast. Whatever the incidentals involved in this, it was going to be a joyous occasion drawing the towns people and mining people together because "that is the Hibbing way, you know."

Mike Godfrey. Approximately 1922, age fifty. He certainly does not look like the cocky young man that appeared in his parents photograph, nor the somewhat full of himself family photo. Here, six years after his wife died, four years after he was first diagnosed with heart problems and four years into the Great Move, he looks like the accomplished administrator and diplomat and man of judgment that so many others saw. The vicissitudes of time had not yet made their entrance. Authors collection.

The day after the banquet the paper returned to the theme without diminishment. The banquet (which the paper still referred to as a love feast) was over and now it was time to live in the atmosphere of the brotherly love that had been talked about when all of Hibbing—over 500 residents, mining officials and politicians (sans the mayor)—filled the armory.

It would seem from references in the article that one of the main forces behind the get together was the business community, which was now stepping up to the plate somewhat belatedly but nonetheless critically. They could not only read tea leaves but maps as well. The trends were all too apparent, the businesses of North Hibbing were about to be "squeezed out" and the politicians and mining officials were having some difficulties in appreciating the urgency of a solution. So the businessmen—the businessmen of Old North Hibbing, not the businessmen of the Pillsbury Addition or the Southern Addition - attended the banquet with not only an appetite but an agenda. They wanted to look over Mike Godfrey to see what he had to say and they wanted to rub some elbows while they were at it. This is assessing, not bonding.

This is the way the *Mesaba Ore and Hibbing News* put it[32]:

> The business people of the community are heartily sick of this bickering and pulling and hauling, the mine workers share the feeling, and if the mining people [in Duluth and points East[33]] do not then they are truly gluttons for assimilating defeat and getting in dutch at every turn.
>
> But our humble opinion is that the mine operators are just as anxious to bask in the sunshine of sweet peace as we are, thought their manner of showing it may possibly be a little strained at the outset of a new condition that is so foreign to their former policy.
>
> . . . .
>
> When the spirit is right it will come to our vision that the gap is not so wide after all, and that with just a few more smiles, just a little more kindness and consideration, just a few more words of encouragement, with the helping hand from each and all of us, we can draw together the edges of the wound and in time there will be scare in sight. Then we can again wear smooth the path of friendship between the different camps.

Once everyone was seated, R.W. Hitchcock acting as toastmaster opened the evening with a thematic toast. "This is a banquet," he began, "of Hibbing people by Hibbing people for two of the ablest and most respected men in this section of the state." The stampede was on.

The Rev. R.W. Adair mentioned that Hibbing has brought forth men of a caliber to compare with its natural endowment. He then called for a toast to welcome Mr. Godfrey and Mr. West; Samuel C. Scott, Hibbing City Attorney stated that Mike's handshake says that he will make a friend and keep him and he went on with the hope that the difficulties of the past would be eliminated and that in the future there will be no differences; the Rev F.C. Coolbaugh of the Episcopal church spoke of the angelic power in the name Michael and he hoped Mr. Godfrey would have success here and that he should be aware of the fact that he was coming to a town where all were not angles[34]; the Rev Father James Hogan who presided over James Gandsey's recent funeral, offered that he liked the sentiment, flowers for the living, flowers for our honored guests, giants in their chosen profession; Frank Webb of the Republic Iron & Steel Company stated that the success gained by Mr. Godfrey was not based on luck but on honest merited advancement accomplished by hard work; C.C. Alexander, and Robert Stratton all gave testimonials to Mike as did A.P. Silliman, real estate developer; Michael Boylan, a friend of Mike's and the mayor of Virginia (attending his second banquet in as many weeks), and Edward Maney (also attending his second banquet in as many weeks).

Mike Godfrey as was his custom spoke briefly about how happy he was to come back to Hibbing and that his policy would be to treat the men underneath him with every consideration in order to win the loyalty of his employees and he wished, further, to remember his friends.[35]

Judge Martin Hughes closed the evening with a solemn speech about the present national crises (the war) that amounted to "one of the most impressive orations ever heard in Hibbing."[36] He managed the solemnity with the artful ploy of never once mentioning either guest of honor.

Every guest received a small lapel flag and the waiters dressed in the nation's colors.

That was one impressive evening.

Two weeks later Godfrey traveled to Norway, Michigan, to visit old friends and some mining colleagues. The *Norway Currant* emphasized that "old time residents of Norway had a kindly feeling for Mike Godfrey who was at one time assistant postmaster here and whose boyhood days were spent here and at Pine Creek."[37] He then left for Duluth for consultations with Olcott and Mitchell.

To Tipple A Prince

Vic Power, who had missed the banquet, did have time to sit down in Fergus Falls, Minnesota, and talk to the local newspaper, the *Wheelock's Weekly*. He seemed in a conciliatory mood as he ended his interview with this:[38]

> The hot fight between the companies and the village has reached a truce now, as a new superintendent, whom everybody respects, has been put in, with unusual powers. Mayor Power explained that the supplanted superintendent was personally a fine man, but that he was continually handicapped by instructions from headquarters which left him no option. Mike Geoffrey, who takes his place, would not come to Hibbing until he was given full authority.

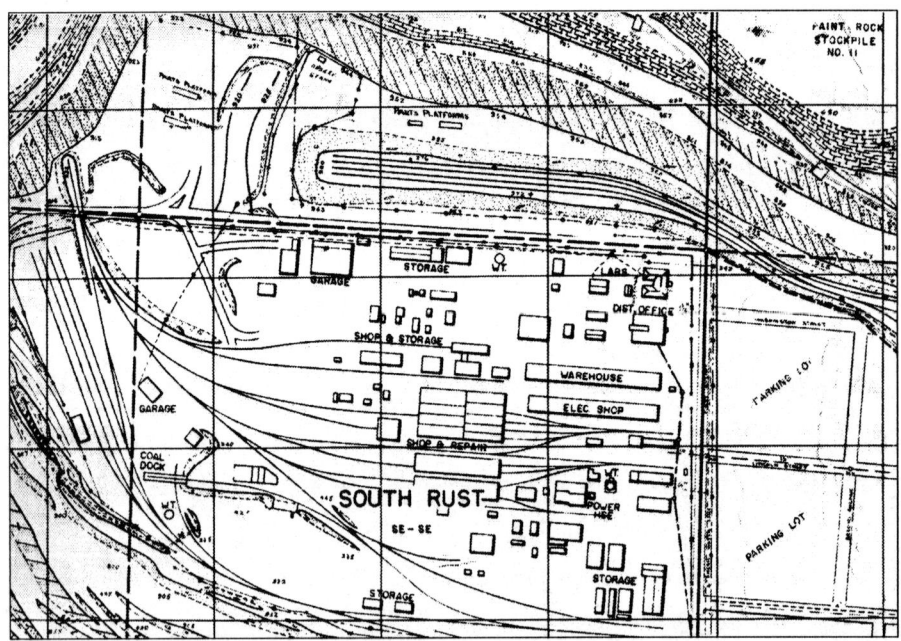

South Rust Headquarters of the Oliver Iron Mining Company in Old North Hibbing. Washington Street is near the top (north) of the property and Garfield St. is near the bottom (south) of the property. The OIM laboratory building is on the northeast corner with the headquarters building next to it on First Avenue. Mike Godfrey's office was to the left of the door in front and faced First Ave. Mike enjoyed this location so near his home and so close to the HRM complex of mining operations. This was his office from 1917 until 1928. Note the prevalence of railroad tracks on the property and just to the north of the property. The thirty-five ft. high railroad (double-track) berm is still (in 2005) there and it looks down upon the present Observation building. The ties are to be found everywhere; the steel vanished with the Oliver. Hanna Ore Mining Company, Map of Pierce Group and Vicinity. Scale is 1" to 200'. Undated.

Daniel W. Lynch

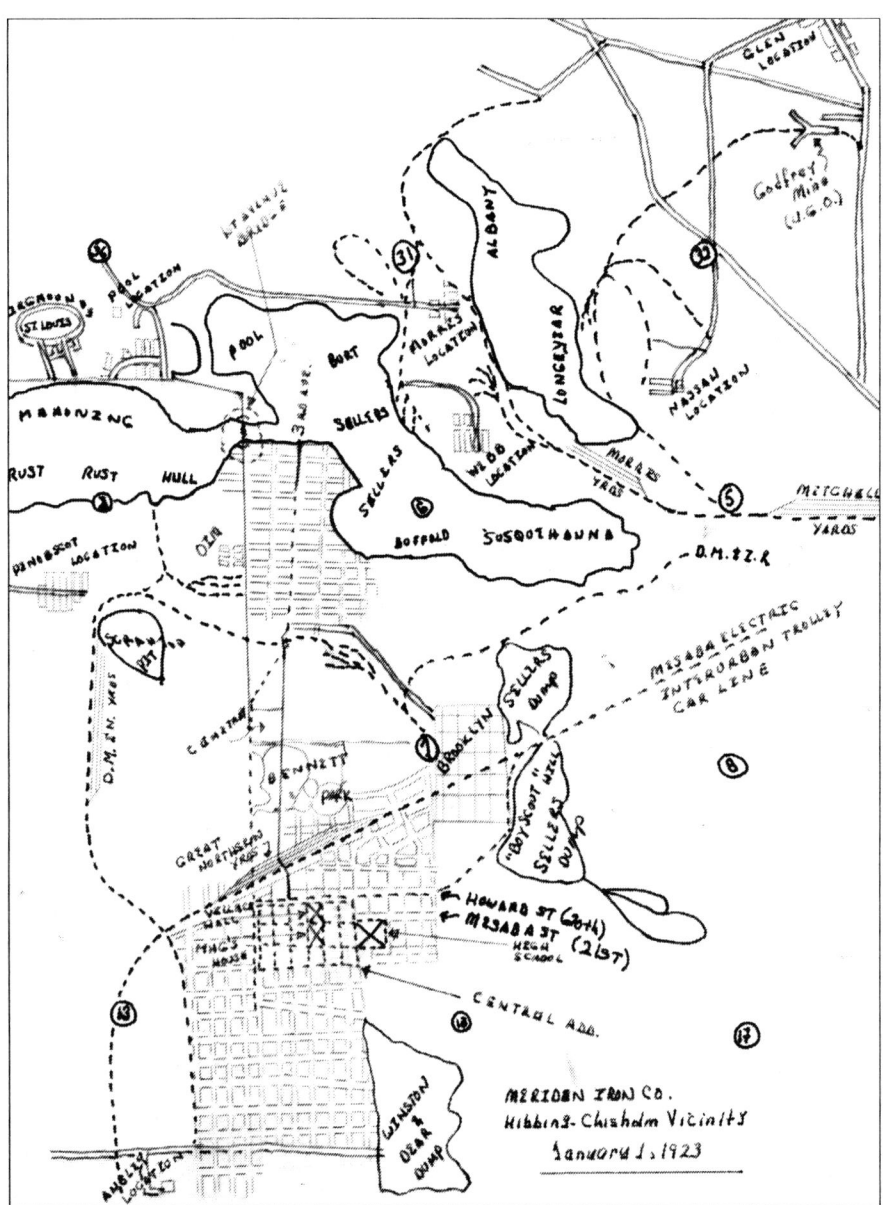

Hibbing District, 1923. This is the layout that greeted Godfrey as he took over the Hibbing District with his unusual powers. The Central Addition is in green outline near the bottom part of the map. The Village Hall and Godfrey's house were in the heart of the new addition. As you can see, the mines surrounded North Hibbing. The Penobscot Location is also in the way of progress as are the St. Louis County Fairgrounds, the Pool Location, the Morris and Webb Locations. However, the Penobscot Location was the only one of those on the south side of the mining operations. Meriden Iron Company, Hibbing-Chisholm Vicinity, January 1, 1923.

To Tipple A Prince

Vic Power was always a very well informed lawyer and politician and it appears quite likely that he was very well-informed on this issue. "With *unusual* powers" sounds immediately different (*unusual*) and hints at something that was definitely not in the papers. And Godfrey did not come to Hibbing *until he was given full authority*. Not only does it appear that Vic was in communication, if not with Godfrey, then with someone inside the Oliver Iron Mining Company (not that that would be unusual but it did mean that the Oliver wanted its change in policy noted for public consumption). A strong wind was surely blowing from the southwest.

By August rumors flew. The *Mesaba Ore* reported, "A rumor that has been freely discussed during the weeks is to the effect that the Oliver Iron Mining Company has purchased the Larrabee Forty, at the Alice Addition and contemplates the moving of their building at the Penobscot Location onto this site. So far, however, this has not been verified. It is also stated that several properties in the village have been purchased by the mining company."[39]

It is difficult if not impossible to believe that at this time the Oliver was not contemplating moving some of their properties, but they testified to that in court when they were sued in 1921. Mike Godfrey, on record, said he was approached by local businessmen and that initiated the moving.[40]

The Larrabee Forty was a very attractive "forty" as it sat in the middle of Alice a more or less large, empty lot with a few trees and a lot of refuse. It was prime real estate located in the heart of Alice and needed a plat. The Old North Hibbing (and maybe the Pillsbury and Southern Additions as well?) businessmen had only one direction to move in if they wished to continue doing business.[41] The Pillsbury and Southern Additions were fully occupied. That left Alice.[42]

The War Beckons

In September of 1917 Godfrey headed up a committee of twenty Hibbing men to help bolster the morale of Hibbing troops going off to war. Before they left for training camp at Fort Dodge, Des Moines, Iowa, the men of the National Army were to be given a public send off. While in boot camp and while they were in Europe they were to be regularly supplied with packages of reading matter, tobacco and letters from a family member or a friend (or the committee if they had no friends).[43]

This was not Godfrey's only civic activity in the service of the village's commitment to the war effort. He was also one of seventy-eight men representing nearly all the range towns from Buhl on the east to Grand Rapids on the west that raised nearly thirty-five million in donations for the YMCA and the War Work Fund. The Oliver not only pledged money but they also put their Oliver Club in the service of holding banquet luncheons where businessmen vied for the privilege of donating funds and raising more.

Credit Where Credit Is Due

December brought more than the cold north winds to Hibbing. The paper was still sounding like it knew more than it was telling. On the 28th it reported that the Oliver was buying up twenty city squares of the old part of town and that *some of the buildings would be removed to another point inside the city limits* [author's emphasis].[44] That *is* what the Oliver had in mind but it had made no public announcement to indicate it. Articles at this time, though, read like the Ore had a fly on a wall inside Oliver headquarters. It is noticeable, for example that the superintendent rarely failed to get a kudo or a mention. In one aside in December, he earned a reference that "under the clear-headed management of Superintendent Mike Godfrey the people of Hibbing and the Steel Corporation are getting along famously and will so continue if the damn fool friends of big business can keep their noses out of our affairs." My.

Events Big and Small

For starters, the war ended. And the Oliver had to adjust to the new reality of a downturn in demand for its sole product: iron ore.

To Tipple A Prince

Thomas Clark Godfrey who was fifteen years old at this time left St. Thomas Academy (the high school) in St. Paul, Minnesota, and enrolled as a junior in Hibbing's High School. Tom was not a serious student and could hardly wait until he graduated so that he could go to work in the mines. He was to get his wish. His Father did not like the idea but Tom had little patience and a heart full of dreams. After all, his Father did not wait long after high school to enter the mines but this was a new era and by entering the work force of an industry that was far more mature than it had been twenty-five years before required more preparation than dreaming provided.[45]

Godfrey was about to embark on a very busy year. He was settling in to his new job as general superintendent of the Oliver's interests in the Hibbing District and putting his house in order, a necessity with eight kids and no wife.[46] This was not the only problem weighing on his mind but it is hard to gauge at this perspective how heavy the worry was.

A Trip to the Southern States?

Godfrey's friend and editor of the *Mesaba Ore and Hibbing News*, C.M. Atkinson, ran a curious mention in his February 8th edition. "Michael Hogan Godfrey, general superintendent of the Oliver Iron Mining Company's operations in this district," he began, "left on Wednesday (5th) for a business trip through the southern states."

This mention is odd not only for its ambiguity (what southern states) but for a different reason as well. Godfrey was off to Duluth just a week later for a business conference with his headquarters managers, Olcott and Mitchell. No mention is made of the previous business trip. Either it was not important or its nature was supposed to be a mystery. After thinking about this and reading ahead in the record, it seems likely that this was a trial balloon.

Godfrey, his sister, Agnes Godfrey who was a nurse, and his doctor, S.S. Blacklock, did indeed take a "southerly" trip in mid-March to

Chicago where Mike was to receive medical attention! Now, that had to be what Atkinson managed to mangle back in February. It was in a fashion a southward journey (Chicago is south of Hibbing) but by no stretch of the language was it through any southern state(s) nor was it a business trip. Godfrey was sick and the nature of the illness either so unknown or so potentially dangerous that he had to travel with a nurse and his personal physician.

Curiouser and Curiouser

Doctor Blacklock returned a week later but Mike and his sister did not. And Mike's brother, Thomas Jefferson, then traveled to Chicago and spent the week there before returning. T.J. had not accompanied his brother on the trip nor was his trip to Chicago mentioned prior to his leaving. It was mentioned only upon his return. T.J. said nothing about his brother's health upon his return but the Ore did learn that Mike would remain in Chicago for two more weeks. According to the story on March 22nd Mike was undecided on where to go once he left Chicago, but he had decided on what he would do: nothing. For the next six months! This makes it sound more like he was on death's door than anything else. A six month's vacation (or a medical leave if you will), at age forty-eight, with eight kids at home? In light of subsequent events something was amiss here.

Nothing more was said as March melded into April and May into June until suddenly summer was in high humid heat. And not one word about Mike's condition appeared in the paper. No mention was made about who took over his job, or if (or, that) Mike had somehow made a miraculous recovery and had returned to work.

This entire episode strikes me as peculiar. Doctor S.S. Blacklock, who accompanied Mike Godfrey and his sister and nurse, Agnes, to Chicago was Mike's physician. He was not along on the trip by accident or coincidence. He did not have a medical practice in the Windy City, nor was he attending a convention. He accompanied Mike Godfrey as his physician, probably he needed to consult with the expects in Chicago (the Mayo Clinic having failed to offer a conclusive analysis) on their diagnosis and preferred method of treatment, if any. He, however, offered no information at all upon returning to the Iron Range, then or later.[47] The Hibbing paper raised the issue of his traveling for medical tests and then dropped the issued without mentioning the results of the tests, if any, or offering a retraction for inaccurate reporting.

What's Up?

In late August the stunning announcement was made that Mike Godfrey and LeRoy Salsich had just been promoted by the Oliver! Mike Godfrey's duties were about to increase, not decrease, at a time when his medical condition was under examination. For the moment this 'condition' was disregarded, forgotten, or misleading.

The Oliver Iron Mining Company was consolidating and combining mining districts on the Mesabi Iron Ore Range and Godfrey and Salsich were at the center of the company's plans. Godfrey was now the general manger of the Western Division of the Oliver which comprised the Hibbing, Chisholm and Coleraine Districts, and Salsich, who had been general superintendent of the Coleraine District, was now the assistant general manger of the Western Division, reporting to Mike. W.M. Tappan, who had been assistant general superintendent of the Hibbing District was now promoted to general superintendent. Tappan, Salsich, and Godfrey each moved up one step on the company ladder.[48] Godfrey had reached the pinnacle of his profession on the Mesabi Iron Ore Range. Any further advancement would require leaving the Range and moving to Duluth.

The Lieutenant Is Discharged

It was little noticed but not long ignored that in December of 1918, Lieutenant John M. Gannon was honorably discharged from the U.S. Army in Fort McArthur, Texas and returned to Hibbing for a visit with his uncle, the Hon. Martin Hughes, before he traveled southwest to his home in Nashwauk to resume his law practice. John as yet had not made any impact on the local political scene but with his connections, legal skills and reputation he was a good future candidate. He would show up in Hibbing soon enough.

The Larrabee Forty Revisited
The end of the year brought with it some reflective rumination on the part of the *Mesaba Ore and Hibbing News*, a sort of recapping and anticipating.

Hibbing had reached a truce in its fight against the mining companies with the assignment of Michael H. Godfrey (the paper quoting Vic Power here) by the Oliver.[49] This was considered a good move by the Oliver almost as if they heard the sound of local aspirations for the first time and decided to act upon them. World War I had increased the demand for iron ore. To increase their mining operations the companies needed more stripping area. Acquiring the title to the remaining properties in the North Forty (i.e., Old North Hibbing) was going too slow according to some company officials. Godfrey's first job was to get that property as the ore underneath the village could be mined.

In that regard the Larrabee Forty, a tract of land to the south of Hibbing proper, was purchased by the Lebanon Iron Mining Company (owned by the Oliver) and platted. It was ready and waiting for occupancy. All that remained was to figure out who was going to make the first move and who was going to pay for this operation.

This was not going to be the same as moving a couple of wooden dwellings from a Location; this was a major and complex operation involving substantial structures of brick and stone, structures that were profit making businesses and organizations that fed, clothed, entertained, supplied, housed, nourished, educated, and governed the growing population

To Tipple A Prince

The view is from the southwest looking northeast and looks directly down upon the remains of the old Oliver Iron Mining Company headquarters complex. The large building in the background is the Pierce Plant. Today, this site is very difficult to 'read' and needs an archaeologist to excavate and explain it. 1956 Postcard photo by David Nordgren.

of one of the major population centers of the Iron Range. Businessmen are loath to commit large amounts of money to civic enterprises that do not at least at face value add great benefits to the organization and politicians are wary of undertaking vast civic enterprises that disrupt the body politic and threaten their chances of maintaining their offices. The old adage that there is no harm in trying is not often quoted in such circles.

* * *

Notes

[1] In the July 19th edition. It would in effect create a 'rapid' transit system between the two settlements.

[2] The Hibbing franchise was granted to a Duluth company, Washburn, Bailey & Mitchell, only the year before.

Daniel W. Lynch

[3] Major settlements were of course represented with stops along the line but Locations were not left out. The orange and dark green trolley cars stopped at Lavinia, Meyers, Croxton, Sharon, Lucknow, Spina, Kinross, Hanna, and Genoa. The route as it left Hibbing was in a northeast direction. However, the route did not include stops at such Locations along the north side of the Hull/Rust/ Mahoning/Burt/Sellers/Susquehanna complex of mines as Penobscot, Pool, Morris, Webb, or Nassau.

[4] The *Mesaba Ore and Hibbing News* of March 15, 1913.

[5] This flap erupted in November of 1913.

[6] A year later his Father took ill after a year of declining health. Vic Power traveled to Chicago where his Father was being treated. His Father a retired judge lived in Escanaba, MI.

[7] While Vic Power was commanding stage center in Hibbing's political arena another (later) player was being noticed for the first time. John Gannon who was soon to begin his legal career in Nashwauk, MN was noted in the local papers as coming home for the weekend to visit with his (very politically connected) uncle, the Honorable Judge Martin Hughes. John was taking a break from law school.

[8] Reported by the *Virginia Daily Enterprise of St. Louis County*, June 1, 1915. The Virginia paper spilled more ink on this story than the Hibbing papers did. Perhaps the fray was more enjoyable from afar.

[9] June first edition of the *Virginia Daily Enterprise of St. Louis County*. Power probably did not play a lot of chess. A player does not Checkmate!! a move. You either remove a Check! by moving the king or interposing a piece between the king and the piece performing the check. If you are unable to do either, it is Checkmate!! and the end of the game.

[10] This was no easy matter for a village the size of Hibbing. It was incorporated in August 1893 with 2,740 acres within its corporate limits and currently contained a population of 16,000 in its 8, 000 acres consisting of 11, 40-acre tracts. The two original plats also were currently sitting on some 27,000,000 tons of very high grade iron ore.

[11] *Virginia Daily Enterprise of St. Louis County*, November 24, 1915.

[12] In the June 6th, 1913 issue.

[13] Stewart H. Holbrook, *Iron Brew: A Century of American Ore and Steel*, The MacMillan Company, (New York, 1939).

[14] As quoted in the August 9th edition of the *Mesaba Ore and Hibbing News*.

[15] *Mesaba Ore and Hibbing News*, June 12, 1915.

[16] In 1913, they were: [1] Hibbing District: Hull-Rust, Burt-Pool-Day, Winifred, Mace, Harold, South Uno, North Uno, Dale, Mississippi, and Mahoning; [2] Virginia district: Alpena, Missabe Mountain, Shiras, Fay, Union, Prindle, Minnewas, Deacon, Wanless, Sullivan; [3] Chisholm District: Leonard-Glen, Leonard-burt, Leonard, Chisholm, Clark, Duncan; [4] Canisteo District: Canisteo, Holman, Judd, North Star, Hill; [5] Adams District: Adams, Leonidas, Hull Forty, Spruce, Norman; [6] Fayal District: Fayal, Genoa-Sparta; [7] Biwabik District: Graham, Vivian.

[17] The *Virginia Daily Enterprise* of November 27, 1915.

[18] Miles was to serve with distinction as Assistant Postmaster to Mike Godfrey's brother, Thomas Jefferson. The Rev. John Hogan served as pastor for James's funeral mass. Hibbing's Irish made a fetish of sticking together.

[19] Eclampsia is the final and most severe phase of preeclampsia and occurs when preeclampsia is left untreated. Preeclampsia is a condition that pregnant woman can get and is marked by three specific symptoms:

water retention, high blood pressure, and protein in the urine. A woman must have all three symptoms simultaneously or she does not have the condition. The causes are unknown even today but poor nutrition, high body fat or insufficient blood flow to the uterus are suspected.

[20] The death certificate does not state the fetus' probable age. Preeclampsia usually appears during the second half of pregnancy, usually after the 20th week, but can appear as early as the fifth month.

[21] The house has since moved to 1805 11th Avenue W. It faces an ore dump but has been restored and looks as lovely as it did the day Cecelia died.

[22] Especially when it was learned that the red-scarfed Elizabeth Gurley Flynn got involved. She drove the officials in Spokane to distraction and was now loose on the Range. She is a story for someone else.

[23] This marks it as an underground operation.

[24] The *Mesaba Ore and Hibbing News*, March 24, 1917.

[25] The *Mesaba Ore and Hibbing News*, March 24, 1917.

[26] The *Virginia Daily Enterprise* of March 27, 1917.

[27] In political-speak this means honest. He was *not* anticipating Roosevelt.

[28] Quotes are from the *Virginia Daily Enterprise* of March 30, 1917.

[29] At this time it seems a bit pedestrian to mention that the menu consisted of Fillet de Whitefish au Beurre Noir, Pommnes Julienne, Fried Spring Chicken a la Maryland, Salade de Laitue aux Tomates, Angel Torte, some After Dinner Mints and to top this (heart attack special) off, cigars. The chef should have been the honored guest.

[30] The *Mesaba Ore and Hibbing News* of March 31, 1917.

[31] *Mesaba Ore and Hibbing News*, April 7, 1917.

[32] *Mesaba Ore and Hibbing News*, April 7, 1917.

[33] Author's interpolation.

[34] The clergy covered the high and the low, again.

[35] *Hibbing Daily Tribune*, April 11, 1917.

[36] *Hibbing Daily Tribune*, April 11, 1917.

[37] *Norway Currant*, April 28, 1917.

[38] *Wheelock's Weekly*, Fergus Fall, MN.. As quoted in the *Mesaba Ore and Hibbing News* of June 2, 1917

[39] *Mesaba Ore and Hibbing News*, August 17, 1917. The Larrabee Forty is better known as the Central Addition. Then and now, it is bordered on the south by Howard Street and on the west by FirstAvenue.

[40] This will come up again in greater detail but for now, it is mentioned to place the time frame for the move as immanent. The Ore moreover was repeating what was all over the street. By late August, rumors had given way to what the paper referred to as "the corporate plan." The Oliver denied it.

[41] It seemed to be some kind of common knowledge that the western forty of the original two plats had approximately 25 to 30 million tons of ore under it. The Oliver played coy with its silence, neither affirming nor denying the rumors or the estimates.

[42] With all the rumors, stories, and articles floating about it comes as no surprise that other newspapers picked up some of the more colorful tales and misprinted them. A paper in San Francisco ran a feature with a Hibbing date line that reported that the Oliver was going to tear down the entire city of Hibbing while in the same breath mentioning that Hibbing had more street lights than the City of Cincinnati (pop. 400,000),

that even the alleyways had the same lighting systems that the streets, avenues, and boulevards of Hibbing did, and as real food for thought the article concluded that Hibbing's village expenses were higher than the state of Delaware's. On the other hand, no one in Hibbing went out of their way to deny the allegations.

[43] His son and oldest child, James Robert, was now eighteen. He visited Minneapolis in September of this year.

[44] *Mesaba Ore and Hibbing News*, December 28, 1917.

[45] His enrollment in the local high school may have had more to do with family circumstances than personal choice as we shall see in a moment.

[46] Still living at home at 411 Sellers Street, Pillsbury Addition, Old North Hibbing, during the 1918-20 period according to the Hibbing census were: James Robert, age 20; Miriam, age 18; Thomas C., age 16; Marjorie, age 15; Paul, age 13; Elizabeth, age 11; Jane, age 9; Agnes, age 5; Agnes (sister), age 35 and working as a nurse, and a maid, single white female, no age or name given.

[47] Michael Hogan Godfrey's Death Certificate tells a third version of the story. It is signed by Dr. S.S. Blacklock as Godfrey's physician, and on it Blacklock states that he has been Mike's physician since 1920. Either the good doctor forgot—he was Godfrey's physician at least since 1918—or he made a misstatement of a kind. He further states that Mike had chronic myocardites for a period of 1 year, six months. He had a heart problem, whatever you wanted to call it, for somewhere near 8 years. A picture of Mike and his second wife, Mary Elizabeth Kramer, taken in 1923 or 1924, on a boat at Lake Esquagama is a picture of a dying man. Godfrey added to the confusion in 1921 when he testified in the Vacation Case. While on the witness stand he was asked to fix the time of his illness that he had mentioned earlier in the morning and he replied, "It was between March and August of 1918." *Henry P. Reed, et.al., Plaintiffs v. Village of Hibbing, et.al., Defendants, State of Minnesota, District Court, County of St. Louis, 11 Judicial District.*

[48] W.F. Kohagen, the General Manager's secretary (meaning Godfrey's) was elected to the Board of Education, succeeding Bruce Middlemiss, who resigned and left to manage a copper mine in Chile. Kohagen is important in this narrative as he kept a diary.

[49] The December 20th edition.

VI

The "Town" That Moved: 1918 to 1922

Introduction

As the turn of the decade approached, Hibbing continued to grow by means economic and natural. The village enjoyed a stable economic base which encourages family growth and to help things along, the Oliver bought and platted two new additions. By 1920 the population of Hibbing approached 18,000 which saw it pass the "queen city" of the Range, Virginia, which had 14,000. Moreover, the population center within the Village was shifting from the Original Townsite to the south, to the old Alice location and the newly platted Central and Eastern Additions. The Oliver Iron Mining Company commanded the lion's share of the ore shipped off the Mesabi Iron Range with fifty-four percent of the total and fifty percent of that came from the mines surrounding Hibbing.

"The move" dominated the lives of those living and running businesses in the Original Townsite. The eastern forty acres had already been swallowed by the mines and now the west forty was about to succumb to the march of mines. Godfrey stage-managed the move for the Oliver, meeting with the Old North Hibbing businessmen at their request (as he recovered from a serious illness). Godfrey had to initially convince his company to back the move and after some initial reluctance, the Oliver did so. And by the time the dust settled, the Central and Eastern Additions had been bought, platted, and were being settled (all spare lots in the Park Addition were also bought up.)

Daniel W. Lynch

By August when Olcott and the Oliver came out publicly the move turned into a rout and six blocks of the Central Addition became the hub of the new Hibbing. This maneuvering and moving of the original west plat to the new Hibbing brought an immediate reaction from the businessmen in the Pillsbury and Southern Additions.

This short period also saw the rise of a newcomer to the Hibbing legal scene, John Gannon, who left the southwest range town of Nashwauk for the more litigious fields of Hibbing. Gannon was eventually to go head to head with Victory Power and with Mike Godfrey. But, not quite yet.

But the Oliver and the move was the major news story for three years. But by 1921, it was almost all over as the Oliver owned all the surface property, private and public, in the original townsite. The rise of the New Hibbing began and the shape that it eventually took is still the main configuration of Hibbing's business district. The rise started in mid-year.

On July 12, 1918, the Oliver-owned Lebanon Iron Mining Company through its officers, Olcott and Swift, platted the Larrabee Forty and renamed it the Central Addition and then they entered it in the book of plats on August 8, 1918. Just in time for Mike Godfrey to begin planning in earnest.

Prior to this time Godfrey had not talked to Vic Power, or the Village Council, or local businessmen, or towns people about the potential move. That the Oliver had been buying up surface property in the west plat of the original Hibbing "80" since 1912 was well known but *what* the Oliver intended to do next and *when* it intended to do it were open questions. People were getting slightly nervous but as Godfrey later put it in court, "the plans were not complete before that time [August 1918]."[1] The plans were not complete before that time because Godfrey had been sick but initiatives were under way. One initiative was the buying and platting of the Central Addition in old Alice, now called 'the New Hibbing'. The other part of the plan consisted of a letter Godfrey wrote to W.J. Olcott, down in Duluth at the Oliver's headquarters.

To Tipple A Prince

He sent the letter on the 9th of August after meeting with some local merchants from north Hibbing.

What Mike Said

He said he had been sick. And not attending to any business at the time. And he said it twice. Godfrey had been in recovery for nearly six months when the businessmen came to visit him.

Two years later Godfrey was in court on the witness stand giving testimony in the civil case brought by Henry P. Reed and seventy-five others (plaintiffs) who, thinking in large terms, were suing the Oliver Iron Mining Company, the Village of Hibbing, the mayor of Hibbing, several prominent citizens, and the Mesaba Railway Company, an interurban electric trolley car line.[2]

In response to a question about the Village's building a post office, Mike admitted that he had heard nothing about it (this was in the Spring of 1918). In response to the next question for the plaintiffs' attorney: "Have you heard anything of that kind?" Mike replied:

> No, I had been sick at that time. They were erecting a building there[3] but I didn't know what the building was for. You see I was sick along in March and we purchased this property along in August; I didn't know. I wasn't attending to any business during that time.[4]

But this was not the only allusion that Mike made to his sickness. Later on in his testimony the following exchange took place:

Mr. Mercer: "Have you talked freely to people about the town, about intending to move to that addition?"[5]
Mike Godfrey: "Yes, Sir."
Mr. Mercer: "How long had that been going on?"
Mike Godfrey: "Well, ever since I was well enough to talk to them."
Mr. Mercer: "You mean since your sick spell?"
Mike Godfrey: "Yes."

Mr. Mercer: "You speak about "ever since you are well enough" and you said something this morning about having had a spell of sickness?"
Mike Godfrey: "Yes."
Mr. Mercer: "If you would fix that time?"
Mike Godfrey: "It was between March and August 1918."[6]

All through this trial whenever the topic of his health came up it is noticeable—and I think important—that Godfrey's usual, "Yes, sir," was replaced with the more terse, "Yes." At three years remove it was apparent that his illness was not a topic Mike was pleased to make part of the public record.

Neither Mr. Mercer nor anyone else asked just what it was that Godfrey was sick with but that wasn't as important as the fact that he was out of commission for seven months. The newspaper had noticed it but did not follow up, or felt that what it knew was better left unsaid. Somewhat of a journalistic rarity.

Godfrey had been sick and this had held up a rather important piece of business.

That business began sometime in August of 1918 when a group of (soon-to-be) Old North Hibbing businessmen situated along Pine Street and Third Avenue paid Mike a visit in the Oliver's South Rust headquarters off First Avenue in the Southern Addition. What was on their collective minds was the developing situation that was all too clear to them: real estate was being bought up by the Oliver in the west part of the original plat, there was little or new construction replacing the old, and the mines surrounding Hibbing on the west, north and east were eventually going to merge as they ate away at the ore in the middle. And they could see the empty quarter down south as well as the Oliver could. What could be done by the Oliver and the businesses of Hibbing to prevent a very nasty situation?

To Tipple A Prince

What Kohagen Wrote

Godfrey had an idea and had his secretary draft a letter for W.J. Olcott with a proposal. Fortunately for us, W.F. Kohagen, the South Rust secretary of the Oliver Iron Mining Company, was the keeper of a private business diary or journal.[7]

An entry dated August 15, 1918, is of particular interest.

The entry states that this is an appropriation request (#2046) from the (Oliver's) Hibbing District for $1,600,000.00 for moving the present townsite of Hibbing to the Central Addition and for the remodeling of seven buildings, as well as for the construction of sixteen *new* buildings in the Central Addition.

And—once again—this was in 1918 and in August Godfrey had just returned to work. The next step was to initiate the move. The Village had not yet been officially informed but it would not be astonished at what was about to happen nor could the mayor object as the Oliver paid a nice amount for his properties plus Mike Godfrey was about to help hishoner with some additional financial advice.[8] Others might object, but that was in the future (a future not that far from making its grand entrance).

Kohagen's record supplies some interesting details:.
Moving from present Hibbing townsite to Central Addition placing on stone foundations and remodeling seven *brick* buildings as follows:

[1] Rogalsky	211 Pine Street	25 x 105	two floors
[2] Barett	101-105 Second Avenue	50 x 55	two floors
[3] Moore	207 Center Street	25 x 105	two floors
[4] Close	223-225 Center Street	50 x 125	two floors
[5] O'Rourke	212-214 Third Avenue	50 x 100	two floors
Lippman		15 x 85	two floors
[6] Reed	310 Third Avenue	25 x 85	two floors
[7] Hibbing Hotel	314 Third Avenue	35 x 105	two floors

Construction of sixteen brick store buildings, two stories each, on stone foundations complete with basement, plumbing, heating, wiring, water and sewer connections, for use as follows:

1 Furniture Store	1 Dry Goods Store
1 Grocery Store	1 Meat Market
1 Clothing Store	1 General Store
1 Hardware Store	1 Jewelry Store
1 Candy Store	1 Restaurant
1 Moving Picture House	1 Pool & Billiard
1 Drug Store	2 Banks

One brick-constructed hotel building on stone foundations, to contain 140 rooms with bath, dining rooms, kitchens, one cafeteria, complete with plumbing, heating and lighting.[9]

Estimated Expenditures for above $1,550,200.00

Acquiring from Victor L. Power, Lots 18, 19, 20 in block 11, Pillsbury Addition, reimbursing him for expenditures in connection with erection of a brick building that had been started thereon . . . $40,800.00

Making total amount of this request $1,600,000.00

Kohagen's journal entry reflected what Godfrey was asking Olcott and the Oliver to do and at the proverbial bottom line, was money. Large amounts of it. This outlay, however, was just the initial one. The future would prove to be ever more costly.

Before we get too involved in what transpired over the course of the next three years ultimately leading to what today we know as "Hibbing," we need to describe the evolutionary course of events that changed everything.

First, a Little History

It is still difficult at this perspective some eighty-five years after the fact to appreciate what caused the original eighty acre plat of Frank Hibbing's to disappear. But disappear it did. No trace remains, no buildings, no streets, no parks, no cemeteries, no trees, nothing but a yawning hole in the ground and what a magnificent hole it is.

To Tipple A Prince

When Frank Hibbing platted Hibbing in 1893 he designated two "forties" for his town. The west plat of the two was settled but the east plat was only occupied by some squatters and little else. Hibbing developed in that west plat simultaneously with the mining of the iron ore deposits to the east that supplied the reasons for the development in the first place. These early mining endeavors were of the underground type and there were quite a few of them. They dotted the landscape.

Time passed and two things about the high quality iron ore that seemed to be everywhere became known: the size of the deposit was far greater than Frank (or anyone else) even dreamed of and, although its "shape" was also unknown its orientation followed the general orientation of the ore on the Mesabi range: northwest to southeast. It was about a mile and a half wide.

In the fifteen years since the mining operations began a giant revolution proceeded alongside: steam: steam to drive giant ore-digging shovels, steam to power giant drag lines (gigantic buckets) that stripped the surface materials off the ore (in some cases over a hundred feet of overburden left behind by the glaciers), and steam to haul it away using giant locomotives called "Yellowstones," the largest steam locomotives of all time. The vast deposits of Mesabi hematite lay exposed to man and man went to work mining it and shipping it to ever-hungry steel mills in Indiana and Ohio and Pennsylvania.

Hibbing, which sat on top of one of these deposits soon found itself surrounded by open pit mines. The area immediately surrounding Hibbing had transformed itself from a collection of fifty-six underground mines into one massive leviathan of a hole, the one we call somewhat misleadingly, the Hull-Rust-Mahoning.

As this was going on another site, called the Alice Location, was forming south of Hibbing near some other underground mines that were gradually being re-shaped into open pit operations.

Daniel W. Lynch

The nation's need for ore took a quantum leap when World War I dominated the political landscape. There was no way Hibbing could sit complacently in the middle of this activity of ever-growing iron ore mining. To make matters worse, Hibbing's population was growing from somewhere around 350 souls in 1895 to nearly 15,000 in 1915. A quick glance at the map might help to understand what was happening.

This was the situation that Godfrey confronted when he was promoted to District Manager and transferred to Hibbing. The Oliver had the mineral rights[10] and was busily buying up the surface rights as well. The business merchants in Old North Hibbing could see the handwriting on the wall. The merchants had made the initial foray and Godfrey had followed up with recommendations to his superiors in Duluth.

Olcott, Mitchell, and U.S. Steel surprised everyone: they backed

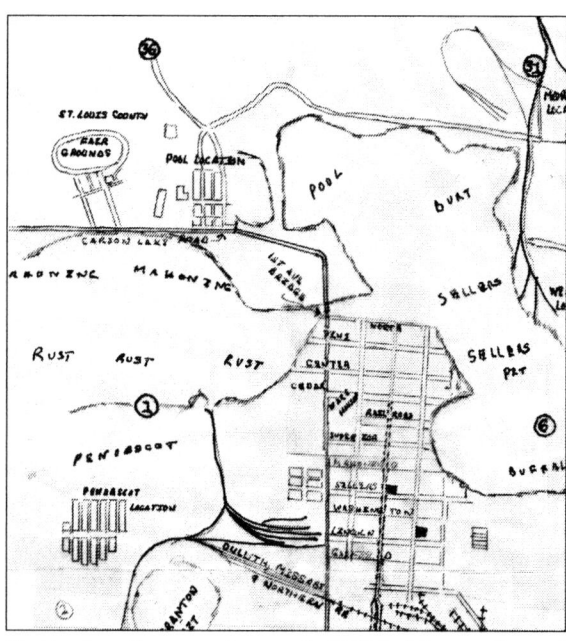

Meriden Iron Company, January 1, 1923. In this map, the east plat of Frank Hibbing is gone, devoured by the Sellers open pit mine. The Mahoning/Rust open pit is eating away on the west and the Pool/Burt are chewing up the north. That arrangement identifies a continuous [author's emphasis] body of ore. Old North Hibbing from North Street to Mahoning Street is in serious jeopardy. The dotted red line depicts the Mesaba Electric trolley car tracks in 1923 as they pass down Third Avenue on their way south. Originally the tracks crossed the First Avenue bridge and connected with Carson Lake Road. The bridge was the sole means for transport vehicles and pedestrians to travel north and south out of and into Old North Hibbing. With the bridge cut off and the town moving a mile or so south to the Central Addition, the Pillsbury and Southern Additions were effectively cut off from the daily commerce of the Village. Reed and others could see this quite clearly. It is still somewhat of a mystery why the Oliver insisted that the ore body under the town was an unknown to them. They owned the mineral rights and they had drill bits. Meriden Iron Company Hibbing-Chisholm Vicinity, January 1, 1923.

To Tipple A Prince

Godfrey all the way even as the costs began to escalate. This was a significant change in policy based on two factors: one was the personality and administrative ability of Godfrey which was the reason he had been transferred to Hibbing in the first place, and secondly, the nation's increasing need for steel was pressing the Oliver to ship ore, lots of ore. What the Oliver and U.S. Steel needed was someone who could make a deal—to their advantage—that would please every one involved. Mike Godfrey was their choice. And he brought it off.

It was, however, not going to be easy.

It was not always understandable, either.

A Continuous Body of Ore

It was obvious to most people in the Village—even if the implications were ignored - and to their representatives that Hibbing was surrounded by ore. The open pits could tell them that much. The Oliver's maintaining its mineral rights was a factor not to be ignored. The potential to exercise them grows with time, it does not diminish. And if you had just awakened from a forty year sleep some corporation buying up all the property in the surrounding area without doing any re-building whatsoever—is a very big headline: We have designs on your land.

And yet, the Oliver, Olcott, Mitchell, and Godfrey, all of them maintained in public and in court that they had no idea at all that there was any ore down there, or what grade it might be, or how much ore there might be. These men were miners, wise and experienced in the ways of marketable rock and the vicissitudes of geology. The Oliver had a posture to maintain, however and maintain it they did.

Here is what Olcott had to say in court.[11]

> "I don't think anybody can give you an estimate [ed: as to ore body size]. It has not been drilled and it is impossible to determine the tonnage until it is drilled."

Again:

"We haven't any information to know anything about it until it is drilled."

We haven't *any* information? *Impossible* to determine the tonnage? Olcott could have leaned over the edge of the pit and figured it out. Everybody else had. What is surprising is that he was not called to account for dragging the verbal equivalent of a hot air balloon into court. But he had his supporters, namely his on-site District Manager. And Godfrey didn't do any better in the veracity department with testimony like this in response to the query:

> "It is your understanding, that there is a continuous body of ore lying under the Hibbing Townsite?"
> "Well, we don't know about that."

Later, he had this to say on the subject:

> "There weren't any drillings there only the two that were mentioned and they weren't made for that purpose (*ed*: sampling the ore). They were made for a different purpose. One of them was for getting water and the other was for a cess pool."

In other words, no test samples were taken to check on the ore body under the townsite. None. Not once. Not at all. The Oliver over Godfrey's signature had just dropped nearly two million dollars to purchase some property in the west plat of the original townsite, and that amount was only the beginning of the financial fun, and *nobody* checked to see if there was *any* ore down there?

Probity seems to suffer best in silence.[12]

Back to the Action

Olcott and Godfrey next asked the Mesaba Electric trolley car people to move their tracks off the First Avenue (the Seller's Bridge) bridge and off Third Avenue—down at Railroad Street—a move the Pillsbury and Southern Addition merchants opposed. The request was a verbal one as

Olcott testified to in court. The intent was clear enough: the Oliver wanted to take that bridge down so they could expand the mining operations in the Sellers pit and they wanted the tracks out so that one more surface obstacle could be eliminated in the west plat.

Summer Turns to Fall
By November the municipal work in the Central Addition shut down in anticipation of the up-coming winter season. But much had been accomplished. Five miles of sewer lines had been put in place and three miles of water mains had been laid by E.W. Coons. Forty men were busily at work and would remain at work for winter's duration on the main sewer line which Coons expected to finish by spring. A building boom was anticipated for the summer of 1919.

The *Mesaba Ore and Hibbing News* understood what the Oliver intended when they ran an article in November pointing out that contracts had already been awarded for the erection of a number of residences for the Central Addition.

Fall to Winter
In 1903, Walter J. Power, Vic's brother, erected the first genuine large theater on the Mesabi Iron Ore range. It offered theater-goers of the various range towns the same class of entertainments as that found in large metropolitan areas (Duluth, the Twin Cities) but even though it had been extensively remodeled in 1913, it had since fallen on hard times and had a two year stint as a vaudeville house and ever more briefly, a motion picture house (talk about hard times). In December of 1918, it was torn down by James Geary on behalf of the Oliver. He kept the interior woodwork.

December saw the Great Northern Railway build a passenger depot just off First Avenue in the Park Addition. It was only a temporary one brought in on a flat car and at first glance looked like a tool shed but it had a station agent and was far more convenient than the one over at

Messabe Park. The Great Northern was also aware of the Central Addition's growing importance.

So was the Mesaba Telephone Company. It was laying underground conduit into the Central and Park Additions so that anyone it those additions who did not have telephone service or had only a party line, would now have a private line and the aerial wires running into those areas were to be taken down. E.P. Houghton, the local manager of Mesaba Telephone figured that would take care of demand until spring. He anticipated increased demand at that time.

The war was over, the Oliver was on the move, the town was growing, the sewers were in, the water lines were ready, the phones were ringing. Now if winter would just go south.

It is instructive that the move south was not done by a vote of the general population but by an open (but not publicized) agreement between Mike Godfrey representing the Oliver Iron Mining Company and Vic Power, representing (sometimes himself) the Village Council and citizens of Hibbing. The move south was not a secret but the assumption that all the townspeople were involved in the move was a flaw in the plan: the Pillsbury and

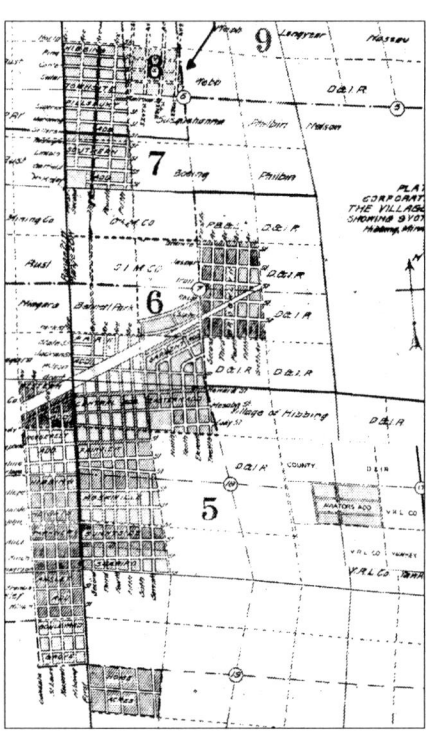

Hibbing in 1921. The existing Additions are all identified. The Park Addition is adjacent to and north of the Central Addition. The Oliver considered platting the Eastern Addition where the High School was built. Howard Street, the main business artery of the Central Addition runs east and west. The main business artery of the Western Addition and the Roosevelt Addition is First Avenue which runs north and south. The intersection of these two roadbeds was the place where the trolley car turned from First to go east on Howard. *Mesaba Ore and Hibbing News.*

To Tipple A Prince

Southern Additions—which had no marketable ore—were left out of the move but they were nonetheless *indirectly* and *powerfully* affected.

The west plat of Old North Hibbing moved to the new location a mile or so south, private residences, businesses and all. The City Hall, Fire Station, Library, Court House were eventually demolished and reborn in the Central Addition. When the First Avenue (or Seller's) bridge was cut and the electric street car service ceased that eliminated the sole remaining link to the settlements and locations to the north and to the south (except for Third Avenue). The old Hibbing was completely cut off and surrounded by mines, except to the south. To get into the New Hibbing you now had to enter from the south or from the east (and at that the route was south of the mines). You did not have to go to Old North Hibbing for anything let alone even pass through it and this resulted in the two remaining Additions to dry up slowly and inevitably.

The New Hibbing (which for a long time was "Alice') accepted the move fully. Business was booming and new businesses were opening all the time. The mayor and his law office were moving into the Central Addition, the Village Hall was being rebuilt there, the Fire Station, the Library, the largest hotel on the Iron Range was going up, apartments were being built, the widest streets on the range were being laid out and were, additionally, serviced by the only electric trolley car line in northern Minnesota, banks were moving to the new townsite, the mines were running at capacity and expanding. The Village Council voted a tax levy of $2,536,114.00 to help pay for municipal expenses and improvements in the Central Addition. The picture was full of sun light and shadow and in the shadow were those who were getting left behind but as plans unfolded, they got steamrolled.

As 1918 was drawing to a close at some point—no one seemed to recall exactly when—Godfrey approached Power and asked him what the Village planned to do with the public buildings (Village Hall, Water and Light Plant, etc) and Power responded with "After you have purchased a substantial majority of the Village property, come and see us."[13]

Daniel W. Lynch

Godfrey added that Power never said he would urge people to move south or advertise the fact that Hibbing was moving south.

Nineteen nineteen was here and the move rolled on.

Cocoons, Butterflies, and Flies

It was obvious now that residences and businesses were being bought up and transported south that *a* movement was fast changing into *the* movement. By the time spring appeared on the Range the Oliver had bought up some ninety-three percent of the property in the twenty square blocks that used to be Hibbing.

Although the Oliver and Olcott (and ultimately U.S. Steel) supported Mike in public, things were not always so behind the scenes a fact that was little known and virtually never referred to. In testimony Mike was rather guarded when he mentioned it but the message was clear enough:

> "Well, I wasn't urged by the company to do this, you know; in fact the company refused to do this. I was urged by the businessmen of Hibbing to take this matter up and I had a good deal of trouble in getting it across. It was the businessmen of Hibbing that got me interested in it."[14]

The businessmen persuaded Godfrey and Godfrey persuaded Olcott. It must have taken some persuading as Olcott did not respond to Mike's August 1918 letter until a year later. The millions of dollars involved may have had something to do with it. In his testimony in 1921, Olcott still did not know when the Oliver would begin mining the ore under the town. This was a decision that had caution for parents.

Godfrey's health wasn't speeding matters along either. The first week in January of the new year had him returning to Chicago for a 'business trip'. He was gone for a week. This was apparently a check up on how he was doing in his recovery rather than another crises or period of treatment. The following week he traveled to Duluth for some more business or as the

To Tipple A Prince

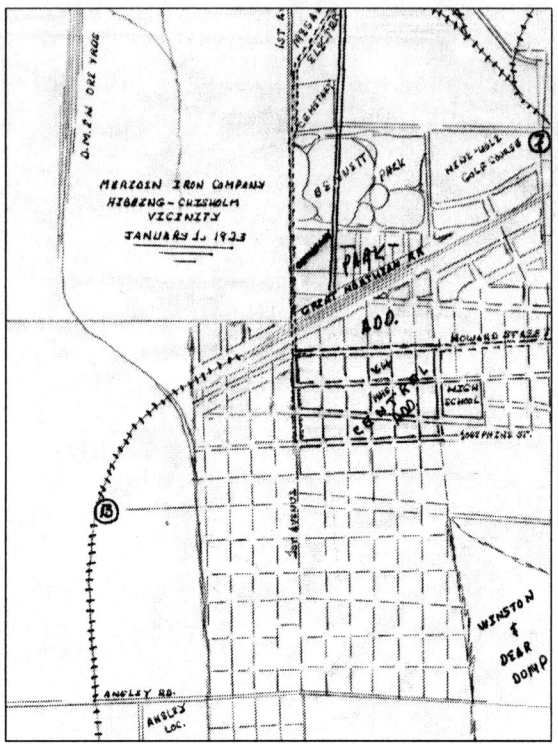

Hibbing on the cusp. The Park and Central Additions which adsorbed most of the new buildings, residences and people are highlighted in yellow. The Mesaba Railway Company tracks are in dotted red, the Hibbing High School is in Green as is Bennett Park which at that time extended to the west side of First Avenue. Copied from a Meriden Iron Company, Hibbing-Chisholm Vicinity, January 1, 1921.

paper put it for the first time he spent the week at the "head office of the company".[15] For a decade Godfrey had gone to 'Duluth on business", "had a business meeting with Mr. Olcott," spent the "time in Duluth talking to Oliver officials" or to "officials of the company". Now he is at the "head office of the company"? Maybe nothing is significant by this change (he undoubtedly was on business), but it is the stilted phrasing has the wrong pitch. I believe it was a lead for the news item a week later. On January 31st, Mike Godfrey, General Manager of the Oliver Iron Mining Company's Western Mesaba Iron Ore Range District office—sounds like the honorarium for an Oriental potentate—spent several days during the week (that's during a *business* week) in Duluth as a visitor.[16] Now, that *is* different. (I think the sentence is too short: it should conclude, ". . . spent the week in Duluth visiting the widow of Hugo Kramer, one Mary E. Kramer, and her son.")

Site Planning

One of the problems with moving a large number of citizens from one place to another is that the destination may lack some services. The Village Council was taking fairly good care of the problem, however, by increased tax levies and the laying in of water mains, sewers, streets, and alleys but education was a little slow in getting there. The problem was where to put the new High School placement dependended on population density. The school goes where the students are; the students do not go where the school is.

Godfrey, the Oliver and the Village Council tackled this difficulty in February of 1919. The Council solved its problem by turning it over to the Board of Education (one board member was Mike's brother, T.J.), and they in turn turned it over to Mike. Mike as it turned out had a suitable site but he had to first check with Olcott. Olcott then consulted with Kerr, vice president of U.S. Steel. This furious letter writing campaign took two months to conclude ending in the School Board's purchasing 7.14 acres for $10,000.00. Mike had assured Kerr and Olcott that testing had insured that no ore surrounded the site.[17] He also noted in passing that the school was close to the new power plant and could probably be heated by steam.

The site was really chosen for two reasons: the Oliver owned the property[18] and it was centralized, laying just to the east of the Central Addition and just to the south of a new forty platted by the Sargent Land company (not much of a surprise resulted when they named it the Sargent Addition; you plat it, your name goes on the plaque). This was merely the start of the process as a considerable distance had to be traveled before the school became a reality. Final approval for just the purchase of the property was granted at long last on September 17th but voter acceptance was not given until October 24th.

March Was a Good Month

For Vic Power as he ran for re-election for the seventh consecutive time and walked to victory winning 1,596 votes to J.L. Williams' (who left no other mark on history) 470. After seven victories in a row it was beginning

To Tipple A Prince

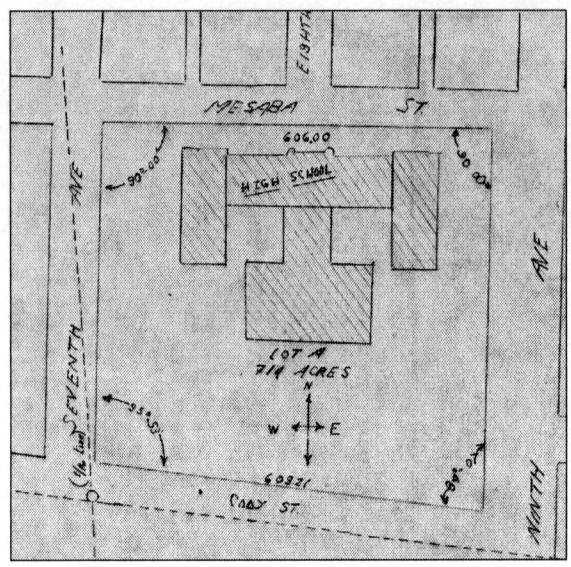

Hibbing High School's location as presented by the Engineering Department of the Oliver Iron Mining Company. The school is between Seventh and Ninth Avenues and Mesaba (Twenty-first) Street on the north and Cody (22nd) Street on the south. The front of the school property is two football fields wide (606 ft). The eventual cost of the school was approximately $3,850,000.00, making the lot's price of $10,000.00 inexpensive by comparison. February 21, 1919.

to look like "Vic" was short for "Victory." Mike Godfrey must have had good news of some sort as he traveled to Chicago for another check up and went right back to work. This was his last visit for quite a while but as time and events played out it became evident he was not a healthy man. Not healthy, but he had staying power as we will see.

While he was in the midst of the negotiations to move a town and find a location for the Village's growing student population, Godfrey still had time to request a $1,000.00 donation from the Oliver to the Catholic Churches in the Canisteo District (Grand Rapids in this case). Back in September of 1916, Godfrey had helped out the same Catholic Churches with $350.00 and he felt that Father P.J. Ryan was doing good work in this community, so he recommended favorable consideration of the request. The request was granted.

Mike Godfrey as the man on the spot for the Oliver fielded many requests during the transition period and it is amazing how many were honored. The Oliver followed Mike's recommendations almost to the (pardon the expression) letter. Here is another example from May. L.C. Newcombe a cashier at the First American National Bank (where several decades later James Godfrey, one of Mike's sons, was to rise to Senior

Vic President) and Chairman of the Elks' Lodge Building Committee wrote Mike requesting his and the Oliver's help. "If the Lodge selects these lots as a site would you consider building us a home consisting of two store rooms, lodge and club rooms above at a cost of about $75,000.00, the Lodge to furnish $35,000.00, you to furnish $40,000.00 taking a first mortgage of same for say ten years at six percent?[19] Again, approved.[20]

Initially, as Mike Godfrey testified to in court, the Oliver was tepid in its enthusiasm for the way he wanted to handle the dismantling of Old North Hibbing and the re-assembling of it further south in the Central and Park Additions but in one way or another using his position, reputation, authority, something akin to what the Roman's used to call *gravitas*, Godfrey won his management over to his side of the effort. It didn't hurt that he was real good at personal public relations and had a flock of kids. He was not only management but he was a Hibbing Pioneer, regular church goer, family man, widower, and straight as a proverbial arrow. It was not lost upon him that there was a gold mine under that section of the original townsite and the Oliver would be buying the rights to mine it at Woolworth prices. After a time even upper management can understand that kind of economics.

The publicity department of the Oliver was now, by May of 1919 at least, thoroughly behind Mike's efforts and began a public campaign to make it obvious that their point man was also their spokesman.

The Memorandum
Buried in the usual stack of foolscap memoranda of discarded Oliver Iron Mining Company office correspondence collected by James Steel for a never published effort at company history, there lies a remarkable internal document dated May 10, 1919 and titled, *Memorandum, Central Addition, Hibbing Minnesota* and it is a priceless piece of thinking precisely because it was not intended for public eyes. It is an insider's look at what the Oliver was

thinking and to what extent they were willing to back Mike Godfrey in his efforts to unlock the clasp around a valuable pocket of ore.

Brass Tacks

One item dealt explicitly with the proposed new Elks club. The Oliver was finally proving adept at understanding the need for good relations as they noted that, "it is of the utmost importance that a publicity campaign be started before the Elks' meeting Monday night, to create public sentiment for the erection of the new Elks' Home in the Central Addition, by stating definitely that a hotel will be built, and by exhibiting plans and drawings of the hospital, mercantile building, hotel, First National Bank building and Congdon & McIntyre's drug store."[21]

The new Itasca Mercantile building (to replace the one in the original townsite) and its owner-operator Mrs. Dottie J. Power were featured players in the move to the Central Addition. "Mrs. Powers agreed" it was noted, "on May 9, 1919, to put down $25,000.00 in cash or more and pay $7,500.00 or more per year and interest on unpaid balance at 6%. She desires that all contracts be referred to her before being signed up." The Oliver's plans and specifications were at this date complete and bids were submitted on May 15th. The Oliver let the contract out for $133,450.00. Without a whimper.

The general design of the new 140-room hotel for the Central Addition had been completed and the cost of the building and the property was projected to run $320,000.00. The plans and specifications were complete and ready for submission to the contractors by July 1st. Godfrey was authorized to offer this package to the potential operators and to conduct negotiations with them. He was further authorized to begin excavations for the hotel *at once*. Before the final details have been agreed upon by the potential owners, let's dig the foundation.

The memo noted that the reinforced concrete skeleton for the new Hospital had been completed in December of 1918 and the plans and specifications for the erection of the complete hospital building had been submitted to the contractors for bids to be opened by June 2nd. This job was proceeding smoothly and would continue that way.

The First National Bank building's plans and specifications were complete and bids for the construction had been received and accepted by the Bank.

The Merchants & Miners State Bank was ready for construction, awaiting only a decision on location.

Congdon & McIntyre had plans and specifications completed for several months but had postponed construction due to inactivity in the new addition. The same observation was made concerning the hardware store of a Mr. Thouin. He was planning to build his store in the Pillsbury Addition unless activity started soon in the Central Addition.

The activity was beginning. And would continue.

An authoritative statement was to be made by Oliver or Godfrey *at once*, that a new union depot for the D.M.& N. and Great Northern railways was to be built and a location made known at an early date. The local press—*Mesaba Ore and Hibbing News*—was to be told personally by Mr. Godfrey that it was going to get its new brick building for the headquarters office and printing plant in the Central Addition.

Another authoritative statement was to reinforce the public belief that the Mesaba electric trolley car line was to get its right of way along Howard Street both east and west. (Ed: it was to only run east as it eventually came south on First Avenue instead of Third Avenue.) And as many buildings as possible would be moved from the original townsite before the tracks were laid for the trolley car line. (Ed: the dwellings were to move under steam powered tractors mostly down First Avenue.)

And to make certain that the message was not lost in the administrative backwaters of in and out baskets, the memo concluded that authority should be given to Mr. Godfrey to employ a publicity agent and provide office space, if necessary. Furthermore, data should be prepared for the Hibbing newspapers and for whatever other arrangements should be necessary to publish articles written and approved by Mr. Godfrey. Advertise, publicize, promote. And make sure that Godfrey either writes or approves of the material. Get the word out. Make sure it reaches as many people as possible. Right now. (A publicist?)

Someone at headquarters got the message. This time there was no turning back. Once a bureaucracy starts moving its like watching an avalanche in slow motion. It does not move fast but it never moves in reverse.

The *Mesaba Ore and Hibbing News* got the message as it demonstrated in print on May 16th. The multiple headline read, "Building Operations in New Business District to Hit a Rapid Stride This Summer. Oliver Iron Mining Company to Erect New Hotel that Will Be One of the Finest in the Northwest, Several Store and Office Buildings. Work on Hospital Will Be Resumed at once. Removal of Buildings on North Forty of City Will Be Carried Out as Fast as Possible." With a headline like that the article is an afterthought.

The article read as if the Oliver wrote it which largely was the case. What the Oliver had done was not exactly an about face but it was close enough. Luke warm support had become a full-fledged backing for moving the North Forty to the Central Addition, just what Godfrey had been advocating since the Summer of 1918. The Oliver was now announcing that the company was to immediately launch a full scale building plan for the *new* Hibbing business district in what was the south end of the city. It wasn't really the south end of the city. It was south of the city. That is more than just a magician's trick, the new Hibbing from the old Alice. This was nothing less than shifting the focus of the town from one business district to another and it was reshaping the Village. The main street business district was moving south a mile or so and reorienting its axis. It was to run east and west instead of north and south, it was pulling itself away from its main business draw to the north (north of the mines) and to the immediate south (the two old additions) and was now to do its business with no less than four to six new additions, one of which, the Central, was about to become a new mini-village all its own: Village Hall, two major banks, Library, Fire Hall, apartment complex, Post Office, major Hotel, train depot, trolley car service, mining officials residences, and new residential neighborhood surrounding everything. What is more, the business district was now brick and stone. Permanent. Long term. Solid. For the future. Courtesy of the Oliver.

The Cleveland-Cliffs mining company joined in with the announcement that they would build an office building and three residences near the new business district.

Not that it was going to surprise anyone but the News also mentioned that while the work of building up the new business district was in progress, the Oliver would proceed as far as it was possible to move or tear down the buildings between North Street and Missabe Park, or in what is known as the North Forty of the City. This was a reminder that as the new was a work in progress the old was devoid of progress. The article further stated that the (same) Oliver officials believed that the new business district would be far enough along by a year from the Fall (that would place it abound the Fall of 1920) to warrant the "general move" of the city's most important business places.

For the time being the politicians would acquiesce in all this. Certain business men would not. The president of the Village Council Vic Power would say little and do less. He was, after all, about to put his building in the heart of the new downtown.

The Hotel

The Hotel was high on the list of showcase buildings that the Oliver intended to use as an anchor for the business district and it was elaborate and impressive. Godfrey and his people chose the site well. It is still the anchor of the business district on Howard Street even though that street is assuming less business importance with each passing decade. Fifth Av-

To Tipple A Prince

enue and Twentieth Street (Howard Street) was in the heart of business activity in the Central Addition. The hotel was not only an anchor it was a hub of social activity for the district and the Village.

The hotel eventually cost some $650,000.00 to construct with an additional outlay of over a $100,000.00 for the furnishings. It was to have three private dining rooms and a Coffee Room. The architectural design was Northeastern Italian with a footprint of 133 (Howard Street) by 125 feet (Fifth Avenue) and it was to be four stories high, with basement (which was to contain a vault for food storage and a separate vault for furs) five chair barber shop. The southwest corner had a sun porch that measured fourteen-foot-wide and fifty-foot-long. For the business man the first floor had a room for a public stenographer. The capital E design (so that every room had an outside view) housed 148 sleeping rooms, sixty-two with both bath and toilet.

Androy Hotel approximately 1925. The capital **E** design enabled every room to have an outside view. The view to the south was of the Oliver Iron Mining Company's clubhouse (today the Library). The main entrance fronted on Howard Street. The hotel's name is derived from the first three letters of the first names of the original owners, Andrew M. Doran and Roy Quigley. Quigley started as a bell captain at the Spaulding Hotel in Duluth and had been most recently the assistant manger of the Spaulding and Holland Hotels. Doran had recently been employed as the chief clerk at the Spaulding. The chief clerk at the Androy was Carl Quigley, Roy's brother. Every room contained a telephone. The grand opening was in June, 1921. From a colorized postcard.

Daniel W. Lynch

The hotel was commissioned for construction at the same time as were twenty residences for Oliver employees. One of those residences was in the form of a duplex and two were triplexes, each unit of a residence to have six to eight rooms. These were among the ones for Oliver employees but Godfrey was also the head of the Commercial Club's Housing Committee which incorporated a Housing Association with a net capital worth of $100,000.00 for the express purpose of promoting the building of homes in the city to help solve the housing problems. The Housing Association was authorized to make loans to citizens of the city with as low an interest rate as possible.

The move may have been all consuming for the citizenry of Hibbing but it was not so for the Oliver and surely for the other mining companies

Buffalo-Susquehanna open pits mines in 1918, looking slightly south and mostly west. The original western part of the Hibbing plat sits right on the precipice of this massive open pit. The Hull, Rust and Mahoning mines 'curve' around the town to the north (right edge of picture). The lighter colored material running around the top of the mine is overburden and the darker stuff is iron ore. In 2005 this portion of the massive complex of fifty-three pits and shafts is still filled partially with water. Aubin Studios.

To Tipple A Prince

on the Mesabi Iron Range. Mining was the chief activity, indeed the crucial activity in this place. The competition for ore was paramount and was divided between independents and the steel-company owned dependents, with the Oliver being the largest of the dependents, as you might expect when you are (depending on your point of view) a subsidiary, a wholly-owned subsidiary, a division, or a integrated department of U.S. Steel. The Oliver had a reasonable degree of success maintaining a certain local flexibility from mother steel at this stage in its history. U.S. Steel set the quotas and allocated the funds and the Oliver managed its affairs under that benevolent umbrella. While it planned the move for Hibbing and ran the show for the better part of three years, it also had to do some mining and in 1918/19 it was doing a fairly good job of doing just that.

In 1918, 126 mines shipped iron ore from the Mesabi Iron Ore Range. These mines were responsible for shipping almost 41 million gross tons of ore, in the neighborhood of 320 thousand tons per mine. The Oliver's share (from thirty-two producing mines) of the total production? Fifty-four per cent! This was some twenty-one million tons. And fifty percent of that amount came from its six Hibbing mines! This puts getting at another twenty-seven million or so tons under the town in perspective.[22] Pickands, Mather & Company came in second with ten mines shipping three million tons. M.A. Hanna & Company had twelve producing mines and shipped about 2.5 million tons. And the Mahoning Ore & Steel Company, an independent, with its one mine, the Mahoning, hit the scales with two million tons.

A Year Later
August 1919 rolled around, hot, humid, and filled with potential.

John Gannon became vice-president of the Hibbing Trading Company along with T.S. Gang and Archie McPhail. Their trading company was situated at 710 Third Avenue and sold dry goods and shoes and men's clothing. That now made three major players in the retail mercantile trade:

Gannon (future mayor), Power (Dottie and the Itascan; she was the wife of Vic's brother), and Godfrey (T.J., brother of M.H, and member of the Library Board and the District 27 School Board). John opened his general law practice above the Woolworth building in April of 1920.

In August the Thomas property passed into the hands of the Oliver during the first week for around $10,000.00 and the St. Paul House, owned by J.A. McCarthy also went to the Oliver, this time for over $50,000.00. The F.H. Dear home, one of the largest structures in Old North Hibbing was put up on blocks to move. Frank Hibbing's old office and first building in Hibbing, situated at the end of North Street was preserved by actions of the Park Board, the Oliver, the Old Settler's Association (Mike Godfrey was a member), and the Commercial Club. They presented a plan to take the cabin apart and rebuild it in the fifty-four-acre Bennett Park. It dated to 1894. The old order and the old townsite were vanishing.

Godfrey delivered Olcott's letter to the mayor.[23] Power had told Godfrey a year before to come see him when the Oliver had bought up a substantial portion of the original townsite and that time was now here. This letter outlined the Oliver's overall plan for the old townsite and the new. The full court press had started in May and now the game was nearing some kind of conclusion.

The Letter, the Court, the Intent
Godfrey asked Power "if it was the proper way to take the matter[24] up and he looked the letter over and said it was; he said that of course so far as the property was concerned he was going to recommend that they appoint a committee to appraise the value of the present buildings to ascertain their cost and see whether it met with the public approval, and that he would proceed along those lines in due course of time. I left the letter," Godfrey stated, "for him at that time. He told me he would present it to the Council."

"I told him what we were going to do, the same as I told many other businessmen of Hibbing, in fact, anyone that asked me could find out what we were going to do exactly."

"The Central Addition was platted for the *purpose of giving the people who we bought out a place to re-locate* [author's emphasis]; we wanted to give business interests at Hibbing a chance to centralize business in some permanent location off the ore body as far as we could tell, *at reasonable cost*." [author's emphasis].

"It was also platted so that we could move a number of our own buildings there." Godfrey went on to say that the Oliver bought unsold lots in the Park Addition for the same purpose and that the Oliver did not own any real estate in the Pillsbury Addition or the Southern Addition (except for his house).

Godfrey was now in full disclosure about the Oliver's plans. He had conceived the strategy, sold it to his management, carried out the plan with a minimum of difficulty, and had the mayor, if not on his side, at least on the sidelines. In a series of exchanges with the defendants' attorneys Godfrey laid it out.

When he was asked if the people whose surface rights he had purchased where to understand that they could buy property in the Central and Park Additions, Godfrey was clear: "Certainly. Everyone had the privilege of going down there."

When he was asked if it was his idea to create that addition [Ed: the Central], to furnish a place so that all of the people whose property you bought in the Hibbing Townsite could go down there and buy it, Godfrey again repeated the message of "Yes, sir." The new additions were for anyone whose property the Oliver had purchased. Just see how much cooperation you get if you dispossess thirty per cent of the town. The back and forth is interesting even if it reads like a polished rehearsal. In a way it was a case of Godfrey quoting himself.

"Did you plan on a new business district down there in the Central Addition?"
"Yes."
"And did you plan on letting the people in the Hibbing Townsite Addition all have business locations down there?"
"Yes. And not only that, but in the Pillsbury Addition and the Southern Addition, the entire Addition."

Now that was a change; the Pillsbury and Southern Additions? That inclusion had not been clear up until now. Previously, all testimony and newspaper accounts dealt with the Original Townsite, or what was left of it. That is, the original eighty acre plats, not the Pillsbury and Southern which were platted later and not by Frank Hibbing. It was a shrewd strategy. Offer the deal to anyone even if you have not purchased their property. You won't be left out. If it is true that the Oliver did not know if marketable ore underlie the other two additions—and it is very hard to believe they didn't—the idea was planted that the Oliver was going to be fair to all businessmen. An idea with not only merit but fruit. The exchange continued:

"The buildings that are constructed on the Central and Park Additions, has your company been financing the construction of those buildings at all?"
"Yes."
"Is it a common thing that you finance them or is it just exceptional cases?"
"Well, we are putting up some buildings down there and we are paying for the buildings; we hope to sell them or rent them after they are completed; the reason we are doing it is so as to have some place to which the people from the north forty can move when we want them to move."
"You are putting up a hospital down there, I believe?'
"Yes. In the Central Addition."
"For public use?'
"Yes."
" Public hotel?"
"Yes. Four Story. 140 rooms."
"Stores?"
"Yes. Twelve to fifteen made of brick."
"Apartments?"
"Yes. The Oliver."

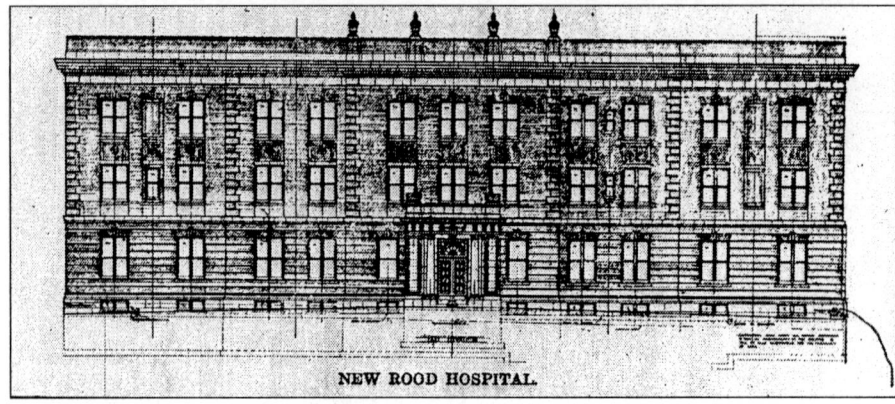

The three-story Rood Hospital that Godfrey referred to in his testimony. Designed by an Oliver architect/engineer. The building faced east overlooking a park. The first floor contained physicians offices and the main operating room; the second floor contained a minor operating room, stations for nurses, two and four bed wards and a diet kitchen and the third floor had an obstetric delivery room, obstetric surgery room, two bed wards and a baby room. The exterior was finished in 1919. The building was ready for patients in October of 1920 and the cost was in the neighborhood of $500,000.00. From the *Mesaba Ore and Hibbing News*, February 1920.

Howard Street being paved in 1921. Notice the Mesaba trolley car tracks in the center of the street. This view is slightly northwest with the First National Bank in the far background, the Merchants and Miners Bank in the center. It is actually in the Power's building. The tracks ran east along Howard Street to Brooklyn, then over to Mitchell Location, then to Kitzville Location and from there to Chisholm. *Mesaba Ore and Hibbing News*, 1921.

"In other words, you are building down there, those buildings which you think would be desirable in a new part of town? And you are doing that irrespective of whether you have tenants or purchasers for them?"

"Yes. There is only one case where we have a purchaser already; for the rest of them why we are just going right ahead and taking the chance putting the buildings and hope to rent them or sell them when completed."

"You haven't limited your buildings to any particular persons?"
"No."
"How big a district do those buildings cover?"
"Four or five city blocks."
"How are the buildings placed in respect to the Interurban road run?"
"Well, the Interurban road is coming in on the main street, Howard Street. That street was laid out eighty feet wide."
"Did you have any talk with Mr. Power about where you were going to locate your buildings down there?"
"No."
"Did Mr. Power buy any of your property down there in that addition?"
"Yes. At the corner of Third Avenue and Howard Street."
"How many acres are there in the Central Addition?"
"About fifty-seven."
"Park Addition?"
"Probably forty-five."

After a brief back and forth about when Mike talked to people about his period of illness, the defendant and his attorney got back to business.

"I wish you would give me a little idea as to what you said to these men about this removal proposition."
"Well, I told them we were going to plat this property down there and anyone that cared to go down there could go down there at a reason able

Victor L. Power Building. This is the building that Vic Power decided to build in new Hibbing after conferring with Mike Godfrey. Power gave up constructing the building he had planned on in Old North Hibbing but he used the construction materials he already had purchased. He received the same deal as any other merchant or businessman. This is on the northeast corner of Third Avenue and Howard Street. The Howard Street frontage was eighty feet and the Third Avenue frontage was 125 feet. Colorized postcard.

price. I called the attention of the business men to the fact that on Third Avenue there wasn't room for all of the business interests to get in there."

"And you gave that notice to them so that they could all get into that addition?"

"Yes, sir. So that they could all get into it."

"And your idea was that if they would go down there it would move the whole town, the whole old part?"

"Yes."

"And now is it the fact that the movement of population to the southern part of the Village was started through the influence of your company or was that movement started itself long before you took any steps to buy land down there?"

"The population had commenced moving down there many years ago. Alice was incorporated in 1910 and admitted into the Village of Hibbing in 1913. We have moved sixty-two residences and if you will allow five to six people to each residence you will find that we have only contributed a population of 300 or 400 people down there among the thousands already there."

Godfrey then summarized his thoughts on Old North Hibbing for the court emphasizing the age and general deterioration of the wooden buildings with maybe twenty or so in good condition as they were constructed of brick. Many of the buildings had no foundations and many were toppling over. Then the conversation got around to what Vic Power knew and when he knew it.

"I will ask you to take as briefly as possible the conversations that you had with Mr. Power with reference to the buying of that property."

"I asked for Mr. Power to come to the house one day and he got to telling me about this new building that he had started down on the corner and I told him that I thought that he was making a mistake and he wanted to know why and I said, 'because I feel that the same amount of money invested in property further south would help to unite the business interests of Hibbing and that you will get just as great a return out of your money.'"

"He said, 'You can send for whoever you want to and have them come in here and fix the price and you can take this and I will go south and put up my building, use the same steel and put up my building in the Central Addition.'"

What transpired here is that Power decided while he was talking to Godfrey that he would put up his building in the Central Addition, the one that eventually went up on Third and Howard and he sold the building he had just purchased in Old North Hibbing to the Oliver. That was the one for $18,000.00.

What Godfrey and the Oliver had done to keep the deals in the open and at the reasonable price so often referred to were two things: the first was to put a layout of the new business district and the Central and Park Additions up on Mike's wall in the South Rust headquarters with individual names and prices placed on the lots purchased and secondly, the Oliver contracts required construction in a short period of time on the lot. These two tactics prevented reselling on the sly and forced the buyer who just had his property purchased by the Oliver to roll over his money for the new lot. The system worked.[25]

> "State whether or not at that time there was any agreement between you and Mr. Power that he as a Village official or otherwise would urge people to move south or anything of that sort."
> "No, sir."
> "Mr. Power is putting up a building in the so-called Central Addition to the Village of Hibbing. Do you know whether Mr. Power purchased the lots on which that building is being built from your company?"
> "Yes, sir."
> "I will ask you whether or not Mr. Power paid either more or less than those lots were offered to the public?"
> "He paid the list price. The price at which we were selling to everybody. We have the price marked on the map. A plat of the Central Addition and the price of each lot is marked on that."[26]
> "That plat was published by our company prior to the time these lots ere sold?"
> "Yes."
> "And was it put out through the Village of Hibbing?"
> "No. I keep it in my office, the price of those lots. Anybody can come in here and see the price."

The rest of his testimony was spent in denying that Vic Power ever mentioned the sale of the Village Hall (or any other public building in the Village) or ever promised to advertise the fact that the Village of Hibbing was moving or would urge the moving of the Village of Hibbing. Godfrey then wrapped up his testimony by stating that he was the main representative of his company, the Oliver Iron Mining Company, in the Hibbing District. The events that Godfrey and others were testifying to occurred in the period August 1918 through the Summer of 1919.

October 1919
In October the City of the Dead closed. No new lots were to be sold and the last half lot in the old cemetery was sold during the first week of the month. The new cemetery at Maple Hill was to open soon.

As soon as the news was out that the Oliver presented its plans to the mayor, and made it known that the Mesaba Interurban Electric Railroad was to move off the Third Avenue bridge, the businessmen in the Pillsbury and Southern Additions[27] who were as aware of the Oliver's plans as anyone, read the direction of the prevailing winds and went to court. Henry P. Read and seventy-five other residents and businessmen submitted a petition requesting an injunction to restrain the Village of Hibbing, the Oliver Iron Mining Company, and the Mesaba Railway

First National Bank, Hibbing. On the northwest corner of Howard Street and Third Avenue. This 104 by 125 foot edifice was two stories high and cost $175,000.00 to build. The exterior was of gray Bedford Stone. The interior of the bank was finished in white marble. Over the center of the lobby was a skylight dome. This was the bank and this was the building that James, Godfrey's oldest son, worked in while rising to the position of Sr. Vice President. James and Margaret lived across the street from Bennett Park. From a colorized postcard.

Company from moving public buildings and tearing up public streets. The petitioners stated they were forced to act because the village authorities had not protected them against the damage being inflicted upon them by a private corporation. That's less oblique than it looks; the petitioners meant the mining companies. They were contending that the Village had no right to sell any portion of the city without the sanction of its citizens. Well, the mayor was saying little or nothing for the record anyway and that left a large public relations gap.

The intent was clear enough. They hoped to restrain the Oliver Iron Mining Company from obtaining a clear title to the original platted portion of Hibbing until the company purchased all the surface property rights in the Pillsbury and Southern Additions. This was not going to happen as the Oliver to begin with didn't own the underlying mineral rights as they did in the case of the original North Eighty and it is doubtful if even they had the financial wherewithal to buy up two more forties.

What was not in doubt was that the real estate value of the properties in the Pillsbury and Southern business areas were about to experience an all time low. Reed and others were trying to do more than save face; they were trying to save their businesses.

It seems that a mere lawsuit was not going to put a stop to the movement that was relocating Old North Hibbing to the new Hibbing. In that regard, Godfrey and the Oliver announced during the first week of 1920 that C.F. Haglin & Sons, building contractors headquartered in Minneapolis, had been awarded a contract to build no fewer than ten new buildings in the New Hibbing. The concrete foundations were to be laid that week.

With that little item of business disposed of, Mike Godfrey spent the rest of the month running the Oliver's operations in the Hibbing District and preparing to marry for the second time. He had been a widower for four years and had eight children still at home. With the help of his oldest daughter, Miriam, now aged eighteen, and a maid, he had managed fairly well.

Reed Building in Western Addition in the new Hibbing in 2003. It's the buff-colored one to the right of the brown brick building on First Avenue West and Cody Street. Reed and others did not get their injunction and the amount they finally did acquire was paltry. The author lived upstairs in the brown two-story for a brief time. Author's collection.

Pictured below are three of those buildings that went up in the 1920s.

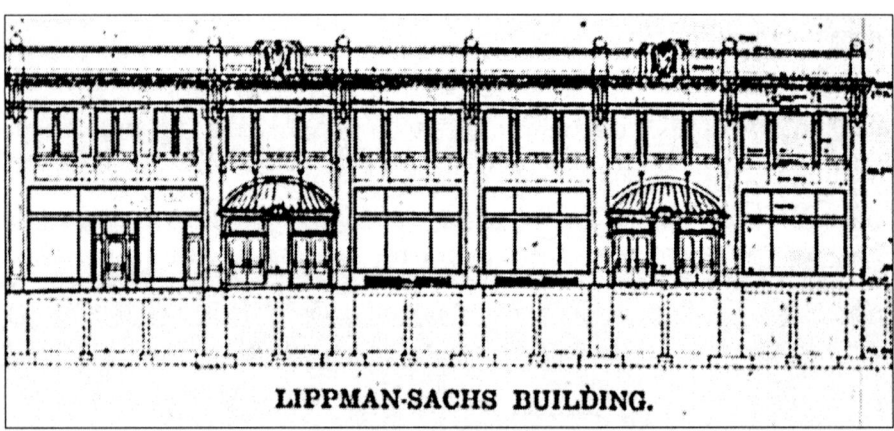

The Lippman-Sachs Building at the southeast corner of Howard Street and Third Avenue, occupying four lots. Frontage was on Howard and the Third Street frontage was 125 feet (it had a side entrance). One hundred feet of the Howard frontage was Mr. Lippman's and thirty-three feet were Mr. Sachs'. *Hibbing Daily News and Mesaba Ore*, February 2, 1920.

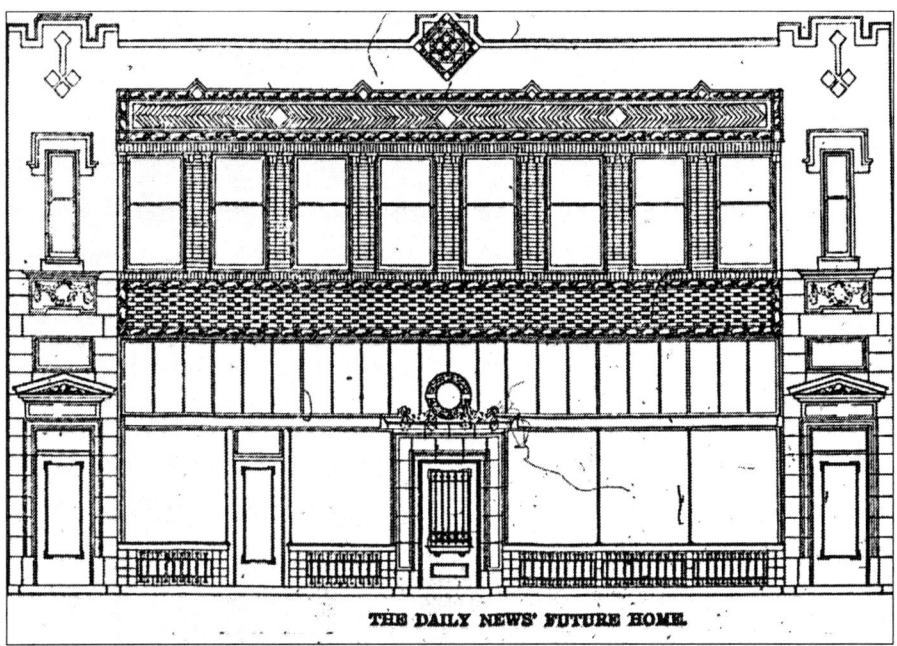

Hibbing Daily News and Mesaba Ore. On Howard Street between Fourth Avenue E and Fifth Avenue E. It occupied two lots. The home of the "Old Man Hereof", C.M. Atkinson. *Hibbing Daily News and Mesaba Ore*, February 2, 1920.

Haley & Rooney building on the north side of Howard Street between Second and Third Avenues E. This building occupied two lots on the main street. The ground floor has two large store rooms and a central entrance leading to the second floor. The east store room contained billiard and pool tables. *Hibbing Daily News and Mesaba Ore*, February 2, 1920.

To Tipple A Prince

But now he had three college-aged children including Miriam and a retarded daughter, he was forty-eight years old, he had had a recent bout of heart trouble that sometimes left him breathless, and his responsibilities as District Manager of the Oliver's operations along with moving a town, were requiring more and more of his attention. In February he married Mary Elizabeth Kramer (neè, Parker), widow of Hugo and late of 2121 East Second Street in Duluth. The new couple took a few days off and then settled into Mike's Sellers Street home in Hibbing.

The Main Business Street
Howard Street (actually 20th Street) is the main business thoroughfare in Hibbing. It was so in 1920 when the Oliver Iron Mining Company chose it as the main artery. It extends east and west for six blocks and is eighty feet wide. At the rear of the business buildings, both on the north

Mary E. Kramer's home at 2121 Second Avenue E. in the fashionable east end of Duluth, Minnesota in 2003. Author's collection.

Daniel W. Lynch

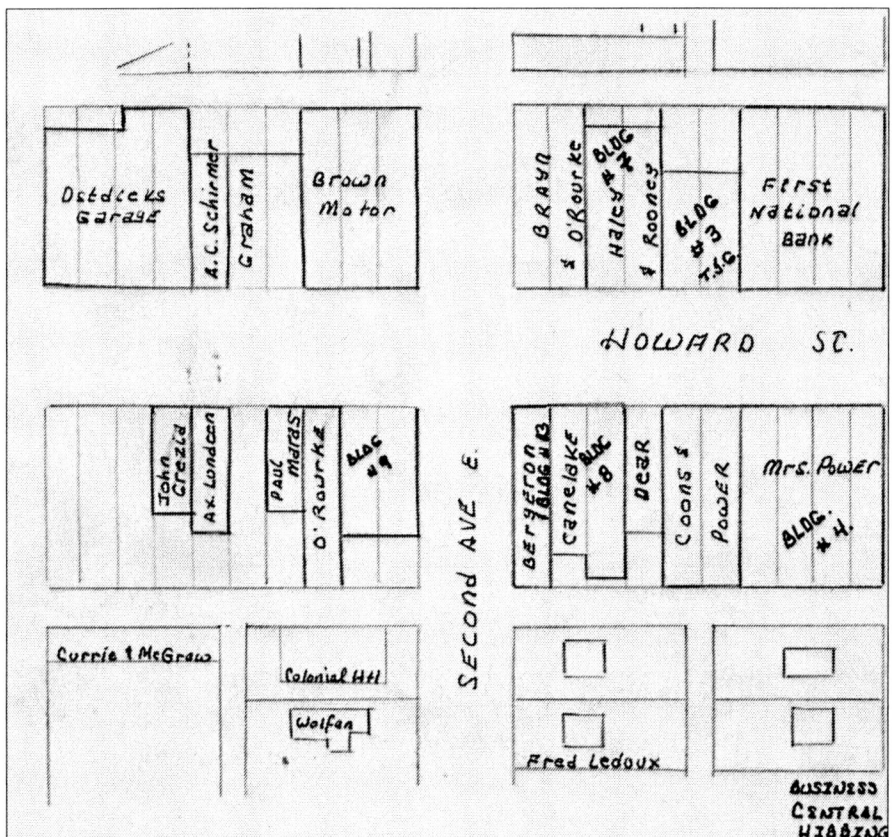

Howard Street is the main business artery of the new Hibbing and runs for six blocks, east and west. The north side of the street is at the top of the graphic. The avenues run north and south. Shown above are the two "westernmost" blocks (First and Second avenues E.). Dottie Power and Thomas J. Godfrey, rivals in Old North Hibbing, now face each other across the main street. Copied from the original map which sat in Mike Godfrey's office at the South Rust complex. It carries a date of July 8, 1921. Author's Collection.

and south sides of Howard Street, are alleys twenty-five feet in width. The north-south avenues in the Central Addition are sixty-six feet wide. To start things off, the Oliver had three fine brick business blocks built on the new business street. The ground floor of each building is divided into two, twenty-five by eighty foot stores.

The move continued unabated throughout the Winter months and the Oliver and the Village started talks about the 40,000 yards of wood paving blocks that were still in good condition, being only seven years old.

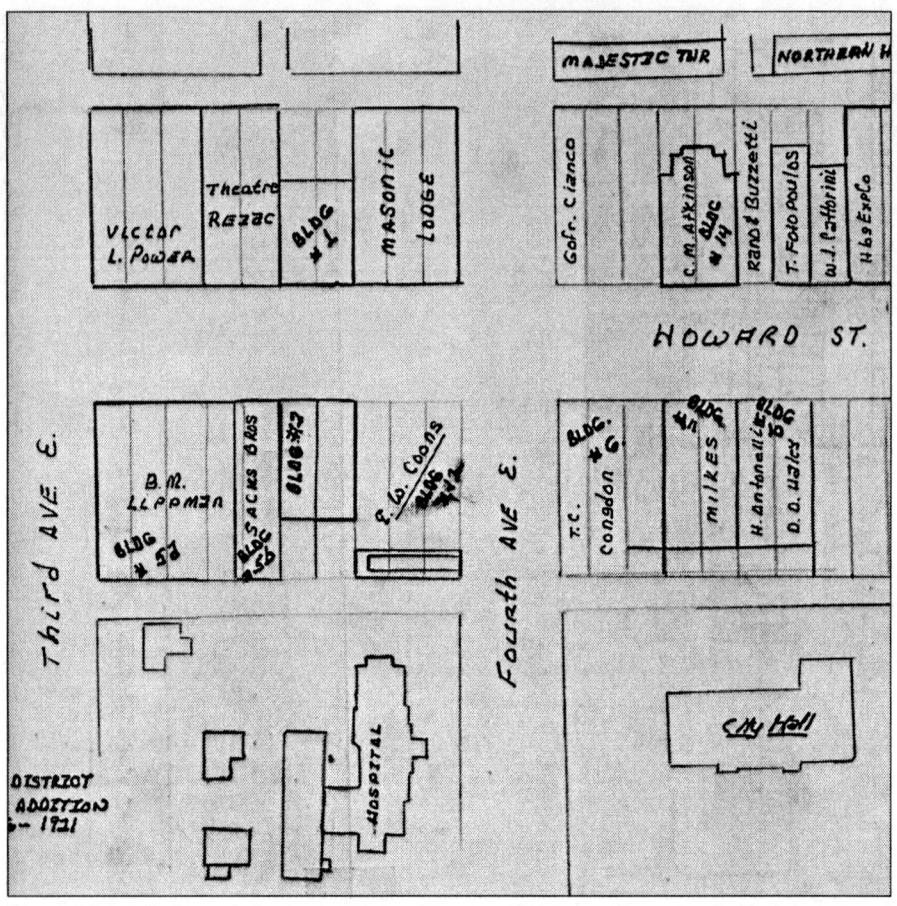

Howard Street is the main business artery of the new Hibbing and runs for six blocks, east and west. Shown above are the two "central blocks" (Third and Fourth avenues E.). The Hospital, City Hall (which had not been built yet) and the Oliver Club House were inline. Mike Godfrey's House at 404 Mesaba Street faced City Hall (it was constructed in 1923). Designations such as "Bldg #1," "Bldg #2," etc specify the order in which they were built, not occupied or sold. Author's Collection.

The Mesaba Street Railway Company started construction of the steel bridge at the southern end of Third Avenue thus allowing the trolley cars to run over the Duluth, Missabe & Northern railroad tracks. The line then turned southwest to go behind the cemetery to enter the new Hibbing at First Avenue and Howard Street where it then headed south along First Avenue and east along Howard. Another part of the line, a triple overpass over the D.M.&N and G.N. tracks just east of the

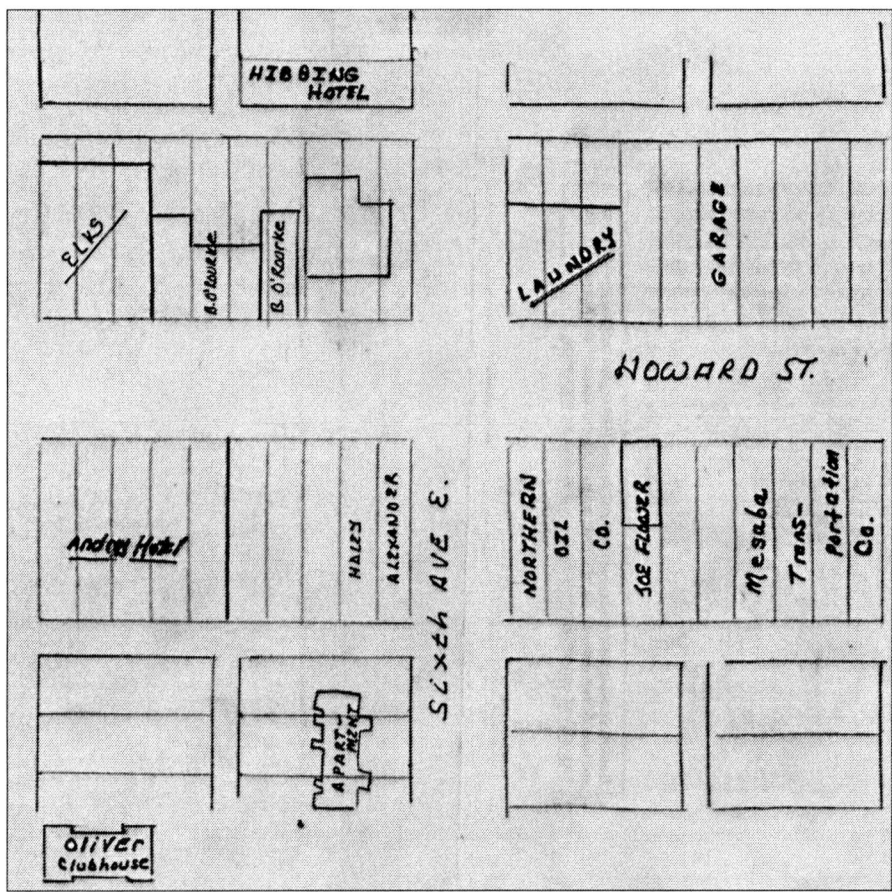

Howard Street is the main business artery of the new Hibbing and runs for six blocks, east and west. Shown above are the two "easternmost blocks" (Fifth—on the left, and Sixth Avenues—in the center, E.). The Androy Hotel anchors these two blocks and dominates the main street (its frontage spanned five lots). The modern library now occupies the space vacated by the Oliver Club House.

Mitchell Yards was also under construction. Projected completion date was August. Travel into and out of the new Hibbing was being assured even if it amounted to the long way around for the locations and settlements north of the Great Pit.

The following map appeared in the *Hibbing Daily News and Mesaba Ore* on March 5, 1920, and shows the area of Hibbing above the heavy dotted line in the "Old North Forty" that was to be moved. It comprised

To Tipple A Prince

approximately sixteen blocks and was the major focus of the move. The stripped area represents the extent of the ore deposit as was then known by the Oliver. The ore quality was the big unknown. Much of what is today's Hibbing, north of the Great Northern railroad tracks—represented by the stripped areas for the Scranton, Hull, and Susquehanna deposits—would not exist if the ore quality had been higher. If they would have had to move Hibbing a second time, considering the turmoil that would have caused and the staggering cost involved, the Oliver would probably have preferred to move the ore deposit instead.

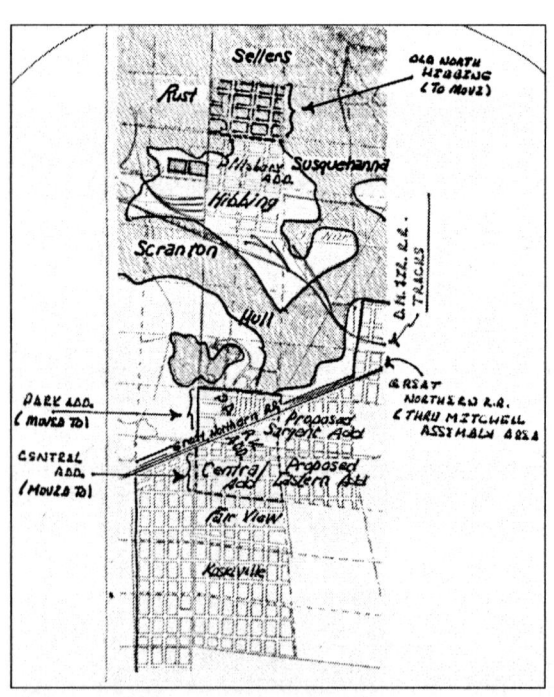

March 5, 1920, map from the *Mesaba Ore and Hibbing News*. The Park Addition remains much as it was back then and so does the Hull-stripped area although development has been minimal. The Pillsbury and Southern Additions are ghost towns. Foundations mark the only remains of the South Rust headquarters of the Oliver. The trackage in the Pillsbury and Southern Additions is gone but the Third Avenue bridge's foundations remain. The Great Northern tracks are still in use.

Rat Tails

Needless to say, moving towns and villages was possessed of its own special hazards. It upset people used to consistency, it cost a ton of money and no one wanted to foot the whole bill. A site to move to was not always easy to induce people to move to, the old place must be leveled (much as the Romans did to Carthage even though the casualty rate was much lower), and then there were the rats! Yes, rats. All over the place. Level the residences and businesses and habitats are lost, rat habitats at that. The *Hibbing Daily Tribune* of September 29th ran it by the populace with the alarming head: "Rat Nuisance Is Dangerous. Moving of Hibbing Causes Rodents to Seek New Quarters." (Just guess where they were going.[28]) Imagine reading that headline over your morning cup of coffee. The health department was quoted as saying that it was planning a drive on rats to prevent the danger of an epidemic with a reminder, in case you weren't taking this seriously enough, that Galveston, Texas had recently been visited by the bubonic plague. The Water and Light Department of Hibbing (I have no idea why it was the charge of the W&L, but it was. They were thinking of raising the bounty on rat tails to a nickel!) The drive was partially successful: the rats are still around but not in such abundance. The bounty proposal appeared only once.

Moving In

But the Central Addition and Park awaited people and while they were waiting the sewer mains had gone in and now Fall found the heating mains going in. Who needs heat in the Fall is not the issue (although it is hard to imagine someone living on the Iron Range who hasn't thought of it), its who wants to anticipate a Winter without heat (when now they do have it) and in the new Hibbing everyone headed for the new additions was going to have heat. Municipal steam heat at that. The finishing touches on installing the last mains between Josephine and Adeline Streets in the alleys on either side of First Avenue were going in during October.

The Oliver employee club house was taken apart and divided into three sections and moved from the original townsite to the location across the street from the not-yet-decided-upon-location-for-the city hall. The hospital was completed in the same month[29] (October), and in December the Oliver announced that it was building 40 new dwelling houses in the Spring of 1921. The new homes were going to be located east of Seventh Avenue E. and southeast of the Central Addition. The Central Addition was fast filling up, the Eastern Addition was now on the spot.

To Tipple A Prince

Spring (in this case April) saw C.W. Ostdick start his garage on the northeast corner of Howard Street and First Avenue. The building was to weigh in at 107 by 135 feet with a showroom that was rated as the largest in the northwest (it *was* large measuring fifty by sixty feet) and contained storage space for some eighty-four cars. In front there would be a drive-in gas filling station (that's the reason for the diagonal cut of the building in front) and there would be two more rooms facing Howard Street for rent. One would later on house Sammy's Pizza.

June witnessed the merchants of Old North Hibbing announce their largest—and probably their first and only—moving sale. Over a million dollars worth of merchandise was put on sale to reduce inventories. Only those merchants who were really moving were eligible and they were led by Mike Godfrey's brother, T.J. T.J. moved into his new digs opposite Dottie Power's Itasca Bazaar in August. A car was put up for a raffle. Since the sale started on July 8th, buntings were everywhere and several speeches were made. Inventories were drastically reduced and profits soared.

The Oliver pushed things along by announcing that all buildings owned by the company must be vacated by August 1st. That was really the death knell for Old North Hibbing as the Oliver owned all but one private building (M.J. Moran's Oliver Hotel) in the original townsite. One of the most interesting phases of the moving program was the removal of residences and business structures of all sizes by loading them on to sets of trucks, attaching a steam tractor and watching the tractors go chugging off down the streets of the old town and along the First Avenue highway to some site in the new Hibbing.[30] At times there were as many as three buildings on the way while several others were being prepared for the journey and still more were being lowered onto their foundations. Of the 200 buildings moved in this way, only one failed to make it to its destination.

The State Theatre opened in mid November and contained a pipe organ that took ten men six months to install. It was capable of furnishing the same amount and variety of music as an orchestra of twenty men. The Rezac's cost was well over $125,000.00. The State was to that part of Howard Street what the Androy was to the other end. It was like its counterpart dominating in its architecture and size and comforting in its presence.

The Oliver now closed in on the final steps for owning all the private property of the original townsite with the purchase of Joe Flower's property on Cedar Street (as well as apparently, his property in Marble or so it was said) for some $55,000.00. It must have been a good deal as Joe then turned about and purchased property on the corner of Fifth Avenue E and Howard Street and a second piece of property between Sixth Avenue and Seventh Avenue E (again on Howard).

Game, set and match took place in December of 1921 when the Oliver purchased all the Village's property for about $350,000.00. The City Hall being the largest single item and one still contested in court. The Oliver donated a piece of land in the Central Addition running 266 feet wide by 250 feet deep for the new City Hall. The land was worth $50,000.00 and the Oliver, glad I think to have the deal done, dropped another $40,000.00 into the deal to help build the new City Center.

That same week the first car of the Mesaba Railway Company left the Great Northern square area at 6:00 a.m. headed south on a bleak winter morning, down Third Ave, then behind the cemetery to First Avenue, turning East on Howard Street and running to Sixty Avenue E., thence south to Alexandria Street where it turned west to First Avenue and headed back. The cost per trip? Five cents.

The Bottom Line

So, the question has to be asked, when the dust settled and the air cleared and the streets were paved and the street lights worked, and the

To Tipple A Prince

politicians finished their speeches, and Mike Godfrey thought about getting a good rest (he still had to dig up all that ore that he said he did not know the amount of), what did the whole thing come to, how much did it cost? Crass as that may sound pipers have to be paid.

For starters however, the Oliver wasn't saying. Officially anyway. But the irrepressible *Hibbing Daily News and Mesaba Ore* had a pretty good fix on the bottom line and wasn't hesitant about sharing the good news. Its estimates on October 1 were:

- New business blocks about $3,000,000.00
- New hotel and hospital about $1,100,000.00
- New power plant about $1,000,000.00
- New homes about $1,000,000.00
- New school buildings, $3,600,000.00
- Water and sewer mains, $650,000.00
- Street paving, $600,000.00
- City Hall, $300,000.00
- Depot and railway improvements, $300,000.00
- Warehouses, $200,000.00
- New residences, apartment buildings and residences moved and repaired, $1,100,000.00
- Interurban car line improvements, $225,000.00
- New county fair grounds, $250,000.00
- New parks and boulevarding, $490,000.00
- City improvements such as gutters, heat, gas, water mains, $1,500,000.00
- Old business district property, $1,000,000.00
- Mineral rights, $2,500,000.00

All of which comes to a bottom line of $18/20,000,000.00.

BandWagon Bob

It seems that with all this plating and expanding going on the mayor decided to indulge himself a bit with some expansion plans of his own. In January of 1921 Power announced his intentions to expand the boundaries of the Village of Hibbing and to incorporate the Village as a City, this being a business proposition, not a political one. That's what he said. The expansion of the village would increase the assessed valuation of Hibbing from around eighty-seven million dollars to around 121 million dollars. In February he continued to talk up the subject without really adding any clarifications. He avowed that it would be good to change the sobriquet by which Hibbing was then known, "The Richest Village in the World" to "The Most Beautiful City on the World." "The Village," he said, "had outgrown its Village clothes."[31] "In five years from the time a charter is adopted there will be pavements surrounding every block in South Hibbing, the alleys will be paved, the streets boulevarded, every park will be beautiful." He stopped short of paving the streets in gold but it didn't matter, he won re-election handily by 890 votes. J.C. Eastman was the sacrificial lamb this time. But Power would not be in office five years hence.

His wife, Mrs. Percy Garner Power, would barely survive her husband's ninth election. They had been married eleven years and she was only thirty-nine years old. She had grown up in the Upper Peninsula town of Manistique. Vic Power had now lost his Father and his Wife in less than a year.

Looking Around

While he was immersed in moving a "forty" from one place to another and running the northern iron ore mining enterprises of the Oliver Iron Mining Company, Mike Godfrey had little time to reflect. He did manage somehow during this period to meet, and marry a woman from Duluth where he traveled frequently but with eight children to keep track of, and the presence of his siblings and his parents nearby, his personal time was rarely his own. He was an avid hunter and fisherman but as the years accumulated, those activities all but disappeared.

His younger brother Thomas Jefferson Godfrey had been running a successful men's haberdashery for several decades which featured Hart, Schaffner and Marx clothes and he had served on the village council a half dozen times and was the Old North Hibbing postmaster from 1910 to 1914. His career started with the Oliver as had Mike's but T.J.[32] was restless to be his own boss and quit the job of chief clerk to go into the clothing business. He had at one time or another served on the Old North Hibbing library committee, and on the park committee. He was a founding member of the country club. He was on the draft board. In 1920 he was elected president of the Board of Education of Independent School District #27, not a bad position to be in when your brother offers the land for the new high school.[33] He was now in 1921 once again in the postmaster's seat but this time in the new Hibbing.[34]

James Robert, Mike's oldest child at twenty-one (born in 1899) was a junior at the University of Minnesota but in November 1921 he was in the Mayo clinic[35] in Rochester where Mike and "Aunt May"[36] visited him a week later. He returned to the University where he graduated. His brother Thomas Clark graduated from high school in 1920 and then attended Notre Dame University in South Bend, Indiana for less time than it took to register. He wanted to be a miner like his Father and hauled a lunch pail into the Mt. Iron mine to start his career. For the most part Mike was not overly pleased with his sons who did not (except for James) seem to be headed for professional careers. Paul was eighteen in 1921 and headed nowhere. Elizabeth, according to the rest of the family the favorite child of Mike's, was an eleven-year-old blond haired blue eyed fun-loving child. Jane and Agnes were nine and five respectively and were known to be above average students. May retained her friends in Duluth for the most part and she and Mike were recorded as traveling to the Zenith City from time to time. Mike's Mother and Father lived nearby in Old North Hibbing but Mike had only brief moments to visit them.

John Gannon

John wasted no time once his law practice opened in April in getting himself on the local map. In May the paper announced that John Gannon a prominent attorney, ex-serviceman, and a member of the American Legion would be the Memorial Day speaker. The World War I veteran was possessed of a fund of information on any subject and was a fluent speaker. He was Irish, mellifluous, and ambitious. In April of 1920 he had opened a law office and now in September he formed a partnership with Thomas Strizich, formerly of the Victor L. Power law office. After only three months in Hibbing Gannon was now traveling in august company indeed. Their shingle was hanging from the Carlson Building on Third Avenue. September saw John's elevation to Chancellor of the Knights of Columbus. He had to wait until late in October to become secretary of the Range Bar Association. But he made up for that oversight early in November by representing the local American Legion post of Cobb-Cook as a delegate to the eighth district board meeting.

Now that he was established he was free to go practice some law. He did that winning in April of 1921 a breakthrough case over in Grand Rapids. It was the first acquittal given by a jury in Grand Rapids that term and it was obtained by a Hibbing attorney! That was not easy especially considering the length of the trial which lasted several weeks (automobile tire theft). John was now both known and established. He was in for the long haul even though he made a misstep or two along the way.

H.P. Reed and Seventy-five Others

Civil law courts present two points of view, one by the plaintiffs who bring the action—here called an injunction (a command to stop an act)—and one by the defendants who resist, or object, to the action. The court is presented with a set of facts presented by the plaintiffs and a set of counter arguments from the defendants that mitigate or deny the plaintiffs contentions. Pro versus con in short. In this case of Reed and his colleagues versus the Village of Hibbing and anybody else involved in the move things were very transparent but not completely so. They were somewhat of a mystery as well.

Looking west from "Boy Scout" hill. This is actually the original Sellers open pit overburden dump. Highway 169 as it becomes Howard Street is in the forefront and marching across the skyline in back are various overburden and waste ore dumps. At one time the dump was covered with only trees but now it also contains apartments. Author's collection.

In August of 1919 the Oliver had its plans out in the open and the mayor and the city council were appraised of the plans for buying the remaining surface properties in Old North Hibbing and the plans for the new Hibbing's development. Reed and others had the same access to those plans as anyone else did and they did not like what they saw. Their reaction took two months to develop.

In October they filed suite to restrain (i.e., prevent) the Oliver from obtaining clear title to the original forty until they had *also purchased all the surface property rights in the Pillsbury and Southern Additions.* The injunction that was being sought also included the Mesaba Railway Company which was moving its trolley car tracks out of Old North Hibbing and running the new trackage to the extreme west of the remaining two additions, and the Village of Hibbing as it still owned several public buildings in Old North Hibbing. Merely filing the injunction was a deterrent and progress in obtaining title was slowed.

This was on the surface at least a bit perplexing. Reed and other businessmen along Third Avenue in the two additions had the same access to the Oliver's plans as did the Old North Hibbing businessmen (one of whom was Mr. Reed) and could have bid on property in the new Hibbing just as easily as anyone else and paid the same prices as did the others.

Asking the Oliver to buy up the surface rights to the Pillsbury and Southern Additions was a pipe dream. The Oliver did not own the mineral rights for the simple reason that the Pillsbury-Bennett[37] interests did and the Pillsbury-Bennett fee owners were not offering to sell the rights. Their records were no better than the Oliver's on this score.

With the large business district adjacent to the Pillsbury/Southern Additions almost a mile away, that spill-over business was going to decline if not vanish and property values would take a nose-dive. But it was not just that a forty was moving; all the new forties were down south. The center of expansion, the center of population growth, the center of population concentration was now elsewhere and that was going to persist. If you owned a business in the Pillsbury/Southern Additions, especially the Pillsbury, your future markets were headed south in more ways than one.

Olcott and Godfrey Testify
W.J. Olcott, president of the Oliver Iron Mining Company and stationed in Duluth, was called to testify on February 24, 1920. Olcott testified that he had no idea (later on Godfrey maintained the same posture) as to the nature or extent of any ore deposit under the west plat of the original townsite.

When Godfrey got on the stand the plaintiffs' lawyer tried to establish some sort of conspiracy between him and Vic Power, a private under the table deal that maybe the public didn't know about that concerned Power's property at Third Avenue and Sellers Street (in Old North Hibbing). That path went nowhere as Godfrey described his conversation with Power in response to the query:

"I believe you stated that you had bought certain property in either Pillsbury or Southern Addition from Mr. Power?"

"Yes, sir."

"That was the building concerning which you have testified had been partially completed?"

"Yes."

"When did you buy that?"

"It was along in August 1918, I think."

"Mr. Power held that individually in his own name?"

"Yes, sir."

"Mr. Mercer has touched upon that and I think I will ask you to state as briefly as is possible the conversations that you had with Mr. Power with reference to the buying of that property. Counsel seems to think that is material here."

"Well, after that I could discuss things fairly well I sent for Mr. Power to come to the house one day and he got to telling me about this new building that he had started down on the corner and I told him that I thought that he was making a mistake and he wanted to know why and I said, 'because I feel that the same amount of money invested in property further south would help to unite the business interests of Hibbing and that you will get just as great a return out of your money.' 'Well,' he said, 'I never looked at it in that way.' He said, 'I think you re absolutely right about it.' And then he went on and told me—and I also called his attention to the fact that of course if any considerable number tried to get in there, property values would increase in price to such an extent that the business men could hardly afford to buy it and do business and he called my attention to the fact that he tried to get one lot adjoining that corner over there, one lot to the north and they wanted $18,000.00 for it, and he asked me if I would try to take the thing off of his hands, and I asked him about the price and he said, 'Let your architects name the price.' He says, 'You can send for whoever you want to and have them come in here and fix the price and you can take this and I will go south and put up my building—use the same steel—and put up my building in the Central Addition.'"

It must have been quite an evening. That was the longest answer Godfrey gave in three days on the stand but he was not finished with fielding questions about this transaction. He was next asked:

"How was the price that you paid to Mr. Power for that building computed?"

"Actual cost."

"To him?"

"Yes, sir."

"With reference to the lots as distinguished from the superstructure, how was that computed?"

"It was absolutely what he paid for them, so far as I know; I think it was; there may have been a difference of a thousand dollars or something in those things but so far as I know it was approximately what money that he had in it."

. . . .

"There has also been some testimony here concerning the fact that Mr. Power is putting up a building in the so-called Central Addition to the Village of Hibbing? That is correct, I believe."

"Yes, sir."

"Do you know whether Mr. Power purchased the lots on which that building is being built from your company?"

"Yes, sir."

"I will ask you whether or not Mr. Power paid either more or less than those lots were offered to the public?"

"Paid the list price."[38]

"What do you mean by the list price?"

"The price at which we were selling to everybody. We have the price marked on the map."

"By the map, what do you refer to?"

"A plat of the Central Addition, you know, and the price of each lot is marked on that."

"That plat was published by your company prior to the time these lots were sold?"

"Yes."

"And was it put out through the Village of Hibbing?"

"No. I kept it in my office, the price of those lots. Anybody can come in there and see the price."

"And Mr. Power bought at those rates and no less?"

"Sure."

What Godfrey's testimony amounted to here is that the Oliver, through Godfrey, bought Victor Power's Old North Hibbing property and sold him the lots for his building in the new Hibbing for the same price that everyone else paid for lots. If you don't believe it, read the map. Everyone was entitled to. The plaintiffs really weren't getting anywhere fast.

Next the plaintiff's tried to prove that the owner of the *Hibbing Daily News and Mesaba Ore*, C.M. Atkinson, was opposed to the injunction because Godfrey and the Oliver promised to build him an office building. That route hit a brick wall as well.

H.P. Reed and A.P. Silliman testified next and concentrated their testimony on thee bridge at the north end of First Avenue the removal of which would be highly detrimental to business in the Pillsbury/Southern Additions. That was obvious by now.

The defense witnesses started off with assistant general mining engineer Deal for the Oliver who testified that seven million dollars of ore could not be mined due to its close proximity to Old North Hibbing. This was not the ore underneath the Village but on the existing mines' slopes. This seemed to be an attempt to establish that if the west plat was not moved a fortune in ore would be lost regardless of whether or not there was more ore underneath the plat.

The mayor was next for the defense and he emphatically stated that the village property would not be sold unless it was the will of the people of the village. The will of the people has to be checked if you intend to run for re-election in the future. More to the point Power stated that the Village Council had no intention of vacating the west plat until (again) ordered to do so by the district court. Furthermore, no action according to the mayor had been taken toward granting the Oliver the right to destroy the Sellers Bridge and that restriction held true again until and unless the district court so ordered. The district court was going to be busy for a while.

And in January of 1921 the district court in the form of a judgment by Judge Edward Freeman gave Power all the leeway he needed. Freeman denied the injunction by Reed and others. The streets could now be torn up, the parks dismantled, the trolley car tracks could be moved, the bridge could be deconstructed, the public buildings sold and torn down, Old North Hibbing could be vacated. The old order was giving way to the new but grudgingly.[39] This suit was not going away, only one injunction was denied. There would be further legal battles along the way.

The Oliver and Four Others

Businessmen and citizens are not the only ones who can launch court actions, so can corporations and the Oliver and four other mining companies (Hanna, Republic, Interstate, and Shenango Furnace) did just that in October in Hibbing against School District #35 of Buhl. An injunction was being sought the object of which was to prevent the completion of the Buhl school buildings under construction and to stop payments on school warrants which the Oliver believed were issued illegally. The Honorable Judge Martin Hughes presided.

The case was argued before the Judge in November with the Oliver, et.al. plaintiffs contending that the 1897 and 1903 laws covering items purchased by the Buhl school board were limited to eight mills on the dollar (the school board had exceeded this limitation as far as the Oliver and its partners were concerned). The items in contention were such things as school furnishings, architects fees, and electrical fixtures that District #35 said fit the definition of expenditures for the purpose of sites and erection of school buildings. The parties to the suit had differing interpretations of that phrase. It was the court's job to decide who had it right.

The New Hibbing

As court battles were waged on the new frontier of iron and ore, life went on elsewhere in the form of new beginnings. Excavations for the new City Hall were begun on December 7th in the acreage donated by the Oliver, across from the Clubhouse, next to the Hospital, behind the Androy in the center of the Central Addition. The links of the new were being joined together one by one as Hibbing took shape.

The year closed with the New Hibbing virtually finished (except for the city hall and the high school), court cases supplying the few remaining spectator sports, and Mike Godfrey enjoying a full family for the first time in years. What would the future bring to Hibbing and its major players?

The drama of building Hibbing was not yet over.

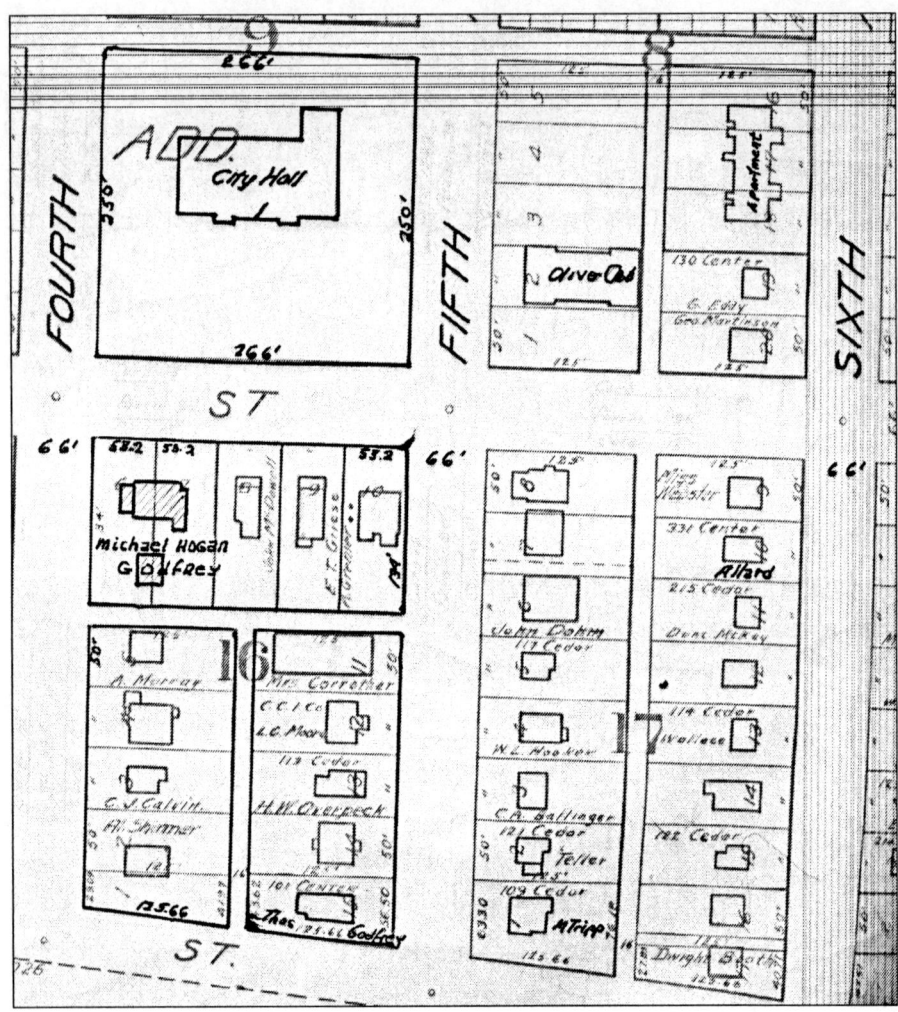

Central Addition center showing the location of City Hall (not yet built in 1921 but the basement had been excavated), the Oliver Clubhouse, the Oliver Apartments, Mike Godfrey's house (not yet built either), Thomas Jefferson Godfrey's house, and two in-laws of Godfrey's, the Tripps and Allards. Author's Collection.

Notes

[1] Henry P. Reed, et. al, plaintiffs vs. the Village of Hibbing, a corporation, et.al., defendants, 1921, page 285.

[2] Henry P. Reed, et. al, plaintiffs vs. the Village of Hibbing, a corporation, et.al., defendants, 1921.

[3] Sellers Street and Third Avenue. Henry P. Reed, et. al, plaintiffs vs. the Village of Hibbing, a corporation, et.al., defendants, 1921.

[4] Henry P. Reed, et. al, plaintiffs vs. the Village of Hibbing, a corporation, et.al., defendants, 1921, page 267.

[5] The Central Addition.

Daniel W. Lynch

[6] *Henry P. Reed, et. al, plaintiffs vs. the Village of Hibbing, a corporation, et.al., defendants*, 1921, page 285.

[7] The business journal of W.F. Kohagen is owned by Paul Aubin of Aubin Studios, 1801 E. 3rd Avenue, Hibbing, Minnesota. It was given to him by his father who was a friend of Kohagen's. Kohagen was also on the Board of Education at this time as was T. J. Godfrey, Mike's brother. .

[8] He was about to have another reason not to object.

[9] With modifications this was to become the Androy Hotel which was originally called the Oliver.

[10] The Oliver had purchased the mineral rights in 1899 for $2,500.000.00 and later in 1918 started buying the surface property.

[11] All quotes here are from *Henry P. Reed, et. al, plaintiffs vs. the Village of Hibbing, a corporation, et.al., defendants, 1921*.

[12] Later we will touch upon the building of the by now famous Hibbing High School but for now a comment is called for concerning the property it sits upon. Mike Godfrey had proposed that the Oliver authorize a price of $10,000 for the land. The school board seemed well disposed towards that amount. Olcott took up the matter with D. C. Kerr, vice president of US Steel in a letter where he said, and I quote: "This forty has not been drilled but the exploratory work that has been carried on on the forties north and west shows that it is located in the slate area, therefore the chances of finding any ore on same would be rather remote." The Oliver didn't drill this acreage for the simple reason that the surrounding area had no ore. They didn't drill the Old North Forty for the simple reason that they didn't have to: they used the samples from the west, north and east of that acreage to tell them what they needed to know: they were sitting on a continuous body of ore, a lot of it.

[13] *Henry P. Reed, et. al*, page 329.

[14] *Henry P. Reed, et. al*, page 337.

[15] *Mesaba Ore and Hibbing News*, January 24, 1919.

[16] *Mesaba Ore and Hibbing News*, January 31, 1919.

[17] Nonetheless mineral rights were retained by the Oliver. What Godfrey wrote was: "We have again taken this matter up with our Engineering Department, who assure us that, in their judgment, there is no probability of ore existing on said land. We, however, will, in case the School District purchases same, see that our rights are fully protected with our usual form of contract reserving all mineral rights." This letter was sent by Godfrey directly to E.H. Gary, Chairman of US Steel. It is dated April 8, 1919. The High School was to occupy acreage in the Eastern Addition which the Oliver also platted. Walter Power's real estate endeavor brought about its development.

[18] The original acreage was joined by an additional 2.36 acres on the south that cut off Cody Street at Seventh Avenue. Cody Street itself was 0.70 of an acre, the three lots dubbed A, B, and C taking up over ten acres in the Central Addition. The school fronted on Mesaba Street which also ran right past the Village Hall and Godfrey's house (built later on) to the west.

[19] The lots were across the street from the hotel and on the west side of Fifth Avenue. The Androy is on the east side.

[20] By the time of approval the mortgage was on the order of 15 years.

[21] All quotes here are from the May 10th memorandum.

[22] Judge Cant was to eventually find that there was approximately 13 million tons of ore down there, worth about eight million.

To Tipple A Prince

[23] This and the following quotes are drawn from the court testimony of *Henry P. Reed, et. al.*

[24] The matter in question was what to do with the public buildings of Hibbing, the Village Hall, Fire Department, Court House and so on in addition to the standing buildings in the west forty and how they would be handled and what the Oliver was going to do with the Central Addition and in what way.

[25] A duplicate of the layout map is dated to July 8, 1920 and was used to continuously update owners names until 1931.

[26] Corner lots were $1,200.00 and inside lots were $1,000.00.

[27] These were platted by Archie Chisholm who also testified in the famous case. He claimed that at the time they were platted it was generally understood they would have to be moved.

[28] According to the article, the rats were finding refuge in local warehouses, sheds, residences and outhouses.

[29] The first new patient with anything serious was one Giacinto Daniani of the Nassau Location who had to undergo a knee operation.

[30] Quite a few trees had to be 'sacrificed' to make way for the tractor's large cargo. First Avenue north of Howard Street still lacks trees as a result.

[31] *The Hibbing Daily News and Mesaba Ore*, February 26, 1921.

[32] Thomas Jefferson Godfrey was always called "T.J." by friend, foe, and family alike but his brother Michael Hogan was never called 'M.H.' His friends called him Mike, his enemies called him Godfrey, and people on the street called him Mr. Godfrey. The local paper called him genial and once called him Iron Mike. His children adored him and fifty years after his death they still honored his memory.

[33] W. F. Kohagen, he of the private business journal, was also on the board. Kohagen was also a boy scout leader and an expert on birds.

[34] There were at this time two post offices in South Hibbing. The other was run by J. B. Connors.

[35] The diagnosis was diabetes.

[36] The children called her this. She was never 'mom', or 'mother', or our 'stepmother'. Mike's second wife was never fully integrated into the family dynamics. When Mike died, May left town and Miriam the eldest daughter was left to take care of the children still at home. This included Marjorie who was retarded.

[37] That's where the park got its name.

[38] The list price for a corner lot was $1,200.00 and for inside lots $1,000.00. So, Power who needed a corner lot and two inside lots paid a total of $3,200.00.

[39] The State Supreme Court sustained the lower courts ruling in October 1921. It found, in part that the private interests of plaintiffs would not be invaded by the proposed vacation of the streets in the townsite nor by mining so long as the streets between them and the mining operations are left safe for public travel.

VII

And the Town That Didn't: 1922 to 1924

Introduction

Sometimes opportunities just don't seem to come your way and sometimes when they do, you watch them pass on by. Such was the case of the Pillsbury and Southern Addition businessmen. They had the opportunity to move to the new South Hibbing as did the businesses in the west plat of the original townsite but they did not avail themselves of the chance. They watched as their northern neighbors moved down First Avenue and settled the Central and Park Additions and then instead of 'kicking' themselves for passing up the golden opportunity to grow with the rest of Hibbing, they did the next best thing: they sued the Oliver: they had missed the window of opportunity, so they went to court.

But, this was not the Oliver's only court case of importance at the time. In the other case of note, the Oliver had the initiative as the plaintiff. This case was a protracted one also. Its conclusion would startle a few officials.

The move from Old North Hibbing to New South Hibbing continued as there was still much to do, principally build a new high school and a Village Hall. The village had to be administered from somewhere and it was obvious that Old North Hibbing wasn't going to continue as a prime location for this activity. Likewise the high school. Ground had been broken for each but designing the buildings and constructing them was to take awhile as these were major undertakings of considerable community involvement and pride.

To Tipple A Prince

Vic Power went through some political misfortunes but seemed to weather them, then failed at a comeback and pretty much "retired" and John Gannon's star reached its public apogee before he started making mistakes.

Through it all Mike Godfrey and the Oliver continued to command stage center by chance and choice. Mike continued to steer "the move" from his vantage point in the Hull-Rust headquarters off the Southern Addition and the Oliver continued to grow its open pit operations. On the Mesabi Range, open pit operations now outnumbered underground operations by about four to one and tonnage from open pits enjoyed a ten to one advantage over undergrounds.

The iron ore shipments from the Mesabi Range for the 1922 season showed a seventy-one per cent increase over those of 1921. In 1921,

The Mesaba Electric Railway company's bridge over the Duluth, Missabe & Northern railway tracks. Dismantling of this bridge would seriously impede business and shopping and travel between Old North Hibbing and the New South Hibbing. The view is to the southwest. Photograph of a photograph from the Hibbing Historical Society display in Old North Hibbing.

eighteen companies operating seventy-one mines produced sixteen million tons of ore, while in 1922 a total of twenty-two companies operating ninety-four mines shipped twenty-eight million tons. Average shipments per mine rose from 230,000 tons to 300,000 tons. Progress on a very big scale. The Oliver had the lion's share of this bounty, with twenty-three operating mines shipping around sixteen million tons of rich red ore. Pickens, Mather & Co, not exactly bashful about their production, came in a distant second with nine mines and two million tons of ore. The range consisted of one real giant and twenty-two pale dwarfs.

Buhl Injunction Case

The Buhl-Kinney injunction case received a quick nod in mid-January as Judge Martin J. Hughes set a civil trial case date of February 6th to hear the arguments of the Oliver Iron Mining Company et.al versus school district #35.

Attorneys for both sides had been sitting down with the contractors to see what could be done at this point as the North wing of the Buhl

The same junction today, looking south from Third Avenue and McKinley Street. The crest in the road bed is the center of the old bridge's span over the D.M.&N. tracks. The concrete supports are still there buried in the weeds even if the bridge is long gone. Author's Collection.

high school and the improvements at the Kinney school were about ninety percent completed, with some additional improvements to the Buhl high school about seventy-five percent complete. The parties reached no agreement. The contractors would not shave their costs, the school district could not abandon the improvements and the mining companies would not pay.

The case continued through February and into March and then into April with significant progress lacking. Mike Godfrey was called—as expected—to testify for the plaintiffs and he stated the case clearly: too much non-authorized monies were being spent on the two schools. His testimony and that of other mining officials went unheeded however. Judge Hughes lifted the injunction and construction proceeded apace. The mining companies' support of higher education through tax levies continued. But the plaintiffs were not going to roll over without appealing the judge's decision and so they went to the Minnesota Supreme Court to have the injunction re-instated. They met the same lack of success at the higher court level in late April.

The final price tag on this issue amounted to over $2,000,000.00. Mike Godfrey, although he, as was his custom, said nothing in public, in private he never forgot the judgment of Martin Hughes. He rarely mentioned legal matters at home but on this score he did and on more than one occasion. He really believed that Hughes's judgment against the mining companies was subjective, that there was something personal here, not quite in evidence but none the less real. His children could recall his distaste with clarity decades later.[1]

This was not the way Mike Godfrey wanted to start year four of the great move. He was getting tired and it was showing somewhat.
But by June he and other Hibbingites had something else to divert their attention from the ordinary cares and concerns of daily life.

Daniel W. Lynch

Oh Boy, Race

Summer on the Mesabi Iron Ore Range brought with it more than just heat, humidity, and bugs by the billions, it also brought the end of the school term for high school students and the beginning of the annual hunt for a summer job. And in this era, summer employment at the many lakes and resorts that abound in the surrounding area, was easy to obtain. Young men and women flocked to the resorts for a hiatus from the concerns of scholarship and weren't seen again for three months. Peace prevailed. And then the unexpected happened in the summer of 1922, something to talk about.

The new hotel, the Androy, needed waiters and waitresses for the tourist season and the labor pool had dried up. Quigley and Doran were not newcomers to the hotel business and they knew what to do, call in the reservists. From the Twin Cities. At this point the local papers got a hold of the story and the summer perked up immediately.

The noted and former head waiter of the Rogers, the Andrews and the Curtis-Court hotels, one Redmond (no last name) was summoned by the Androy management to enlist a core of waiters from the Twin Cities to come to Hibbing to help out for the summer. He did and they did. But Redmond was, in the vernacular of the day, "colored" (in other words, black) and his waiters were, ahem, colored as well. Hibbing and the other Range towns had had their share of ethnic problems over the years and these could rise to the point of real, genuine passion but everyone involved in the dual of differences was for lack of a better word, "white" and these newly minted waiters at the Androy were not.

As Quigley and Doran pointed out, on the plus side, each of the waiters employed had considerable experience in serving at many of the best hotels in the country and perk of perk, they had also had Pullman Dining Car service. The experiment worked for the summer and trouble never did develop. The summer ended, the students returned, the tourists went home and life went on but the experiment was not repeated the following year. The novelty did not last long enough to produce real objections that could cause concern but neither was the case repeated. It was not for another forty years before blacks re-entered the context of the all white range and this time real trouble ensued.

Another Pioneer Dies

In late September, Mrs. Barbara Hibbing, widow of Frank, died suddenly one evening of a heart attack. She had been living with her only child, Mrs. Herman Keller of Minneapolis. Barbara Hibbing had been visiting her (adopted) daughter for the summer but her health had turned bad. She left behind an estate valued at $228,000.00.

There would be other Hibbing pioneers during this decade who would also leave the Iron Range to history.

A Power Failure

John Gannon, who's star had been on the ascendancy for the past two years, decided in February to take advantage of public recognition and filed for village council president which after much dithering and dathering forced Vic Power's hand at the last moment. He too, filed for the position. This year it looked like a real election contest.

Power wasted no time in hitting the stump addressing the women of Old and New Hibbing and of Brooklyn with two speeches in early March. The speeches essentially defended his administration's last nine years in office. In each speech he was quoted as saying, "Hibbing is a community where people do things. Once you start the movement for extensive improvements it does not stop in Hibbing. This movement has continued until all the towns on the range are the best communities in the United States. If you don't want to continue the improvements, don't vote for me."[2] He probably wished he hadn't said that even though the paper supported him strongly. A massive parade in his honor on March 12th seemed to indicate that his popularity was never stronger and a headline on March 14th, "Power Shreds Opposition Claims" seemed to confirm it. But it was not to be this time, for the first time. John Gannon won the election by 686 votes in a record turnout year: five thousand, five hundred and six voters visited the polls. Hibbing had its first turnover in its top public office in a decade.

Power, declaring that he never felt better, decided that a vacation was in order and visited the Taggart Resort in French Lick, Indiana for two weeks. He took along Mike Godfrey's brother T.J. for company. The rest of the year he pretty much focused on practicing law and staying out of the news. Circumstance would all but guarantee that he would be back.

New South Hibbing

Village Hall

Elections aside, the move that was making, or rather, remaking Hibbing, continued. Businesses and residents from the original townsite had been continuously moving to their "new" village and it was obvious that as the population center shifted so too must the political center: bids went out in March 1922 for construction of the new Village Hall. Nine bids were received with $108,000.00 being the low bid and $130,000.00 being the high bid. This being a government contract, the winner was the low bidder, Phelps-Drake of Hibbing.[3]

The 125-foot-wide, sixty-eight-foot-deep building was to face Mesaba Street and contain a ten cell jail on the first floor. The second floor would house a municipal courtroom and the village offices. The west side ground floor entrance (Fourth Avenue E.) would contain a Gents room and the east side (Fifth Avenue E.) would have a Women's Comfort Station (still so labeled) and the doors to the stations and into the building would be so arranged as to afford access to the rest facilities twenty-four hours a day, even though the building would be closed after public service hours ceased.

To Tipple A Prince

The front entrance faced Mesaba Street (now, Twenty-first Street) and across the street (at a very slight angle) 404 Mesaba Street, the home of the man who donated the land the Village Hall rested on. The mayor's office, however, faced Fourth Avenue E. and could not see its benefactor. The office faced the hospital. The Women's Comfort Station faced the all-male Oliver Club.

Initial estimates were that the building would run around $200,000.00 and like a typical government project this estimate proved to be widely, spectacularly low: the final toll hit $400,000-plus and that didn't include the cost of the clock tower. (The halls were finished with imported Italian marble.)

The Clock Tower

The most dominating feature of the entire structure was to be the three-story high clock tower and like any proud tower hovering above a town, this clock tower had its own pedigree.

The tower was part of the building but the contract for the tower and for the clock were separate budgetary items. The installation of the clock *system* (that's what they called the combination tower construction and clock mechanism; also included were other clocks in various rooms of the village hall) was entrusted to H.G. Burnham, a jeweler (the E. Howard Clock Company built the clock, nothing else) which had entered the high bid of all things. That should have been a tip-off right there. The bid was $14,190.00 for the entire job. That was in October of 1922.

The mayor, John Gannon, and the Village Recorder, Everett, voted against giving the contract to the E. Howard Clock Company. They were in the minority.

That was in October. In January of 1923 they were still in the minority and still refused to sign off on the clock system. Gannon and Everett contended that the contract awarded H.G. Burnham by the votes of three members of the Village Council did not conform to the

Daniel W. Lynch

The Hibbing Village Hall. This is what nearly $400,000.00 built. Its front entrance faces Mike Godfrey's house on Mesaba Street and the mayor's office on the second floor (on the far side in this photograph) faces Rood Hospital on Fourth Avenue E. The Women's Comfort Station can be seen on the right side of the building in the center on the ground floor. This is an imposing structure even if it does not resemble either Faneuil Hall in Boston or Independence Hall in Philadelphia. The structure curiously enough faces south, almost as if it were deliberately turning its back on the huge mining operations, especially the Oliver's, to the north. Ironically enough, the New Hibbing's main business district centered on Howard Street is one block north. Aubin Studios.

specifications called for in the bid. It seems that along with a standard bid (in correct form), Burnham also submitted alternative bids in which prices were quoted on various other styles of dials and equipment, and it was on one of those alternate proposals that the contract was awarded. District Judge Edward Freeman in a decision in Virginia court upheld Gannon and Everett.

Contract canceled. Bids had to go out again.

Burnham it seems was ready again and again got the contract. By mid September, the parts for the clock began to arrive. But it took two weeks for all the parts to get to Hibbing. Installation could not begin until all the parts had arrived even though the clock's chimes, weights, and bolts were sitting there waiting for assemblage.

To Tipple A Prince

Preliminary work on assembling this system began on October 20th but as the nature of the task and the weather made clear this would take a couple of weeks. That, of course, was the estimate. In any case, an over night job it wasn't especially in light of what the crew was dealing with: four bells in all with the largest one weighing in at 1,500 pounds and measuring forty-two inches in diameter at the base, and the smallest one weighting in at 300 pounds, measuring twenty-six inches in diameter at the base.

The bells were to be installed in the uppermost section with a floor between them and the actual clock. The bells were to chime four times on the quarter hour, eight on the half. The clock was fixed in a cast iron frame and the frame was sixty-six inches in diameter. Finally, on November 24, 1923, the clock rang its chimes for the first time in Hibbing history. In spite of the late start, they have been ringing ever since.

The south face of the clock tower in 2003. Still going strong. Author's Collection.

The Women's Comfort Station on the ground floor of the East side of the Village Hall. Author's Collection.

The High School

The high school was also taking shape at this time and the plans for it were as impressive as the size. Situated on former Oliver property offered by Mike Godfrey and the Oliver, and selected as the site (in part) by Mike's brother, Thomas Jefferson, this 420-foot-wide structure was to cost nearly four million dollars and contain over eighty classrooms for 3,000 students from kindergarten through two years of junior college. It also featured dormitories for the teachers, a swimming pool, basketball court, and an auditorium that could seat 1,800 (better than half the student body at one time) and was modeled after the Capital Theatre in New York.[4]

The main entry way is designed to command your attention the minute you walk in the door with six murals, three on each side, that depict Columbus Discovering America, the Signing of the Declaration of Independence, Trading with the Indians, Westward Ho (the opening of the western frontier), Lumbering in Minnesota, and a Naturalization Court. This feature of the school ran to nearly $10,000.00 in 1920 dollars.

The construction effort was so extensive and the materials so massive in size and quantity that a railroad spur had to be built through the front of the property on Mesaba Street to handle the loads. This was a massive undertaking and the resultant structure, basically a capital **W** that faced north (facing the mines), is still the single most impressive public structure on the Mesabi Iron Ore range.

Hibbing High School looking southeast. It was first conceived by the board of education in 1918; construction began in 1919 and was finally finished in 1924. It occupies four city blocks, could easily intimidate an Egyptian pharaoh, and graduated the likes of a former Minnesota governor, a professional basketball player, and the founder of Chun King. Colorized Postcard.

To Tipple A Prince

Municipal Building

The New Hibbing was nearly done, the Village Hall was being constructed, the high school was under way, and Howard Street merchants were in business, streets were being paved, sewer lines were in, churches were being constructed, what was left? Well, a municipal recreational building, according to the Village Council. Today this would be called a sports arena but the concept is the same: a publicly financed sports facility for the general public to both watch sporting events and participate in them. The council put $275,000.00 of the public's trust into the venture in January of 1924, subject to a referendum (which passed). It was to be built in the Fairview Addition in the New Hibbing. The site chosen was Fifth Avenue East between Joseph and Adeline Avenues (Twenty-third and Twenty-fourth avenues today).

It was a beautiful building until it burned to the ground in 1933. The current arena was erected in 1935.

The original memorial recreational building which cost $275,000.00. The replacement in 1935 cost about double this but had only half the character. Its frontage was 225 feet and its depth was 282 feet. The ice arena is 200 by 100 ft and it's on the second floor! That makes it the second largest second floor ice area in the country. It had a sixty-by-forty-five-foot dining room and an auditorium that seated 1,800. Colorized Postcard.

Daniel W. Lynch

The Case That Would Not Die
for the Town That Did Not Move

In spite of previous rulings that went against them, or maybe because of those rulings, Reed and others proceeded to fight their court battle with the Village, its officials, the Electric Trolley Car line and the Oliver in court where, until now, they had found little success. But with each loss came renewed vigor to find yet another legal avenue to pursue. The Pillsbury and Southern Additions weren't going anywhere and seventy some respondents wanted to be compensated for their inertia.

Back in September 1919, when it became obvious to even the slowest of minds that the Oliver Iron Mining Company, the Village of Hibbing, and the residents and businessmen of Old North Hibbing were going to conduct a move to the Central and Park Additions, the merchants of the two additions to the immediate south went to court to try and stop the move and when they couldn't they wanted compensation.

To refresh our memories Reed and others claimed that all the defendants entered into an unlawful conspiracy to (1) vacate—hence the name of the court action, "vacation"—the streets, (2) change the route of the electric railway, (3) unlawfully dispose of the village's public property and (4) engage in unfair competition to remove the businesses and residences of the original townsite to the Central and Park Additions. The plaintiff's claimed they were damaged to the tune of $500,000.00 and asked for a court appointed referee to ascertain the damages accruing to the property holders of the Pillsbury and Southern Additions. They wanted the Oliver to stop what they were already doing which was moving the North Forty somewhere else.

Judge Martin Hughes issued a preliminary restraining order that commanded the defendants to stop digging up Old North Hibbing. On January 20, 1920, Hughes issued a temporary injunction against the defendants. The battle was now joined. At the end of the year in December, Judge Freeman ruled that the plaintiffs were *not entitled* to the relief they were seeking and he lifted the temporary injunction. The plaintiffs took that in stride and appealed to the Minnesota Supreme Court. The Minnesota Supreme Court in October 1921 upheld Judge Freeman in all respects of fact and conclusion. That must have lifted the plaintiffs' spirits somewhat as they then appealed the judgment to the U.S. Supreme Court. In October of 1922, the U.S. Supreme Court refused to order the Minnesota Supreme Court to report its findings for review. But the U.S. Supreme Court retained the case on a Writ of Error.

There the matter stood until January 1923 when the Supreme Court ruled that the Oliver Iron Mining Company had the right to move the property in the west plat of the original townsite of Hibbing in order to mine the underlying iron ore.

John Gannon now acting, in March, as an official representative of the Village asked for a minimum of $900,000.00 from the Oliver to compensate the Village for the many thousands of dollars the village had spent on municipal improvements. The mining companies in his legal view had enough data concerning the ore deposit under Old North Hibbing to know that the taxes they had been paying on 5,000,000 tons of ore was a gross under payment.

In May of 1923, Judge Cant ruled out all claims for damages made by the city, except for improvements located in the North Forty. He further granted the petition of the Oliver for a complete vacation of the North Forty plat. No general or specific damages were awarded to the Pillsbury or Southern Additions. But Judge Cant did leave a bone for some to chew on: he ruled that the property owners at the *north end of the* [Seller's pit] *viaduct* were due special damages as they would be cut off from free access to their property. What he meant is that they could no longer access their property from the south as the Seller's viaduct was to be removed, leaving only a yawning hole between their property on the north side of the viaduct and anything on the other side. They would now have to take an extremely circuitous route north and west and then south and east to reach the New Hibbing. And that giant open pit hole in the middle was only going to get bigger.

In June, Judge Cant defined the extent of the Village improvements that required compensation and awarded Hibbing $296, 841.53. Once the Oliver paid that amount the Village had sixty days to remove what property it needed and then the Oliver could begin stripping.

However, Mike Godfrey and the Oliver did not even have time to exhale before the next suit landed on their headquarters complex off the Southern Addition. In July, 177 property owners in North Hibbing filed a motion to have Judge Cant's June ruling thrown out on the grounds that his court was without jurisdiction. They further claimed that they—not the Village—would suffer damages to the tune of $3,281,354.00 if the streets and alleys were vacated. This was clearly upping the ante. This appeal was also carried up to the Minnesota Supreme Court. It was denied.

Meanwhile, in the background but not very far back, John Gannon and some other property owners were still at work determined to keep this case alive. To every denial there is an appeal gathering momentum. In December of 1923 Gannon and what the *Hibbing Daily News and Mesaba Ore* called a large delegation of property owners met in the Library for the purpose of preparing a transcript to present to the state supreme court as part of yet another appeal.[5] This would take a fair amount of cash, some $2,000.00, and some means had to be devised for raising it.[6]

Gannon went on record as stating that [Old] North Hibbing was being cut off on the east, west and north and would be nothing but a "back up" town and would never amount to anything. (Gannon was on the basis of current observation, absolutely correct.) A back up town is a town that has to be reached by first going through another town. His case was that only the Minnesota Supreme Court had the power to say whether or not the Seller's Viaduct could be cut off. The roads to the west—through Penobscot, and the east—through Brooklyn, were private roads owned by the mining companies and could be cut off by them but the viaduct over the Seller's pit was not part of, in his opinion, a private road.

This appeal was also headed for the Minnesota Supreme Court. That bridge was of critical importance. It was the only road to the locations on the other side of the complex of open pits that ringed Hibbing (Pool, Sturgeon Lake, Carson Lake, Bear Country). The eastern route around Hibbing to say, Chisholm, was not yet paved over the entire distance. There was no "western route" around the other side of Hibbing.

The Rumors of Winter

Rumors raced through Hibbing in January 1924 that the Oliver was about to blow the Seller's viaduct to bits with a very large cache of dynamite. The prophecies failed to materialize but the Oliver did have its steam shovels situated in the southwest corner[7] of the viaduct now known as the Sellers-Hull-Rust Approach, nibbling away at the frozen ground. Signs had been posted in the New Hibbing on First Avenue, nailed to the barricades that the company had erected. Special Oliver police manned the position. That bridge was not long for this world. Stripping operations had begun.

Late in November or early in December yet another appeal was being readied to stop this mining operation.

John Gannon Stirs the Political Pot

John Gannon had hardly hung up his hat in Hibbing when he became mayor of the growing village of Hibbing in April 1922. His election after ten years of Victor Power's administration may have been due more to the desire for a change in the Village's administration rather than any real disappointment in Power's accomplishments. Then too, there may have been some resentment from the voters in the Pillsbury and Southern Additions over not being made part of the deal that moved Hibbing south. If so, Gannon's victory was not a clarion call but rather a muted toot.

Daniel W. Lynch

John read it otherwise. With C.E. Everett, county probation officer and member of the school board, and T.J. Madden, village trustee, at his side, Gannon announced a retrenchment.

Gannon's first announcement was that members of the staff of the state public examiner's office were taking charge of the books of the Village for a thorough audit. An entirely new set of books would then be opened for the new administration. A clean slate, so to speak. If there is a more blatant way of saying your predecessor was doing a ballet with the books without saying so explicitly, it hasn't yet been found. This also serves the purpose of covering your own financial miscues as you initiate yourself in the finer points of local governance.

What Gannon had in mind was that the new improvements necessitated by the great move, such as paving roads, installing sewer and drainage systems, supplying power and water to all the new dwellings, was going to cost a real bundle and economies would have to be found somewhere in the Village budget.

He thereupon laid off thirty-one policemen. His rule had begun.[8]

The Next Step
What does one do after establishing oneself as the new hard charging lawyer in town and then shortly thereafter get yourself elected mayor? You get married.[9] Since he was originally from Wisconsin[10], it was only natural that he marry a Wisconsin girl, Margaret Loney, from Superior, who had just spent the last three years teaching school in Hibbing (her sisters, Mary and Nora, were also teachers, Mary in Hibbing, Nora in Wisconsin).

More Retrenchment
The economies promised by Gannon continued through the rest of August and into early September. Thirteen more members of the police force were laid off, the library fired its janitor, stopped buying books and subscribing to periodicals, the street department cut its work force in half and so did

the park board. The city health officer, Hugh Reynolds, cut his own pay in half. Even at that this was only a beginning. More cuts were to follow before the year's end. Hibbing appeared to be in dire financial straights.

Hoisted with His Own Petard

John had returned from his honeymoon to work with the Village Council on these budget cuts so as not to appear either casual or unconcerned but this gesture cost him and his new bride some embarrassment.

It seems that one evening John had parked his car near the city hall while helping work on the budget and upon finishing and returning to his car, discovered that his wedding presents had been stolen![11] It may be academic or not, but perhaps the current budget cuts affecting the police force had something to do with the boldness of the maneuver: the police department is in the same building as the mayor and the Village council and they didn't see it happen, right outside their door.

One Good Turn Deserves Another

If you are going to paste your political opponents with financial extravagance it is almost a necessity that they return the favor and so they did. Financial malfeasance may not be practiced by everybody but that has never diminished the popularity of the claim. John Gannon's response to the accusations (which his rule had been making in one form or another as well) was to call for a public meeting to refute the charges. As he put it, "some refutation of the charges of reckless spending was necessary and a mass meeting was the best method of getting the truth to the people."[12] The mass meeting was held in the Coliseum on First Avenue the second week in September.

While this was going on Gannon was also hiring laid off miners at least for part time work to help them through the long winter months. This was announced in late November. The Oliver was at this time employing some 1,400 men in its operations in the Hibbing District and it was the usual custom, as Mike Godfrey said on this and many other occasions, to lay off men in the winter months as open pit mining was nearly impossible due to the brutal weather. Only stripping was done during such a period.

But Gannon and his administration had come to office to do more than just balance the books and watch the Central Addition thrive. Something else was in the air and it did not take long to find out what it was.

Talk about Rash

On November 28, 1922, John Gannon and the Village Council made it clear that they were breaking with the previous administration's policies in regard to the Oliver and the vacating of Old North Hibbing. Three plans were formally drawn up and publicly put forth.

The first plan presented was a promise that Hibbing would completely vacate all streets and alleys in Old North Hibbing *if* the Oliver would promise to purchase all the property in the Pillsbury and Southern Additions! That kind of generosity was going to go unappreciated but what it did illustrate was that the merchants and residents of the two additions were now out in the open with their mistake and they wanted the Oliver to rectify the matter.

The second plan had an equal lack of appeal for the Oliver. In it, Hibbing again agreed to vacate all the streets and alleys in Old North Hibbing if the Oliver would pay Hibbing the exact and *total* replacement cost of *all public improvements* made in Old North Hibbing. This kind of approach was almost guaranteed to have your opponent wondering if you had lost your sanity.

The third plan at least had a real dollar figure to it. Hibbing would again agree to vacate the streets and alleys of Old North Hibbing for a million dollars.

In all, it is still hard to understand even at this perspective just what it was the Hibbing Village Council and/or John Gannon were thinking.

To Tipple A Prince

The Oliver had never expressed any interest in buying anything in the Pillsbury or the Southern Additions, and as far as they were concerned their taxes had already paid for all the public improvements in the Old Village, why do it again? Besides, it looked very much like the courts were going to favor the mining companies anyway. Whatever financial judgment the courts would require of the Oliver would be paltry compared to what the Oliver had already spent. If an elephant is sitting on you it makes little sense to try and fine him for the privilege. Gannon declared that the mining interests had never made any effort to compromise on the matter. Pouting is not a good negotiating ploy either.

This was a critical juncture for both the Oliver and the Village. Tensions were running high and the move to the Central Addition was nearly complete, at least the initial phase was complete, and time was needed to settle things down. But appeal after appeal was dragging a legal resolution past the breaking point, Gannon was pressing for a financial settlement independent of the courts, and Mike Godfrey who

Howard Street Hibbing, circa 2000. The view is to the west. Beyond the town and in the background, stand the ever present overburden dumps. The buildings erected in the great move of 1919, 1920, and 1921 are still here for the most part in 2000. But the First National Bank and the State Theatre formerly on the north side of Howard Street are long gone. Author's Collection.

had engineered the move and spent more of his time in court than was healthy, had little room to maneuver caught as he was between the court, the mayor and his boss, William J. Olcott. It was not a good place to be late in November 1922.

Mike's Year in Review

First, One Funeral

Mike left his home at 411 Sellers Street in the Pillsbury Addition early on the morning of May 2, 1922, to attend the funeral of the man he replaced as District Manager of the Hibbing District for the Oliver, William West. West was a more than capable District Manager, as he had proved for the last five years in Virginia, but he did not have the political and administrative skills necessary to handle two demanding jobs at once, one of them having little if anything to do with managing mines. The funeral was in Dodgeville, Wisconsin, and the trip and funeral would take the better part of two days. For Mike, it was a sad visit to a member of a very elite peer group, a member of the upper management echelon of the Oliver Iron Mining Company, one of the very few who had commanded the Oliver's massive operations in the Hibbing District. Olcott was there as well.

Godfrey no sooner returned from that sad visit, than he had another one to face as well: his mother, Bridget Hogan was very ill. She lived around the corner from Mike on Garfield Street and both her husband and one of her sons was in attendance. She was holding her own for the present but it was obvious that her end was coming. May was the beginning of the end.

Then, Another

June 6th managed to liven things up a bit for Mike Godfrey and some other "rough necks" of the Iron Range. Douglas D. McEachin had reopened the Hotel Hibbing after its journey from the corner of Cedar Street and Third Avenue in Old North Hibbing to 6th Avenue East just off Howard Street in the Central Addition. As many of the original band of pioneers that had dedicated and opened the hotel back in 1896 were on hand to celebrate the new grand opening and Michael Hogan Godfrey was there front and center, albeit somewhat somber. His brother, T.J. was there, as was Fred Twitchell and Leroy Salsich. It was a time to celebrate and an orchestra was there to help, playing far into the night but all was not well with this group and they must have gone home in the wee hours feeling a real mix of emotions.

Many had lost wives, or parents, or siblings or children while carving out a life in what had been a true wilderness on the extreme edge of what civilization there was in those northern swamps of north central Minnesota. Mud streets had been replaced with paved ones, and the horse had been replaced by the electric trolley, and sewer lines had replaced outhouses, and telephones had replaced the occasional letter but nothing replaces the friends you have lost or members of your family you can no longer talk to.

And time waits for no man and fate can be a very indifferent master and Godfrey's life was no different than any one else's. On June 8th his Mother died at home at 415 Garfield Street in the Southern Addition. She was nine days past her seventy-sixth birthday. Another funeral, another link to the past gone.

Memories pile up as time runs out.

Back in Public
In early August arrangements had to be made for a mine inspection tour during a late August convention, whatever the other circumstances and obligations, for 200 members and guests of the American Institute of Park Executives who would be arriving by train from Minneapolis. Luncheons would be served at the Androy on the day of arrival and an informal banquet would be served in the evening. Godfrey, Salsich, Tappan and Kohagen were in charge of arrangements and tours. Mike

arranged for the Oliver's special touring train, the *Northland*, normally reserved for officials of the Oliver, to be used for a tour of the giant Hull, Rust and Sellers open pit mining operations.

Events on the Mesabi then settled down a bit for the remainder of the summer and the early fall as mining activities hit their summer high output stride. Godfrey had only his normal duties to discharge along with keeping abreast of the court cases that he was involved in. He took a brief moment to deny rumors that the Oliver was planning an injunction to block the purchase of a Sargent Addition school site by the local school board. "There is no injunction even under consideration," he stated for the October 12th edition of the *Hibbing Daily News and Mesaba Ore*. In mid-November he noted that the layoffs that were occurring were normal for this time of year as the company readied itself for the upcoming winter slow down in the mines. As was the usual custom, stripping overburden was to take precedence over mining ore.

In Private
When the daily obligations of running the largest iron ore operation in the world were not pressing down on him, Godfrey could usually take Sunday off as a real day of rest for him and his family. His children remembered Sundays as a special family get-together time after church services. The ritual was much the same over the years as they and their Father seemed to enjoy the regularity of sitting down to breakfast, with Father dressed impeccably in full suit and tie and watch fob, and reading the Sunday funnies to his captive audience before breakfast brunch could be served. The family favorites as recalled years later were the Katzenjammer Kids, Little Jimmy, Down on the Farm and Bringing Up Father.

The Idle Ends
John Gannon and the Hibbing Village Council used the Thanksgiving period to present their three plans for settling the Vacation Case. Mike

and the Oliver responded a few days later in front of the Commercial Club gathering at the Library.

E.A. Bergeron opened the meeting by explaining that he was trying to bring all factions to the argument together to hear each other out. Bergeron circled the room calling for various citizens and businessmen to speak out on the issues but no one would. That is until Bergeron called on Godfrey. The right button got pressed.

Mike jumped on the opportunity to tell of conferences that the Oliver had with members of the Village Council during which John Gannon had asked the company to pay a million dollars for the streets and alleyways. He said Oliver executives felt that since the company had paid approximately ninety per cent of the tax money that had been used in making the improvements in the North Forty and had purchased all of the property that had benefited from those improvements, it was a stretch to ask them to pay again.[13]

In response to a question from the audience, Godfrey stated that the company's lease on the ore under Old North Hibbing had thirty-two more years to run. And when he was asked how much overburden the company expected to have to strip off the Old North Hibbing plat before they could begin mining operations, he replied that it was somewhere in the neighborhood of 13,000,000 cubic yards.

The meeting ran late so it was decided to form a committee of seven to keep the dialog going and Mike Godfrey and John Gannon were both appointed to the job. Less than two weeks later the roof fell in.

John Gannon's Strange Trip to New York

At first it looked like things may have settled down a bit. Mike Godfrey and John Gannon were both sitting on a committee charged by a group of local civic leaders and merchants to see if they could work out a solution to the vexing question of what to do about those streets and alleyways that the Village had maintained and improved and that the

Oliver had supplied the tax money for. The mines were quiet, the end of the year was approaching, stripping was taking place as expected, the snows and the cold were keeping everyone indoors whenever possible and Christmas was approaching, a season mostly known for its goodwill.

The paper broke the news on December 12th: John Gannon and the Village Council announced a settlement![14] That must have startled most of the Village and not a few officials as well. A settlement just before the Holiday Season was one very large Christmas gift for everyone. Or so it appeared.

John Gannon the Village president and John T. Madden, a Village Councilman, had traveled to New York the previous week and had a series of talks with Judge E.H. Gary, the chairman of U.S. Steel and owner of the Oliver Iron Mining Company.

These discussions led Gannon and Madden to conclude—or maybe believe or even just rationalize—that U.S. Steel was going to settle, was promising to settle, the problem that had developed when the Oliver started moving Old North Hibbing; that is, what to do about the streets, alleyways, parks, and municipal buildings that were not moving from the original townsite.

But this is *not* what Gannon and Madden addressed when they made their announcement.

What they announced was that U.S. Steel and the Village had agreed that the Steel Trust *would purchase the Pillsbury and Southern Additions*! The public approval must have amounted to a roar with a settlement like that. There was a small 'ahem'! however. The price asked by the property owners in those additions had to be satisfactory. But that little problem seemed minor when compared to the next piece of news. Mike Godfrey and the other local officials of the Oliver—and that included W.J. Olcott—had not even the foggiest idea of what was going on. Nobody, it turns out, had talked to them, not Gannon, not the Village Council, not judge Cary, nobody. *That* was strange.

To Tipple A Prince

"Corporate" had not told them of the deal—if there had been one —although it would have been a little out of place not to have a least rung the locals up about the situation but the Village Officials had gone off and negotiated directly with U.S. Steel and completely by-passed the Oliver, the organization most directly affected by the deal. Godfrey and Olcott must have been livid. They had no idea this was in the works and must have been perplexed at the very least. Madder than a hornets nest also comes to mind.

Godfrey wasted no time putting out that no local mining official and that included Olcott, had received any word from the New York offices regarding any such agreement nor had they been informed officially of the visit to New York of Messer's Gannon and Madden.

Godfrey then traveled to Duluth to meet with Olcott and others. He could not be reached for a quote but he did put out a statement that

Hibbing from the air, 2002. Looking northwest. The large, white roofed building in the left center is the "new" municipal auditorium. The Blessed Sacrament catholic church is at the bottom left and the high school is just peaking out at the bottom right. Author's Collectioon.

his visit to Duluth had no connection with the purported "agreement" between the Hibbing officials and the Steel corporation heads.

That was about as likely as birds flying backwards.

Gannon was not to be deterred. He published a statement that as a result of his visit to New York all that stood between the reuniting of North and South Hibbing through the purchase by the Oliver- who did not seem to be part of the deal—of the Pillsbury and Southern Additions was a reasonable attitude on the part of the property owners—apparently Gannon had left them out of the discussion as well—in those additions in fixing the price at which they would sell their property.

He said he would appoint a representative committee of businessmen to negotiate with individual property owners in these additions to the end that complete and detailed figures as to the price fixed on each parcel of property in those additions could be laid before the mining interests. (Perhaps like a sacrificial offering.)

It was generally conceded that should the Steel corporation purchase the property in the two remaining forties in North Hibbing, the purchase would be made on the basis of actual property values and not on the presumption that the two forties were overlying rich iron ore bodies.

There it was anyway. Hibbing would be re-united. The west plat of the original townsite would be joined with the two remaining siblings that had not moved but how this was to be accomplished was in the rush of euphoria, overlooked. That part of the town that had not moved and indeed at first did not want to move, would now be moved.[15] The largess of the mining companies was suddenly boundless.

Godfrey and Olcott said nothing. Strangely enough U.S. Steel wasn't saying much either.[16]

Something got messed up somehow but no one seemed to know just what was correct and what was not.

To Tipple A Prince

New York, Again
Judge Gary had sent a telegram to the Village Council summoning them to his office for an 11:00 a.m. Monday morning meeting. So, it was back to New York. And more talks. This time though the Village blew the budget on travel. The entire Council took the train trip along with all members of the Commercial Club.

The local Oliver officials apparently took their own train.

What exactly transpired on this trip was not clear either. The meeting seemed to take place at the appointed time and place but continued at Judge Gary's home later that evening. The participants this time included W.J. Olcott, Penticost Mitchell, and Frank Adams from Duluth and Michael H. Godfrey from Hibbing. The matter was then referred to the finance committee of U.S. Steel for evaluation.

On December 22nd the combatants returned to Hibbing, via separate trains. This time silence reigned supreme. Nobody issued any announcements. And the Court case, the Vacation Case, continued unabated. Whatever happened on this trip, it looked like everyone was told to put the lid on and wait.

Mike returned to his family and waited for winter and the courts to resume their journey. James, his oldest and Marjorie, who supposedly was retarded, returned to the University of Minnesota to resume their studies.

An Editorial by Walter W. Brown
This saga must have gone on just a bit too long and as journalists like to fill up silence with something important this was the perfect opportunity for the *Chisholm Tribune-Herald* to speak. Walter Brown, the editor took the time to pen a thoughtful essay. What he had in mind must have also been on the mind of others. He had excellent pitch.

> When Mayor Gannon of Hibbing made his first trip to New York to interview the "higher ups" in the U.S. Steel Corporation rumors were circulated about Hibbing that the impression the Mayor would make would result in

a regular volcanic upheaval in the Oliver Iron Mining Company and many a High Official would be dropped into the pick and shovel brigade in the shake-down that would follow. But the wise ones in Hibbing and elsewhere on the Range shook their polished domes [Ed. Note: *that was unnecessary.*]. Taking local affairs over the heads of capable men who were paid for considering just such affairs seemed a waste of time and an additional expense in money and idleness to the community which needs employment for its citizens more than anything else.

Mayor Gannon created an impression all right but it appears to have been with the people of Hibbing rather than with the United States Steel Corporation and the impression created sums up now to be *that the wrong thing was done in decidedly the wrong manner* [Author's emphasis].

Gannon was stumbling, whether from inexperience or just decidedly bad ideas poorly implemented is hard to tell but he was creating problems instead of finding solutions. The sort of thing voters and potential rivals notice.

And notice he did.

He's Back

Vic Power was a lawyer as was John Gannon but Power was also a politician of somewhat finer instincts than Gannon and he had the right sense about this moment. It was time to maneuver himself back into the Village's limelight. A mass meeting was held in the Flower Auditorium on the 18th of February to test the political waters. A committee of seventy-five concerned citizens, representing various political factions and individual groups, talked to the former mayor and learned that he was willing to become a candidate only if a majority of Hibbing's citizens convince him. Why should I run if it looks like I am about to be trounced?

Public support was there and so was the necessary financial support: businessmen in large numbers were there with funds to support a campaign. Power was in, the race was on.

The first week in March saw over two hundred businessmen and other professionals meet to see what had to be done to, as they put it, "give Hibbing a chance."[17] The meeting was chaired by Con Keppel who had good words for Gannon, but he pointed out that John had only been in Hibbing for three years and did not have the local experience, knowledge and trust necessary to solve issues that had a long, local history, some twenty-five years of history in fact. Keppel next sounded a typical Power theme: in that the prosperity of Hibbing depended wholly upon the mining industry, it was a suicidal policy to fight that industry. A more refined way of saying Don't Bite the Hand That Feeds You. Gannon, he noted, used rhetoric that set up the mining industry as an opponent that had to be fought to the finish.

The Flower Auditorium was packed for a second time in a month while thousands cheered Power as he delivered a speech on the Village's economics. His point was that books can be juggled to make sound fiscal policy appear as extravagance and his administration was more fiscally conservative than Gannon's.

The public "bought" it. Power won handily, 3,068 to 2,787 with Hibbing's fourth ward providing the winning margin. The paper called the incumbent and asked him if he was conceding and he shouted "No!" loud enough to be heard all over St. Louis County. Then he hung up the phone.[18]

Vic Power was back but he did not intend to stay.

Power for Senator
Power won his local election, the tenth of his career after a year's hiatus where he had time to consider what to do next. I think he concluded that as rewarding and satisfying as practicing law was and as fulfilling as being mayor was, maybe it was time to make laws for a larger audience. At this juncture in his life he was not going to have the extravagance of waiting awhile and taking a shot at the larger limelight later on. Time to go for broke.

He filed for the un-expired term of the late Senator, Knute Nelson. He had been mayor ten times.

Hibbing High School under construction. This is in 1923. The view is looking south from Mesaba Street. Notice the railroad spur that was needed to haul in the heavy stone for the building. Aubin Studios.

The former mayor, John Gannon, was asked if he had any comments on Vic Power's new candidacy and he was quoted as saying, "I cannot say that I would endorse Mr. Power. I shall have to wait and see who else files. Maybe someone else from Hibbing will file."[19]

He needn't have been so lukewarm. Power got plastered in the primary, losing by a margin of 4 to 1. Now, however, he had the bug. He'd be back for the big prize again.

Summer Returns

There is little time for long reflection on the Mesabi Iron Ore range. The four seasons make certain of that. As soon as winter is over, equipment must be readied for the summer mining activities and the hoards of other activities that have been postponed for months waiting for the chance to travel without getting caught in a blizzard.

Mike Godfrey managed to keep busy with his day-to-day activities as spring dictates long hours of preparation, not to mention the necessity of proving to the corporate heads that you are ready in report after report. Toss in a court case or two and you have the makings of a busy schedule. June saw Olcott, Mitchell, Hearding and others visit Chisholm, Hibbing, and Coleraine for an inspection tour. They were accompanied by the fee holders who wanted to take a look at their investments. The parties arrived on the special Oliver train car, the *Northland*. Since Mike was at one time head of each of these districts he was put in charge of the briefing. He probably could have done it in his sleep.

In August you could probably have pardoned him if he gave a silent groan or two. This time he was in charge of entertaining, educating, and touring with all 250 members of the Lake Superior Mining Institute. Their president, Francis J. Webb, wanted his institute to have the full tour of all three districts but naturally the biggest of the three, Hibbing, was the most important site. The Hull, the Rust and the Mahoning were then and are now, impressive.

The Androy Hotel hosted the banquet at 7:00 pm after the all day tour. By this time 300 guests had managed to finagle an invitation to dinner (wives usually skipped the excitement of touring the largest man made hole on earth but dinner was a different story and the Androy was a first class hotel). Toasts flowed freely and Mr. Webb led the parade with, "It gives us great pleasure to be in Hibbing tonight. The last meeting here was in 1913 and the next one is in 1928 and if your entertainment is as good as it was in 1908 and 1913 and tonight, then I think that we might make it every three years."[20]

One another thing Webb made note of is worth recording. He mentioned that the LSMI was first organized in Iron Mountain, Michigan in 1893 and several of its charter members were in attendance that evening, among the notables was the host, Mike Godfrey. And Webb went right to him: "We would now like to hear from Mr. Godfrey, District Manager of the Oliver Iron Mining Company in the Hibbing District." Mike was gracious as always mentioning that, "the mayor had been called from the city and could not be here tonight to welcome the guests. I am extending to the members a hearty welcome to Hibbing. We trust that you will enjoy every moment of your stay while in our midst and hope that it will not be many years before you will make us another visit."[21] They came back in 1928.

Autumn Returns

The summer passed and autumn arrived. Traditionally, the mining companies took a look at their production records for the summer and added an extra shift or two if some quotas fell short but for the most part things merely slowed down as equipment was banked, ore was stockpiled or rushed to market and men got ready for unemployment and the deer season. This was always a good time to hand out a few rewards for good service or good performance.

Oliver's Safety Record

One emphasis that permeated the entire operation on the Mesabi range for the Oliver was safety, a prime concern of Mike Godfrey's since his younger days in Michigan's upper peninsula mining industry.

Two months after the Lake Superior Mining Institute was feted the Oliver's General Safety committee which Mike Godfrey was the general chair of, met in Hibbing to, well, gloat for a bit. In September the Oliver's Lake Superior operations, comprising over 12,000 employees had only eighteen lost time accidents.

John Gannon as he appeared on November 12, 1922 adorning the front page of the *Hibbing Daily News and Mesaba Ore*. He was being profiled as one of Hibbing's Community Builders. *Hibbing Daily News and Mesaba Ore.*

To Tipple A Prince

Godfrey opened the morning sessions by commending local committees and employees of the company for their efforts to make safety effective. He stressed that officials of the company were as enthusiastic as ever to safeguard the health of its employees. He closed by reminding the group that vigilance had been shown so far was just the beginning.

U.S. Steel is credited with being largely responsible for the progress made in the promotion of safety methods and appliances in the industry, and the meeting in Hibbing established Steel's mining division as being in the front of the procession.

The Androy hosted the hot turkey luncheon for 190 people and served the entire crowd in just thirty-nine minutes. It seems that everyone was going for one kind of record or another.[22]

One Case Settled

In an unusual legal move, attorneys' Gannon, Strizich, and Farnand, representing L.H. Milkes in a civil law suit for damages against the Oliver, moved for a dismissal of their own case. The lawsuit was launched to recover alleged damages against the Oliver in the amount of $43,000.00.

Milkes had been a Old North Hibbing merchant who moved his business south to the new Central Addition of Hibbing (to Howard Street) and felt that misrepresentations made by Mike Godfrey caused him to lose money. It was Milkes' contention that Godfrey led him to believe that all businesses in the New Hibbing would be on Howard Street (which was nearly the case) and that the Kerr and Penobscot locations would be moved east of their current locations (west of the main body of the Village). For one reason or another, Milkes felt he was also due some compensation for the higher operating expenses of his new store (the old one cost less to run).

The request was denied. A small victory for Mike and the Oliver but a victory nonetheless. Along with testifying in the Vacation Case, Mike must have felt he should take up quarters in the court house. He practically lived there in April.

Daniel W. Lynch

Open Pits Do Not Have All the Ore
Even though open pit mining operations outnumbered "shafts" (a miner's reference meaning underground mine) by a margin of four to one, they could still be economically viable. The Oliver was certainly not against making a profit and would from time to time open an underground mine in the Hibbing District. They opened one in November of 1923, slightly south of Chisholm, northeast of Hibbing and it was called the Glen. It was to employ some twenty-five crews of miners to operate. The Glen underground mine spawned a well-known Location, complete with school, location recreation center, and a first rate train depot. It also progressed to an open pit mine where the ore was milled.[23]

Another "Shaft" Proposed
Mike Godfrey had now worked for the Oliver for nearly thirty years. His endeavors had taken him from bookkeeper to district manager. He had headed the three major districts in the heart of the Mesabi Iron Range: the Virginia, the Canisteo and now the Hibbing. He originated, planned, and carried out the moving of one Forty in Hibbing to another, established safety as the prime concern of his mining operations, and was virtually untouched by the periodic labor problems that plagued the range. He loved a good story, drank little, smoked less, fathered eight surviving children and buried one wife. He was also an absolutely horrid driver and never mastered the art of steering the damn contraptions where they were supposed to go. His driving experiments to Duluth and back were frightful ordeals and the children, his oldest daughter Miriam for one and his next to the youngest, Jane, were looking foreword to their father's next promotion, which was to be the Oliver Headquarters in Duluth. No more trips over that hill.

Mike did not know it but the Oliver had something else in store for him and sometime in 1922 they started to make it a reality. In a remarkably well-preserved map with the Meriden Iron Company signature stamped in the lower right-hand corner, their map of the Hibbing-Chisholm and Vicinity mining areas, dated January 1, 1923, the Glen mine and location are shown clearly but the real interest in this document is a label just south of those points, 2,500 feet due south of the Glen School, 2,000 feet east of the Alexandria No. 2 underground mine. On a Wellington R. Burt fee holding, there is a spot clearly labeled "GODFREY."

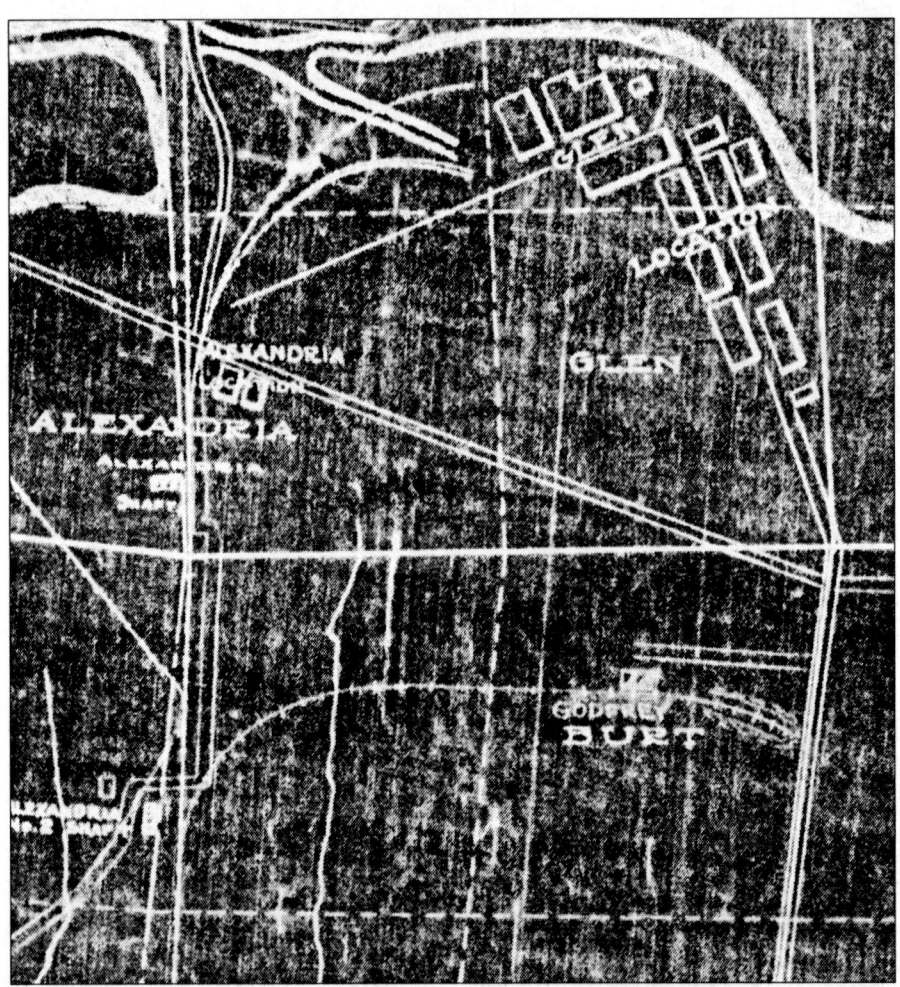

The Meriden Engineering Map, dated January 1, 1923, is the earliest indication so far uncovered that the Oliver Iron Mining Company had something special in mind for Mike Godfrey. They were going to name the most modern underground mine on the Mesabi after one of the best known, most able, and most popular mining men on the range. It is in a minor way also significant because Mike, who earned his spurs running some very large open pits, notably the giant Hull/Rust/Mahoning complex, first started working for the Oliver in an underground operation.

Mike was near the apex of his career and he was surrounded by friends and family. He had moved into the new home that the Oliver had built for him and his large family at 404 Mesaba Street. This place was built for someone with a large family having eight bedrooms and seven bathrooms. The first floor had a living room with a fireplace, a breakfast room, a kitchen and servants' rooms. A beautiful oak spiral staircase led to the upstairs sleeping quarters. The garage had an upstairs living area for the chauffeur.

Another Go for Gannon

Vic Power spent much of 1923 coasting and staying out of the public eye which is not a good thing for a politician to do. But he had other political plans and they did not include running for mayor. John Gannon did run for mayor and easily defeated Ray Keis 3,382 to 2,870.

The General Manger's house at 404 Mesaba Street. This is the back of the house and a portion of the garage can be seen on the right side of the picture. The girls had the bedrooms on the second floor and the boys had the dormitories on the third. The blue spruce on the property were apparently planted when the house was built. The dwelling faces the Village Hall. The original phone number was **100**. The picture was taken in 2003. Author's Collection.

To Tipple A Prince

At this time Mike could see most of his family. Agnes Eleanor, his youngest, was nine and living at home[24]. His eleven-year-old daughter, Jane Winifred, livedat home and going to school. Elizabeth Ann was thirteen and in school. James Robert was twenty-four and his occupation was given as bookkeeper. He was still living at home. Marjorie Helen was twenty and living at home. Paul Francis was eighteen and was employed as a laboratory technician for the Oliver. He was living in the garage apartment (instead of the chauffer). Miriam, twenty-two, was living with her brother Tom, at 411 Sellers Street. She was teaching part time in the Hibbing school system. Tom was a fireman for the Oliver. In addition to this bunch, Mike's siblings and Father are all living in or near Hibbing: William Emmett lives the furthest away, about four miles, in the Mahoning Location.[25] This clan got together with friends during the New Years' holidays at the patriarch's home for a picnic supper. The new Mrs. Godfrey was fond of such ideas.

The Spoils

John Gannon had been out of office for a year but was still burning with the fire of a zealot as he took the reins of his second administration. He promised a one hundred per cent change in policies. That sounded a lot like heads will roll and sure enough they did. On April 1st sixteen political plums were distributed to loyal supporters. John T. Naughton got Special Village Attorney so that he could oversee the legalities in building the new recreational arena which was to be built with a new $400,000.00 bond issue. This passed in June.

Power Makes His Move

Vic Power was virtually assured of the Republican nomination for congress in the eighth district when he ran in June. He trounced his nearest opponent by nearly 3,000 votes. That was the primary, the general election was different and here Power lost a close one to Congressman William Caras. Power's political days were over.

Daniel W. Lynch

Business as Usual

As Vic Power returned home to spend time on his farm and John Gannon figured out how to run the Village smoothly, Mike Godfrey got on with the usual business of running the Hibbing District for the Oliver. Iron ore was much in demand in the early part of the twentieth century for the building of the industrial giant that was the United States between the Wars and the Oliver and Mike Godfrey were in the forefront of that industry.

In July of 1924, the Oliver played host to the financial officials of numerous U.S. Steel's subsidiaries, twenty-five U.S. Steel managers, and a number of Duluth-based officials of their own. These parties were given tours at the eastern end of the Mesabi and then the next day they were given the royal treatment in the Hibbing District, Mike Godfrey presiding. Dinner was at the Oliver Club a block east of Godfrey's house.

For many of these men this were their first hands-on introduction to iron ore mining and their first view of the largest open pit iron ore mine in the United States, if not the world. Mike Godfrey made sure they were impressed when they boarded the special deluxe Oliver train and took a ride down into the complex known as the Hull-Rust-Mahoning.[26] When they were done with that experience, off they went to an underground operation, the Pioneer.

As soon as that chore was done, Mike attended the Safety First meeting in Iron Mountain, Michigan, where he presided. His party returned on the 22nd of July.

In August, parental responsibilities took over when Mike's twenty-five year old banker son, James, was seriously injured in an automobile accident near Ely. The details never were made clear but the accident probably occurred when James' car was side-swiped six miles outside of Ely. James suffered a skull fracture and was hospitalized in Ely. Dr. Blacklock rushed from Hibbing to Ely to treat James, who recovered.

To Tipple A Prince

Oliver Clubhouse in 1921 after the move from Old North Hibbing. To the north of it the large building in the background is the Androy Hotel. If you stood on the front porch of the building you could see the Village Hall, the Rood Hospital, the Androy of course, and Mike Godfrey's house. If the streets in the photo, Fifth Avenue East and Mesaba Street look unpaved, they are. The block in front of Mike Godfrey's house was the last one paved in the Central Addition after the great move.27 Aubin Studios.

Nineteen twenty-four ended with Vic Power off in semi-retirement, John Gannon again trying to see what he could do to re-shape Hibbing and somehow make it less dependent on the Oliver (or at least less responsive), Mike Godfrey at the top of his game and with the Vacation/North Forty legal quagmire as unresolved as ever. What had not changed and, what wouldn't, was the status of the Pillsbury and Southern Additions: they weren't going anywhere regardless of how much time was spent in court.

Notes

[1] The leading spokesman for the family was Miriam as she was the oldest daughter and quite close to her father. She was also by this time a graduate of Barnard college and was a substitute teacher. Other family members would from time to time buttress her comments with some of their own. It may have been hindsight on Mike's part when he recalled this court case as Hughes was a relative of John Gannon, who in subsequent years also took issue with the Oliver and Mike Godfrey. It was one of those, "if its not the judge, it's the mayor" things.

[2] The *Hibbing Daily News and Mesaba Ore* of March 10th.

[3] Buildings require excavated foundations and this award went to the McGovern-Wring Company with its bid of just under $5,000.00.

Daniel W. Lynch

[4] The auditorium was the last part of the school to open. It was dedicated in January of 1924 with a week of festivities.

[5] December 15, 1923.

[6] At the same meeting Gannon dropped a bombshell: he claimed that the attorneys in the North Forty Vacation Case had never asked for nor ever received any compensation for their efforts. He was not challenged on this assertion. Whether or not he was correct, it certainly made for good drama.

[7] That is on the Old North Hibbing side, not on the Pool location side.

[8] The *Hibbing Daily News and Mesaba Ore* was of the habit of referring to the 'Administration of Vic Power'and in referring to the "Rule of Gannon".

[9] August 16th.

[10] Greenbush.

[11] They were not recovered.

[12] *Hibbing Daily News and Mesaba Ore* of September 7, 1922.

[13] As quoted in the November 30, 1922 edition of the *Hibbing Daily News and Mesaba Ore*.

[14] *Hibbing Daily News and Mesaba Ore*.

[15] On or about January 10th, Gannon put a price tag of $5,000,000.00 on the surface rights in those two additions.

[16] What Gannon and the officials of U.S. Steel actually discussed will never be known for sure for the parties involved starting issuing statements as soon as the meeting was over indicating that they were either in separate meetings or on different planets.

[17] *Hibbing Daily News and Mesaba Ore*, March 2, 1923.

[18] As reported in the *Hibbing Daily News and Mesaba Ore* on March 11, 1923.

[19] *Hibbing Daily News and Mesaba Ore*, May 26, 1923. Reading between the lines, that's lukewarm support. John and Vic were never the closest of friends.

[20] *Hibbing Daily News and Mesaba Ore*, August 31, 1923.

[21] *Hibbing Daily News and Mesaba Ore*, August 31, 1923.

[22] Mike Godfrey's brother, T.J., had some welcome news himself that fall. Washington D.C. notified him that he was now Hibbing's Postmaster. He expected to take the oath of office in November.

[23] More about this later as the milled ore was 'dropped' into an underground drift into a much better known underground operation that we will discuss in detail later. For now suffice it to say, that Mike Godfrey was involved.

[24] The addresses can be found in the Virginia City Directory for 1924.

[25] Mike, his Father Robert, Mother Brigit, brothers Thomas Jefferson, William Emmett, sons, Tom, James, daughters, Elizabeth, Miriam and Marjorie, are all to die in Hibbing.

[26] This reference to the "Hull-Rust-Mahoning" is the first time I encountered the triadic reference. The phrase became such a regular staple that it sounded more like a litany that an identification. This was the verbal and written order that the names were—and still are—given, with never a variance. And along with any conversational reference to "the Oliver"—never, "the Oliver Iron Mining Company"—passed into history as the accepted custom until either or both became legendary or mythical.

[27] It is not known if Mike appreciated the irony.

VIII

Where the Wind Hangs Heavy: 1925 to 1928

Introduction

The court case that wouldn't go away, didn't go away. It reconstituted itself with the litigants changing from acting in concert to acting individually, thus giving the case a new perspective: the North Forty acquired singular points of view. The Buhl/Kinney school district court case also picked itself off the floor to take another swing at the Oliver.

Minnesota's Mesabi Iron Ore Range was not—during this period of time that we have been describing—for the faint of heart or the delicate of constitution. The weather on the range can run the gamut from tropical heat and humidity in the summer months to brutal sub-artic colds in the winter. And this land with its extremes of heat and cold can be a depressing place as well. The leaden gray skies that dominate the days during any time of the year do not lend themselves easily to goodwill and cheer.

And in the 1890 to 1930 time frame that we are looking at, this entire area, known as the Mesabi Iron Ore Range was a frontier, every bit as much a frontier as the one that faced the first pioneers when they left St. Louis for the coasts of California. Hibbing in 1890 was a couple of huts huddled in a stand of pine. Outhouses were the bathrooms of the day and disease was everyone's companion. Medical care was no better than medical concern.

And death was never far away. Hibbing's pioneers knew that well: Frank Hibbing had died nearly a decade ago, James Gandsey (second mayor of Hibbing and father of Mike Godfrey's wife, Cecelia), Vic Power's father, his wife, Frank Hibbing's widow, Leonidas Merritt—all gone from the scene.

A Good Start

The first three months of 1925 were typical gray, cold, blustery days on the range with not much in the way of the unusual happening but when it was time for Cal Coolidge to be inaugurated everyone at the Oliver's South Rust headquarters complex off First Avenue in the Southern Addition was granted the opportunity to listen to the ceremonies courtesy of Mike Godfrey. He had a special aerial installed on the roof of the headquarters building and a special radio installed in his office for anyone to listen to. No one could remember that happening before. The staff spent the better part of half a day listening in.

Later that month, Mike held the regular Safety First meeting in the Oliver Clubhouse on Fifth Avenue. But this was not the usual dull, pedantic presentation of awards and precautions that marked most of these meetings. This one came complete with cartoons for the kids and a Hollywood production for the adults. Then came the safety talk.

Hibbing continued to grow from a collection of huts in 1893 to over seventeen thousand people in 1925. The new Hibbing was looking like an attractive place to live after all.

But Then

It seems that the Buhl school district court case ruling against the Oliver was not going to end the matter for all parties concerned. One party in particular, the National Contracting Company, felt that it suffered losses during the construction delays resulting from the Oliver taking school district #35 to court over the issue of proper expenditures for schools. They believed that the Oliver should pay them a half a million dollars damages. The Oliver felt otherwise. Judge Martin Hughes, presiding.

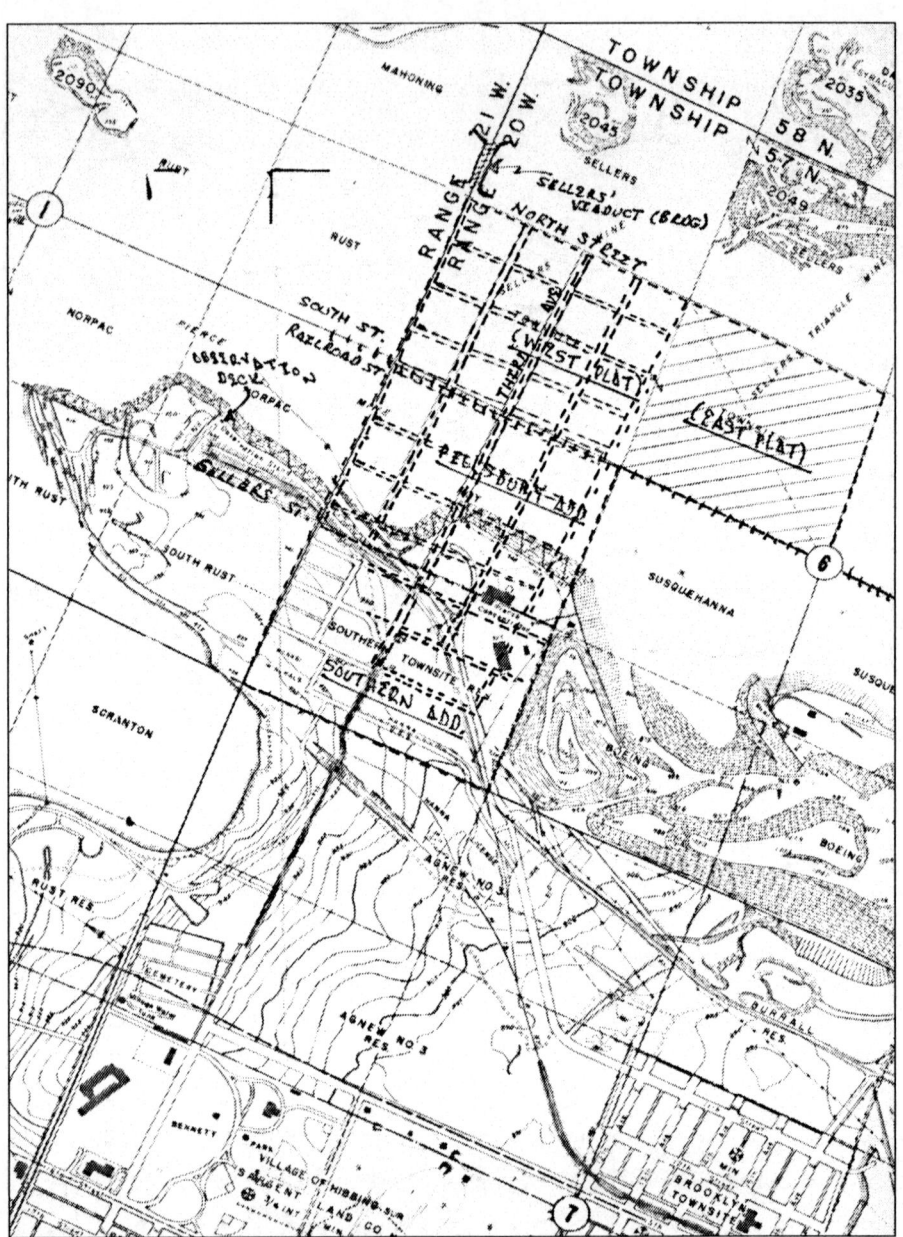

Where was the original townsite of Hibbing? Today, nothing of the original plat remains or of the Pillsbury Addition but a few streets and avenues from the Southern Addition have been preserved. Everything else has been swallowed up by the Hull/Rust/Mahoning open pit. The = = = = and ////// lines represent the four forties. Present day Brooklyn is in the lower right hand corner and present day Hibbing begins in the lower left hand corner. Today's Observation building is called out on this map as an Observation "deck." Hand drawn overlay is the author's. Original is U.S. Steel. Hull Rust Group. Plate 13, 1929.

Daniel W. Lynch

Was It?

On June 19th the *Hibbing Daily News and Mesaba Ore* carried the announcement that the NORTH FORTY APPEAL LOST. MINING COMPANIES WIN IN DECISION OF HIGHER COURT. Did this mean that the case was finally settled, once and for all, with this decision (which was the result of yet another appeal)? Four of the five judges of the Minnesota State Supreme Court upheld Judge Cant's original "Findings of Fact and Conclusions of Law," with only Judge Homer B. Dibell, dissenting and then only on one point.

Judge Cant found that there were thirteen million tons of ore in the slopes of the North Forty worth about $8,000,000.00 and that those tons could not be mined unless the plat was vacated. There were a number of other findings but as finds go there was nothing truly spectacular about them although one did stand out: there was no practical or feasible way of maintaining a highway across the North Forty (the west plat of Hibbing), except at a prohibitive cost, and that the advantages to the public would be slight.

However . . .

There remained Judge Dibell and his dissenting opinion. In it he said, "I do *not agree that the damages suffered* by the owners of lots south of the vacated forty are *all general and none special, and that none of the owners can be compensated.*" He felt that some owners could be compensated. His reasoning was that "a great traffic has passed for years over the viaduct and through the North Forty to the property to the south. *Property has been bought and improved with that situation in view.* So far as anyone knows there is not to be again direct access to and from the north. The property is less valuable for use, less productive of rents, and less salable. It might as well be surrounded by a river or lake incapable of bridging. No one at present sees a way of bridging them or passing through them. *The property has a use and value still.* The use, *at least of some of it*, will be restricted."[1]

To Tipple A Prince

But that dissent was enough. So, in late August, some 100 property owners, nearly all of them litigants in the original action, voted to appeal this decision all the way to the U.S. Supreme Court. In December it was announced that the Court would hear the case in April. In April the law firms of Gannon, Strizich & Farnand, and Anderson & Reed, and T.S. Silliman, announced that the date was pushed back to October. In October the U.S. Supreme Court rejected the appeal on the grounds that there was no federal question involved. The court did not even require the Oliver to present its case. And that was, well, it was not the end of that.

"The lawyers" said that as a group[2] [the Pillsbury and Southern Addition property owners] they can no longer hope to recover damages due to the decrease in property valuation that they allege followed an order which closed North Forty streets and alleys and in particular, the viaduct which spanned the mine and connected the north section of Hibbing with the Sturgeon Lake country. "As a group" was the telling phrase. And in the event that you were asleep, they spelled it out, "their *only* recourse now was to *take individual action against the mining companies* for damages allegedly occurring because of dirt and noise." These guys were reading Dibell's notes.

Back at the Pit

While claimants and their lawyers appealed decision after decision and the mining companies slogged their way through one court action after another and the residents of Hibbing tried to get on with life, the mining companies kept making *that* hole bigger and bigger and bigger.

By then, in 1927, the Oliver had a 350-ton steam shovel chewing away at the famous North Forty. The Hibbing Townsite was now a layer of dirt about 150-feet deep and covering an area of forty acres and it was gradually being transported to and piled on top of some very big stripping dumps. What remained wasn't much. The original townsite was now sixty feet of overburden.[3]

Daniel W. Lynch

In the last two years, the old viaduct that connected Old North Hibbing to every location, town, village, and lake side settlement was becoming more and more inaccessible, in fact it was not accessible at all. The southern end of the viaduct/bridge was three or four hundred feet from the original townsite and the northern end was nearly the same distance from a landside connection. The bridge was now an island in the middle of one gigantic hole. Only a stray bird could reach it.

A Few May Have Noticed the Passing

Not that it would have rated a national news headline but it did rate a headline in a New York Italian newspaper: Teofilio Pietrella, labor agitator and leader of the strike of Mesabi Range miners in 1907 was killed in June 1925, in Brazil, following a dispute over a loan. (His wife and son may have been killed with him.) Pietrella had left Hibbing, some said with the strike funds, and returned to Italy where he took a degree in languages and taught for a number of years in an Italian university. He also had served in the Italian chamber of deputies for a couple of years. Herman Antonelli was of the opinion that not many would find the time to deeply mourn Pietrella's passing.

But the men who made the news on the Iron Range were growing fewer in number.

Power Dies, Godfrey Is Seriously Ill

Almost a year later, a real giant of the Iron Range, Vic Power, died. On the day of his death the front page article could not have been more startling. The headline told a part of the story: VIC POWER 10 TIMES MAYOR OF HIBBING DIES SUDDENLY EARLY TODAY. He was forty-five years old. His father and wife had already died and Power had no children. He was to be buried in the family plot in Chicago, Illinois, where his wife and father were also buried.

To Tipple A Prince

Vic Power. Front page of the *Hibbing Daily News and Mesaba Ore* of April 6, 1926. The front page carried a double blow: Vic Power had died and Michael Hogan Godfrey was seriously ill with heart trouble. Power's wife had preceded him in death and they had no children. He himself was one of seven children. *Hibbing Daily News and Mesaba Ore*, April 6, 1926.

He died at home in bed in the Aviation Field Addition of Hibbing. He was found by the caretaker on the farm. Dr. Howard R. Weirick, after whom the main business thoroughfare of Hibbing was named, pronounced Power dead at 8:00 a.m. An era was closing.

Prior to Power's taking office in 1913, Hibbing had no paved roads, its fire department was horse-drawn, and its parks amounted to some grass and a tree or two. Power transformed that, turning a tax levy of $278,000.00 into one of $760,000.00. At that point Power and Hibbing went on a municipal roll of improvements and expansion until the Oliver starting playing the same form of hard ball. "The move" complicated matters but it succeeded in transforming Hibbing from a Village into a progressive voice on the Iron Range. Power himself was involved in the real estate development of Hibbing, investing heavily in the Park, Boulevard and Aviation Field Additions.

His funeral service was at the Assumption Hall Catholic Church in the New Hibbing. All business in Hibbing was suspended from 10:00 until noon in his honor.

Daniel W. Lynch

Hibbing Looks Back

The original townsite of Hibbing consisted of two "forties," (eighty acres) that were carved out from the lumbering interests of the Saginaw, Michigan, Lumber Company. Hibbing secured a lease from the lumber company and with the help of A.J. Trimble and H.L. Chapman platted the land and laid out the town's foundations. Pine Street became the town's main business street (it ran east and west) but by 1913, it was still a quagmire of sticky, stinky red mud, with the sidewalks over three feet above the mud level. Most buildings were wood and ramshackle and street lights lost the battle with the darkness. Power, who originally worked for the Oliver, changed all that after obtaining his law degree. Five years into his efforts to change Hibbing, the Oliver exercised the power of the purse and starting buying up the surface rights to the west plat of the townsite in order to mine the ore underneath. Hibbing would have to move but the consequences of that necessity spawned some very bitter court battles that ultimately the Oliver won.

Godfrey Seriously Ill

The same page that announced the news that Vic Power had died also carried with it another piece of sad news: the man who more than any other had designed, planned, carried out and wrapped up the details of the Great Move (and then spent the remainder of his career in and out of court defending it), Mike Godfrey, was seriously ill with heart problems.

What is unusual here is not the announcement that Mike had heart problems but that it was promulgated as something of a surprise. It shouldn't have been even (or maybe especially) to the public. Mike's illness had been public for sometime but perhaps his near miraculous recovery in 1918 had fooled everybody. He had been treated at the Mayo Clinic in Rochester, Minnesota but without too much success. Mike had then gone to Chicago where treatment was conducted for a period of two weeks, whereupon he returned to Hibbing. His sister, Agnes a

To Tipple A Prince

trained nurse, and his personal physician (also an Oliver employee), S.S. Blacklock, accompanied him while he was at the Mayo. Agnes accompanied him to Chicago as well.

This was all reported in the local papers although the nature of the illness was not specified.

Godfrey had also seen his health read into the public record in court when he was asked about a sequence of events that had occurred prior to the Great Move. He was quite clear about the date and the duration of the illness, from March to August of 1918. The nature of the illness again was not given.

Also not given public voice was the intention of the Oliver (since 1923) to open a mine south of the Glen underground mine and they were planning on calling it the Godfrey. They may not have told Godfrey about this but that is extremely unlikely as he was the district manager of that part of the Mesabi Iron Ore Range and he knew the industry, the major players and personalities like the proverbial back of his hand. Not much happened on his territory, significant or otherwise, that he didn't know about. Then too, he was being honored ahead of his time and that can make a man uneasy.

Mike Godfrey and his second wife, Mary, aboard a boat on Lake Esquagama southeast of Gilbert, Minnesota. This picture was probably taken in the Summer of 1925. Compare this to the other pictures of Mike Godfrey. He is thin, hollow-eyed and has the look of a man who has experienced just about all the pressure he wants or needs. The haggard expression and the body English spell exhaustion. Author's Collection.

Godfrey was in the Kahler Hospital, a part of the Mayo Clinic organization, where he had been taken during the day. His daughter, Miriam, and his wife, had been notified by telegram from L.C. Newcombe, who had accompanied Godfrey, from the Oliver's South Rust headquarters to Rochester. By the next day, he was in better shape but was still listed in serious condition. He was now surrounded by family.

On the eighth Vic Power's funeral was held.[4]

At first, Godfrey seemed to improve rapidly and was animated and talkative with family and friends but this did not last and he spent the better part of two months at the Mayo.[5] At that time he was sent home and it was noted by a reporter for *Skillings* that—quoting a Duluth source—Godfrey was much improved.[6]

A Death of a Kind

The Mesaba Street Railway Company which had a rough time of it on the Iron Range was facing the real possibility of dissolution according to a *Hibbing Daily News and Mesaba Ore* article on June 12th. Operating expenses for May had been $800.00 more than revenue. June looked worse and July looked worse still. The electric trolley car line had had a colorful history and had shown a profit, albeit a small one, for a few years but had been in the hands of a receiver for at least two years. The automobile and the bus had cut heavily into business—between Hibbing and Gilbert - and so too had the economies of the Great Move. The line had been forced to re-route its trackage, build overpasses[7] and pave between its tracks and none of this had been in the budget. Cutting off *that* bridge at the end of First Avenue hit the hardest, however. The tracks serving Old North Hibbing had been taken out in 1921.

The rolling stock (two cars still exist) in the Hibbing terminal building (which also still exists) was hauled off to Virginia for storage. That stock was never used again on the Iron Range. Holders of ninety-two percent of the stock, which local papers took considerable glee in mentioning were "Eastern investors" would receive nothing when the interurban line's affairs were liquidated.

The Mesaba Street Railway tracks in 1921, running down the center of Howard Street in the New Hibbing. The view is looking west and the photographer took this picture just east of Sixth Avenue E. with the trolley car's wye (to the right) just in front of the camera. According to folk lore, the tracks are still underneath Howard Street. That's the Androy Hotel dominating the south (left) side of the tracks. Aubin Studios.

Mike's Progress

In August of 1926, the Oliver let it be known that Mike Godfrey, who had been quietly recuperating at the Mayo Clinic in Rochester, was being transferred to St. Mary's Hospital in Duluth. The reason for the transfer was that Mr. Godfrey's condition was so serious that doctors feared a resurgence of his summertime hay fever would kill him. Duluth, with its summer weather conditions more subjected to cool breezes off Lake Superior was known for its low hay fever pollen count.

Interurban electric trolley Car No. 15 southbound on its Third Avenue tracks in Old North Hibbing. The Hotel Hibbing is on the right at the northeast corner of the intersection and the Congdon Drug Store is on the left (southwest corner of the intersection). The year is not given but it is certainly prior to 1921. The line went into receivership in 1927. It did not recover. Oliver Iron Mining photograph. Wayne C. Olsen Collection.

In September, Godfrey's condition was rated as "more encouraging."[8] His family visited in October for a few days and by November his condition was upgraded to "much improved in health."[9] Sometime early in November, while *Skillings* was going to press, he returned home to Hibbing. The date of his return is not exact but there was a reason to be at home if at all possible by the last week in November.

Recognition Goes Underground

The Oliver had as far back as 1922, reserved a "forty" for the digging of a new underground mine. This underground operation was going to be one of the, if not thee, most modern underground operations on the Mesabi. It was relatively soft ore and it was in an area known to be "wet." But the ore was of a very high grade, especially the western half of the deposit.

Right now for our purposes, its importance was in its dedication. It was being named after one of the best Oliver men the Mesabi Range had ever seen, Mike Godfrey. The name of the mine had appeared as we saw earlier on a Meridian map dated 1 January 1923, but that was a company held (private) document. Now, on November 11, 1926, the Oliver went public: OLIVER TO START WORK SOON ON NEW UNDERGROUND MINE. SHAFT, TO BE LOCATED NEAR GLEN, WILL BE CALLED "GODFREY" AFTER DISTRICT MANAGER.

The announcement specified that the work would begin immediately on the sinking of an underground mine shaft and the other necessary development work in connection with the opening of a new underground mine which was vaguely placed a half mile south of the Glen mine.

According to the announcement, it would be a year before ore would ship. The shaft would be a standard shaft with a steel head frame and other modern underground mining equipment would be installed.[10]

Ever mindful of the basic issues involved, the article in the *Hibbing Daily News and Mesaba Ore* went on to say that the opening of the new

To Tipple A Prince

November 24, 1926. Sinking the main shaft. There are three men digging in the holes with picks and two more with shovels on the perimeter. This is the first photograph of what was to become the Main Shaft of the Godfrey Underground Mine. The view is to the southwest from the crest of a 1,200-foot entryway that would serve as the D.M.&I.R. track bed to the site.11 Minnesota Historical Society.

mine in the Chisholm district would not mean an increase in the number of men employed, as diminishing operations in other underground mines of the district would release veteran employees of the company, who would be put on at the new property.[12] In other words, employed.

This was somewhat unusual for the Oliver as they generally did not announce the naming of a mine after a living employee and must have come as somewhat of a surprise to the miners on the range, particularly those who worked for the Oliver. The announcement was not only an honor but a precursor. Mike probably recognized it for what it was but he was both sick and isolated by family and friends who weren't going to tell him anything that would upset his recovery (as would happen a year later). Sometime on or before November 20th, about a dozen men took spades, shovels, drills, and other digging equipment to the top of a rise overlooking a rugged, barren stretch of land, and started to dig the main shaft to the mine. Work progressed rapidly. Winter was coming and the ground that far north can harden in a hurry. The miners quickly reached a depth of thirty-seven feet where they encountered bedrock. (It was from this level to the surface that the walls of the shaft would be lined with concrete, and from here to the bottom of the shaft that steel plates would line the walls.)

Skillings Mining Review published their article on December 11th.[13] The headline was brief and to the point: OLIVER IRON MINING CO HONORS M. H. GODFREY. The article reinforced and expanded on the lead:

> The Godfrey mine, soon to be opened by the Oliver Iron Mining Co in the Chisholm district, on the Mesabi Range, has been named in honor of Michael H. Godfrey, district manager of the company, with headquarters at Hibbing. Mr. Godfrey was the first general superintendent of the Chisholm district, when that district became an integral part of the company's operations some twenty years ago.
>
> No higher mark of merit can be gained by any man than to have his name given to a big industrial enterprise by the industry he serves. It is a fitting tribute to achievement. Mr. Godfrey's high standing in the Lake Superior Mining District amply attests that the distinction was deserved.
>
> The Godfrey mine will become one of the largest underground producers on the Mesabi Range. It will hoist not only the ore from the Burt Property, on which the shaft will be sunk, but also the ore from the adjoining Glen Property (i.e., to the north of the main shaft.)[14]
>
> The shaft will be of steel and concrete construction. Its five compartments will include two skipways, one ladderway, one cage compartment and one compartment for pipes and power cable. The head frame, stock pile trestle, and idler stands will be of steel construction. There will be built a combination hoist-compressor house, a blacksmith shop, and a change house thoroughly modern in its appointments.
>
> In the hoist compressor house there will be installed a cage hoist, and two air compressors each of 750 cubic feet capacity. All machinery will be electrically driven.[15]

The mention and emphasis on modern machinery and electricity was important. Open pit mines on the Range were taking over and if an underground mine was to compete, it had to use the latest in equipment and facilities. The drilling was to be electric (not steam), the transport of ore along the drifts as well as up the shaft, cage movement, all were to be powered by electricity. All major drifts were to be lit by electric lights. Fresh air was to be pumped into the mine and water pumped out. Creature comforts were not neglected either; the change house, or dry house, as it was sometimes called, had hot running water for showers, metal lockers, wooden benches, lots of windows to let in sunlight, and was surrounded by flower beds and shrubbery. The graded parking lot was to be a few feet away.

A Smaller Honor
In December, thirty-one service medals were distributed to Oliver employees who had put in at least twenty-five years with the company or its subsidiaries. The medals were shaped as watch fobs "as a token of appreciation of such loyal and faithful service and as a constant reminder of the friendship and personal interest that exists between the officers and employees of the Oliver Iron Mining Company."[16]

Work Progresses
On January 8, 1927, *Skillings* returned to the theme once again, reminding its readers that "the mine will be electrically equipped and will be served by a 300 feet, five-compartment shaft with steel head frame and modern surface buildings."[17] This was going to be more than a mine; it was going to be a showcase. To make sure that the showcase could be seen, the (disassembled) 100 feet steel head frame from the Alpena underground mine in Virginia, Minnesota. arrived on January 11th. (The Alpena had last shipped ore in 1920; its head frame needed some first rate maintenance after years of neglect.)

And the work of digging the main shaft continued, with a depth of 100 feet reached on March 5th. In this same article, it was stated that the Blacksmith shop had been completed and that the Change (Dry) house and Engine (Hoist) house were under construction.[18] Sixty more feet had been dug by April 2nd, remaining surface buildings were nearing completion, machinery was being erected on concrete foundations, and the head frame was in place (but reassembly was not yet finished).[19]

Olcott Breaks Tradition

W.J. Olcott, a man not known for his loquaciousness or his desire to give public speeches, showed up in Hibbing at the end of January 1927, and surprised everyone by giving a public speech of some duration in Hibbing. It was the first time Olcott had in fact given a public speech in Hibbing. He spoke for over an hour. He began his talk before the rotary club by describing his mining career and his presidency of the D.M.&I.R.

Olcott began his career, as had so many others, in the Upper Peninsula of Michigan right out of mining school. He, like Mike Godfrey, was forced to act as miner, bookkeeper, and accountant and inventory clerk. Later he went to the Gogebic Range and worked there as an engineer, chemist and draftsman. From 1901 until 1909, he served as president of the Duluth, Missabe & Iron Range railway before joining the Oliver.

Olcott had the good fortune in August of 1892 to accompany Frank Hibbing from Duluth to Biwabik by train. Arriving at the station they then rented two horses and proceeded to the 4,520 acres that Hibbing had taken an option on. Frank's headquarters consisted of three log huts and a couple of tents that housed, as Olcott phrased it, "bartenders and some persons that were worse than bartenders."[20]

The only mining that had taken place up until then consisted of some test shafts and the only record they had was a blueprint of what was known of the Burt Forty.

Then everybody got lucky.

As he related the story, you could almost hear his relief at his good fortune. The mineral rights holders, or as they are also known, the fee holders,[21] who controlled the Mahoning holdings, had held a survey of the ore supply in what is now known as the Mahoning Pit. When the survey was finished the fee holders concluded that they were standing on far more ore than there would ever be a demand for and decided to unload their fee rights. The Oliver took over but even they felt that maybe they had purchased a white elephant. Time and market conditions would prove them to be very poor prognosticators.

And to quiet rumors, Mr. Olcott spent time giving the highest tribute to Michael H. Godfrey, who Olcott recognized, was the man largely responsible for the successful operations of the Oliver Iron Mining Company on the Mesabi Range. He recognized that Godfrey had been sick for some time and was unable to engage actively in his work but nonetheless he was still the general superintendent of the Western Range District. Godfrey had the full support of the Oliver and it was on the record. This was a real change for Olcott; he was a man who preferred the anonymity of authority. His appearing in public to praise a subordinate was a radical departure from his normal business behavior.

Olcott stopped in and visited with Mike and his family before leaving. Mike was improving.

April 1927

In April the Godfrey mine entered shipping class status (as opposed to just digging the stuff up and storing it above ground). It was in the process of sending four cars a day to market. This was a record and the *Hibbing Daily News and Mesaba Ore* of April 24 rushed out with the news. The headline ran, "NEW GODFREY MINE, HEAR HIBBING, SENDS OUT FIRST CAR OF ORE IN RECORD TIME." The article noted that the Godfrey had rung up a new record in range mining history by shipping ore from the property within 142 days after the first shaft work was started. This was officially on April 12th. The shaft had reached a depth of 240 feet on April 24th. It isn't clear, as there are no direct, clear references, at what depth this ore was mined but it is known that the ore body surrounding the main shaft at the Godfrey was reached at a depth of approximately 227 feet and it is most likely that that depth is the source of the ore.

Daniel W. Lynch

Car 19063. The first shipment of ore from the Godfrey mine and some of the men (eleven) who made it possible. Mike Godfrey was healthy enough for the picture taking. He is kneeling in the front row on the right. The head frame is off to the left and the trestle is about 200 feet off to the right. Minnesota Historical Society. Album III. 14.6.

Coleraine Pays Tribute

The editor of the Coleraine paper—as quoted by the *Hibbing Daily News and Mesaba Ore*—had some kind words to say about Mike Godfrey with the Coleraine homecoming just around the corner (June/July).[22] It is couched in the form of a special invitation to Godfrey. "Just because a man does not live a thousand miles away from Coleraine," editor Lammon wrote, "is no sign that he will not be welcome at the Coleraine homecoming."

Lammon must have been around when Godfrey took over for John C. Greenway. He states:

> One of the most welcome will be Mike Godfrey, Hibbing District manager for the Oliver Iron Mining Company of which the Western Mesaba is a part. Mr. Godfrey followed the late John C. Greenway into this district. He is acknowledged both by miners employed by the Oliver and by independent concerns as *the best miner ever in charge of iron mining on the Mesaba Range*. (Author's emphasis.) Godfrey could make the dirt fly, he could get out the ore. That was his job, and believe us, he could do it.

> The past couple of years Mr. Godfrey has not been in the best of health, and his condition has been the concern of his wide host of friends, beginning with the man on the job and going all the way up.
> Everybody in Coleraine wants Mr. Godfrey to regain his old time vigor. He has been making a fight that only a man like Mike Godfrey could make, and he is reported as gaining. He says he is going to get well, and because of his pluck and determination his friends expect him to so we will all be surely looking forward to seeing him, and if puling for him will help any, every old timer in the district is doing that.

That was quite a tribute from "Greenway Country" where John C. was more revered than any politician or businessman in the Canisteo District. But Godfrey was remembered by the miners, the men whose safety Mike Godfrey had always put first. Reading between the lines, it would also be entirely possible that Mike on some occasion had reason to give Mr. Lammon a good quote or two. Godfrey made the dirt fly. He got the ore out. He did his job. We remember.

June 1927

On June 4th, another important step was completed out at the Godfrey mine. The cage hoist that carried men down into and back up out of the mine, was put into service for the first time.[23] By this date, the shaft had reached a depth of 235 feet, the massive headframe was in place, the main shaft was finished with concrete to a depth of forty-three feet, the shaft had been collared, the main buildings had all been constructed, and the first railway car of ore had been shipped. Not bad for a dig that saw its first shovel full of earth just eight months before. The work was on schedule in spite of the usual difficult conditions that so characterize a northern Minnesota winter.

The progress at the mine was noted by *Skillings* in its June 11th issue.[24] "Work," it said, "of cutting an underground station and ore pocket is now in progress at the Godfrey Mine. This underground construction is of steel and concrete, and fire-proof in every detail." The article goes on to mention that a new electric skip-hoist manufactured by the Lake Shore Engine Works was to be installed during June. As a reminder to its readers, *Skillings* mentioned that the cage-hoist and the air compressor were already in service (fresh air in abundance is a necessity when you are several hundred feet below the surface). Skillings also noted that the American Bridge Co. had completed the steel work on the head frame, stockpile trestle,[25] and the 16,000 gallon water tank.

On June 25th, the new electric skip-hoist left the confines of the Lake Shore Engine Works. Its duty was to operate the two five-ton balanced skips.[26] It too, was equipped with all the latest safety devices.

At the end of June, the digging of the main shaft was completed.

The table below briefly summarizes some of the milestones for the Godfrey Underground Mine.

The heart of the Godfrey underground mine was on the surface 940 feet above Lake Superior. This photograph shows head frame, trestles and idler stands under construction in May 1927. The view is to the northeast but the head frame itself is on a north /south axis with the "face" to the south. The mid-level trestle platforms structurally supporting the tram car tracks are forty-five feet from the ground and the head frame measures seventy-six feet from the ground to the center of the upper sheave wheels. Each tram car reaching the surface held approximately 27,000 pounds, about ten tons. Just out of the picture to the right is the Engineering House. From the air, this structure closely resembled a capital Y lying on its side with the stem facing East. The main drift also ran East for 3,000 feet. Minnesota Historical Society. Album III. 14.6.

To Tipple A Prince

November 20, 1926, (the Oliver Iron Mining Company official history uses the 30th).	Digging of the main shaft begins. W.R. Harkins in an article in Skillings in 1958, also places the date on the 20th.
Mid/late December	The Main shaft was collared at a depth of 4 feet.
January 11, 1927	Head frame arrives from the Alpena mine that Mike Godfrey had once supervised.
March 5th	Digging reaches 100 foot level.
April 12, 1967	First car of ore shipped.
July 30, 1927	Sinking of main shaft completed. Initial depth of 257 feet eight inches. This was the bottom of the ore deposit at this location. The ore at this depth was thirty-two feet thick. The main shaft eventually reached a depth of 311 feet six inches.
Godfrey ships 4,813 tons.	The OIM officially employed three men at the Godfrey site. Their average wage was $3.18 a day.

While his mine was becoming a reality, Mike and his family returned to the business of getting on with their daily activities. His first duty was playing hostess to a luncheon at the Mesaba Gold Club on the 29th of May. Mike's daughter Miriam was known to have visited friends at Lake Esquagama in July and attended a party for forty some people in Virginia later in the month. Mike was requiring less care than before.

U.S. Steel Pays Tribute

D.G. Kerr vice president of United States Steel Corporation headquartered in Pittsburg, Pennsylvania. was on the Iron Range in August in connection with his annual tour of properties and subsidiaries of U.S. Steel and he stopped by to see Mike and express great pleasure at his progress toward recovery. Things were looking up but it was more of a case of inching back from the edge a pit. Mike was better but he was not going to return to work anytime soon, if at all.

The visits from the upper echelon of the Oliver and of U.S. Steel were certainly morale boosters for Mike in this period and the well wishes were as sincere as realistic businessmen can make them but on occasion when you think about it, those wishes must have been as much like farewells as getwells.

October Leafs

The famous North Forty case was coming to an end. That's what the *Hibbing Daily News and Mesaba Ore* said on October 19th, 1927 in a burst of relief. The case was dismissed by the U.S. Supreme Court on the grounds that there was no federal question involved. In dismissing the writ of error and denying the application of the group of plaintiffs for a certiorari which would have required that the records of the case be called up for review, the high court stated it did not care to hear the Oliver's side of the case. This should have brought the case which at one time or another had nearly 400 Old North Hibbing residents / property owners filling claims against the Oliver, to a close.

However.

That bridge that last connected Old North Hibbing to the north side of the Hull/Rust/Mahoning where there were still numerous Locations, villages, towns and settlements, some of which are still there today, was still there. Out in the middle of emptiness, nothing immediately surrounding it, like the lone and level sands stretching far away. Like in Shelly's poem.

Hopes faded, said the article. The article did not say dashed, quashed, or crushed. It said faded. You could almost see the paper lower its editorial head below its newsprint shoulders as it went on to say, "as a group they [the plaintiffs] can no longer hope to recover damages due to a decrease in property valuation they allege followed an order which closed the North Forty streets and alleys and in particular, the viaduct which spanned the mine and connected the north section of Hibbing with the Sturgeon Lake country."[27]

To Tipple A Prince

The only recourse now according to the lawyers (C.G. Anderson, Gannon, Strizich, Farnand, and T.S. Silliman) was to take individual action against mining companies for damages occurring because of dirt and noise. This particular leaf would drop in January.

As a spectator sport this was one long contest to watch.

November's

Doctor S.S. Blacklock, for years Mike Godfrey's personal physician, had a decision to make, a difficult one. Should he recommend the family remain quiet, based on his medical opinion, or should he, fearing that someone would say something accidentally, recommend that the family "break the news gently" to Mike. His daughter Elizabeth Ann, his favorite daughter, a recent graduate of St. Mary's high school in Fairbault, Minnesota, had just died, four days after her seventeenth birthday.[28] She was the darling of the family, the studious one, the cute one, the frail one, and Mike had always found a special place for her in his life and now . . .

Mike was in bad shape, right on the edge between maybe getting a little better and prolonging his life, or slipping once more into an acute cardiovascular state. Blacklock recommended caution and the family decided not to tell their father. That must have been a very difficult decision as it would be next to impossible to keep his daughter's death from him for very long but it was felt that telling him now without first some improvement in his condition would deal too severe a blow to his health.

Where the Wind Hangs Heavy

Once again the North Forty case proved it was not dead. On January 7, 1928 a spark from the ashes nourished itself into a flame of litigation.

Ralph and Mark Erspamer who together ran a thriving hardware business on Third Avenue in the Pillsbury Addition launched an action against the Oliver (sued them, in other words) claiming that the mining company wrongfully cut the highway (the bridge) which was an outlet to the North country, cut the principal retail business street (Pine Street and Third Avenue) off from access to various centers of population and destroyed a highway that was never vacated. The sum of these actions cut into the brother's hardware business to the tune of some $59,000.00. The Hibbing law firm of Anderson and Reed were representing the plaintiffs. Reed certainly had the necessary experience.

Michael Hogan Godfrey

I doubt if Mike even knew that the court case his actions did so much to create was once again in the news. He was simply too sick by this time to care. He was bedridden and his bedroom was now on the first floor of his house, in front of the fireplace, looking out the window, to the Village Hall across the street. His Oliver, the company he had worked for going on thirty-five years, had donated that land to the Village of Hibbing for

The Hull/Rust from a thousand feet, looking East, in 2001. Much of this water has been pumped out but the water at the far east end has not. It is considerably deeper than the central part of the mine. The observation building run by senior citizens sits on the south face of the mine—your right—in the center of the photograph. Follow the road behind it as it curves around to the east and you will see a group of building foundations that represent all that is left of the mighty Oliver's South Rust headquarters where Mike Godfrey guided the company's fortunes and influenced those of Hibbing for over a decade. Hibbing is to the right, a mile or so to the south. Author's Collection.

Looking east across the Hull complex from the air in 2003. The water is lower now but the east end is another 150 feet deep and the water may never be pumped out. Author's Collection.

their showcase political center. It is still so today. The Oliver Iron Mining Company that had been his professional home was the single most powerful mining company on any of Minnesota's three iron mining regions. It does not exist any more. The Hull/Rust/Mahoning/Burt/Day/Sellers/Scranton and so on, mine, almost three miles long and a mile and a half wide has been a deep and dangerous lake for thirty years.[29]

Mike would not see any of that unfold.

Friday, January 13, 1928

T.J. had just come from a private meeting with Howard Weirick, Hibbing's mayor and a few village council members who happened to be in the building. Tom had just informed them that there was little or no chance that Mike would live through the night. His doctor had told the family that this was the end and to make Mike as comfortable as possible. His wife, Mary, and his children began the process of preparing for the worse. Even Mike's Oliver driver, John Fetzik was told of Mike's condition.

The temperature outside on this dark gray morning was twenty degrees above zero. Snow was steadily falling and would reach four and a half inches before letting up late in the afternoon. The wind was coming in from the west at about ten miles an hour. Hibbing was getting its usual blanket of early-in-the-year snow and since the sky was so overcast and the snow so thick and wet and dense, the Village left the street lamps on. Christmas was over but the holiday season had only subsided, not vanished.

Mike was aware only dimly of his surroundings as it was clear that he no longer had the energy or interest for anything but rest. His bed was on the first floor just to the right of the front entrance, next to the fireplace.

Tom walked across the street and talked to Mary Elizabeth (Aunt May to her step children) and then went back to the post office to give the employees there the bad news. Then he went walked home and

The living room fireplace in Godfrey's house on 404 Mesaba Street. If you stand here you can look over your right shoulder and see the Village Hall and if you twist a bit further to your right you can see the library, site of the old Oliver clubhouse. Mike had his bed here on the first floor for over six months as he could no longer climb the stairs. This picture was taken in 2003. Author's collection.

started to make calls. A prince of the range was dying.

Early that evening the entire family was aware of the situation and had begun to gather. Mike's seven surviving children were there, his wife, nine siblings, and his father, Robert.[30]

At 10:50 pm Mike Godfrey died.

The *Hibbing Daily Tribune* broke the news Saturday evening.

M. H. Godfrey, District Manager Oliver is Dead

The *Hibbing Daily News and Mesaba Ore* carried a similar story on Saturday evening.

The *Duluth News Tribune* carried the news on Saturday under the head, "M.H. GODFREY, OLIVER MINING OFFICIAL, DIES," and beneath that head the lead, "DISTRICT MANAGER OF FIRM AND MESABA RANGE PIONEER SUCCUMBS AT HOME."

The *Duluth Herald's* headline read, "DEATH TAKES MINING CHIEF," with a lead for the story, "M.H. GODFREY, MANAGER OF O.I.M. CO., AT HIBBING 11 YEARS, DIES."

Each of the articles reviewed Mike's history from his birth in Michigan's Upper Peninsula town of Champion, through his stint at the Post Office in Norway and his time with the Penn Iron Company to his arrival on the Mesabi Iron Ore Range in 1893. His career with the Oliver was recapped and everyone carried a notice of the funeral services scheduled for the following Monday at Assumption Hall.

R.W. Hitchcock in his editorial column in the *Hibbing Daily Tribune* wrote a personal obituary of Mike.[31] It is worth quoting in full.

> All Hibbing, all the iron ranges, all the great Lake Superior mining region sorrows in the death of M.H. Godfrey. The loss to Hibbing is a particularly heavy one.

Daniel W. Lynch

The mining of iron ore, linked as it is with the greatest, industrial and business enterprises of the world, naturally attracts as its executives and its operators men of unusual ability and attainments. Mr. Godfrey was not only a peer among these men, but in the many years he worked beside them and with them, his accomplishments were conspicuous. From one position of trust and responsibility he rose to another and then to another. Finally one of the greatest tasks[32] ever set before a mining executive in America's greatest iron mining region fell inevitably to his lot. He was the one man to do the work. He did it, did it kindly, did it nobly, did it brilliantly. Perhaps the toll and the burden of it broke down his health and cost him his life.

It is said that a prophet is not without honor save in his own country, but Hibbing always knew that Mike Godfrey was a great man. It respected, honored and loved him in his life time among us, it does so today in the sorrow of its loss, it will always be so.

It may well be said of Mike Godfrey: "Well done, good and faithful servant; enter thou in the joy and the reward that thine own uprightness hath prepared for thee."[33]

The funeral was set for Monday, January 16th.

Denouement

Monday arrived with sleet, gray skies, and a wind out of the northwest that cut skin.

At 10.30 a.m., Monsignor J.A. Limmer of Hibbing presided over a mass before a packed audience of several hundred in Assumption Hall for a Requiem High Mass. Father Powers reviewed Mike's career, calling attention to his many virtues, his reverence, his support of education, his tolerance, his love of his fellow man, his almost infinite patience, his devotion to duty and his great abilities.

Flags flew at half-mast in Hibbing, Coleraine, Chisholm, Virginia, Mt. Iron, and elsewhere along the iron range. The Oliver shut down its entire operations for two hours across the range in honor of one of their best known executives. Olcott attended the mass and funeral, J.H. Hearding,[34] assistant general manager was there, in fact, the entire Duluth office was there. The mining community weighed in with general managers, general superintendents, vice presidents, chief engineers, and presidents from Republic Iron and Steel, International Harvester, Cleveland-Cliffs, M.A. Hanna, Inter-State Iron, Meriden Iron Company, Winston-Dear, Donner Mining, Inland Steel, Great Northern Iron Ore Properties, McKinnery Steel, Butler Brothers, and representatives from three law firms.

Gravestone of Michael Hogan Godfrey. His grave is next to the grave of his first wife, Cecelia, who died in 1916. He and many other members of his family are buried in the family plot, Calvary Cemetery, Block 37. The plot is noted for its eight pine trees planted by Mike to honor his eight children. His estate in 1928 consisted of stocks, bonds, notes and cash and was valued at $260,000.00. This photo and previous photo are in Author's Collection.

Daniel W. Lynch

When the mass was over the procession motored to Calvary Cemetery in Virginia where Mike Godfrey had purchased a family plot when he lived across the street. He had loved the view from a high corner of the property and had told his family that is where he wished to be buried. He was accorded his wish.

While he lived he looked over the place where he was to be buried; while he was dying he looked over the section of a town he gave new economic life to. He would have appreciated the reminder.

A Reminder
Mike Godfrey was dead and much of what he did and accomplished resides in the Village of Hibbing. The part of the town that he moved is still there, businesses have come and gone, residents have left or died and their houses have been resold several times over but those dwellings, like the other buildings along Howard Street, and those scattered about the Central Addition, remain. Who built them or who moved them has long been forgotten but they are, for the most part, still there.

Another reminder of Mike Godfrey and the mining company he represented for so long was just getting under way, three and one half miles northeast of what is today the corner of Howard Street and First Avenue: the Godfrey underground mine.[35] The mine is now closed, the main shaft buried behind a ring of weeds and dying trees. It is some 1,200 feet east off the old Babcock Highway, just north of the Mitchell Yards' overpass and in 1928, it was thriving. It operated continuously for twenty-eight years.

Mike Godfrey's role on the Mesabi Iron Ore Range of Northern Minnesota ended over seventy-five years ago. Much has happened on the Iron Range since then that has obscured his role: the Great Depression which began a year after his death, a very slow mining and steel industry recovery, a war which saw not only the most massive iron ore shipments in history but which also completely depleted those deposits far faster than anyone imagined (in the twenties it was estimated that the ore deposits would last seventy-five to one hundred years), the closing of those empty pits in the 1950s, the development of a taconite industry some years later which has all but obscured the long, colorful, difficult, complex history of some of the largest man-made holes in the ground ever created and the men responsible for them.

So many changes, in fact, have occurred on Minnesota's Mesabi Iron Ore Range that the beginnings have been lost and it was just so, so, long ago.

The Prince Has Been Tippled.[36]

The heart of the Godfrey Underground Mine in operation in (approximately) 1950. The tramway half way up the head frame is forty-five feet above ground. The head frame is 100 feet high measured from the ground to the top of the structure. The ore cars are D.M.&I.R. cars and as they are filled they can be released and backed up to the right onto the 400 ft long trestle (the remains are still there). The ore pocket bin above the cars holds several cars' worth of ore. Aubin Studios.

Daniel W. Lynch

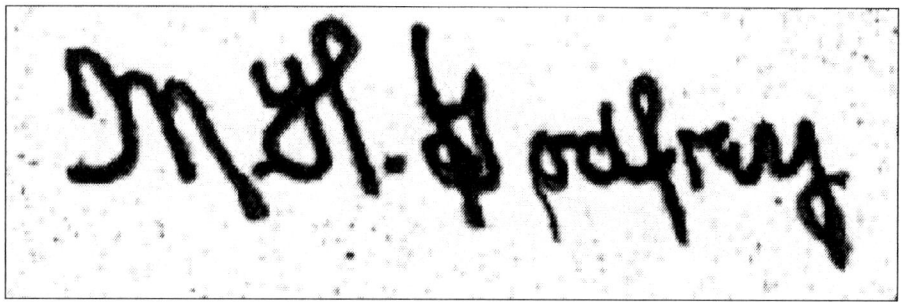

Notes

[1] Judge Dibell as quoted in *the Hibbing Daily News and Mesaba Ore* on June 19, 1926.

[2] As quoted in the October 24, 1927, *Hibbing Daily News and Mesaba Ore*.

[3] In 1908 the Oliver Hotel was built on the north end of Third Avenue and in April of 1926 it remained the only building on the north end of Third Avenue in Old North Hibbing. On the 24th it sustained fire damage of $1,000.00. The hotel was owned by the Oliver at the time. The damage was not repaired.

[4] On May 11th, Leonidas Merritt a pioneer, woodsman, iron ore discoverer, capitalist, soldier and Indian fighter died at home in Oneota. His parents had preceded him in death.

[5] His death certificate listed chronic myocardites as his malady. The only worthwhile treatment at that time was rest and plenty of it.

[6] *Skillings Mining Review*, May 29, 1926, Vol XV, No 3, page 11.

[7] The one on Third Avenue over the D.M. & N. tracks was over 100 feet long and made of steel. The double bridge over the Mitchell marshalling yards' tracks —which we will come to later, was 1221 feet and made of timber. It crossed over the D.M.& N. and the Great Northern railroad tracks.

[8] *Skillings Mining Review*, September 18, 1926. Vol. XV, No. 19, page 13.

[9] *Skillings Mining Review*, November 13, 1926. Vol. XV, No. 27, page 13.

[10] Essentially, the mine would be an all electric mine. The shaft would be ready for shipping its first car of ore in record time, less than a year would pass from first breaking ground.

[11] The caption for this photograph which is on file with the Minnesota Historical Society, Album III. 14.6, is formerly titled, "Sinking Shaft at Godfrey Mine". The caption does not refer to the footings were also dug at the same time.

[12] *Hibbing Daily News and Mesaba Ore*, November 11, 1926.

[13] *Skillings Mining Review*, December 11, 1926. Vol. XV, No. 31, page 1. As the masthead reminds us, Skillings was Published Every Saturday Morning. (This issue also gives the official beginning of the dig as November 30th.)

[14] It would also hoist ore from undergrounds to the west and the southwest.

[15] 440, direct.

[16] *Hibbing Daily News and Mesaba Ore*, December 15, 1926.

To Tipple A Prince

[17] *Skillings Mining Review*, January 8, 1927. Vol. XV, No. 35, page 15. This issue also contains the earliest photo I can find of the head frame. The original plans for the shaft, presently on file at US Steel's MinnTAC headquarters in Mt. Iron, MN., called for the shaft to be 311 ft 6 in down from ground level to the bottom of the sump.

[18] *Skillings Mining Review*, March 5, 1927. Vol. XV, No. 43, page 20. This article contained the first set of location clues as to the placing of the shaft: it was between the Leonard and Alexandria mines.

[19] *Skillings Mining Review*, April 2, 1927. Vol. XV, No. 47, page 20.

[20] *Hibbing Daily News and Mesaba Ore*, January 31, 1927.

[21] Also known colloquially as 'miners hemorrhoids'.

[22] *Hibbing Daily News and Mesaba Ore*, May 1, 1927.

[23] The hoist is an apparatus that consists basically of a generator with a cable attached to it that runs from the Engineering House—directly opposite the head frame—over supports called idler stands, up to and over some rotating wheels on top of the head frame and then down to a cage (to us an elevator) which is lowered taking men into the mine. Reverse the hoisting apparatus to bring the cage up to return the men to the surface. More about this later but for now let's note that the cage itself is not generally in the center of the shaft but in one of the compartments. In the case of the Godfrey, it is on the west side, and opens behind the head frame. The view as you step out of the cage is into the lumber yard.

[24] *Skillings Mining Review*, June 11, 1927. Vol. XVI, No. 5, page 7.

[25] The head frame is a very large steel structure that serves a number of functions. One function –and it is the primary one—is to haul ore up to the surface where it is placed in a large container called a bin to be gravity fed into a waiting ore car, or placed into a waste ore pile, if the grade is too low. If it is the non-shipping winter season, the ore is placed in a separate pile called the reserve. The skip cars will be directed to one of the three places by someone on the surface. There is also a third trestle but it is for stockpiling ore cars and is off in the corner of the site. On the Godfrey site, it is 400 ft long and runs northeast/southwest.

[26] The skips were ore cars that were filled with ore from just below the main hauling level below the main shaft. The ore was dumped into a steel bin down there and the skip cars were pulled to the surface by the hoist in the Engineering House (it operated on a separate set of idler stands, shaeve wheels, and pulleys. Its cable was in a different compartment from the cage's cable.)

[27] *Hibbing Daily News and Mesaba Ore*, October 24, 1927.

[28] The primary cause of her death was endocarditis of five and a half month's duration. She died in Rood Hospital in Hibbing, one block from where her father lay dying. Her heart gave out before her father's did.

[29] It is being pumped dry at the present time so that Hibbing Taconite can mine the 'new iron ore", taconite, on the north side of the mine and eventually from the bottom of the old dig. There is something, however, about gray ore that lacks the resonance of red ore.

[30] They were: his sons, James, Thomas, and Paul, daughters, Miriam, Marjorie, Jane, and Agnes; siblings, Robert, Thomas, Winnifred, Mrs. M. Allard, Mrs. A. F. Hein, Mrs. H. Tripp, Mrs. J. J. Cox, Mrs. John Ring and Miss Agnes Godfrey. The Irish of that era and place had a habit of coming from and leaving behind, large families. Death, however sad, was usually well-attended.

[31] *Hibbing Daily Tribune*, January 14, 1928.

[32] Hitchcock is referring to the moving of Old North Hibbing to the Central Addition of the New Hibbing.

[33] A bit over the top but well meant. On occasion, well meant gratitude can slip loose from the bonds of sensible discourse.

[34] He lived in Mike Godfrey's house in the late fifties.

[35] The fee holders at the time belonged to the estate of Wellington R. Burt, oft times referred to as the "fabulous" Wellington R. Burt. The five compartment main shaft for those who use GPS readings, is located at 47 27' 98" N & 92 53' 88" W. This unusual mine will be described in an Appendix.

[36] Stewart H. Holbrook, *Iron Brew: A Century of American Ore and Steel*, the Macmillan Company, (New York, 1939). The full quote on page 109 is as follows, "A veritable price of the range for many years was the late Mike Godfrey, who had charge of the great Oliver-Frick properties and bossed more mine captains - some of them as temperamental as opera stars—than any superintendent up to that time. Godfrey was rated a genius on the range and had a mine named for him, a positive accolade either of stature of wealth. In Godfrey's case it was stature."

Appendix A
Locating the Godfrey Underground Mine[1]

The Problem

Traditionally, neither open pit iron ore mines nor underground ones on the Mesabi Iron Ore Range have signs posted identifying them. Normally, the best indication that there is a mine nearby is a warning not to trespass. But most of those signs have been removed and the ones that remain identify nothing. If you know enough to have a USGS map, however, it will identify the mine by name. That, however, only applies to *open pit* mines. Underground mines are a different story.

Normally, you can walk right by one—if you are out in the woods on the Mesabi—and you will never know it is there, let along what its name is. On USGS maps there will be an 'underground mine' designation (but no name) or a warning that an area is a 'caved area', meaning a closed underground operation, but again, no name.

So, if you wish to find an underground mine (they are all closed now, none have been in operation for decades), how do you go about finding one? *Assuming* you want to.

The Simple Answer

You visit your nearest library or a local or regional historical society or the Minnesota Historical Society in St. Paul, Minnesota and ask for a copy of the *St. Louis County Inspector of Mines Annual Report*.[2] The mines are listed in alphabetical order by mining company so it is helpful, but not critical, to know the name of the mining company involved. In the case of the Godfrey Underground Mine, it was[3] the Oliver Iron Mining Company for most of its existence.

Digging of the main shaft began in November of 1926 and ore shipping began in 1927, so it is to that year that we go. And we find under the Oliver Iron Mining Company heading an entry for the Godfrey Underground Mine of:

SE-SE, Sec., 29 & NE-NE, Sec. 32 of T. 58, R.20W[4]

But only a geologist, map maker, or farmer would treat this as anything but hieroglyphics.

This is actually *not* the location of the Godfrey Underground Mine or the location of the main shaft (where you enter the mine) but rather it is the *area in which the main shaft is located* and the area where the fee owners own the mineral rights. The size of that area is forty acres and the somewhat cryptic designation above locates the Godfrey's forty acres where the main shaft is located. That's forty *acres*.

The Better Answer

In the late 1840s, the federal government began to survey the area that is now the state of Minnesota as part of the Public Land Survey (PLS) project. What the surveyors did was to take every six mile column between the Meridians on the globe (imaginary lines running north and south from pole to pole every fifteen degrees) and call it a Range. The ranges were then numbered consecutively from east to west starting at Range 1, immediately west of each meridian. The survey further divided the land into six miles between lines—from a baseline—running east and west. Where the north/south lines intersect the east/west lines the resultant 36-mile squares were called *townships*. Each township was then further subdivided into one mile squares called *sections*, thirty-six to a township.

That makes for a large number of identically sized townships scattered across the length and width of a very large country. But this system is amazingly flexible and can be used to identify virtually every forty-acre plot of land we have. So, how do we do that, how does it apply to the Mesabi Iron Range in northern Minnesota, and how does it help us find the main shaft of the Godfrey Underground Mine?

Minnesota falls into two township numbering *zones*. Townships in the west and south of the state are numbered from the Fifth Principal Meridian (PM) of the PLS system, and those in the northeast of the state from the Forth Principal Meridian. The result is twofold: all the Fifth PM township numbers are above 100 and all the Fourth PM numbers are numbered below 100. The second result of this is that there is an

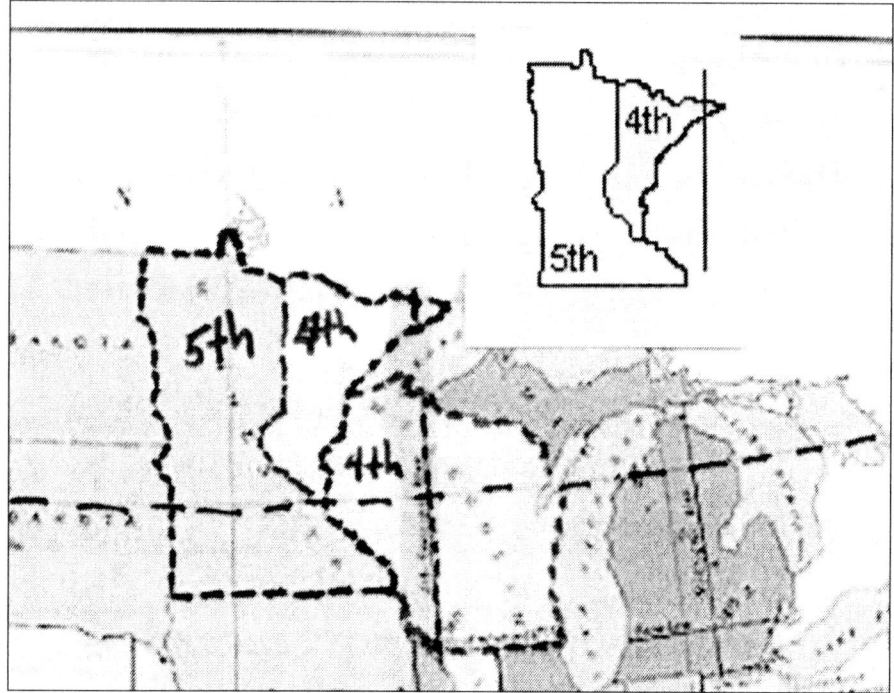

This is what the PLS surveyors created. The townships west of the 5th PM are numbered from 100 on up and those of the 4th PM are numbered below 100. However, there are townships on either side of the 4th PM resulting in the need to distinguish between them (see inset). St. Louis County where the heart of the Mesabi Range is resides in the western 4th PM. The broken line in the center of the graphic is the baseline.

anomaly because the Fourth PM passes *through* the state at the easternmost tip.

So, the townships to the east of the Fourth PM have an attached "E" and those to the west of the Fourth PM have a "W" to indicate which side of the line they fall on.

This helps to explain the "T. 58, R. 20W" reference: township 58, range 20 W(est) of the Fourth PM. (Another way to say this is that the reference is to the twentieth six-mile column to the west of the Fourth PM line.) Remember when we said that each township was subdivided into 36, one mile squares called sections? Well, our shaft is somewhere in Sections 29:32. That's two square miles of bog, swamp, river, forest, ore piles, overburden dumps, fifty years of overgrowth, and some wild life that doesn't appreciate your presence.

So, we have to narrow our search some more.

Narrowing the Focus: the 'Forty'

Each square mile (of the 36) is 640 acres (23,040 all together) but surveyors don't stop there, they further divide the 640 acres into four parts of 160 acres each. So, for each square mile section there are four parts, each of 160 acres and each with a designation befitting its position in the quadrant: NW, NE, SW, SE (upper left, upper right, lower left, lower right).

Each of these four quadrants of 160 acres is then divided again into four parts, this time of forty acres, each division carrying another two character alphabetic designation specifying its place in the smaller quadrant: NW, NE, SW, SE.

6	5	4	3	2	1
7	8	9	10	11	12
18	17	16	15	14	13
19	20	21	22	23	24
30	**29**	28	27	26	25
31	**32**	33	34	35	36

Daniel W. Lynch

There are thirty-six squares in the grid with each square representing one square mile. The surveyors numbered the squares in the grid beginning in the **N**ortheast (NE)-most corner (1) and "snaked" their way back and forth until all thiry-six squares had been surveyed. Square 6 was the Northwest (NW) corner, square 31 was the Southwest (SW) corner and number 36 was the Southeast (SE) corner.

Each square mile section was then subdivided into four quadrants, each quadrant representing 160 acres and carrying a designation:

NW   NE
SW   SE

Each of these 160 acre quadrants was then further subdivided into 40 acre quadrants carrying the appropriate designation. The result is that each section has sixteen-addressable forty-acre pieces called "forties."

Section 29   N   Godfrey Plot

NW	NE	NW	NE
NW	NW	NE	NE
SW	SE	SW	SE
NW	NW	NE	NE
NW	NE	NW	NE
SW	SW	SE	SE
SW	SE	SW	SE
SW	SW	SE	SE
NW	NE	NW	NE
NW	NW	NE	NE
SW	SE	SW	SE
NW	NW	NE	NE
NW	NE	NW	NE
SW	SW	SE	SE
SW	SE	SW	SE
SW	SW	SE	SE

W (left side)   **E** (right side)

Section 32   S   Godfrey Plot

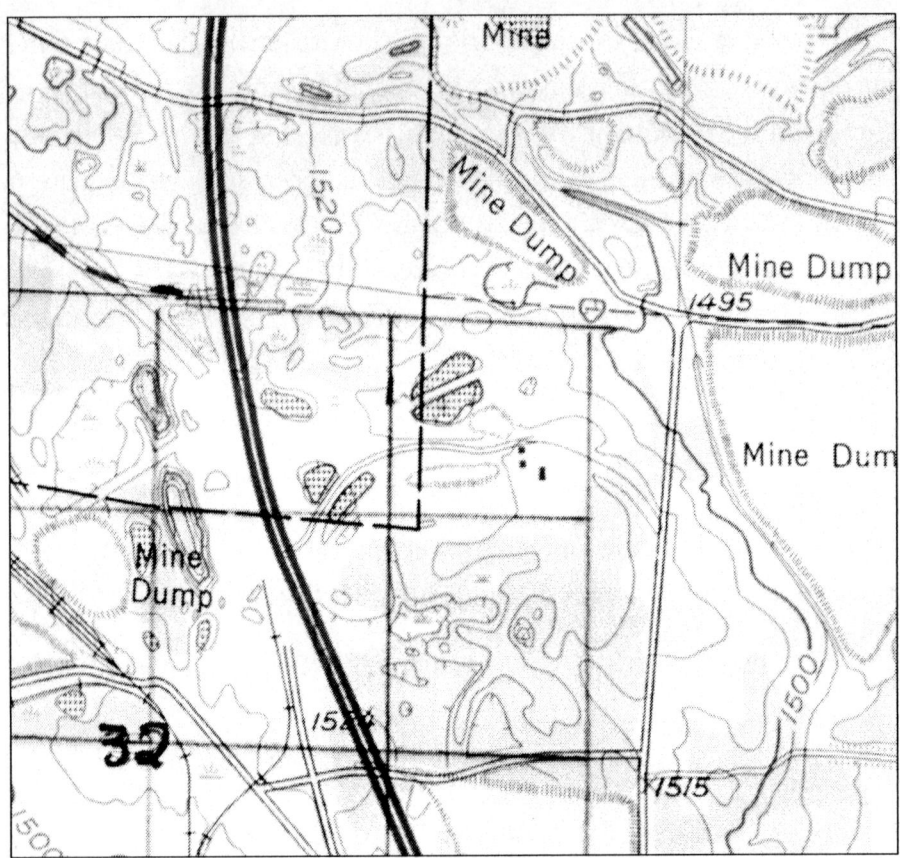

The Godfrey's main shaft is in the center of the USGS Quadrangle map which shows four forties. The site was last used for mining by the Snyder Mining Company which shipped ore from a reserve ore pile on the surface. A concrete mixing company used the water supply from the Godfrey mine for many years. It is now gone and only the building foundations from the Dry House/Heating Plant, the Hoist House and Cooling Plant remain. United States Geological Society.

Highway 169 is the heavy double line running down the left side of the map. The two full squares (top and bottom) on the right (east side) of Hwy 169 are the ones designated in the St. Louis Country Inspector of Mines Annual Report as SE-SE, Sec.29 & NE-NE, Sec. 32 of T. 58 R.20W. The shaft is just to the north of the three dark rectangles in SE-SE 29. The faint s-curving double line running east right up to the dark rectangles from Hwy 169 is an old DM&IR double railroad spur that served the mine.[5] Today, it's a gravel road.

The gravel road to the Godfrey Underground Mine main shaft in 2002. There are buried railroad ties on each side of this road. The view is to the east from Hwy 169. Current maps do not identify the mine or its shaft but for the modern generation the GPS coordinates are: 470 27' 98" N and 920 53' 88" W. The intersection of First Avenue and Howard Street is 3.4 miles to the southwest of the main shaft. Author's Collection.

After a 1,200-foot walk up a low grade this is what greets the summer visitor. This is the area surrounding the main shaft in August 1999. The heavy foliage obscures the 'chicken-wire' fence and posts that enclose the capped shaft. A concrete mixing company ran a water line into the shaft and pumped out all the water they needed, free. Today, even that operation has been plowed under. Author's Collection.

Same view in spring. Now you can see the small mound that surrounds the "chicken-wire" fence. The footings that you see are actually taller than a man and were embedded in the ground for stability. The two in front supported the cantilever that went to the Reserve ore bermed-in area. The fence is not designed to hold anything out; it's just a sign to avoid the area. Sometimes the shafts are capped, sometimes backfilled but they are not reliability filled in. Author's Collection.

The remains of the 400-foot-long trestle in the southeast corner of the property. The ore cars would be filled with ore at the tipple (the head frame) and then backed up to the end of the trestle which held about twenty cars. Then a steam locomotive would back up to the lead car and hook up. Then it was down hill over the Pillsbury grade to the Mitchell yards for sorting and eventual transport to the Head of the Lakes. Author's Collection.

The water tower at the Godfrey Underground Mine held 16,000 gals of water and supplied, using a four-inch underground pipe, both the Godfrey Location and the Glen Location which are off to the right outside the photograph (north). This picture was taken in 1998 and the tower was torn down in 2002 and the out buildings were also removed. The view is to the west from the trestle. Author's Collection.

This is the opening to one of the shafts of the Godfrey Underground Mine. At one time it had been back-filled but time and the power of erosion have exposed the collar and yoke. This can provide a very nasty surprise when you are walking the woods anywhere on the range where the map says "caved area." The area is not going to cave in but it does mean that underground operations once flourished in the locale. The shaft has since been back-filled again. Author's Collection

To Tipple A Prince

The graphics and the pictures in this appendix should give you not only an idea on how to locate an underground mine but what you will see when you get there. Shafts do not have the glamour of pits; there are no panoramic vistas, no sheer cliffs leading to piles of stratified rock, no lakes where mining operations used to be, no giant machines becoming derelicts of rust. What you will find in some quiet corner of the range tucked away behind some popular and birch trees on the edge of an ore dump, is the memory of who worked and what transpired, here.

Notes

[1] Chapter 1 contains material similar to this appendix. For anyone finding that sufficient, you can ignore this material. It is a slight elaboration on that material with some up-to-date photographs.

[2] If you do not find the mine you are looking for in the Annual Report, look in another. A closed mine is generally not listed in the report only active ones or ones that have been closed for a 'temporary' period. If the mine you are looking for was once active, it will be in some year's report. The *Bulletin of the University of Minnesota*, School of Mines can also be a helpful resource.

[3] Mining companies portfolio of mines change about as often as the holders of your mortgage paper.

[4] There were no GPS devices in those days so we have to use the rectangular method established by Congress in 1787 as part of the Public Land Survey system.

[5] In Minnesota this is really all you need to go to your nearest USGS office and pick up a United States Department of the Interior Geological Survey Quadrangle map. If you are lucky somewhere on the map you will see a designation for an underground mine. It will have no name attached to it and when you find the main shaft (and you should) it will have no designation either. Very old mines like the Godfrey are no longer marked at all but the map will show you what you are confronted with in the way of streams, rivers, swamps, forests, and so forth and it will also carry important clues to long lost activity: old abandoned roads, rail tracks, mine dumps (ore and overburden), the concrete platforms of old abandoned buildings. And when you go out in the field you are in for a surprise. More about that later.

Appendix B
Defining the Mine

Introduction

The Godfrey Underground Mine first became an idea sometime in 1922. The mineral rights had been purchased, the nature and extent of the ore body was known, and the main shaft was pinpointed on a map. It started to become a reality in 1926 when the main shaft, running par-

The Godfrey Underground Mine circa 1951. The 16,000-gallon water tank in the foreground supplied water to the Godfrey site, the Godfrey Location and the Glen Location. The Dry House when the men showered and changed clothes is right behind the water tower. The Hoist House which brought the ore to the surface and took the men up and down in their cage is in the center of the idyllic picture. The head frame is in the center background and the cantilever for the Reserve Ore is on the far left. The power to the site was 440 direct current. It was landscaped and flowers were planted when the construction was finished but that work lasted one Summer. After that, ore dust, coal dust, weather, weeds, economic factors, general neglect, and the passage of time took over. Colorized Postcard.

allel to the ore body, was dug into some very hard ground in November of that year. Full time operations began in 1928, the year Mike Godfrey died. It left the shipping lanes in 1963.

In May of 1954, the Godfrey underground iron ore mine, situated near the northern edge of the Mesabi Iron Ore Range was sold. Its operations, begun with some measure of fanfare on a long ago cold day in November, 1926, had run continuously for twenty-eight years, extracting over fifteen million tons of soft, non-Bessemer hematite ore to feed the nation's hungry steel mills. In 1930, the Godfrey shipped an amazing 889,000 tons of ore and in one twelve year stretch (1939 thru 1950) had annually shipped an average of over 450,000 tons of ore. During the World War II years the Godfrey shipped over four million tons and in fact, the Godfrey shipped over half a million tons annually sixteen times, shipping records never again contested by an underground mine on the Mesabi Range.

But in 1954 things were different. Three hundred men were laid off, approximately the same number that had been released from the Fraser Underground Mine, south of Chisholm, six months earlier. The era of underground iron ore mining, begun with the Soudan underground mine near Tower-Soudan in the 1880s, was rapidly drawing to a close. From here on, underground ore would be shipped mostly from above ground reserve stockpiles, as the cost of extracting the ore and hauling it to the surface was prohibitive. The Godfrey mine had been operated during these years by the Oliver Iron Mining Company, with the last four of those years as a division of U.S. Steel Corporation and it was now changing ownership. Its ore was to become an asset of the Snyder Mining Company. The mine stayed, the owners changed.

1928 and 1929

Nineteen twenty-eight and nineteen twenty-nine at the Godfrey mine tells us that iron ore was a hot commodity: over half a million tons were extracted in the first three years. Employment levels further reflected this by increasing from thirty-seven to sixty-three men employed above and from eighty-seven to 159 men employed below ground. And with over two hundred men working the site, there wasn't a disabling injury to record and that would have pleased Mike Godfrey no end.

The average miner during the 1920s earned $4.20 per day.

	Iron Range: Ore Shipped	Godfrey Mine: Ore Shipped	Men Working Underground at Godfrey	Men Working Aboveground at Godfrey	Injuries or Fatalities at Godfrey	Total Number of Mines Worked on the Iron Range
1927	24 million tons	4,813	3	*	0	*
1928	35 million tons	119,000	87	37	0	*
1929	43 million tons	406,200	159	63	0	*

The 1930s

The 1930s saw a sustained, high-level output from the mine except in 1932 and 1933, when production took a real plunge (along with the workforce) which is understandable given the world economic outlook. The Mesabi Range as a whole took a real beating, dropping from thirty-one million tons in 1930, to fifteen million in 1931 and a staggering two million in 1932. In this regard, the Mesabi was following the rest of the nation down the economic ladder.

What is less easy to explain is 1938, where output dropped sixty percent, while the workforce dipped twenty-five percent. Nineteen thirty-nine clearly reflects the blowing winds of war and the Godfrey output responded accordingly, with a record of over 750,000 tons (this increase is partially explained by the fact that the Glen mine's shipments were included in the total and would continue to be until 1950)! This was once again achieved with a workforce of over 200 men. But five million tons of ore extracted over a decade takes it toll. This decade saw two men lose their lives and eight men sustained injuries worthy of lost time.

At the Godfrey mining site, the tables also show a rather consistent relationship between the number of men below- and the number of support and administrative personnel above ground. The ratio remains remarkably consistent - throughout the mine's history it took about one man above ground to support two and a half men below.

The average miner during the 1930s earned $3.75 per day and the year 1938 saw the first mention of "vacation wages."

	Iron Range : Ore Shipped	Godfrey Mine : Ore Shipped	Men Working Underground at Godfrey	Men Working Aboveground at Godfrey	Injuries or Fatalities at Godfrey Mine	Total Number of Mines Worked on the Iron Range
1930	31 million tons	889,032	170	56	1 fatality	*
1931	15 million tons	666,801	106	40	0	*
1932	2 million tons	237,243	*	*	*	*
1933	13 million tons	204,146	46	31	*	*
1934	14 million tons	351,112	105	54	3	*
1935	18 million tons	438,674	121	53	1	*
1936	31 million tons	649,143	156	61	0	*
1937	45 million tons	607,663	167	52	3	52
1938	13 million tons	254,492	126	47	1	38
1939	30 million tons	750,241	157	54	1	43

Nineteen thirty-nine was the year the W.P.A. came to the Iron Range as Project 6926, which filled in test pits and shafts, repaired fences, blasted down smoke stacks. Every piece of metal that wasn't being used was hauled off for the war effort. Underground mine shafts (for mines that were no longer being worked) were backfilled and fenced, engine houses leveled and slabs of concrete were used to cover shafts. Layers of rails were used to cover some shafts (but the author was not able to locate any; as the war progressed, I think the WPA came back and removed the rails).

The 1940s

The 1940s saw the mines go into high gear for the war effort, with record tonnage shipped every year to meet demands. This success came at a very high price as high-grade ore was leaving the Mesabi Iron Range at a rate that had never been foreseen.

The underground mining industry was getting more popular by the year. In 1940, there were eleven working underground mines and the

Oliver ran seven of them. In 1941, there were twelve working underground mines, and in 1942 there were fifteen.

From 1940 through 1943, ore shipments rose every year as more and more steel was needed for the war effort but as soon as the end was in sight ore shipments started to slip. The economy leveled off after the war but it didn't exactly plummet: demand by industry and construction still remained high. Shipments stayed in the vicinity of 500,000 to 600,000 tons every year until the end of the decade. Interestingly, employment at the Godfrey rose (instead of leveling off) to an average of over 250 men working at the mine between 1946 through 1950. In 1947, the work force topped 300 at the site a feat never before reached.

This was to prove a high water mark for both the Godfrey and the mining industry as a whole. For the moment things couldn't have been better. The total number of operating mines throughout the Mesabi Range, which had averaged around sixty during the war, now raced ahead at an average of over ninety.

The average miner during the 1940s earned $5.11 per day.

	Iron Range: Ore Shipped	Godfrey Mine: Ore Shipped	Men Working Underground at Godfrey	Men Working Aboveground at Godfrey	Injuries or Fatalities at Godfrey Mine	Total Number of Mines Worked on the Iron Range
1940	45 million tons	549,686	161	51	0	*
1941	59 million tons	594,805	170	53	*	*
1942	70 million tons	636,909	185	57	3	60
1943	64 million tons	674,026	183	66	2	62
1944	62 million tons	568,398	193	42	7	66
1945	58 million tons	473,618	179	39	12	56
1946	46 million tons	424,165	232	50	*	60
1947	59 million tons	621,682	263	63	9	79
1948	64 million tons	609,495	239	37	4	80
1949	52 million tons	467,487	198	41	3	94

The 1950s

The 1950s began well enough with the number of mines on the Mesabi increasing immediately from 109 in 1950 to 122 two years later. Initially, it appeared as if the Godfrey would also enjoy prolonged prosperity. It shipped

To Tipple A Prince

600,000 tons of ore in 1950. Three years later, 650,000 tons, but that was the high water mark as costs were cutting into profits at a heavy rate and market forces were forcing the price of ore to an all time low. By 1954, the Oliver announced that it would have to close the mine in mid-1955 (leaving only seven underground mines on the Mesabi), citing declining ore quality, increasing operating costs and increasing competition from abroad.

The average miner during the 1950s earned $9.48 per day.

	Iron Range: Ore Shipped	Godfrey Mine: Ore Shipped	Men Working Underground at Godfrey	Men Working Aboveground at Godfrey	Injuries or Fatalities at Godfrey Mine	Total Number of Mines Worked on the Iron Range
1950	60 million tons	611,776	248	32	5	109
1951	73 million tons	303,248	*	*	*	*
1952	59 million tons	552,005	245	41	3	122
1953	75 million tons	646,207	285	40	7	122
1954	45 million tons	507,230	245	23	10	121
1955	64 million tons	132,560	80	14	0	121
1956	58 million tons	<closed>	*	*	*	127
1957	64 million tons	300,000	0	213	22	124
1958	40 million tons	194,000	134	0	15	91
1959	33 million tons	169,000	110	0	6	89
1960	*	360,000	*	*	*	*

When the Godfrey was first excavating its ore, it drove its first drift 2,500 feet north and reached the limit of its mineral rights when it ran head on into the Glen property. The ore in the Glen plot was mined using a combination of open pit and underground methods. The pit was mined by the Milling method which is used for mining ore in the bottom of a deep trough, the upper part of which has been mined out by steam shovel. The overburden is first stripped off by steam shovel (124,000 cubic yards of the stuff for the Glen), a hoisting shaft is sunk down and close to the ore body and horizontal drifts are run out from the shaft at fifty to sixty foot intervals under the ore deposit.

Raises are then driven up through the ore to the surface and the ore around the raises is milled or broken down into the raises, from which it is drawn off from the bottom, transported to the main shaft (in this case, the Godfrey) and hauled to the surface.

Looking down on a milling pit, it has the appearance of a series of funnels with intersecting or touching rims, the raises forming the spouts. Milling starts around the tops of the raises and extends outward in a widening circle as the excavation deepens, the excavated ore falling down the sloping sides of the mills into the raises.

The Torch Is Passed—December 13, 1956

Mines with rich deposits (as well as stockpiles) of ore are not easily abandoned. Skillings on December 22, 1956, carried an announcement that must have been warmly received by more than one mining family. Under a banner headline, "SNYDER MINING CO. LEASES GODFREY MINE (Formerly Oliver Mine on Mesabi Range)," the article announced the completion of negotiations assigning the lease on the Godfrey underground mine near (south of) Chisholm, Minnesota, Mesabi Iron Range, to the Snyder Mining Company by U.S. Steel's Oliver Iron Mining Division. This was announced on December 13, 1956, in a joint statement by R.T. Elstad, Oliver president, and W. P. Snyder, Jr., President of Snyder Mining.

The Snyder Mining Co., owned by the Shenango Furnace Co., and the Crucible Steel Co, plan to operate the Godfrey in conjunction with its own adjacent South Tener Mine using the hoisting and surface facilities of the Godfrey for both properties. Mr. Snyder said they expected to re-open the mine in the immediate future.

The Godfrey underground mine was owned, operated and run continuously by the Oliver Iron Mining Company from 1926 until 1955. In 1952 U.S. Steel absorbed the Oliver into its corporate fold and continued operating the Godfrey mine. In 1955 the Godfrey was closed by the Oliver and it was not immediately re-opened in 1956 when it changed hands.

In 1957, the Snyder mining company bought the rights to extract ore from the Godfrey and the Oliver was left to operate its other mining interests.

To Tipple A Prince

February 2, 1957

Snyder didn't wait long. The new superintendent in charge of the Godfrey mine, Harry Haller, arrived on the Mesabi Range in February fresh from an underground limestone mine in Ohio. He announced that hiring would begin immediately. The mine had been pumped continuously by a skeleton crew since the Oliver had shut the mine down and much of the equipment was still there. Over a million gallons of water a day had been removed from the mine to keep it operable. Snyder thought at the time that 200,000 tons of ore a year could be removed. (In 1957, Snyder mining activities ranked 13th in iron ore shipments in the Lake Superior region. It shipped about a million tons of ore annually.)

By April, a major conveyor belt installation program at the mine was underway. This was to be 3200 feet of thirty-inch wide conveyor belting and the system was the cable suspension type. From now on, belts would take the ore from the mining areas to the main shaft for hoisting to the surface. During 1958, plans did not quite live up to expectations but by then about 200,000 tons of ore were shipped anyway.

July 12, 1958

The passage of time does not always go unnoticed and Skillings paid homage to thirty years of mining at the Godfrey in its July 12th issue. It noted that the Godfrey was one of the few active underground mines on the range and reminded its readers that the head frame was still quite visible from highway 169. Some really choice historical information followed with the mention that the mining area for the Godfrey now covered 19 'forties', up from the original grant of four. The growth was accomplished by assimilating the East Morris, Glen, Leonard, Monroe and Wellington properties (the equivalent of rural sprawl, I think).

Then the writer W.R. Harkins, who also did the photographic work, dug a little deeper and told us more: the ore body was wide (and on this score he was not specific) and consisted of a thin layer of limonitic ore in the lower cherty horizon and had an average thickness of twelve feet! To get to this "pancake"-like deposit, you had to dig through 240 feet of paint rock, slaty rock, and the usual glacial drift. Also down there were over twelve miles of track haulage and over one and a half miles of conveyor belt. This was not a small operation.

The 1960s

Snyder operated the Godfrey from 1956 through 1961 extracting and shipping the ore. But in 1961 Snyder closed the mine without fanfare. It was closed for good, even though it shipped ore from the on-site reserve stockpile in both 1962 and 1963.

The Eveleth Fee Office records had this to say about the mine: "On December 29th, 1961, our mine inspector and engineer made a symbolic trip to the Godfrey, witnessing the actual physical closing of the mine. The last act performed by Snyder's salvage crew was the removal of the hoisting cage [which the men used] and skips [for the ore] from the shaft and securely covering the openings. Major salvage operations had been completed during the week. An around-the-clock watchman schedule is being carried out by supervisory personnel and Oliver has given Snyder six months time to remove the salvage equipment. An estimated 93,774 tons of Burt ore [the W.R. Burt estate owned the mineral rights] remained in the common stockpile at the mine as of January 1st, 1962. Plans are to ship out the stockpile during the coming ore season."

The average miner during the 1960s earned $17.04 per day.

	Iron Range: Ore Shipped	Godfrey Mine: Ore Shipped	Men Working Underground at Godfrey	Men Working Aboveground at Godfrey	Injuries or Fatalities at Godfrey Mine	Total Number of Mines Worked on the Iron Range
1960	51 million tons	281,850	164	0	11	95
1961	42 million tons	270,515	107	0	1 fatality; 11 injuries	85
1962	42 million tons	97,407	None	None	None	46
1963	43 million tons	115,091	None	None	None	61
1992	806,966 tons	*	*	*	*	9

To Tipple A Prince

In 1992, only nine open pit mines were left. There were no more operating underground mines.

Since then, it has become increasingly difficult to even locate one of those mines let alone describe what the above ground site facilities looked like. As far as the belowground operations are concerned, well . . . Head frames, standing like proud, silent sentinels of a timeless industry, have been torn down, and the shafts that they stood guard over, have been back-filled, covered with planks and rails, or with cement slabs, and fenced off.

But this is only part of the story.

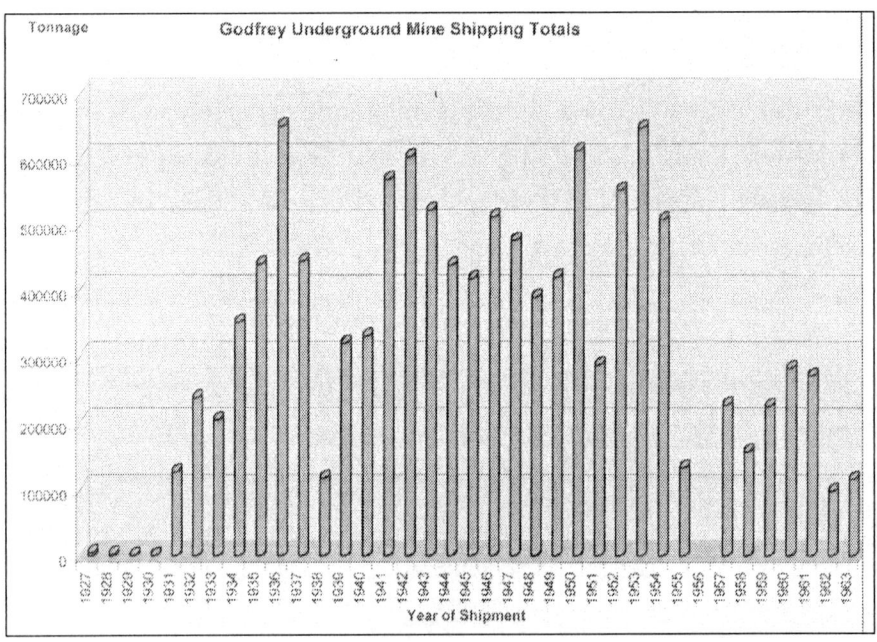

Standing at Ground Zero for a Look Around

It is difficult, today, to imagine what the original site or the underground operations looked like but let me stand for a moment where the massive 100 foot high head frame once stood, to describe what I do know and can see.

Daniel W. Lynch

As I look around, not much remains of what was once one of the busiest underground mines on the Mesabi Iron Range. It was closed for good in 1964, salvage crews tore out every piece of metal in sight, and the elements and several desultory businesses have since ravaged the site further. Time and the tides have taken their toll.

The main shaft is now capped by a concrete slab that has been thoroughly eroded by the elements and is surrounded by some half-upright wooden posts that are supposedly supporting a wire fence. In the summer, a few poplar and birch trees scattered between some growing-out-of-control bushes, hide the derelict from view but in the fall or winter the emptiness of the place is evident. A few feet away to the southwest two of the old head frame's concrete footings still remain and beyond and in a straight southwest angle from these are several more concrete support footings. The various footings still posses some of the original, but now twisted, rebar.

Immediately to the north of the main shaft is a pile of rapidly depleting low-grade ore, last used for aggregate and behind it, a caved-in area that now serves as a swamp (it was originally the timber yard). It is bisected, East-West, by the remains of what used to be DM&IR spur (plenty of ties remain; no tracks). A road moving uphill in a gradual S-curve from the west—of the main shaft- from what is now highway 169 (169 used to be the old fur trader's trail, and then became the DM&IR tracks) is filled with remarkably well-preserved railroad ties (again, courtesy of the DM&IR), partially buried, on both sides of the incline. As you approach the main shaft, about 100 yards short of it, the ties on the right hand side of the road arc off to the southwest. A caved-in swamp area now borders each side of the road. The south side of the road used to be the ore stockpile area. The tracks on the north side of the road used to run right under the head frame; not anymore. All that remains of the hoist house, south of the head frame, and the dry house are remnants of the original cement slabs they rested on. The garage, the parking lot, the timber yard, the 16,000 gal water tank, all gone, traces obliterated.

To Tipple A Prince

However, some 400 feet from the head frame, off to the southeast there is a rather curious earthen berm that runs about 450 feet, arcing slightly to the southeast as it does. At its end it faces an intersection of two trails in the woods and stands thirty feet or so above ground. All along its surface as it raises slowly, the ground falling off rapidly on either side, the litter of railroad ties clutters your progress. There is little or nothing here to indicate that I am standing at the heart of an underground mine that shipped better than 14,000,000 tons of iron ore, over a thirty-five-year stretch, to the nation's burgeoning steel industry.

Let's see if we can re-create what the site looked like originally and, once we have finished that exercise, let's go underground.

The Site

The Head Frame and the Skips

If you stood in front of the main shaft, facing south and looked up, you would be looking at a massive steel edifice that loomed over all that surrounded it. This was the head frame. The front of the head frame looked north, the back faced south. From where I am now standing, it was seventy-six feet straight up to the center of the sheave wheels, (measured from the concrete collar). This collar was placed six ft below ground level and 940 feet above Lake Superior. Forty feet or so above your head ran a single line of tram car tracks that ran due east for some 200 feet and west for about fifty feet before forking into a "Y" that angled northeast and southwest to the waste ore area and the reserve ore, respectively.

The ore was brought to the surface in a metal bin called a skip. The skip was hoisted via steel rope cable, originating in the hoist house where it was wound around its drum. The skip was guided in its journey up the shaft by wooden guides on each side of the compartment. The compartment for each skip (they were side-by-side) measured five-feet two-inches by six feet and when fully loaded could carry 27,000 pounds (ten tons!). These were balanced skips: as one was raised, the other was being lowered: as the cable was winding around the drum hoisting one skip, the other skip was being lowered as its cable was unwinding.

Then the ore was dumped via a trap door in the skip into a large container bin poised above the DM&IR ore cars or it was shoveled into a tram car on the elevated track way. Each tram car held one skip's worth of ore. The ore from the container bin was then dumped into the railroad cars thru chutes using the natural force of gravity. Once a car was full it was moved one car length east along the tracks (the adjoining, parallel, track held empty cars for the next shipment), the next car was filled and so on until approximately twenty cars were filled, all that the trestle had room for. Once the cars were loaded, the locomotive (in our case DM&IRR #191) pushed the train back down the incline to the west where Hwy 169 is and then started the journey south down the Pillsbury grade to the Mitchell Yards. The DM&IR tracks, incidentally, were standard gauge, some fifty-five inches apart.

If the ore was not dumped in the bin (usually because it was winter and Lake Superior was frozen), it was put into the tram cars on the track above the container bin and hauled off to the stockpile area to the southwest. This usually amounted to half a year's production. This track off to the southwest is the steel structure (unfinished) to the right of the head frame. The section shown in the picture also had a 120-foot-long cantilever, the center of which is the pole with the guide wires attached.

All this activity was regulated from inside the Shaft House, the white building half way up the back of the head frame (not shown in photograph on next page). The Shaft House measured twenty-four feet by thirty-six feet and needed only one operator to run the equipment.

The Cage, the Cable and the Hoist House
Miners going down into, and coming up out of the mine rode an "elevator" a single deck (one floor) cage which held approximately fifteen men within its eighty-four cubic feet. The cage—like the skips —had

The head frame complex under construction in May of 1927. The head frame is in the center of the photograph and the ore container bin is the dark area in the lower part of the frame. The rail platform extending to the right and the left is forty-five feet above ground and its purpose was to move the tram cars off to the side (east side, on the right) for later dumping if it was waste ore (off to the left rear) or reserve ore (to the front left). Minnesota Historical Society (also used in Chapter 8).

Looking to the northwest in August, 1936. Head frame complex in operation. In the foreground are DM&IR ore cards waiting to be filled from the bin. The Shaft House is the white building half way up the frame. Tram cars are moving off to the right and behind the head frame waste ore is accumulating. The cable wires that operate the cage and the balanced skips are visible near the top of the structure as they run over the top of the Sheave wheels. The cables are anchored to drums in the Hoist House. The timber for the supports underground is stored in the background. Minnesota Historical Society. HD3.122. # 74127.

Daniel W. Lynch

Inside the Hoist or Engineering House. One drum can be seen but there were two. The cables ran from here to the head frame via Idler Stands for support and guidance. The curious disks on either side of the drum (one for each drum) are elevation indicators with the needle arm indicating the location of the transport cage for the men or the skip cars. The hanging cords are used to communicate with the miners in the cage or at the bottom of the shaft. Minnesota Historical Society. HD3.122. #24120.

wooden guide rails on each side of its compartment, which measured five feet eight inches by ten feet, was located on the west side of the shaft. (The cage door was on the north side.) Illumination inside the cage was provided by one bare light bulb and the cap lamps each miner wore.

The cage was lowered and raised via a steel rope cable that extended from the top of the cage, to the top of the head frame, over the sheave wheels, and then back down (south) at a 350 angle into the hoist house, where it wound around a cylindrical drum. The drum was turned by a generator. And the operator communicated with the cage, back then, via a kind of Morse code triggered by a man in the cage when he pulled on a

Shift change at the Godfrey Underground Mine sometime in the Summer of 1937 (notice the flowers in bloom in the foreground). The men are wearing heavy coveralls in spite of the heat as the temperature in the mine, summer and winter was a constant 550. In this photograph, looking northwest, a new shift is headed for the main shaft's cage on their way to work. The DM&IR ore cars are being filled and the tram cars are on the move. This is a mine at work, not a still life: men coming and going, waste ore piling up, an ore train getting ready for its eventual journey to American Steel and Wire (in Duluth). Even the shrubs cooperated. The ones in the foreground are blooming. Minnesota Historical Society. HD3.122. #74130.

cord that rang a buzzer back up in the Hoist House. Signals were worked out in advance to indicate when the men wanted to go down, or up, or that they had stepped out of the cage (i.e., they were releasing it) so that someone else could use it. Since a shift had approximately eighty men, it took awhile to lower all of them down.

The cable was one and one-eighth inches in diameter and 700 feet long. This meant there was little danger of its running short: the drum was about twenty-one feet in circumference; the hoist house was 175 feet from the head frame and another 100 feet from there down to the top of the cage or skip, plus another 250 feet or so down to the ore.

The Hoist or Engineering, house was 175/180 feet away to the south of the center of the head frame and was approximately 100 ft long by thirty/thirty-five feet wide. The long axis of the structure ran east—west and the front of the building faced the head frame and could view every detail of the site's operation. It was connected by phone to OIM headquarters in Duluth and to the South Rust headquarters complex in Hibbing, and to the other OIM mines on the range. It not only contained the hoist equipment (drum, cabling, air compressors, etc.) but the mine's general administrative offices as well. Topping the building at the eastern edge was the shift siren which signaled shift changes and other important events. It could be heard in either Chisholm or Hibbing. Clearly.

The cage hoist was a geared hoist driven by a 200-horse-power General Electric motor and the drum for the hoist had a 640-foot capacity. The skip hoist was also a geared hoist driven by a 200-horse-power General Electric motor and like its counterpart, had a 640-foot capacity. Both GE motors were in the Engineering house and so were the two Ingersoll-Rand, duplex, two-stage, belt driven, 150-horse-power motors that delivered the necessary 750 cubic feet per minute of forced air down the main shaft into the mine workings.

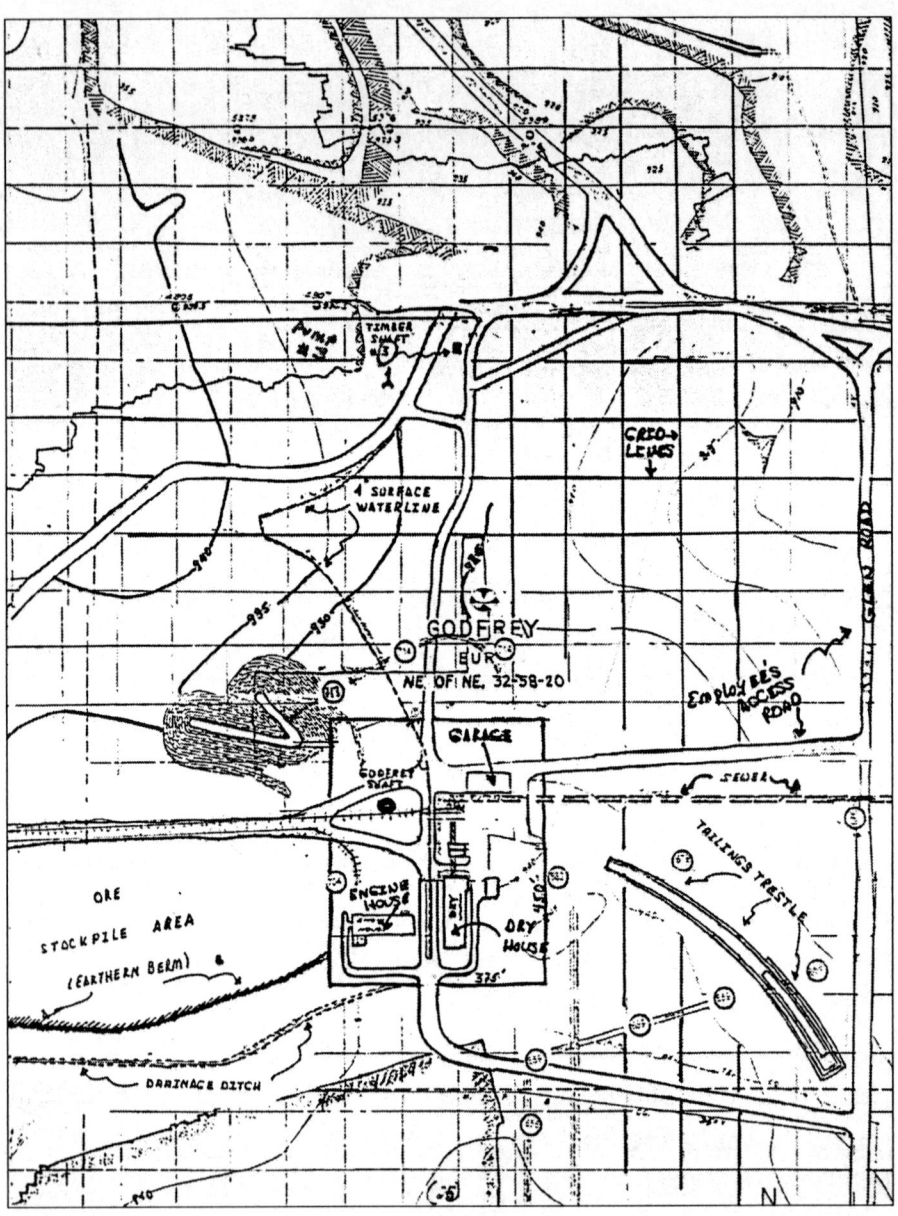

Bird's-eye view of the surface. The grid lines on the drawing are 100 feet apart; the north-south lines were of critical importance in understanding the underground workings in the mine. The circles with numbers in them represent elevations in the mine above Lake Superior; the other numbers represent elevations on the surface above Lake Superior. Engineering Department, Oliver Iron Mining Corporation, courtesy of the Eveleth Fee Office, Eveleth, Minnesota.

Daniel W. Lynch

The Dry House

The heart of the site was contained in a rectangular area that ran about 450 feet north-south and 375 feet east-west. The elevation above Lake Superior was about 930/935 feet. The sewer line ran under the Dry House in a northerly direction for about 100 feet and then left the site to the east.

The dry house was yesterday's equivalent of today's shower room. Here, a man coming to work changed out of his street clothes, hung them in his assigned and numbered locker, put on his coveralls and lamp cap, and headed for the cage. When his shift was over, it was up the shaft in the cage, off with the clothes and into the shower to try and get

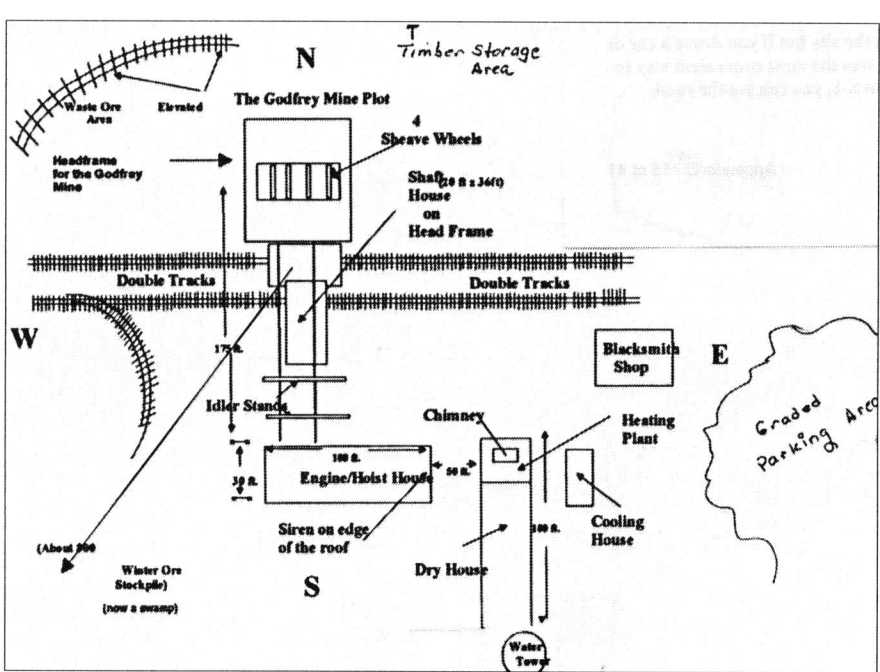

Site schematic. The arrangement is simple, compact, and functional. The Engineering or Hoist House raised and lowered the skips and miner's cage. The ore was brought to the surface and fed into the pocket bin or the tram cars. The miner's Dry House faced the Hoist House and was heated by a furnace/boiler arrangement. Each man had a locker. The blacksmith shop repaired equipment. The water tower supplied surface water to the site, the Godfrey Location and the Glen Location. The sewer line ran off to the east. The double tracks ran down grade to the west. The employees even had a parking lot for those owning cars. Drawing courtesy of the U.S. Steel MinnTac, Mt. Iron, Minnesota.

some of that rust-red paint dust off his skin. The water was as hot as you could tolerate and the boiler was on other side of the wall on the northern part of the building.

The Dry House was fifty feet to the east of the Hoist House. This structure had approximately the same dimensions as the Hoist House (some thirty feet wide and 100 feet long) but the long axis ran north-south and it was divided into two unequal rooms, the larger for the men, the smaller for the heating Plant (the northern part of the building). In photographs it can be seen as the long building with all the windows. It is a low building but when the chimney was completed, you couldn't miss its function. From there you could walk directly to the graded parking lot at the eastern extremity of the site complex.

The Cooling House and the Blacksmith House

To the east of the Dry House was the Cooling House which also had a north-south axis. The Blacksmith House was situated some thirty feet to the northeast of the Dry House and its major axis ran east-west. In photographs the Blacksmith House is the building with the air vents on top center and the stove pipe on the southern pitch of the roof.

The Blacksmith House was adjacent to the graded parking Lot which was reached from the west. The road runs slightly uphill to reach the site. This road ran perpendicular to and connected with an older road now occupied by the Northwestern Bell telephone lines. This of course was not the only way to reach the site but if you drove a car or some relative wished to visit the site—it had been graded, flowered and shrubed—this was the most convenient way to drive to the mining operations (without getting in the way of the mining operations).

The Trestle

Earlier I introduced an earthen berm of some 400/450 feet in length (and about fifty feet wide) that starts some 400 feet east of the main shaft, at ground level, and gradually rises until it ends high above the juncture of two trails. This berm is what remains of a tailing trestle and appears in dozens of O.I.M photographs (all taken between 1926 and 1927) but in not one of them is its relation to or direction from the head frame either given on a photograph or by clues contained in the photographs. Next to the head frame, this feature would have absolutely dominated the site. One photograph does mention it was completed on the 5th of January, 1927.

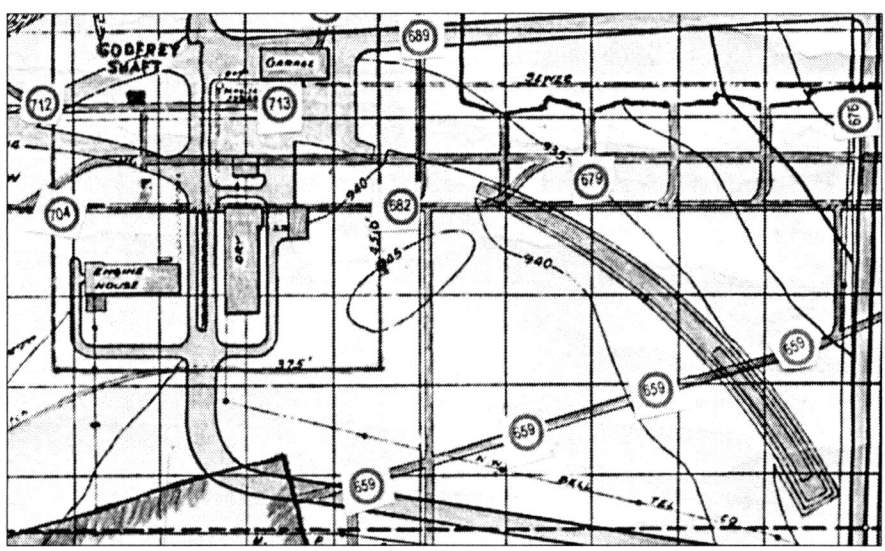

Site layout and trestle location. From a site map copied at the Eveleth Fee Office. The trestle is in pink on the right side of the map. It is an imposing structure (most of it is buried however) but fifty years of overgrowth has obscured its location and size. The green areas are graded or paved surfaces. The red double parallel lines in the center of the graphic represent underground drifts running east 3,000 feet from the base of the main shaft. Engineering Department, Oliver Iron Mining Corporation, courtesy of the Eveleth Fee Office, Eveleth, Minnesota.

The trestle was extended from an existing slope on the southeast corner of the property, then the supports, usually wooden (Tamarack was preferred), were constructed and lastly the steel tracks were laid on top on the cross member. But a fully loaded train would collapse this structure unless some fill was supplied between the uprights which were spaced 20 ft apart. So, locomotives were used to push side-dumping cars out onto the trestle to dump the dirt or rock (low grade ore) on both

To Tipple A Prince

The trestle under construction. The locomotive is pushing ore cars loaded with overburden (earth) to a point on the wooden superstructure where it will tip the cars to fill in the space between the supports for permanent stability. Aubin Studios.

Another view of the trestle under construction in 1927. The men at the end of the trestle are readying the wooden supports. The structure is about two thirds complete. From this point on the ground falls away rapidly. The steel rails have not yet been placed on this section. Aubin Studios.

Daniel W. Lynch

sides—the outsides—of the wooden supports, until the result reaches the height of the trestle. The material would build on the sides, running downhill outside and inside underneath the supports. The inside would eventually form an inverted triangle "∇" of 370, the natural angle of repose for loose material, forming a three-four-five triangle (with the four on the top, three on the vertical, five on the sides: the base of the triangle runs parallel to the ties). The timbers are, in this scheme, left to rot under their cover as they are no longer needed.

The Main Shaft—From Collar to Sump

Now, let's see what's underground by taking a look at the main shaft, the chief means of reaching the ore, the single most important physical connection between the surface and the ore deposit below.

The Five Compartments

That shaft, because it moved men, ore, air and electricity, along its interior compartments, was known as the main shaft. (There were other special purpose shafts as well and we will come to these later.) The shaft which was dug in approximately 200 days was designed with five compartments within its eighteen feet wide by eleven feet deep dimensions. It extended from the surface (approximately 930/35 feet above Lake Superior) down some 311 feet, six inches.

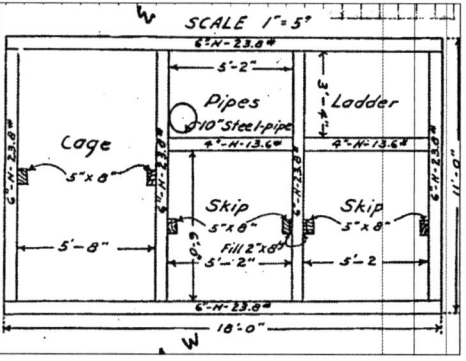

Cross section of the main shaft compartment, eighteen feet by eleven feet. The Cage compartment was the principle way down into the mine and the principle way out but the Ladder compartment could be used in an emergency. The Cage opened on the north side (the top in this drawing). The Skips were balanced: as one descended the other ascended. The Cage compartment and the Skip compartments each had wooden guides for stability. The ten-ince steel pipe was used to force fresh air into the mine. The compartment also contained the electrical conduits. Drawing courtesy of U.S. Steel MinnTac, Mt. Iron, Minnesota.

To Tipple A Prince

The five compartments that comprised the shaft consisted of: the Cage compartment, which moved men down to the ore and up from it; a compartment for the piping which carried fresh air into the mine (its dimensions were five feet two inches by three feet four inches); a third compartment with those same dimensions, which contained a ladder for emergencies, a forth and fifth compartment with identical dimensions, which held the (2) balanced skips that hauled the ore out of the mine (in 27,000 lb bundles). Each skip compartment measured six feet by five feet eight inches. As mentioned before, the skips and the cage had wooden side rails for guidance and stability.

The Godfrey head frame and site, April 12, 1927. The head frame has been positioned for operation but the trestle track for the tram cars has not been erected and the Dry House is not completed either. Note the double tracks, one running under the frame and the other outside it. The photograph also shows the tracks curving off to the right with a steam shovel parked on the end. It was used to excavate the Reserve Ore area and build the bordering berms. The view is to the east. Minnesota Historical Society. HD3.122. #77799.

The Main Shaft—In Cross Section

The collar for the Godfrey underground mine was about six feett below the surface which put it above the clay (there was eight feet of clay). Below the collar and extending down another thirty feet, the shaft passed through

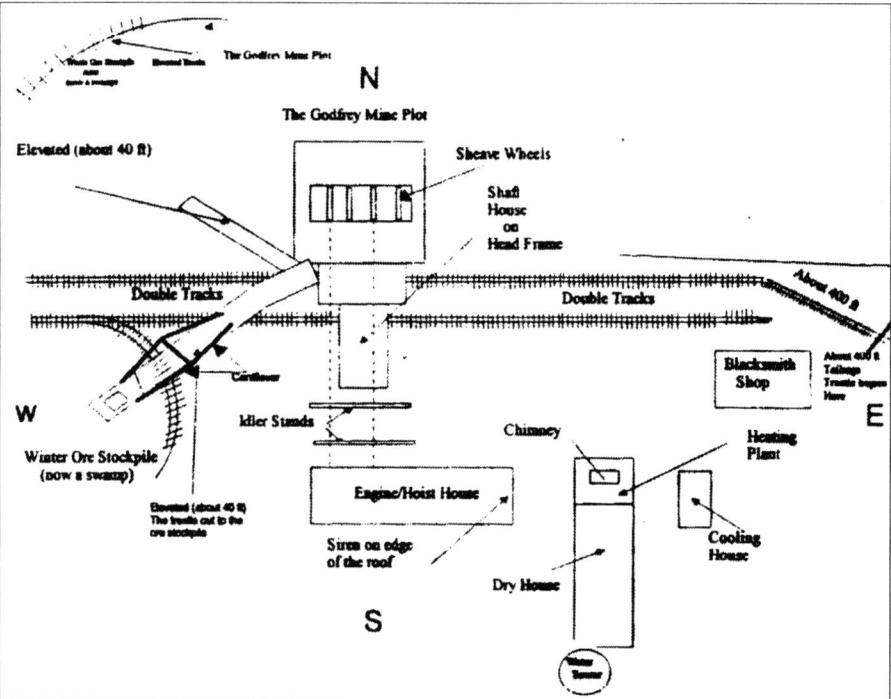

The site layout of the Godfrey Underground Mine with the Reserve Ore and Waste Ore trestle shown. The trestle extended off to the east at the same height of forty-five feet and was used to back up the tram cars. The tracks to the northwest of the site took timber to the storage area. Underground mines on the Mesabi (and the Godfrey was no exception) used immense quantities of wood for shoring. Drawing courtesy of the U.S. Steel MinnTac, Mt. Iron, Minnesota.

sand and rock at which depth it reached its first taconite strata, ninety feet of it in fact. That was followed by some seventy feet of slate rock. The back of the ore body at this location sat some 227 feet down from the surface. The shaft was on the north side of the deposit.

The Importance of the Placement

The bottom of the shaft at 312 feet, however, was not the level at which the ore deposit was mined for this area was taconite and since it was not economically sensible to mine it, the area comprising the last fifty feet or so was the sump, where water collected before being pumped out. Immediately above this was the main body of ore. Since the ore deposit was virtually flat, this meant that the main haulage level would be at the highest point in the deposit. The main haulage drift would decline from this point. Looked at from the east end of the drift, the haulage levels at the Godfrey all rose slightly as they approached the main shaft.

227 Feet Down at 92° 53' 88" W/47° 27' 98" N

As the layout shows, the ore body's depth was measured from the collar and at the Godfrey this meant that the ore body that yielded 14 million tons of ore was taken to the surface from a depth of 227.79 ft, below the collar (712.21 ft above Lake Superior). This was the heart (if not the center) of the mine, this is where the men entered the ore body that they were mining and this is were the major drifts radiated from and this is where the ore started on its upward journey, in one of the skips, to its rendezvous with the surface where the head frame loomed.

Shift Change at the Godfrey

This is one rare photograph, and is the only one I could find in the entire Oliver collection, taken here at the main haulage level, at the underground entrance to the main shaft. Here the ore was dumped from the side-dumping

A vertical cross-section of the main shaft of the Godfrey Underground Mine. Note the ore "pockets" where the ore was dumped before being taken to the surface. This is the central part of the underground operation. All the mined ore had to reach this place to make it to the surface. This station was 227.79 feet below the collar. Drawing courtesy of U.S. Steel MinnTac, Mt. Iron, Minnesota.

ore cars, one at a time, to the left or right of the locomotive where you can (barely) see the gratings on either side, at the ground. These gratings are worn in the center from adsorbing the impact of the ore as it was being dumped into the pockets below before being raised to the surface in the skips.

Shift change at the Godfrey Underground Mine. Even though this is only one photograph, taken in the fairly dark confines of a small area, the amount of detail, historical and otherwise, is priceless. Note for example, the trolley extending from the back of the electric locomotive, the worn pocket gratings, the cage door entrance partially raised waiting to take the men to the surface, the bare bulbs hanging from their single cords, the supervisor casually leaning against the tram car, and the lumber and timber everywhere. This scene was rarely seen by an outsider. Minnesota Historical Society. HD3.122. #24138.

The Base of the Main Shaft

This was the busiest and most complex area in the mine. The immediate area around the base of the shaft was not "mined out" as it was used to support the shaft. Whatever the quality of the ore (and the quality here

Here is another view of the same train approaching the main shaft. This picture was taken as the train rounded a curve just to the west of the main shaft. There were usually ten to fifteen cars in a train. Notice the electric cables just above the men's heads and the timbering everywhere. The rails are twenty-four-inch narrow gauge. *Minnesota Historical Society. HD3.122. #78377.*

was high) it remained as is and the deposit at this 'vertical', rested on taconite and extended, without interruption, to the surface thereby creating a very competent pillar of support.

The narrow-gauge railway ran right in front of the cage (as it had to) so that it could dump the contents of its tram cars into the ore pockets at the base of the main shaft. The tram cars, which had panels on either side, were unloaded using either a hook and hoist or a "camelback" arrangement, where the outside track was humped, tilting the car, spilling the ore on the other side, as it passed by the pocket. The locomotive ran off a direct electric current of 440 volts as did the bare-bulb lights.

The curious lopsided oval loop that ran in front of the shaft accommodated the bi-directional locomotive and its chain of cars, numbering normally about ten to fifteen cars per train to fill a pocket. At fifty-eight-cubic yards of ore a car, this was a large pocket. Using the oval, the locomotive—traveling from one of the major drifts from a cross-cut—could arrive from either direction (east or west), in-front of the shaft to dump its ore into the pockets in the floor and leave in the same or in the reverse direction. If two trains were involved, one waited in the loop while the other unloaded.

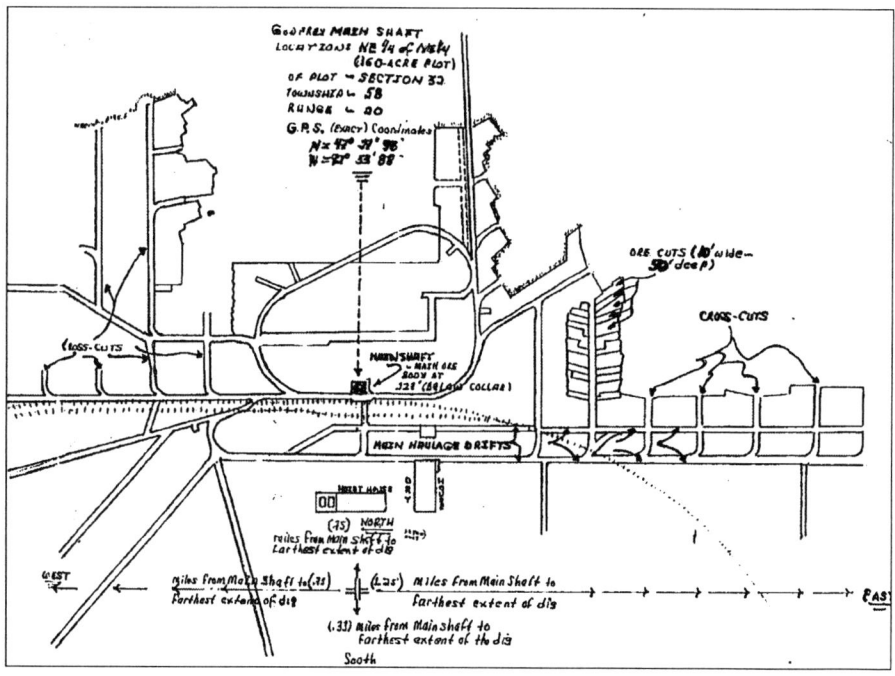

The area in and around the main shaft at the haulage level. The oval could be approached from any direction to unload at the ore pocket at the center. The lines radiating north and south are drifts, with the intersecting lines being cross-cuts (where the ore was extracted). The north/south cross cuts were 100 feet apart. Layout graphic courtesy of U.S. Steel MinnTac, Mt. Iron, Minnesota.

The passageway in the center of the oval served as a repair shop for both cars and locomotives.

To Tipple A Prince

... And Beyond
By going to their left, the miners could take any number of drifts that radiated out from the main shaft, crossing beneath present-day U.S. 169 to head in the direction of the Hull-Rust or East Morris or Alexandria mines. The Alexandria ore was taken over by the Oliver and that rich deposit, nearly sixty feet thick at one point, had its ore taken to the surface via the Godfrey main shaft. By turning right and following the passageway a short distance in a northerly direction, a miner could then enter a diagonal drift that headed to the northeast to the workings (way out) there (over a mile from the main shaft). The drifts ran under and past the Monroe yards.

The two drifts headed due east extended to the very edge of the deposit, gradually sloping ten degrees as they did so. The first of the two drifts contained the 3,000 frrt long conveyor belt that brought ore from the far edge of the deposit to the center of the dig.

Sometime in 1953 or 1954, the Oliver and Wally Beam tried to establish a washing plant for the ore—an underground try at beneficiation—along the conveyor drift. At a ninety-degree angle to the axis of the drift they cut a fifty feet deep, eighteen feet high, thirty-five feet wide room in which they set up a tilted, rotating slurry tank. The ore was put into the rotating tank, water was pumped into this, the slurry came off the top at one end, the washed ore at the bottom of the other end—and into the conveyor. The slurry was pumped to the surface. The experiment did not survive a lack of funds and never was put into regular practice.

Every 100 feet, running due north or south, were the cross-cuts where the actual "mining" took place at the outer edge of the ore deposit.

The Extent and Location of the Deposit
The ore body occupies a rather large, and somewhat amorphous, area underground. In the Soudan mine that deposit was at a seventy-eight degree angle to the surface. The deposit that the Godfrey mined was (mostly) horizontal in nature and occupied an area beneath nineteen surface "forties."

Daniel W. Lynch

The original mineral lease called for two forty-acre sections (eighty acres) for the Godfrey lease but over the years, the leases and the areas they controlled expanded and contracted, but at its greatest extent, the Godfrey underground mine claimed an area of 760 surface acres.

The principal axis ran west and east for a length—at its greatest extent—of two and a half miles; the shorter axis ran north and south for a width—at its greatest extent—of (not quite) three quarters of a mile.

Some orientation is in order here. The names of the open pit mines to the north of the Godfrey "shaft" are still the same—Pillsbury, Glen, Leonard/Burt, Monroe/Tener—but if you visit the area today, it is one large, water filled hole. Hwy 169 slices through the property more or less bisecting NW-NE, 32 and SW-NE, 32, passing right over the western extremity of the Godfrey. The present gravel road leading from the west to the east for about 1,200 ft to the Godfrey is just across the highway from the Godfrey's Timber Shaft #5. (Today, this is a very dangerous area. This shaft was back-filled and is now a water-filled sink hole surrounded by a fragile wire fence and a couple of rotting fence posts.)

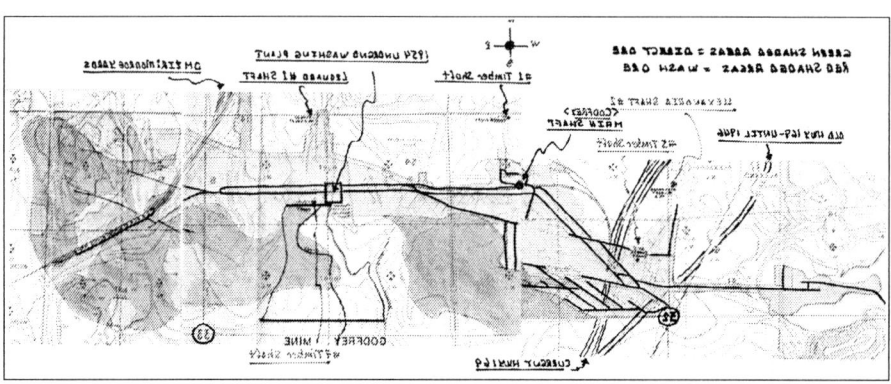

The Godfrey deposit. The green coloration represents direct shipping ore (no treatment required-dig it and ship it) and the red represents ore requiring beneficiation (washing and separating ore from impurities, mostly sand). The dark red lines represent some of the major drifts. The pre- and post-1946 Highway 169 road beds are shown and so is "Beam's Folly," the washing plant. This depiction in from U.S. Steel's file at its MinnTac facility in Mt. Iron, Minnesota, #9-2407-18, Sect. A, DWR/CPT 54F, on the Oliver Iron Mining Co., dated 1929. Original is in the author's collection.

To Tipple A Prince

The Shape and Nature of Things
As you can see, the ore body was extensive and at the same time it is fairly clear that the deposit to the east of the main shaft was considerably more extensive than to the west. What you can't see from the outline is that the deposit sloped down and out from the main shaft and did so at about a ten-degree angle, and from west to east, the lowest point of the ore (and the lowest point in the mine) being to the southeast of the main shaft. This would be the general area labeled, SE-NE, 33.

Drifts and Things
Imagine that you are among the men digging that shaft down into the earth back in November of 1926. When, on July 30, 1927, you reached the depth you wanted and noticed that it was cool down there compared to above, where did you go from here? Previously taken core samples indicated that it was best to go north for the initial extractions. And so north you started to dig.

What you dug was a drift, which is a sort of horizontal tunnel, about eight feet to ten feet wide and about the same height with massive timbering every ten feet to fifteen feet to shore up the back (to us civilians, the top or ceiling; and while I am at it, the floor is called a sill) of the drift and the sides.

As the drift was excavated and the ore and rock were transported to the main shaft and taken to the surface in skips, wooden beams, averaging twelve inches thick, the size of telephone poles (in one picture a No Parking sign is still on the pole), were used for support. The vertical support columns were called posts and the horizontal logs near the ceiling were known as caps. Tamarack was preferred for posts, Split Cedar for the caps. Jack and Norway pine were also highly-prized for their durability.

Timber and Timber Shafts
The posts and the caps would have to be periodically replaced, every three or four years, however, as wood with bark or in constant contact

with water—and the Godfrey was one very wet mine—rots and with that much timber downstairs, whole forests were in danger. This obviously ran up the overhead costs of mining ore so, in the last (although this was not known at the time) years of mining the Godfrey, a second attempt was undertaken to establish a washing and treatment plant for the timber. This treatment facility was to operate in the mine near Timber Shaft #2 and was built by the Rogers Iron Works but never used.

Because of the tremendous need for wood as a drift was cut into the ore (and the equal need for regular replacement of that wood) some means had to be found to easily deliver that wood that didn't involve the Main Shaft, which could be quite literally, miles from the place where the wood was needed.

The correct way to handle the slusher cable. This picture was taken in one of the Godfrey's drifts and is demonstrating how to pull the cable on a double-drum slusher, a scoop-like device for handling ore and transporting it to the tram car. Note the abundance of timber. The year is 1938, eight years into operation. Minnesota Historical Society. HD3.122. #43505

The miner here is signaling the slusher operator by electrical switch and buzzer that the ore is in position for the double-drum slusher (the separate rotating drums are in the background). Minnesota Historical Society. HD3.122. #19521.

The solution was to place timber shafts where they were needed the most, be that along a drift or off some cross cutting area. There were between six and eight such timber shafts where timber (and remember this was very heavy stuff) was placed in a cable sling and lowered down a shaft. The shafts were scattered about the deposit and so were not of uniform depth and individual shafts could and did serve different functions in addition to supplying the mine's timber needs.

Timber Shaft # 1
Timber shaft # 1, was located about 900 feet due north of the main shaft and at an elevation of 925 feet above Lake Superior. This was the direction taken by the first drift. It needed a lot of wood right away. This was a dual compartment shaft with the 2.5 feet by 6.0 feet smaller section to

Daniel W. Lynch

be used for ladders and, potentially, for the pipes necessary to bring fresh air into the cut. The larger section, used to lower the timber by cable and sling, was some 207 feet down into the cross cut area where the ore was being extracted, and it was six feet by six feet. The shaft was cribbed using eight-ince round timbers. The shaft at this location was entering an ore body forty-four feet thick.

Timber Shaft #1 was started on August 7th, 1927, and was finished five months later on December 31, 1927, just before midnight.

Timber Shaft # 2

Timber Shaft #2, was located 1,600 feet north of the Main Shaft and slightly to the west of TS # 1, at an elevation 928 feet above Lake Superior. It located in SE-SE, 29. This shaft contained only a single compartment. The opening for the timber was six feet by six feet and the shaft was a relatively shallow one (being on the edge of the deposit), bottoming out at 118 feet. The ore was nineteen feet thick in this area. As was standard practice, the shaft was cribbed using eight-inch round timbers.

Timber Shaft #2 was started on October 3, 1927, and was finished eleven months later on September 2, 1928. Obviously, it too was in that part of the ore body that was dug initially.

Timber Shaft #3

The third timber shaft was north of the Main Shaft and located in SE-SE, 29. This places it to the north and east of TS#1. The elevation here was 939 feet above Lake Superior and the shaft, like Timber Shaft #2, consisted of a single compartment. The opening was also six feet by six feet and the shaft was a relatively shallow one reaching its optimal depth at sixty-six feet below the surface. The ore was about sixteen feet in depth here. As was standard practice, the shaft was cribbed using eight-inch round timbers.

Timber Shaft # 3 was started on December 2nd, 1927 and was not completed until May 25th, 1929, an elapsed time of eighteen months. (Maybe things move slowly this far out from the center of the deposit.)

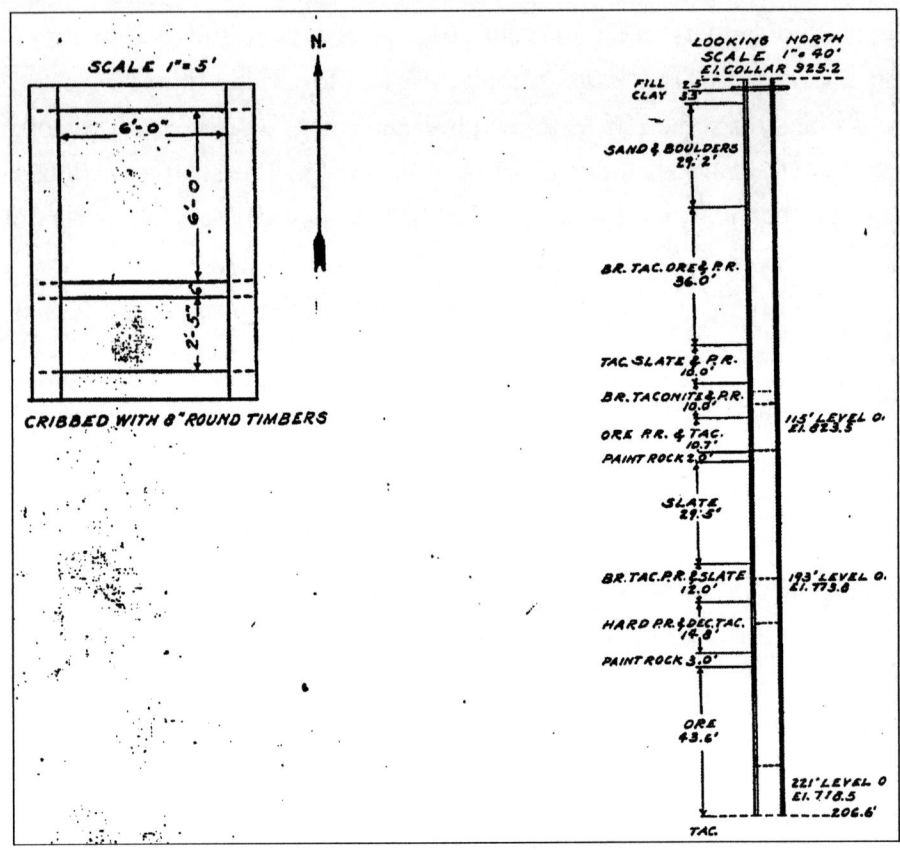

Timber Shaft # 1. Courtesy of US Steel Corporation, MinnTac, Mt. Iron, Minnesota.

Timber Shaft # 4

Timber Shaft # 4, got its start 950 ft above the blue waters of Lake Superior and it broke ground about 1,300 feet from the Main Shaft. It was located in NW-NE, 32. This would shift the mining of the ore deposit from an initial, generally northerly direction to a western one. This was a dual compartment shaft with the 2.5 feet by 6.0 feet smaller section used for ladders and, potentially, for the pipes necessary to bring fresh air into the cut. The larger section, used to lower the timber by cable and sling, was some 190 feet down into the cross cut area and it was six feet by six feet. This shaft was also cribbed using eight-inch round timbers. It entered an ore body (we are working out from the center again) sixteen feet in depth.

Timber Shaft # 5

Timber Shaft # 5 got its start 941 feet above Lake Superior its exact location is not given in the documentation at MinnTac and neither is the date of its digging. What we do know (again) is that it was located in SW-NE, 32. This would place it to the south and somewhat to the west of TS #4. The shaft is in a somewhat complicated area as it would appear to be between two drifts, a few hundred feet west of where they cross. We are about 250 feet west (and below) of present day Highway 169 and southwest of the Main Shaft.

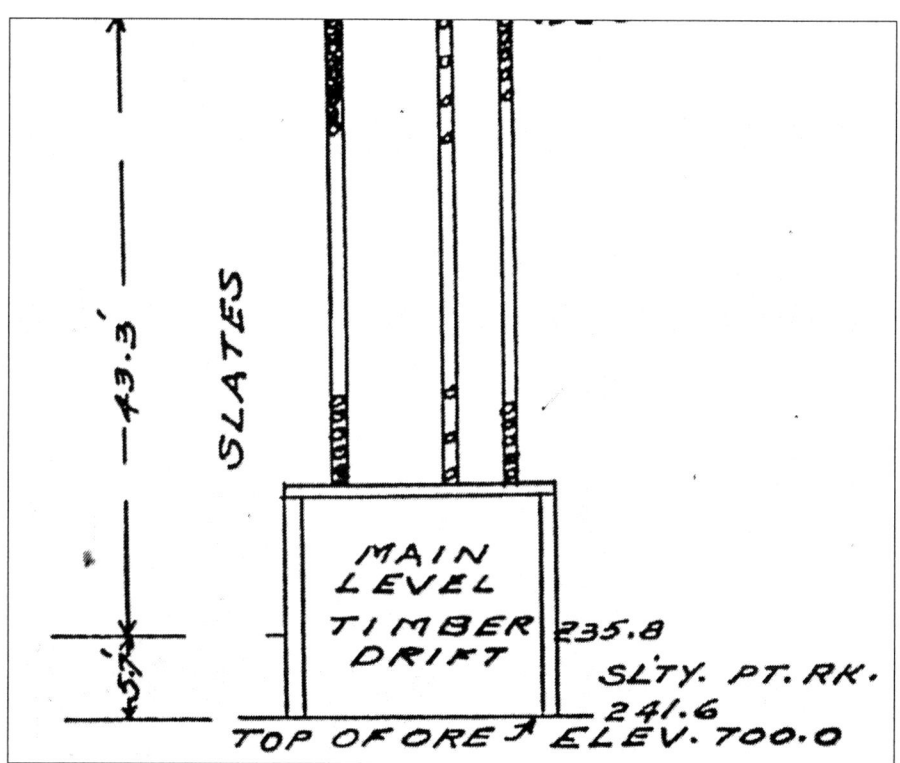

Timber Shaft # 5 on the main level. Courtesy of U.S. Steel MinnTac, Mt. Iron, Minnesota.

Cross Cuts and Top Slicing

The cross cuts were driven into the ore body at right angles to the drifts (or as close to a right angle as possible). The cross cut was then taken to the edge of the ore body or to the end of the property, whichever was reached first. As the cross cut was driven, say to the north, the ore was removed by the electric locomotive, pulling the inevitable ore cars behind it.

Since the cross cuts were 100 feet or so apart the ore was now extracted by blasting and/or digging into the ore on each side of the cross cut (using the jumbo drills) and out from it for a distance of fifty feet. The ore was first drilled from the top of the cut to prevent it from collapsing of its own weight. The ore was then removed or, sliced, from the ceiling working down to the floor of the cut, out fifty feet on either side of the cut, retreating back along the cut (in the direction of the drift) for a distance of ten feet. Thus ore was removed from the immediate area leaving an empty room behind which was ten/fifteen feet high, by 100 feet wide, by ten feet deep, or about 15,000 cubic feet of ore. The ceiling was then drilled to collapse the slate and paint rock before gravity did the job for them. The ceiling that remained was taconite which creates a "very competent surface expression."

When the ore collected on the floor of the cross cut, it was broken up with "Jack-Leg" drills and was dragged away using a scoop attached to a steel cable (pulled back and forth by an electrically driven double-drum hoist) called a slusher. (Take note, again, at the amount of timber in these photos. The Iron Range is

In the photograph above the slusher is pulled by an unseen operator, toward a vertical chute (see next photograph). The chute was usually a cut-out in an elevated platform with a loading ramp in front, and when the slusher was pulled over the opening, the ore would spill into a tram car underneath. When all the cars were loaded, the electric locomotive would haul them to the main shaft. The ramp would be moved in the direction of the digging as room after room was emptied. Minnesota Historical Society. HD3.122. #78170.

Daniel W. Lynch

certainly not, even today, noted for its majestic trees. One of the reasons may be found underground.)

A double-drum slusher hoist is constructed so that power is applied to each drum separately. One drum is used for pulling the loaded scraper and is called the haul drum or pull-rope drum. The other drum is called the tail-rope drum. The rope from the haul drum is attached to the bail or drawbar of the scraper, and it is then passed over a sheave or pulley, which is anchored in the drift somewhere above and behind the material to be moved and attached to the back of the scraper.

By engaging the clutch on the haul drum, the operator pulled the scraper forward, enabling it to dig into the material and gather its load. On reaching the unloading point, the clutch on the haul drum is disengaged and the tail rope drum clutch engaged, thereby returning the

The photograph shows an ore chute in the upper right. It was used to funnel ore into the tram cars each of which held 27,000 pounds. The miner in the picture is opening the chute at the end so that the ore from above can empty into the tram. The electric locomotive is at the bottom left in the picture. *U.S. Steel News.* June, 1937. P14.

scraper to the muck pile or the material to be moved. The movement and the productive action of the scraper are controlled by the alternate action of the hoist at the will of the operator.

The slusher is still used to scrape muck, or broken rock or ore, into chutes or mill holes from which it is usually loaded by gravity into rail cars on a lower level. When the ramp is mobile and the slusher is mounted on it, the device is usually referred to as a scraper or loading slide.

An electric locomotive hauling a string of ore cars behind it was not the only way, however, of getting ore cut out of the ore body a mile or so away to the main shaft. Back in 1958 it was noted by Skillings that the use of a conveyor was being studied. In fact, such a conveyor was used in the main haulage drift running due east of the main shaft for 3,200 feet.

Blasting It Loose
The blasting was done according to a pattern that varied from room to room and was based on the ore's composition. The number of blast holes varied but on average, seven to nine holes were common reaching a maximum of fifteen in places. Miners used an auger drill driven by compressed air to bore holes in the ore. Each hole was six feet deep and was loaded with eight sticks of dynamite; the first stick was called the detonator because it contained the cap and the fuse. The fuse burned at the rate of one foot per forty seconds.

The blasting sequence saw the center sticks (DuPont dynamite) set off first, to weaken the core of the wall, followed by the next circle of dynamite-filled holes, until the last blasts went off on the outermost ring of blast holes. This careful arrangement and sequencing of blasts was fairly easy given the fixed rate of primer cord burn. The shortest fuses were on the inside and the longest ones on the outer rim. The blasters counted the charges as they went off. Any charge that failed to go off was noted on the blast chart in the Dry House, for the next shift. By tradition, blasting generally occurred at the end of a shift.

Daniel W. Lynch

These men are preparing a wall of ore for blasting in the Godfrey Underground Mine. The holes have been drilled and the dynamite is being inserted. It was a safety requirement that two men perform this operation to reduce accidents. The blasting sequence arrangement has already been determined by a blaster skilled in determining the composition of the ore. This photograph shows that one of those fifty feet deep rooms in the process of being created. This next step is shown in the next photograph. Minnesota Historical Society. HD3.122. #19520.

Blasting could cause considerable amounts of smoke in addition to the congestive blasting effects but this did little harm to the rats, bats, or silverfish that plagued all underground mines: the bats liked the cool darkness, the silverfish liked the saturated wood and the rats had a daily banquet of food scraps left behind by three shifts of eighty miners each eating lunch "downstairs." Poisoned wheat was used on the rats and the bats took care of themselves.

By the time all the ore that could be taken out of the Godfrey was taken out not only had a great deal of ore been removed but also a con-

Secure the area after blasting. Put up the timber and then trim the loose ore. Minnesota Historical Society. HD3.122. #78366.

siderable number of forties had been mined. At the end, a reference to the Godfrey Underground Mines would be given as:

SE-SW, Sec 28, SE-SE, Sec 29 & NE¼ & SE-NW, Sec 32, T.58, R.20
& NW-NE & N½-NW, Sec 33, T.58, R.20

Notes

[1] Under the headline, "Oliver to Close Godfrey Underground Mine, Mesabi Range," R.T. Elstad, president of the U.S. Steel's mining division, is quoted as saying that "every effort would be made to provide employment of these men in the division's surface operations, providing their length of service permits it." Although Mr. Elstad did not mention it, that would leave the Oliver with only two operating underground mines, the Pioneer Mine in Ely and the Soudan Mine near Tower-Soudan. Both of these mines were on the Vermillion, not the Mesabi, Range. Quoted in *Skillings Mining Review*, Charles D. Skillings, editor and publisher, 319-320 Bradley Building, Duluth, Minnesota. Vol. XLIII, No. 50, March 19, 1955, page 4.

Daniel W. Lynch

[2] Rodney J. Lipp, editor, and Kenneth J. Reid, director, Minnesota Mining Directory, page 100 (Mineral Resources Research Center, U. of Minnesota, 56 East River Road, Minneapolis, Minnesota. 55455, 1989).

[3] Frank Sevshek, forty-eight years of age, married and the father of four was the first recorded death but not the last. Over the life of the mine, however, fatalities were low.

[4] There was one fatality: thirty-seven-year-old Joe Micheletto died on July 13th. Underground mining at the Godfrey may have been somewhat safer than it appears as half the injuries were aboveground. One miner, John Komidor, broke his elbow in a fall in the Dry House.

[5] 1945 marked a watershed year for two reasons: the first was the record number of injuries at the Godfrey and secondly, it marked the first time that women on the Mesabi Range are mentioned as working in the "pits."

[6] Anton Oberstar hurt himself on March 15th, and Rudolph Paripovich, not be to outdone, injured himself on November 12th when he 'bruised' his ankle. He was out for eight days.

[7] This one is dear to the author's heart: on November 25th, Joe Gamboni making like an aerialist, walked out to the end of those railroad ties near the end of the Godfrey trestle, and as the tie cracked, fell 20 feet and broke his right knee.

[8] Shutdown in April of 1955, even though, as *Skillings* noted, "there is still substantial tonnage remaining." But a small maintenance crew was kept on the property to keep the pumps working and to maintain other, necessary equipment. That crew was still there when Snyder re-opened the mine in February 1957. The Oliver's estimate had 8,000,000 tons of direct shipping ore remaining; 4,800,000 tons of crude, washable ore, and 3,000,000 tons of concentrates.

[9] A very good description of milling can be found in *Iron Range Country: A Historical Travelogue of Minnesota's Iron Range*, page 103; published by The Iron Range Resources and Rehabilitation Board, Eveleth, Minnesota and The State of Minnesota.

[10] *Skillings Mining Review*, December 22, 1956, Vol. XLV, No. 38, page 6.

[11] Actually, to the north and east of the Godfrey.

[12] Two pumping stations operated twenty-four hours a day, discharging over 800 gallons of water a minute. This amounted to about 1.1 million gallons every twenty-four hours.

[13] *Skillings Mining Review*, Jul 12, 1958. Vol. XLVII, No. 15, page 5. Not only did the Godfrey head frame make the cover under a bright orange banner, but this marked a new format for the magazine. It now resembled popular magazine formats.

[14] Eveleth Fee Office, Eveleth, Minnesota, Burt Reports, 1955 to 1974.

[15] There are Godfrey mine photos (almost 200 of them) on file at the Minnesota Historical Society in St. Paul, MN. There are several collections but the best and most extensive is that of the Oliver Iron Mining Co. labeled Collection III.14.1-6. The photographer is usually identified by name and city.

[16] From the original plans and drawings for the Godfrey mine, dated May 2, 1927, on file at the US Steel's MinnTac Headquarters in Mt. Iron, Minnesota. These plans (at least the ones that could be located nearly seventy-five years later) consist of ten carefully drafted, inked, cross-sections depicting shafts, ore bodies, drift depictions, and letter-prefect hand-drawn textual characters all drawn on light blue-grey linen paper sheets. The care and professionalism that went into the creation of that material was worth the effort tracking it down.

[17] I would like to thank William Rolfe of Chisholm,, Minnesata, for some of his observations on the sights and sounds of the Godfrey. The cage he remembered went up and down the 300-foot shaft very rapidly. It seems there was one speed to the mechanism: fast. Information is from a conversation with Bill on November 23, 1999. Bill worked in the mine from 1951 through 1954.

To Tipple A Prince

[18] These and other details were culled from numerous sources, including walking the site, the OIM photographic collection cited earlier, and a site layout drawn up by the Engineering Department of the Sherman mine, for the US Steel Corp, on January 1, 1968.

[19] The gear ratio of the cage was set for 4.5:1 and the gear ratio for the skip, which could carry a much heavier load (obviously) was set to 15:1. The cage carrying 15 men (say, 2,500 lbs in total weight), would require the 200 hp GE motor's shaft to turn four and a half times to rotate the drum one full revolution; the skip when fully loaded with 27,000 lbs would require the 200 hp GE motor's shaft to turn fifteen times to rotate the drum one full revolution.

[20] I am indebted to Ben Imbertson's, *"Oliver's Railroads-Steam"*, for this description. *The Missabe Railroad Historical Society, Vol. 12, No. 3, Fall 1999.*

[21] Ore bodies do not run in a nice, neat horizontal line, parallel to the surface. The Godfrey deposit, while remarkably level, declined from west to east at about a 10^0 angle. The Godfrey deposit averaged 12 ft in depth. The best ore was on the west and the east held a poorer quality. The Godfrey was also known as one very wet mine.

[22] This photograph is catalogued as HD3.122, and was taken on September 12, 1936 by Robert Yarnall Riche. All the elements are here: the open cage door, the congregation of men waiting to be taken to the surface, the electric locomotive arriving with a 'train' of tram cars, the ore pocket with its steel grating waiting for the ore cars to dump their load of ore (at the men's feet), the claustrophobic closeness at the place. Note the wooden beam above the locomotive engineer's head that protects the men from the electric trolley arm that powers the train. There were over 12 miles of track in the mine.

[23] This information was worked up from an April 14, 2000 conversation with William Rolfe. The plant was located about 100 ft to the east of Timber Shaft #7 and to the west of the Monroe Yards. The Pioneer Underground Mine also tried this but they put the washing plant in the head frame.

[24] An exception to this was the first drift that was dug at the Godfrey, which ran due north to the edge of the deposit.

[25] The Godfrey Underground Mine, like all such mines in the area, was a constant $50/55^0$ year 'round. The local papers put the temperature in Hibbing that day, at a high of 89^0.

[26] By reading some faint, reversed imagery on the bottom of the specification sheet, it would appear that the shafts (timber shafts #4 and #5) were started sometime in 1943, which places them 15 years later than the other two timber shafts (assuming that the date on the sheet really does refer to the sinking of the shaft and not something else). The faint traces of a reversed date on the two sheets could be the date of the drawing and not the date the shaft was started or finished. The other sheets for the timber shafts have separate dates for the drawing and sinking.

[27] Sometime around 1920, slushing began to replace hand shoveling which nearly doubled output. The hoist varied in horsepower, from $2^{1/2}$ hp for a single drum to 10 hp, for a double-drum.

Appendix C

Siblings

Introduction

When Michael Hogan Godfrey died in January of 1928 he left behind more than an estate and a legacy. He left behind a window and seven children by his first marriage to Cecelia Gandsey, who had died twelve years earlier. At the time the children ranged in ages from thirteen to twenty-nine.

What became of them at least in brief is the subject of this appendix.

Michael Hogan Godfrey—the patriarch, Stewart H. Holbrook's *"Prince of the Range"*, was born on April 13, 1872, in Champion Michigan's Upper Peninsula, one of ten children. He died on January 13, 1928, in his home in Hibbing, Minnesota, across the street from City Hall, leaving behind a widow and seven children all of whom were living in Hibbing. He had risen from clerk at the Oliver Iron Mining Company to the pinnacle of success as Western District Manager of the Oliver's operations on the Mesabi iron ore range (his salary at the time was $11,000.00 a year) and had been the chief architect behind the move of North Hibbing to New South Hibbing. He had an underground mine named in his honor two years before his death. He was Irish by birth, Catholic in religion, tall, about six-foot-two and left-handed, and rare for an Irishman of the era, a rare drinker.

His estate was valued at nearly $290,000.00.

To Tipple A Prince

Mary Elizabeth Parker Kramer Godfrey—his widow. She was fifty years old at the time of her husband's death and supposedly had a teen-aged son by her first marriage (I can find no evidence of this). She inherited some $120,000.00 as her part of the estate. She was a widow living in Duluth's fashionable East End at the time of her marriage to Michael Godfrey. She was seriously ill, living in Duluth once again, when she dies apparently in 1943. Mike's children rarely if ever mentioned her unless they had to out of necessity. And then they called her "Aunt May" without ever explaining why.

James Robert Godfrey—twenty-nine at the time of his father's death and the first born. He was a graduate of the University of Minnesota and working at the First National Bank in Hibbing. His portion of the estate was 12.5 percent. Between graduation from high school and entering the Univ of Minn, he supposedly joined the army in 1918 and was medically discharged with diabetes. He married Margaret McHardy and had three children, Michael, Claire and a child that died in infancy. He dies of a heart attack in Hibbing in January, 1953 while living at 512 Sixteenth Avenue East.

Miriam Cecelia Godfrey—twenty-six at the time of her father's death and the second born. She was a graduate of Barnard and never married. She was a substitute teacher all her life and took care of Marjorie. Her portion of the estate was 12.5 percent. When her Father died she took her sisters Jane, Marjorie, and Agnes to Duluth (1929-1933) where Jane and Agnes finished high school and Jane finished stenography school. According to one of the local librarians in Hibbing she had read every book in the library. She died in June 1975 while living at 917 East Howard Street in Hibbing.

Thomas Clark Godfrey—twenty-five at the time of his father's death and the third born. He attended Notre Dame for a semester and then left never to return to college. He entered the mines immediately thereafter and finished his forty year career as a Foreman in the massive Hull/Rust/Mahoning operation his Father had supervised for so long. His portion of the estate was six percent, probably because he and his Father had had difficulties over his career. He married Delia McHardy, Margaret's sister and they had three children. He dies of heart failure in January, 1973 while living at the Androy Hotel on East Howard Street.

Marjorie Helen Godfrey—twenty-four at the time of her father's death and the fourth child. She attended the University of Minnesota with her brother James but returned home after two semesters. Her portion of the estate was nineteen percent. She accompanied her sisters to Duluth when their Father died. Lived with her sister, Miriam, her entire adult life and never worked. She was retarded most of her life. She died of heart failure in July 2000, in Hibbing while living at the Leisure Hills Health Care Center.

Paul Francis Godfrey—twenty-one at the time of his father's death and fifth child. He is the family mystery. Not much is known of him but it is a family tale that he rarely worked (he did not have a Social Security number), never married, sponged off siblings, had a history of drinking problems and died in January, 1957 of kidney failure while in the Anoka, Minnesota State hospital. His portion of the estate was 12.5 percent. His last known residence was listed as Hibbing. He was sometimes alluded to as the cause of Marjorie's retardation but no details accompany the reference.

Elizabeth Ann Godfrey—was the sixth child and does not outlive her Father. She died of nephritis in November 1927 but the family does not tell Michael for fear of his heart failing. She was a student at the time.

To Tipple A Prince

Jane Winifred Godfrey—sixteen at the time of her father's death and seventh child. Graduated from Duluth's Central High School and later from the University of Wisconsin. Her portion of the estate is 12.5 percent. She lived in New York City for a time, had dinner with the Sulzberger's from time to time, took steno from Arnold Toynbee, joined the Red Cross during World War II, married in Alexandria, Egypt (1943) and lived in Saudi Arabia for twenty years. Along with her sister Miriam, she was a voracious reader. She had no children. She outlived her husband and died of lung cancer in May 1992, in St. Paul, Minnesota.

Agnes Eleanor Godfrey—was thirteen at the time of her father's death and the eighth and last child to survive. Graduated from Duluth's Central High School and later from the University of Wisconsin. Her portion of the estate was 12.5 percent. She married and has four children. A son died at the age of three. Died of lung cancer in July 1988.

Bibliography and Sources

Books

John C. Greenway and the Opening of the Western Mesabi. Boese, Donald L. Grand Rapids, Greenway Book, 1975.

Three Iron Mining Towns. Landis, Paul Henry. Arno Press & The New York Times, 1970.

Iron Mining In Minnesota. Van Barneveld, Charles E. University of Minnesota, Minneapolis, Minnesota, 1912.

Iron Brew: A Century of American Ore and Steel. Holbrook, Stewart H., The MacMillan Company, 1939.

Overburden: Modern Life on the Iron Range. Brown, Aaron. Red Step Press, 2008.

A Century of Iron and Men. Hatcher, Harlan. The Bobbs-Merrill Company, Inc. New York, 1950.

Hibbing Minnesota: On the Move Since 1893. Hibbing Public Library, 2020 East Fifth Avenue, Hibbing, Minnesota. 1991.

The Menominee Iron Range: Its Cities, Their Industries and Resources. Nursey, Walter R. Iron Mountain, Michigan. 1891.

We're Standing on Iron: The Story of the Five Wieland Brothers 1856 – 1883. Skillings, Helen Wieland. St. Louis County Historical Society, Duluth, Minnesota. 1972.

Mesabi Pioneer: Reminiscences of Edmund J. Longyear. Longyear, Robert D. Minnesota Historical Society. St Paul, Minnesota. 1951.

North Hibbing: Reminiscences of a Ghost Town. Compiled by Krier, John G. & Krier, Jonelle J., Tribune Graphic Arts, Hibbing, Minnesota 1976.

A Photo Essay of an Iron Mining Community Hibbing, Minneosta. DeMillo, Lorraine. Iron Range Historical Society, Gilbert, Minnesota 1982.

Just Like Bob Zimmerman's Blues: Dylan in Minnesota. Engel, Dave. Amherst Press, P.O. Box 296, Amherst, Wisconsin. 1997.

Iron Frontier: The Discovery and Early Development of Minnesota's Three Ranges. Walker, David A. Minnesota Historical Society Press, 1979.

The Mesabi Iron-Bearing District of Minnesota. Leith, Charles Kenneth. Government Printing Office, Washington, D.C. 1903.

Duluth and St. Louis County, Minnesota: Their Story and People. Van Brundt, Walter. Ed. American Historical Society, New York. 1921.

To Tipple A Prince

The Missabe Road: The Duluth, Missabe and Iron Range Railway. King, Frank A. Golden West Books, San Marino, California. 1972.

Source Locations

St. Louis County, Minnesota, Inspector of Mines Annual Reports: 1919-1931; and 1933-1950.

Dickinson County Library, Iron Mountain, Michigan, has microfilm copies on file of the *Norway* (Michigan) *Current* newspaper back to at least 1897.

Menominee Range Historical Museum
300 E Lundigton St
Iron Mountain, MI 49801

Hibbing Public Library
2020 5th Ave E,
Hibbing, MN 55746

Virginia Public Library
215 5th Ave W
Virginia, MN 55792

Duluth Public Library

520 W Superior Street
Duluth, MN 55802

Minnesota Discovery Center
(Temp Closed)
Chisholm, MN 55719

Eveleth Fee Office
301 McKinley Ave
Eveleth, MN 55734

U.S. Steel Headquarters
MinnTac Headquarters
Mt. Iron, MN 55768

Great Northern Iron Ore Properties
801 E Howard Street
Hibbing, MN 55746

Meriden Engineering
1910 8th Ave E
Hibbing, MN 55746

[A special note is required here when using such places as fee offices or corporate administrative centers for research: these are not public resource centers and are not open to the general public. Special permission is required to enter these facilities let alone use their materials. Having said that, let me mention that some of the best research I ever did was in these offices.]

> Minnesota Department of Natural Resources
> 500 Lafayette Road
> St Paul, MN 55155

Daniel W. Lynch

Walter Library (East Bank)
University of Minnesota
117 Pleasant St SE
Minneapolis, MN 55455

Minnesota Historical Society
345 Kellogg Blvd
St Paul, MN 55102

[Absolutely the best single source of materials for the study of Minnesota History. For my study, their materials on the Oliver Iron Mining Company, for which Michael Hogan Godfrey worked for over thirty-five years, contained, among other items, over 1,350 photographs. And the newspaper archives can keep anyone busy for years.]

Other Sources

Conversations with William Rolfe in 1999 in Chisholm, Minnesota. Bill was a miner in the Godfrey Mine. His recollections were extensive and as I later learned, quite accurate. He worked in the East End of the Godfrey but said he could reach Chisholm via underground drifts, cuts, and cross cuts without ever "going surface."

Conversations with John Suihkonen, Sr., a site engineer in the Godfrey Mine. He did ore sampling and mining safety inspections in the mine and remembers the mine with clarity.

Phone conversations with H.E. Lager, a dentist who worked summers as a teen-ager with his brother hauling timber to the area north of the Godfrey Headframe. He also provided a hand-drawn map of the probable location of the main shaft of the Godfrey (location at that time unknown to the author).

Richard K. Sellman for providing me with a complete transcript of the famous "Vacation Case."

The Missabe Ore and Daily News, later renamed *Missabe Ore and Hibbing News*. Every paper from 1893 until 1930. The microfilm copies at the Minnesota Historical Society are priceless.

Index

$18/20,000,000.00, 228.

Alice, 2, 39, 41, 45, 67, 68, 78-80, 91, 129, 133-135, 138, 144, 174, 184, 185, 190, 196, 204, 214.

Androy Hotel, 5, 53, 206, 223, 239, 272, 280, 292, 373.

Atkinson, Claude (or, C.M.), 49, 50, 62, 72, 76, 81, 85, 86, 115, 117, 127, 129, 132, 176, 177, 219, 235.

Blacklock, S.S. Dr., 176, 177, 183, 279, 290, 304.

Brown, Walter W, 268, 375.

Buhl injunction case, 129, 237, 243, 244, 282, 283.

Burnham, H.G., 248, 249.

Calvary Cemetery, 159, 310, 311.

Canisteo district, 39, 71, 74, 108-111, 113, 115, 119, 122-127, 133, 148, 151, 152, 155, 181, 200, 275, 300.

Central Addition, 1, 4-6, 68, 76, 88, 173, 182, 185, 189, 191, 194-196, 199, 201-204, 206, 210, 211, 213-215, 221, 225, 227, 234, 235, 237-240, 259, 261, 262, 274, 280, 311, 314.

Champion, Michigan, 16, 18, 20-25, 28, 31, 35, 308, 371.

Chisholm District, 100, 101, 112, 113, 126, 151, 181.

Coleraine, 11, 47, 78, 90, 108, 111-119, 121, 122, 149, 151, 152, 178, 272, 299, 300, 309.

First National Bank building, 202, 203, 212, 216, 260, 372.

Forties, xvii, 5, 12, 14, 15, 27, 29, 44, 67, 68, 75, 76, 78, 83, 87, 93, 133, 175, 179, 181, 182, 184, 185, 190, 199, 204, 205, 211, 217, 223, 229, 232, 233, 239, 241, 253, 254, 264, 267, 275, 280, 281, 282, 284-286, 297, 303, 304, 312, 318-320, 322, 334, 338, 356, 357, 368.

Gandsey, Cecelia, 22, 25, 40, 47, 48, 159, 371.

Gandsey, Gladys, 41.

Gandsey, James, 17, 22, 23, 36, 40, 41, 43, 46, 48, 69, 70, 130, 159, 171, 282.

Gandsey, Mary, 25.

Gandsey, Miles, 41, 48.

Gandsey, Susan, 41.

Gandsey, W.E., 41.

Gannon, John, 41, 163, 178, 181, 185, 208, 209, 230, 231, 242, 246249. 254-260, 263-265, 267-271, 273, 274, 277-281, 286, 304.

Godfrey, Anna, 25.

Godfrey, Cecelia, 23, 42, 45, 47-49, 51, 55, 63, 69, 70, 75, 91, 96, 100, 113, 115, 116, 125, 126, 131, 149, 152, 153, 157-159, 182, 283, 310, 371.

Godfrey, Michael Hogan (Mike), 1, 2, 4, 6, 11, 14, 16, 17, 19, 22-30, 32, 35-39, 41-43, 47, 51, 52, 68, 74-76, 81, 91, 93-97, 100-104, 108, 110133, 143, 144, 148-

171, 174-179, 181, 183-189, 191-205, 207, 209-217, 226, 228, 229, 233-240, 243, 244, 247, 249, 250, 255, 259-268, 271-281,283, 284, 287-295, 297-302, 304, 305, 307-315, 319, 326, 328-335, 357, 371, 372.
Godfrey, Robert, 19, 20, 35, 36
Godfrey, Thomas Jefferson (T.J.), 1, 4, 35, 36, 41, 45, 47, 50, 115, 116.
Godfrey Underground Mine, 317-319, 322, 323, 325, 327, 328-335, 342, 345, 350-353, 356, 357, 359, 367, 368-370.
Godfrey, W.E., 41.
Grant, Bill, 57, 58, 334.
Greenway, John C, 39, 59, 72-74, 108-113, 115, 116, 124, 127, 131, 151, 165, 299, 300.
Hibbing District, 51, 94, 99, 117, 144, 156, 162, 163, 168, 173, 176, 178, 181, 188, 216, 217, 258, 261, 272, 275, 279, 299.
Hibbing, Frank, 1, 11-15, 17, 28, 36, 37, 43, 69, 77, 83, 93, 95, 189, 190, 191, 209, 211, 247, 282, 283, 297.
Hibbing Village Hall, 1-5, 27, 41, 97, 98, 130, 173, 196, 205, 215, 239-241, 247-250, 252, 277, 280, 305, 307.
Hibbing High School, 70, 198, 200, 239, 251, 271.
Hibbing Hotel, 42, 43, 93, 188.
Hogan, Bridgit, 19, 70, 281.
Howard Street, 4, 5, 49, 68, 95, 136, 137, 182, 195, 203, 205, 206, 212, 213,216, 218-223, 226, 227, 240, 249, 252, 260, 262, 274, 292, 311, 323, 372, 373, 376.
Iron Mountain, Michigan, 26, 31, 36, 272,
279.
Itasca Mercantile building, 91, 202.
Joliette Collage, 23.
Judge Cant, 87-89, 239, 254, 255, 285.
Judge Homer B. Dibell, 285, 286, 313.
Judge Martin J. Hughes, 82, 84, 90, 129, 130, 171, 179, 181, 237, 243, 244, 253, 280, 283.
Kohagen, William F., 97, 183, 188, 189, 239, 240, 262.
Kramer, Mary Elizabeth, 183, 198, 220, 272.
Larrabee Forty, 175, 179, 182, 185.
Liend, Elizabeth Hukari, 74, 81-86, 92, 129.
McPhail, Archie, 208.
McPhail, Mrs John, 67, 73.
Merchants & Miners State Bank, 159, 203.
Mesaba Street, 3, 99, 22, 239, 247-249, 251, 271, 277, 279, 280, 291, 292, 307.
Mitchell Hotel, 67.
Mitchell Location, 65-67, 72, 73, 77, 136, 212, 223, 311, 313, 329, 339.
Mitchell, Pentecost, 17, 18, 39, 41, 43, 46, 49, 52, 54, 62, 72, 101, 102, 104, 112, 128, 149, 151, 156, 163, 171, 176, 191, 192, 268, 273.
Mitchell, Richard J., 155.
Mitchell, Robert C., 93.
Municipal Building, 252.
Norway, Michigan, 21, 25, 27, 29-32, 35, 38, 70. 100, 116, 171, 182, 308.
Olcott, William J., 16, 41, 42, 52, 59, 69, 72, 74, 191, 194, 109-113, 119-125, 128, 129, 133, 135, 149, 154, 156, 157,

163, 165, 171, 176, 185, 188, 189, 191-
194, 197-199, 209, 233, 239, 261, 265-
268, 272, 297, 298, 309.
Old North Hibbing, 5, 12, 15, 17, 27, 40,
44, 46, 76, 98, 129, 137, 138, 161, 164,
170, 172, 174, 179, 183, 184, 187, 191,
196, 201, 209, 213-215, 217, 221, 226,
230, 232, 233, 235, 236, 241, 242, 253,
254, 259, 261, 264, 265, 274, 280, 281,
287, 291, 292, 303, 313, 313.
Oliver Apartments, 238.
Oliver Clubhouse, 4, 5, 175, 222, 238, 279, 283.
Oliver, Henry W., 9, 14, 54.
Oliver Iron Mining Company (the Oliver), xi, xii, 3, 5, 6, 9, 11, 14, 16, 27, 28, 30, 39, 41, 44-47, 49, 51-54, 59-61, 65, 67-72, 74-76, 81-92, 94-97, 99, 100, 102-111, 113-115, 117-120, 122-126, 128-133, 137, 139, 141-146, 148-152, 154-157, 162, 163, 165-168, 172, 174-176, 178-180, 182, 184-189, 191-195, 197-212, 215-217, 220-230, 232, 233, 235-243, 248-250, 253-256, 258-281, 264-268, 272-283, 286, 288-299, 302-309, 313, 315, 318, 328, 331-335, 344, 347, 352, 357, 368-371.
Oliver Park, 152.
Park Addition, 184, 194, 195, 201, 210, 211, 213, 215, 226, 241, 253.
Penn Iron Mining Company, 17, 26, 27, 30-32, 35, 308.
Pillsbury Addition, 17, 44, 45, 47, 49, 50, 75, 78, 129, 138, 161, 165, 170, 183, 189, 203, 210, 211, 261, 284, 304.
Pioneer Ball, 40.
Power Building, 212, 213.
Power, Dottie, 57, 202, 208, 221, 226.
Power, Percy Garner, 229.
Power, Victor L., xi, 39, 49, 56, 57, 72, 74, 76, 82, 86, 89-93, 129, 130, 134, 137-148, 150, 156, 158, 162, 166, 167, 172, 174, 179, 181, 185, 189, 194-197, 199, 205, 209, 213-215, 228, 229, 231, 233-236, 239, 240, 242, 247, 256, 269, 270, 271, 277-281, 283, 287, 289, 291.
Power, Walter J., 2, 49, 50, 56, 72, 73, 75, 194.
Powers, Rev. W.J., 165, 309.
Reed Building, 218.
Reed, Henry P., 28, 69, 78, 91, 139, 183, 188, 191, 217, 218, 231-233, 236, 238, 239. 253. 286. 305.
Rood, Dr. D.C., 43.
Rood Hospital, 5, 129, 157, 212, 249, 280, 314.
Southern Addition, 44, 45, 78, 88, 106, 129, 130, 138, 164, 170, 174, 185, 187, 191, 193, 196, 210, 211, 217, 218, 224, 232-234, 236, 241, 243, 253-256, 259, 261, 262, 265, 267, 280, 283, 284, 286.
Township 57, 11, 15, 77, 79, 83, 86, 101.
Township 58, 8, 11,-13, 15, 29, 77, 83, 120.
Township 59, 8.
Trout Lake, 112, 114, 118, 119, 121, 124, 125, 165.
Vacation Case, 44, 183, 263, 268, 274, 281, 377.
Virginia District, 143, 149, 152, 155,-157, 159, 162, 168, 181.

To Tipple A Prince

von Ahlen, Franz Dietrich, 10.
Weirick, Dr. Howard R., 137, 288, 306.
Webb, Francis J., 272.
Webb Location, 16, 66, 73, 128, 171, 173, 181, 272.